THE POLITICS OF MANHOOD

The Politics of

PROFEMINIST MEN
RESPOND TO THE
MYTHOPOETIC
MEN'S MOVEMENT
(AND THE MYTHOPOETIC
LEADERS ANSWER)

Manhood

EDITED BY

Michael S. Kimmel

Temple University Press : Philadelphia

Temple University Press, Philadelphia 19122
Copyright 1995 by Temple University
All rights reserved
Published 1995
Printed in the United States of America

Text design by Erin Kirk New

Library of Congress Cataloging-in-Publication Data

The politics of manhood : profeminist men respond to the
    mythopoetic men's movement (and the mythopoetic leaders answer) /
    edited by Michael S. Kimmel.
        p. cm.
    Includes bibliographical references.
    ISBN 1-56639-365-5 (cloth). — ISBN 1-56639-366-3 (paper)
        1. Men's movement—United States.   2. Men—United States—
    Psychology.   3. Feminism—United States.   I. Kimmel, Michael S.
    HQ1090.3.P65   1995
    305.32'0973—dc20   95-34527

for

MICHAEL KAUFMAN

*colleague, comrade, collaborator
and constant friend*

Contents

V. THE STRUGGLE FOR MEN'S SOULS: MYTHOPOETIC
MEN RESPOND TO THE PROFEMINIST CRITIQUE

VI. CONCLUSION: CAN WE ALL GET ALONG?

Preface

THIS BOOK HAS ITS ORIGINS IN REJECTION. Michael Kaufman
and I had been working on an essay about Robert Bly's book *Iron John*,
trying to engage critically with the ideas of the mythopoetic men's movement.
A friend had mentioned that Kay Leigh Hagan was editing a book to be
called *Feminists Respond to the Men's Movement*, and I thought that this might
be an appropriate arena for Michael and me to publish such a critique.

Kay Leigh Hagan thought so too until her publisher insisted that the
book's title be changed from "Feminists" to "Women." (She did manage a
subtitle with the word "feminist" in it.) That meant we were out, so Michael
and I searched for another outlet for the essay, which had by now grown
quite long. *Feminist Issues*, a scholarly journal, published a shortened version,
but friends and colleagues who read the essay pushed us to publish it in its
entirety, and to consider the many other profeminist men who might be
looking for a forum to respond to the visibility and popularity of the mythopoetic work.

When I became editor of *masculinities*, a new journal devoted to exploring
the "problem" of gender identity from a variety of disciplinary perspectives,
I invited a number of profeminist men to contribute essays representing their
diverse disciplines. All of them—philosophers and theologians, psychologists and historians, sociologists and therapists—obliterated the dichotomy
between scholar and activist. That journal issue formed the basis for this
book.

Our encounter with the mythopoetic men's movement also began in rejection. Profeminist men categorically repudiated the work of the mythopoetic
leaders, finding in it everything from antifeminist backlash and patriarchy

redux to racist appropriation, misleading theology, misguided anthropology, and misogynist political ideology. To most of us, the mythopoetic men's work reinscribed patriarchy as a political system by asserting men's need for *more* power and refusing to move beyond an individual version of empowerment.

Something was missing in this staking of turfs: the mythopoets were reaching large numbers of men, the same good, caring, mainstream men we profeminists had been trying to reach for years without much success. I knew that this book could not stand simply as the profeminist men's critical rejection of mythopoetic work. Therefore, I invited several of the mythopoetic leaders to respond to our writing, hoping that what began as rejection could begin to shift to a sorely needed dialogue between these two camps. The essays collected here significantly expand that common ground and more carefully demarcate the boundaries between our positions. Of course some essays focus more vigorously on boundary maintenance and others on exploring areas of agreement. But the net result is to push the outer limits of our political discourse into new terrain and open up possibilities for conversation and collaboration in unexpected ways.

Thus, though this book began in rejection, it has become a vehicle of inclusion. As a result of our correspondence, for example, Kay Leigh Hagan invited me to appear on *Donahue* when she was scheduled to square off against some mythopoetic men's movement leaders and fellow travelers. Since that time, she and I have worked together and developed a series of workshops and lecture-performances that we present at colleges and secondary schools around the country. In these, we explore the dilemmas and issues facing young women and men on campus today and, not incidentally, explore the ways in which feminist women and profeminist men can work as allies. I am honored to work with such a forthright and brilliant "feminist hothead" and deeply grateful for her ability to work with me to embody the wary alliances forming between feminist women and men.

And I am also thankful that the work on this book has brought me in touch with Robert Bly. His initial interest in the book and his careful and conciliatory response showed me how much room there is for dialogue. And subsequent contact has borne that out. We have now each agreed to try to provide venues for a public dialogue on men's issues, and I have invited him to be the keynote speaker at a forthcoming National Conference on Men and Masculinity, the annual profeminist men's conference sponsored by the National Organization for Men Against Sexism (NOMAS). I hope that my initial critical response to his ideas in this book does not completely obscure my respect and admiration for his work.

Some of that badly needed dialogue among the various strains of men's work has already begun. Marvin Allen, who organizes the annual International Men's Conferences, has always believed that his conferences need a profeminist voice, in addition to the voices of other men he presents, and he has consistently invited me as a featured speaker. My public debate with Shepherd Bliss at U. C. Berkeley, organized by Bob Blauner, was bracing and arduous and showed me how much work there is yet to be done in creating meaningful dialogue grounded in mutual respect without defensiveness. I am grateful to Iona Mara-Drita for her debriefing sessions about that event, and discussions about the possibilities of political rapprochement, in the ensuing years.

As always, Michael Ames was an exemplary editor. He believed in the project from its inception and responded with engagement and enthusiasm. Michael is more than an editor; he is a trusted colleague and friend, as are my agents, Frances Goldin and Sydelle Kramer.

I also acknowledge the community of family, friends, and colleagues who provide the intellectual, emotional, and political foundation for my work. My thanks to: Amy Aronson, Tim Beneke, Bob Blauner, Bob Brannon, Judith Brisman, Harry Brod, Bob Connell, Barbara and Herb Diamond, Marty Duberman, Pam Hatchfield, Oystein Holter, Lars Jalmert, Sandi Kimmel, Ed Kimmel, David Levin, the late Marty Levine, Iona Mara-Drita, Mary Morris, Mike Messner, Tim Nonn, Larry O'Connor, Joe Pleck, Lillian and Hank Rubin, Don Sabo, Vic Seidler, Mitchell Tunick, and Eli Zal.

And to Michael Kaufman, to whom this book is dedicated. His friendship embodies the best of that potential confluence between the mythopoetic and the profeminist men's movements—a caring and nourishing emotional connection, an attention to process, and an uncompromising political vision. He is a constant source of love, support, and inspiration.

M.S.K.
New York City

Publication Information

Articles by Clatterbaugh, Kimmel ("Born to Run"), Beneke, Dash, Gutterman, Kupers, Murray, Schwalbe ("Why Mythopoetic Men . . .") originally appeared in *masculinities*, 1(3), 1993. Reprinted by permission. "Born to Run" will appear in the author's forthcoming book *Manhood in America: A Cultural History* (New York: The Free Press, 1995).

Articles by Sabo, Brod, Bliss, Kipnis, Diamond, Weed, Allen, Benjamin, Nonn, Bullock, and Bly are original to this volume.

"Weekend Warriors" (Kimmel and Kaufman) was published in abbreviated form in *Feminist Issues*, 13(2), Fall 1993; and a full version in *Theorizing Masculinities* (edited by Harry Brod and Michael Kaufman), Newbury Park: Sage Publications, 1994. © by Michael Kimmel and Michael Kaufman. Reprinted by permission.

"Men at Bay" (Connell) is an expanded version of the article "Drumming Up the Wrong Tree," originally published in *Tikkun*. Reprinted by permission.

" 'Changing Men' and Feminist Politics in the United States" (Messner) was originally published in *Theory and Society*, 22, 1993. Reprinted by permission.

"Mythopoetic Men's Work as a Search for Communitas" (Schwalbe) was originally published in *Men's Lives*, 3rd edition (edited by Michael Kimmel and Michael Messner), Boston: Allyn and Bacon, 1995. © by Michael Schwalbe. Reprinted by permission.

Introduction

MICHAEL S. KIMMEL

He who makes a beast of himself gets rid of the pain of being a man.
  Dr. Johnson[1]

I.

"Do you want it tame or do you want it wild?" group leader Shepherd Bliss asks the assembled 60 or so men in a meeting room of a luxury hotel in Austin, Texas. Bliss is running a workshop on "Exploring Masculine Ground" at the First International Men's Conference in October 1991 — a gathering of over 750 men from all over the country who have come together to retrieve their deep, wet, hairy, wild masculinity. There can be only one response to Bliss's question. "Wild!" shout the men in unison.

We're off to explore masculine ground, a "sacred masculine space" to be retrieved through ritual incantation and guided fantasy. This is my introduction to the actual work of the "mythopoetic" men's movement, and, although I have read most of the major texts, I am still somewhat surprised by how uncomfortable I feel. I am politically and intellectually skeptical, and emotionally uneasy. Such feelings are usually a tip-off that I need to pay greater attention to my experience, that I need to be more open to what is happening around me than usual. So I try to let it in.

We've begun our session with a West African chant of welcome, while we participants move around the room welcoming one another to our shared ritual space. I am unable to ignore that I am in a pricey hotel meeting room, with light grey wall to wall carpeting, buffed black metal track lighting, and vertical blinds. And I can't ignore that these white men chanting and dancing to the beat of the conga drum have dreadful rhythm. Unable to suspend disbelief, I nod at a few of them.

Our first task in this workshop will be to explore our playful male natures through getting in touch with the earth, which Bliss invites us to do by taking off our shoes. "Feel the earth beneath your feet, the ground tilled by your ancestors," Bliss suggests. The carpeting is soft.

Bliss leads the group by suggesting what some of us might feel like doing. "Some of you might want to get on all fours and explore the ground with your hands as well," he suggests. All the men drop to their hands and knees to feel the earth tilled by their ancestors. "Some of you might feel some noises coming into your throats, the noises of male animals," he mentions. Everyone immediately starts growling, snorting. A few howls.

"Some of you might feel like moving around the room, getting in touch with other animals," Bliss predicts. Everyone is now moving slowly around the room, growling and snorting, occasionally bumping into one another. The most I can manage at this point is to remain on all fours, swaying back and forth and watching.

"Some of you might even feel yourselves recalling that most repressed sense, our sense of smell, and begin sniffing." Suddenly men are sniffing one another as they move through the room on all fours, resembling a group of suburban dogs in a large pen, checking each other out. Someone bumps into me and sniffs my rear. I turn and frown. He moves on to a better playmate.

Now Bliss escalates. "Some of you might find yourselves feeling like that most masculine of animals—the billy goat. Billy goats are very rambunctious and playful and they love to butt heads." Suddenly everyone is jumping around the room butting and sniffing and howling. Barely able to suppress a giggle, I kneel and sway silently.

After a few minutes of playing human bumper cars, Bliss closes the exercise, asking the assembled how they felt about it. Men shout out their emotional responses, which range from "free" to "playful," with no ambivalence or awkwardness, not a hint of self-consciousness. I develop a sense that these men know the routine, and can retrieve the appropriate emotion and behavior at will. This suspicion is confirmed by our next exercise.

Lights off, blinds drawn against the midday sun, Bliss invites us on a guided meditation to encounter our fathers. Lying on the floor, eyes closed, we move through several fantasy doors, down paths, and toward clearings in the fields until we encounter him. We are each invited to walk with our fathers for a few steps, telling him the things we always wanted him to hear, and listening to the things he never told us.

I am smiling now, imagining myself at about age three, walking hand in hand with my father through Prospect Park to the zoo, which was our early Sunday morning ritual when I was a young child. Around me, I begin to hear sniffs and a few sobs. As the exercise continues, the sniffs deepen to sobs and the sobs descend further to deep heaving and crying.

I'm astonished—not at the outpouring of grief about father–son relations, because I am always aware that my close childhood connection with my father is quite unusual among my men's movement friends. But weren't these the same men who, three minutes earlier, were bounding around the room, butting heads and howling like billy goats? How could they move from exhilarating animal liberation to deep grief so quickly?

My introduction to the mythopoetic men's movement, then, is an immersion in a therapeutic culture in which emotions are constructed and displayed at appropriate moments. It's the same social construction of emotions that finds people, myself included, having what appears to be a fine day, feeling great, but then walking into a therapist's office and suddenly getting in touch with a deep well of pain and anger—all within two minutes of reciting the events of the day. How many of our emotions are *not* the products of recognizing a situation in which such emotions are appropriate and then deciding to deploy them?

I was fascinated nonetheless, perhaps because this kind of workshop and retreat has become so popular among men around the country (and so profitable for their organizers). After all, we social scientists had long held as axiomatic that men don't express their emotions, don't reveal their feelings, don't cry—most especially not around other men. And feminists had for decades urged men to open up and share their feelings. And here men were doing just that, or so it seemed. Is this what we'd been waiting for, the breakthrough moment when men finally let down their character armor and reveal themselves? It is, I admit, somewhat startling to be surrounded by men who appear not only to be in touch with great wells of feeling but willing to share them with utter strangers. Who wouldn't be interested?

Since that time, I have attended workshops, retreats, and conferences organized by the mythopoetic men's movement in an effort to understand the chord it has struck among American men, and the brief hold it exerted over media discussions of the contemporary "crisis" of masculinity. In particular, I have sought to set this "men's work" of the mythopoetic men's movement against the backdrop of the extraordinary efforts of feminist women to claim their voices of anger, passion, and pain over the past thirty years. Is the mythopoetic men's movement what feminists have been yearning for, or is it part of the backlash against feminism, as journalist Susan Faludi suggests in her pathbreaking indictment, *Backlash*? Does the mythopoetic men's movement simply respond to *men's* needs, independent of the way the women's movement addresses women's needs, and is it, therefore, in a sense, indifferent to feminism? And how do the profeminist men, that diverse group of activists and scholars who consider themselves the allies of the women's movement, respond to the mythopoetic men's movement—its signal successes in reaching American men, the media's sarcastic dismissal of its more hokey rituals, and the ire it has inspired among feminist women? Those are the questions I have raised in this book.

II.

The mythopoetic men's movement, inspired and led by poet Robert Bly and his followers, seized the public imagination with the publication of Bly's best-selling book, *Iron John*, in 1990. Heralded by the media as the birth of a "men's movement," the phenomenon was seen as a moment when men were finally answering the claims of the women's movement. Suddenly, men across the country were trooping off to the woods on weekend retreats to drum, chant, be initiated, bond, and otherwise discover their inner wildmen or retrieve their deep masculinity.

As a media myth, the men's movement held the public's attention for its allotted fifteen minutes of fame, but then its minions quietly retreated to their lairs to nurse their wounds and sulk about how they were misperceived by the media. Of course, they were right: the media seemed to delight in deliberately distorting the aims of these movements, and reveling in the photo opportunities afforded by middle class, middle-aged white men in war paint and loin cloths, whooping and hollering like fantasized wildmen.

Still, there was a lot more to this movement, this "men's work" as they called it, than suggested by caustic dismissals. More than sweat lodges, animal noises, and hugs. And there was more to it than Robert Bly himself. The mythopoetic men's movement was as much a textual phenomenon as it was a ritual process. Books by other leaders quickly followed, with diagnoses of the male malaise and self-help strategies from a host of therapeutic traditions. Since I will discuss Bly's work at some length in an essay in this book, here I will comment only briefly on a few of the other works of the genre.

Sam Keen's *Fire in the Belly* was the only work other than *Iron John* to hit the best-seller lists. Michael Meade used stories and legends to make his case in *Men and the Water of Life;* therapists John Lee and Jed Diamond harnessed New Age insights and the recovery movement in their books, *At My Father's Wedding* and *The Warrior's Journey Home;* and therapists Aaron Kipnis and Marvin Allen used more mainstream group therapy insights in their books, *Knights without Armor* and *In the Company of Men.* All these latter books sold only modestly.

Robert Moore and Douglas Gillette became something of a publishing industry themselves, as their *King Warrior Magician Lover* was followed by what I came to call "the inner books"—four separate volumes on the "inner" king, warrior, magician, and lover. Their work is worth looking at for a moment, in part because it represents the worst of these texts and in part because it is typical of the genre.

Drawing on Jungian depth psychology, and mythology, Moore and Gillette, a Jungian therapist and mythologist, respectively, claimed these four as new archetypes for a conscious manhood. Moore and Gillette dilute Jung's evocative archetypal analysis (by way of Joseph Campbell) into a thin, watery soup in which the world's store of myths and legends is used illustratively to spice up an otherwise tasteless broth. In each volume, they take the reader on a breathless world tour, snatching bits of theory from Native American cosmology, and images of kingship from ancient Egypt, 7th century Tibet, the Aztecs, the Incans, the Sumerians—anyplace, in fact, that seems to fit their theory. King images included Chinese emperors, Egyptian pharaohs, Assyrian kings, all of whom, we read, were "committed to the preservation and the extension of a civilized, yet vigorously instinctual way of life" (*Inner King*, p. 156).

At times, their vision of kingship sounds rather grand: he is a protector, provider, procreator, who is capable of love, care, wisdom, embodying fulfillment, authenticity, and maturity (pp. 148, 207). Sometimes, he's simply grandiose, the fruit "of the cosmic phallus," and "the source of useful divine energy in the world" (pp. 127, 114). And sometimes, he sounds downright terrifying, "a warrior who enforces order within his kingdom and who may take military action to extend his kingdom" (p. 52). (Readers may note the cosmic appropriation of women's reproductive power in some of these images; at times a mother is usurped by a "more fertile" Queen, whose major duty seems to be standing by her man.)

Moore and Gillette believe that these archetypal elements of manhood are "hard wired components of our genetically transmitted psychic ma-

chine"—an apparently unself-consciously mechanical rhetorical flourish—
which still must be activated and developed within culture. Despite the fact
that we're born as kings, warriors, magicians, and lovers, then, we still have
to be made—which should be good for book sales. Fortunately, the making
of men is facilitated by the detritus of popular culture. A small crystal pyramid, they declare, can be a "useful portable icon," and the soundtracks to
the films *Ben Hur* and *Spartacus* are excellent background music for activat-
ing archetypal awareness, and are "particularly evocative of King energy."

Such a descent from the pinnacles of cosmic awareness into the mundane
world of a New Age Kmart does not obscure these gurus' frighteningly reactionary politics. Jimmy Carter, for example, is their example of a bad, weak
king:

> Emblematic of his weak thinking was his absurd attempt to dramatize energy
> conservation by not lighting the national Christmas tree, an ancient symbol of
> eternal life and ongoing vigor. Of more consequence was his impotent reaction
> to the Iran hostage crisis.

Most mythopoetic men's movement leaders would be as appalled by such
claims as I am. Bly, himself, after all, was one of the nation's most visible
opponents of macho militaristic posturing during the Vietnam War; Shepherd Bliss recounts meeting Bly at an induction center, and how Bly helped
Shepherd begin to resist the draft. And, more recently, Bly risked some of
his cultural capital among his new male followers by visibly—and admira-
bly—opposing Operation Desert Storm.

Sam Keen is probably the most antagonistic opponent of the false equation of militarism with masculinity. In his best-selling book, Keen rails
against the "heartless functionaries" of the Reagan-Bush years. "A man who
has not been morally anesthetized cannot have his eyes opened to unnecessary suffering, disease, and injustice without feeling outrage and hearing the
call to arms" (p. 166). Keen relies more on Kenneth Burke and Gabriel
Marcel than he does on Jung or mythic dieties, which makes him more ambivalent about questions of power.

And Keen does believe that men can reconnect with powerful adult
women at the end of their journeys, although even he relies on simplified
Freudian notions of separation from mother (here called "WOMAN" in all
capital letters) as the essential first step on the masculine quest. But like
several of the other theorists, Keen posits a facile symmetry between
women's and men's experiences. Male and female, each in his or her sphere,
living lives of meaning and coherence. Each gender is "half of a crippled

whole." Men get the "feeling of power" and women get the "power of feeling"; men get the "privilege of public action" while women get the "privilege
of private being," as if these were equivalent. Or this:

> The wounds that men endure, and the psychic scar tissue that results from
> living with the expectation of being a battlefield sacrifice is every bit as terrible
> as the suffering women bear from the fear and reality of rape. (P. 47)

I wonder if he'd want to swap places with them.

Leaving these textual analyses, pop psychology bromides, mythological excursions and exhortations to heroic manhood, the mythopoetic men's movement did, after all, move a large number of men. Far more was involved than
simply rhetorical musing, and far more than the mass media acknowledged.
There were, for example, efforts to help men acknowledge and challenge
their deep fears about connecting with other men, to enable men to explore
some of the vitality they lost on their way to sober sensible American manhood, including a sense of joy and playfulness. There were outpourings of
deeply felt grief and despair about fathers who had abandoned or abused
their now-adult sons. These retreats helped men begin to dismantle the
walls men build to make themselves feel strong, powerful, invincible—to
shield themselves from vulnerability, pain, need. This work was enormously
valuable. In a sense, these retreats invited men—as the women's movement
had been asking, even cajoling, demanding, and urging, for several decades—to "get in touch with their feelings."

It was not necessarily a pretty sight, especially to feminist women who
listened in horror as they learned what kinds of feelings were being released
at these retreats. Undiluted rage against mothers, who were blamed for entering into incestuous relationships with their sons, thus preventing fathers
from being close to their boys. Venomous anger at wives (mostly ex-wives,
actually) who had expected their men to renounce boyhood pleasures and
shoulder all family responsibilities to provide for their wives and children,
only to grow first disgusted at the inability of their husbands to communicate
and then vindictive during divorce proceedings that left the men childless,
impoverished, and bitter. And seemingly incomprehensible fury at feminist
women who have been agitating for transformation of institutional and interpersonal relations between women and men for over three decades. (I say
incomprehensible because women, after all, brought these issues to men's
attention in the first place. It has always seemed to me that we owe women
an enormous debt of gratitude for caring about women enough to help them
resist oppression, and caring about men enough to believe we were capable
of change and to engage with us as we tried to enact it.)

The response of feminist women to this men's movement ranged from furious dismissal at the ways that masculine retreat could reproduce gender inequalities (if they're off in the woods, who's going to do the housework and childcare?) to a wary skepticism that such retreats could advance an agenda of mutual understanding or gender reconciliation. While the mainstream media's dismissals were more caustic and casual, feminist women engaged with the ideas of the movement, concluding that *Iron John* was, in the words of one journalist, "no gift to women." Susan Faludi's best-selling book, *Backlash*, listed Bly as one of the agents of the backlash. Kay Leigh Hagan's *Women Respond to the Men's Movement* presented feminist women's anger, frustration, and confusion about the mythopoetic men's movement. But even that book referred to Bly's groups as "the" men's movement. One of the most common cries from feminist women was "where are the men who support feminism?"

To listen to the media hype, and, to a lesser extent to the feminist women's response, the mythopoetic movement was *the* men's movement. The only sounds from men were the sounds of drumming and chanting in the woods. That there was *another* men's movement seemed to have escaped notice.

III.

For the past two decades, profeminist men have worked quietly and vigilantly to support feminist women, to help reorient masculinity to a more nurturing direction by embracing—not evading—a feminist political vision. Profeminist men work with batterers, convicted rapists, and sex offenders to stop the violence. We work with athletic teams and fraternities, and offer workshops in dorms on ways to prevent sexual assault on campus. We work with corporations to prevent sexual harassment and warm the "chilly climate" for women in the workplace. Profeminist men believe that men have a collective responsibility to work against the violence, injustice, and inequality that define and confine the lives of women in our society.

So how have profeminist men responded to the mythopoetic men's movement? Essentially, several themes were always present: political distress at the antifeminist rumblings that occasionally broke the surface at the mythopoetic men's gatherings; theoretical, academic criticisms of various anthropological, philosophical, and psychological assumptions; literary discomfort at the use of myths and archetypes. I shared these reservations, and more. I found the mythopoetic men's work unsettling because it seemed "off," marked by a profound misdiagnosis of the current male malaise, and yet was enormously popular, apparently speaking to many more men than feminism ever had. I was, frankly, envious of their successes while shocked at some of their messages, which seemed to me to repudiate three decades of feminism and gay liberation. I wondered whether their success was related to that antifeminist message, or whether, perhaps, it was independent of it, and whether a profeminist message could be harnessed to their retreats.

I invited a number of profeminist men to respond to the work of the mythopoetic men's movement in an effort to bring these critiques together in coherent form. When I published some of these in *masculinities* (1993, vol 1, no. 3–4), a scholarly journal I edit, I hoped that these essays would provoke dialogue, debate, and discussion between mythopoetic and profeminist men in the areas on which we agreed and disagreed. I then invited several of the most visible leaders of the mythopoetic men's movement to respond to these essays, in a sense, to take up the challenge and dialogue with us.

Robert Bly was the first to respond, promising me an essay and also inviting me to participate with him on some public dialogues about these issues. Acceptances followed from Marvin Allen, Onaje Benjamin, Shepherd Bliss, Jed Diamond, Aaron Kipnis, and John Lee, who later dropped out. Initially, Sam Keen accepted as well. His letter chided me for suggesting there is division between profeminist and mythopoetic men, and indicated that he was "a bit tired of the 'men's' issue thing." He also pleaded "not guilty to being a mythopoetic type." In my response, I mentioned that several of the authors in the book had included him in the genre, and that this might be a good opportunity both to disavow the mythopoetic label and to explicate his position more clearly. I sent him a few articles that made explicit use of his book, and he called me back, indicating that he would definitely contribute something to clarify his position. All of my subsequent letters went unanswered, and I never heard from him again.

IV.

This book, then, gathers together the writings of profeminist men on the mythopoetic men's movement and the responses by some of the leaders of the mythopoetic men's movement to our critique. It is a necessary first step toward open discussion and dialogue. But it is incomplete. It begins dialogue among men about the appropriate models for masculinity at the turn of the new century, a debate about the origins of the current crisis of masculinity, and a series of responses to what should be done about it. More than that, it is an open dialogue with feminist women, a response to their responses, an effort to broaden the discussion of the ways we can collectively transform sexist society. In those two dialogues, a new set of voices emerges into the current national discussion of the transformation of masculinity.

I believe that the mythopoetic men's movement does valuable work in breaking down men's isolation from one another, and giving permission for men to experience deep feelings. Here I part with some profeminist contributors, who claim that even these apparent benefits are suspect. I also believe that, unless these potentially counterhomophobic activities are harnessed to a larger vision of gender and sexual equality by embracing difference, the mythopoetic men's movement will remain a feel-good mass therapy. And in the current backlash against women, a movement devoted *only* to men feeling better about themselves as men cannot help but oppose sexual equality and gender justice.

I see the mythopoetic men's movement as being at a crossroads. Will it continue to honor men's feelings of powerlessness, pitting women against me, straight men against gay men, and white men against men of color? Or will it join with those of us who have already committed ourselves to those struggles for equality as a way of redefining masculinity? Can the mythopoetic men's movement claim the rich historical legacy of profeminist men who have publicly stood up for equality? Or will they continue to run away?

Watching the movie *Wolf,* I was again reminded that the descent to a primal, natural, animal-like masculinity can cut either way. For the Jack Nicholson character, the descent toward animality permits reconciliation of his public persona, that of a somewhat stuffily effete book editor, with a fierce, heroic, and sensual nature that civilized discourse had all but completely sapped. (Even his vision gets sharper.) But for James Spader, as his rival, the descent brings out a deeper cruelty, less concealed by social convention. Nicholson uses his descent to elevate his manhood, while Spader uses his descent as an invitation to unchecked depravity. Nicholson becomes a passionate lover, Spader a rapist.

The men of the mythopoetic men's movement also face a choice — not as draconian, perhaps, nor as starkly drawn. They can use their newfound and hard-fought insights to make the world better for others, connecting themselves to those political movements — the women's movement, the gay and lesbian movement, the civil rights movement — that seek to claim the voices they have traditionally been denied. Or they can retreat, in defensive anger, protecting themselves against those who might challenge their gender, race, and sexual privilege. In short, I believe, the mythopoetic men's movement can become either profeminist or antifeminist. But it cannot remain neutral, indifferent, impartial, and unengaged. It can witness these political struggles neither from the sidelines nor, as some of its leaders suggest, from the "woods" in their own ritual space, the last refuge against the oncoming tide.

NOTE

1. Attributed to Dr. Johnson in James Boswell, *The Life of Samuel Johnson*, edited by G. B. Hill, revised by L. F. Powell (New York: Oxford University Press, 1965), volume 2, p. 435.

I

CONCEPTUAL

CRITIQUES

Weekend Warriors: The New Men's Movement

MICHAEL S. KIMMEL
AND MICHAEL KAUFMAN

Held up as the end-all of organization leadership, the skills of human relations easily tempt the new administrator into the practice of a tyranny more subtle and more pervasive than that which he means to supplant. No one wants to see the old authoritarian return, but at least it could be said of him that what he wanted primarily from you was your sweat. The new man wants your soul.

William H. Whyte, *The Organization Man*[1]

ACROSS THE UNITED STATES AND CANADA, men have been gathering in search of their manhood. Inspired and led by poet Robert Bly, the *eminence grise* of this new men's movement—and whose book, *Iron John*, topped the best-seller lists for more than 35 weeks in 1991—dozens of therapists and "mythopoetic" journeymen currently offer workshops, retreats and seminars to facilitate their "gender journey," to "heal their father wounds" so that they may retrieve the "inner king," the "warrior within," or the "wildman."[2] And hundreds of thousands of men have heeded the call of the wildman, embraced this new masculinity, and become weekend warriors.

The movement has certainly come in for its share of ridicule and derision. Countless magazine articles, newspaper stories, and even several TV sitcoms have portrayed the movement as nothing more than a bunch of white, upper-middle-class professionals chanting and dancing around bonfires, imitating Native American rituals, and bonding. Recently, feminist women have indicated their suspicions that this men's movement is patriarchy with a New Age face, a critique that is explicitly political. To date, the new men's movement has received virtually no serious analytic scrutiny from men. This essay is an attempt to make sense of that movement, to subject the new men's movement to serious analysis.

Like any other social movement, the new men's movement can best be examined through a set of analytic frames, each designed to illuminate a specific part of the movement. Through an analysis of the major texts of the movement, as well as through participant observation at several men's retreats, we will attempt to make sense of this phenomenon. Specifically, we will want to pose four sets of questions:

1. *Historical and Political Context.* What specific historical conditions have given rise to this new men's movement? What does the movement have to do with the women's movement? Why now?
2. *Social Composition.* To what specific groups of men does this new men's movement appeal? Why these men? What is the class, racial, and ethnic composition of these weekend retreats?
3. *Ideology of Masculinity.* What is the vision of social change that the new men's movement embraces? From what sources do they derive their vision? What is their diagnosis of the causes of malaise among contemporary men?
4. *Organizational Dynamics.* What are the organizational vehicles by which the men's movement will accomplish its aims? What does the evocation of ritual, chanting, drumming, and initiation mean in the context of the movement?

By exploring these four aspects of the mythopoetic men's movement, we will be able to assess the consequences of the movement, both for men and women individually, and for the larger framework of other movements for social change. In talking about this men's movement, we see it as distinct from the pro-feminist men's movement, even though at least some of the men attracted to Robert Bly also consider themselves pro-feminist. It's also distinct from the self-consciously anti-feminist and misogynist men's rights movement although, again, some other mythopoetic men wander into this camp.

THE MEN'S MOVEMENT AND THE REAL WORLD

Contexts and Composition

The first two dimensions of the new men's movement can be fairly briefly summarized. In the past two decades, masculinity has been increasingly seen as in "crisis," a widespread confusion over the meaning of manhood. (Much of this discussion applies specifically to the United States and Canada, although there are some points of contact with Australia and western Europe.) From the earliest whines of "men's liberation" in the mid-1970s, to the current "Great American Wimp Hunt," and the preoccupation with the diets and fashion tastes of "Real Men," questions of the definitions of masculinity have been contested. That men are confused over the meaning of masculinity has become a media cliche, and hundreds of advice books and magazine columns today advise men on gender issues.

The contemporary crisis of masculinity has structural origins in changing global geo-political and economic relations, and in the changing dynamics and complexion of the workplace. Our traditional definitions of masculinity had rested on economic autonomy: control over one's labor, control over the product of that labor, and manly self-reliance in the workplace. The public arena, the space in which men habitually had demonstrated and proved their manhood, was racially and sexually homogenous, a homosocial world in which straight, white men could be themselves, without fear of the "other." Economic autonomy, coupled with public patriarchy, gave men a secure sense of themselves as men. And if they should fail, they could always head out for the frontier, to the boundaries of civilization, where they could stake a new claim for manhood against the forces of nature.

That world is now gone. The transformation of the workplace—increased factory mechanization, increased bureaucratization of office work—means that fewer and fewer men experience anything resembling autonomy in their work. This century has witnessed a steady erosion of economic autonomy; from 90 percent of U.S. men who owned their own shop or farm at the time of the Civil War to less than 1 out of 10 today. The continental frontier was declared closed at the turn of the century, and since that time we have invented a succession of frontiers to take its place—from the Third World, to outer space (the "final frontier"), to the corporate "jungle." The current global restructuring finds many former outposts on that frontier demanding inclusion into the economy; decolonization and movements for regional or ethnic autonomy destabilize American hegemony.

Perhaps nothing has had a larger cultural impact in this crisis of masculinity than the recent rise of the women's movement, and also the gay and lesbian movement. By the late 1960s, the civil rights movement had already challenged the dominant view that the public arena and the workplace were virtually preserves for whites. With the rise of the women's movement, there was a challenge to older and even more fundamental beliefs about men's place in society. Old certainties and gender divisions were challenged, a process augmented by the gay and lesbian movement, which challenged the heterosexual assumptions of those old gender arrangements.

Although these economic, political and social changes have affected all different groups of men in radically different ways, perhaps the hardest hit *psychologically* were middle-class, straight, white men from their late twenties through their forties. For these were the men who not only inherited a prescription for manhood that included economic autonomy, public patriarchy, and the frontier safety valve, they were also men who believed themselves *entitled* to the power that attended upon the successful demonstration of masculinity. These men experienced workplace transformation as a threat to their manhood, and the entry of the formerly excluded "others" as a virtual invasion of their privileged space.

As a result, many middle-class, white, middle-aged heterosexual men — among the most privileged groups in the history of the world — do not experience themselves as powerful. Ironically, although these men are everywhere in power, that aggregate power of that group does not translate into an individual sense of feeling empowered. In fact, this group feels quite powerless. Entitled to partake in the traditional power of masculinity, these men feel besieged by new forces outside of their control, and somewhat at a loss as they observe the women in their lives changing dramatically while they feel increasingly helpless.

It should come as no surprise, then, to observe that the overwhelming majority of the men who are currently involved in the new men's movement are precisely middle class, middle aged, white and heterosexual. The men who feel most besieged, and who have the resources with which to combat that siege, are the most frequent weekend warriors. Attendance of men of color ranged, over a variety of retreats and conferences in various parts of the United States that we attended, from zero to less than 2 percent, while never greater than 5 percent of the attendees were homosexual men. The majority of the men are between 40 and 55, with about 10 percent over 60 and about 5 percent younger than 30. Professional, white collar and managerial levels were present in far greater proportion than blue collar and working class men, in part because the expense of the weekend retreats (usually $200 to $500 for a weekend) or the day-long seminars ($50 to $200) make the retrieval of deep manhood a journey open only to the economically privileged.

The men's movement is the cry of anguish of privileged American men, men who feel lost in a world in which the ideologies of individualism and manly virtue are out of sync with the realities of urban, industrialized, secular society. It retells the tales of over-dominant mothers and absent fathers who have betrayed the young boy and deprived him of his inheritance of a sense of personal power. The men's movement taps a longing for the lost innocence of childhood, and a cry for certainty about the meaning of manhood in a society where both men's power and rigid gender definitions are being challenged by feminism. These themes, trumpeted by Bly and his followers, link up with the experiences of predominately white, heterosexual, middle-class and middle-aged readers who have made his book and the movement which surrounds it such a success. Movement leaders speak directly and with compassion to men's uneasiness and discomfort: eloquently to their grief about their relationships with their fathers, to their despair over their relationships with women, their pain and sense of powerlessness and isolation. What exactly does the men's movement say? What is its diagnosis of the masculine dilemma?

The Search for the Deep Masculine

The men's movement has many different voices, drawing on many different traditions. Some rely entirely on Greek and Roman mythologies for images of heroic manhood; others use Jungian archetypes or Eastern religions as the foundation for new visions of masculinity. But certain themes are constantly sounded, especially essentialist assumptions about gender distinctions, a contemporary diagnosis of feminization of American manhood, the search for lost fathers (and father figures), and a vision of retrieval of heroic archetypes as models for men. Bly's argument rests on the fusion of (1) a psychological analysis of Jungian archetypes, in which a retelling of fairy tales and myths serve as illustrations; (2) a historical interpretation of the progress of industrialization and modernization on men's lives; (3) an anthropological survey of non-industrial cultures and their rituals of initiating men into society and providing secure identities for adult men. These are sandwiched between a political critique of contemporary men, and a vision for the future of manhood that reclaims lost rituals and grounds men's identities more securely. Since *Iron John*, based on an explication of a Grimm fairy tale, is the touchstone of the men's movement, we can explicate its ideology by deconstructing its seminal text. The fable goes as follows:

> Once upon a time, a hunter volunteers to go into the woods and find out why the King had lost several of his men. The hunter returned with a Wild Man, who had lived at the bottom of a lake, and had apparently been devouring the

others. The King put the Wild Man in a cage in the courtyard. One day, the King's 8 year old son was playing near the cage with a ball. The ball rolled into the cage. To get it back, the Wild Man made the boy promise to get the key to his cage and free him. The key was under the boy's mother's pillow. The boy stole the key from under his mother's pillow and opened the cage. The Wild Man walked off into the woods with the boy. (They have set each other free.)

In the woods with Iron John, the boy fails to follow Iron John's instructions, so he is sent off to work, first as a cook's apprentice, later as a gardener. Here, he meets the daughter of the king. He goes off to war, proving himself in battle, although he doesn't take credit for it: At a post-bellum festival, he catches three golden apples tossed by the king's daughter in a competition, but the boy rides off in a different suit of armor, after catching each one. Eventually, he is brought before the king and asks for the girl's hand in marriage. The big wedding celebration is suddenly interrupted by the entrance of a great King, who walks up to young man and embraces him. "I am Iron John, who through an enchantment became turned into a Wild Man. You have freed me from that enchantment. All the treasure that I won will from now on belong to you."

Bly uses the Iron John fable to several ends—to suggest manhood as a quest, to heal the split between the dutiful son and the Wild Man, to imply that the son's healing of his own wound will simultaneously heal the father's wounds, to suggest the possibilities of manly nurture and initiation of men by other men, and, most centrally, to launch his critique of contemporary men.

The New Man as Wimp

The mythopoetic men's movement agrees that something is dramatically wrong with American manhood; the "the male of the past twenty years has become more thoughtful, more gentle. But by this process he has not become more free. He's a nice boy who pleases not only his mother but also the young woman he is living with," Bly writes (p. 2). The evidence of feminization is abundant; in an earlier essay Bly pointed to

the percentage of adult sons still living at home has increased; and we can see much other evidence of the difficulty the male feels in breaking with the mother: the guilt often felt toward the mother; the constant attempt, usually unconscious, to be a nice boy; lack of male friends; absorption in boyish flirtation with women; attempts to carry women's pain, and be their comforters; efforts to change a wife into a mother; abandonment of discipline for 'softness' and 'gentleness'; a general confusion about maleness.[3]

The new man is incapable of standing up to women, so eager is he to please. "If his wife or girlfriend, furious, shouts that he is 'chauvinist,' a 'sexist,' a 'man,' he doesn't fight back, but just takes it" (p. 63). In short, the new man turns out to be a wimp; he is the problem, not the solution, and manhood needs to be rescued from such sensitive Mama's boys.

The men's movement assumes a deep, essential manhood, and its retrieval is the solution. Manhood is seen as a deeply seated essence, an ingrained quality awaiting activation in the social world. Intrinsic to every man, manhood is transhistorical and culturally universal. "The structure at the bottom of the male psyche is still as firm as it was twenty thousand years ago," observes Bly (p. 230), while Moore and Gillette claim that the deep elements of manhood have "remained largely unchanged for millions of years."[4] And it is the exact opposite of the essence of woman:

> Male and female make up one pair. . . . One can feel the resonance between opposites in flamenco dancing. Defender and attacker watch each other, attractor and refuser, woman and man, red and red. Each is a pole with its separate magnetic charge, each is a nation defending its borders, each is a warrior enjoying the heat of extravagant passion, a distinguished passion which is fierce, eaglelike, mysterious. (Bly, pp. 174–75)

Though masculinity is seen as an inner essence diametrically opposed to femininity, individual men do not inherit manhood through their biological composition. Manhood must be achieved. And it must be validated by other men; women cannot validate manhood. "It takes work to become a man," write Moore and Gillette (1992, p. 234). "Achieving adult male status requires personal courage and the support and nurturing of older men." It is the task of the larger society to facilitate this achievement, because when the actualization of manhood is thwarted, dire consequences result. "If a culture does not deal with the warrior energy . . . it will turn up outside in the form of street gangs, wife beating, drug violence, brutality to children, and aimless murder" (p. 179)—all of which sounds remarkably similar to the words of right-wing ideologue George Gilder (1974).[5] The route to manhood is perilous, but the consequences of failure are far worse.

What then are the appropriate stages of manhood, the stages that each man should follow if he is to activate his deep, essential masculinity? In sum, there are four stages of manhood, each with an accompanying scholarly and mythical apparatus to facilitate its passage: (1) bonding with the mother and breaking away from her (psychological level); (2) bonding with the father and breaking away from him (historical critique of modernity); (3) finding the male mother (anthropological reclamation of initiation ritual); (4) the reentry into adult heterosexual union (reproduction of heterosexuality, gender roles). Each of these is central to the mythopoetic vision.

BAD DEALS FROM MOMS AND DADS

The men's movement embraces a traditional, and rather conservative, rendering of psychoanalytic theory. The task of becoming men requires a break from our initial identification with the mother. In today's world this isn't simple; men's repudiation of the feminine is thwarted. More than one man "today needs a sword to cut his adult soul away from his mother-bound soul" (Bly, 1990, p. 165). There are two reasons why men have not broken the bond with mother. First, mothers won't let them, remaining locked in somewhat incestuous flirtations with their sons. (This is why the young boy must steal the key from under his mother's pillow—she will not voluntarily give it, and thus him, up.) Second, fathers are not there to facilitate the transfer of identity. Separation from mother is traditionally facilitated by father who provides a role model for his son and presents to him an alternative to femininity. But sadly, men are not doing their job as fathers. It's not entirely men's fault but rather a consequence of modern society. Here, the men's movement adopts a somewhat mythic history of the Industrial Revolution and its consequences for male development.

If we state it as another fairy tale, this myth goes something like this: Once upon a time, the division of labor was fully gendered, but both father and mother remained closely bound to the home and children. Fathers were intimately involved with the development of their sons. As artisans, they brought their sons to their workplace as apprentices; the sons had an intimate appreciation for the work of the father. But the Industrial Revolution changed all that; the separation of spheres imprisoned women in the home, as feminists have long argued, and it exiled men from the home (a fact curiously absent from feminist analysis, Bly seems to think). Now fathers are nowhere to be found in the lives of their sons. The "love unit most damaged by the Industrial Revolution has been the father–son bond," writes Bly (1990, p. 19). This, mythopoets label the "father wound."

The consequences of the father wound are significant, including adolescent male rebellion:

> The son does not bond with the father, then, but on the contrary a magnetic repulsion takes place, for by secret processes the father becomes associated in the son's mind with demonic energy, cold evil, Nazis, concentration camp guards, evil capitalists, agents of the CIA, powers of world conspiracy. Some of the fear felt in the 60s by young leftist men ("never trust anyone over 30") came from that well of demons; (Bly, 1982, p. 45)

feminism, since father absence:

may severely damage the daughter's ability to participate good-heartedly in later relationships with men. Much of the rage that some women direct to the patriarchy stems from a vast disappointment over this lack of teaching from their own fathers; (1990, p. 97)

and feminist-inspired male bashing:

The emphasis placed in recent decades on the inadequacy of men, and the evil of the patriarchal system, encourages mothers to discount grown men. . . . Between twenty and thirty percent of American boys now live in a house with no father present, and the demons have full permission to rage. (1990, pp. 86, 96)

(The reader is left to figure out exactly which demons those might be.)

The absence of the father leaves a void in the center of every adult man, a psychic wound that yearns for closure. Without healing the father wound, men are left only with mother, left literally with women teaching them how to become men. But, Bly and his followers argue, only men can really teach men to be authentic men, validate masculinity, and provide a male with a secure sense that he has arrived at manhood.

Masculinity as Praxis

Fortunately, the men's movement has discovered such a mechanism, developed in non-industrial cultures over thousands of years, that can substitute for the absent father and provide the young male with a secure grounding in gender identity. It is the male initiation ritual, symbolically reproduced by thousands of weekend warriors across the nation, men who flock to male-only retreats to tell stories, beat drums, and recreate initiation rituals from other cultures. These non-industrial cultures are seen as providing a mechanism for young boys to successfully pass through an arduous rite, at the end of which he is secure in his manhood. It is never again a question. There is no "man problem."

In each case, initiation centers around separation from the world of women and rebirth into the world of adult men. This is achieved in spatially separate men's huts or retreats, and during specific temporally demarcated periods. Like baptism, there is symbolic death of the boy (the profane self, the self born of woman) and rebirth. Bly recalls one Australian culture in which the adult men construct a twenty to thirty foot long tunnel of sticks and bushes, and push the young boys through, only to receive them with much ceremony at the other end, having now been reborn "born out of the male body" (Bly, 1982, p. 47). Or the Kikiyu, who take young boys who are hungry after a day-long fast and sit them down by a fire in the evening. Each adult male cuts his arm and lets the blood flow into a gourd which is passed to the young boys to drink "so that they can see and taste the depth of the older males' love for them." This represents a shift from "female milk to male blood" (Bly, 1982, p. 47).

The purpose of the initiation has a long theoretical legacy. Mircea Eliade argued that initiation "is equivalent to a revelation of the sacred, of death, of sexuality, and of the struggle for food. Only after having acquired these dimensions of human experience does one become truly a man."[6] And sociologist Max Weber commented on the consistency of these ritual structures in his epic *Economy and Society.* "He who does not pass the heroic trials of the warrior's training remains a 'woman' just as he who cannot be awakened to the supernatural remains a 'layman'," he wrote.[7]

At the conclusion of the initiation ritual, the young male is socially a man. He has been prepared psychically by separation from mother and identification with father, and sociologically by leaving the individual father and becoming one of the band of brothers. Now he is ready to reconnect with woman in spiritual and sexual union, seeking joyous connection, not neurotic demonstration of manhood nor narcissistic self-pleasuring. He is ready for marriage.

Thus, the spiritual quest for authentic and deep manhood reproduces traditional norms of masculinity and femininity, of heterosexuality, and, in our culture, monogamous marriage; in short, the men's movement retrieval of mythic manhood reproduces the entire political package that Gayle Rubin called the "sex-gender system."[8] In the present, as in the mythical past, the demonstration of manhood becomes associated with a relentless repudiation of the feminine. Since, in our era, the father's absence makes this separation difficult, weekend retreats offer an emotional substitute for real fathers. At these retreats, men can heal their "father wound"—the grief men feel that their fathers were not emotionally or physically present in their lives. They can feel a sense of intimacy and connectedness to other wounded and searching men. They can discover the depths of their manhood. This is the men's movement's promise for masculine renewal.

FALSE PROMISES

It is a false promise. In this section of this essay, we will develop a broad-based critique of the mythopoetic men's movement, bringing to bear a variety of social scientific literatures to understand the limitations of each phase of the men's movement's promise. We will discuss (1) the limitations of essentialism; (2) the psychoanalytic misdiagnosis; (3) the anthropological context of male bonding; (4) the historical search for masculinist solutions; and (5) the sociology of regression. We will conclude with an analysis of the value of the feminist critique of masculinity as a blueprint for men's transformation.

The Construction of Essentialism

The central assumption in the mythopoetic vision is an ontological essential difference between women and men. For all theorists of the movement, the male-female difference is not socially constructed and does not vary cross-culturally. Whether based on Jungian archetypes or bowdlerized readings of Eastern religions, or the selection of myths and fairy tales, the men's movement claims that men and women are virtually different species. The mythopoetic search for the "deep masculine" and the psychically "hairy man" is a search for something that exists as a natural, biological reality. Moore and Gillette claim that the central elements of manhood are the "hard wired components of our genetically transmitted psychic machine" — without a hint of awareness of how gendered and mechanistic is their language (1992, p. 33).

The men's movement, therefore, misses one of the central insights of social science — that gender is a product of human action and interaction, that our definitions of masculinity and femininity are the products of social discourse and social struggle. Being a man is distinct from being biologically male. Essentialism leads the men's movement to adopt a version of manhood that corresponds rather neatly with our society's dominant conception of masculinity — man as warrior and conqueror — and to suggest that this represents the quintessence of manhood. Thus Moore and Gillette venerate Ronald Reagan's courage during the hostage crisis and vilify Jimmy Carter as a wimp: "Emblematic of his weak thinking was his absurd attempt to dramatize energy conservation by not lighting the national Christmas tree, an ancient symbol of eternal life and ongoing vigor. Of more consequence was his impotent reaction to the Iran hostage crisis" (1990, p. 167). That this definition of masculinity rests on men's gender power does not have to enter into the equation — rather, the mythopoetic warrior's quest is to rediscover his masculine core and experience a bond with his psychic ancestors.

Healing the Mother Wound

These essentialist assumptions lead Bly and others to an inversion of feminist psychoanalytic insights of the past three decades. Following Chodorow, Dinnerstein, Rubin, Benjamin, and others,[9] we think that the core psychological problem of gender formation for men is, in a sense, not too little separation from mother but too much. In societies where men do little parenting, both young boys and girls have a primary identification with mother. However, the establishment of a boy's identity and his individuality is a psychic process in which the boy struggles to renounce identification with mother, and the nurturing she represents, and embrace identification with father. It is a process with enormous costs. "Boys come to define themselves," writes Chodorow, "as more separate and distinct, with a greater sense of rigid ego boundaries and differentiation. The basic feminine sense of self is connected to the world, the basic masculine sense of self is separate" (pp. 174 and 169). Such a process has political ramifications:

> Dependency on his mother, attachment to her, and identification with her represent that which is not masculine; a boy must reject dependence and deny attachment and identification. Masculine gender role training becomes more more rigid than feminine. A boy represses those qualities he takes to be feminine inside himself, and rejects and devalues women and whatever he considers to be feminine in the social world. (Chodorow, p. 181)

Manhood is defined as a flight from femininity and its attendant emotional elements, particularly compassion, nurturance, affection, and dependence. This does not mean that men completely lose these capacities. Rather it means that these things become more-or-less muted and often experienced as inimical to male power. Though the definition of manhood varies by class and culture, by era and orientation, our hegemonic definitions of masculinity are based on independence, aggression, competition, and the capacity to control and dominate.[10] This helps to explain men's rage at women, men's rage at their own dependency and weaknesses, and the rage of so many men at gay men (whom they misperceive as failed men).

As a result, most men are afraid of behavior or attitudes that even hint at the feminine. So many men are willing, even eager, to engage in all manner of high-risk behavior, lest they be branded wimps or tainted with the innuendo that they might be homosexual. The whole quest for masculinity is a life-long set of high-risk behaviors. The costs to men may be on a different level than the costs to women, but men's lived experience involves consider-

WEEKEND WARRIORS : 27

able alienation and pain. Men remain emotionally distant, aggressively risk-taking, preoccupied with power, status, money, accumulating sexual partners, because these are all badges of manhood. We call this obsessive flight from the feminine the "mother wound." Through the mother wound the boy internalizes the categories of gender power of a patriarchal society. The social project of suppressing women and their social power is internalized and unconsciously recreated in the psychic life of the young boy.

The men's movement claims that the root psychological problem for men is that we have not yet cut our psychic umbilical cord. By contrast, we see the problem as the opposite: the relentlessness by which we consciously and unconsciously demonstrate that the cord is cut. From this difference comes the men's movement's prescription for retrieving manhood: to wrench men away from the home, off to the woods with other men, into a homosocial space where men can validate one another's masculinity. It's a feel-good response, but it does little to address the roots of the problem of either a father or a mother wound. Men breaking down their isolation and fears of one another is important, but to get to the core of the problem requires men to play a role in domestic life through equal and shared parenting. Boys would experience men as equally capable of nurture, so that they would not associate nurturing with only one gender, leaving "people of both genders with the positive capacities each has, but without the destructive extremes these currently tend toward" (Chodorow, p. 218). Men would find their defensive shells pierced by affection and interdependence, thus transforming the definition of masculinity itself, no longer "tied to denial of dependence and devaluation of women." And politically, shared parenting would "reduced men's needs to guard their masculinity and their control of social and cultural spheres which treat and define women as secondary and powerless" (p. 218).

Perhaps more than anything else, it is through the social practices of parenting that men may connect with the emotional qualities that they have rejected in real life—nurturing, compassion, emotional responsiveness, caring. These emotional resources will not be adequately discovered reading a book or stomping through the woods hugging other men who have taken totemic animal names. They are to be found in the simple drudgery of everyday life in the home. Cleaning the toilet, ironing, or washing dishes are not romantic—you don't have to be a "golden eagle" to keep your nest clean. But they are the everyday stuff of nurture and care. They are skills that are learned, not received by divine revelation after howling at the moon in the forest. We need more Ironing Johns, not more Iron Johns.

Although men's entry as equal parents becomes a key part of intergenerational solutions, it isn't only biological fathers who can rediscover their capacity to nurture. Gay men, largely in response to the AIDS crisis, have developed inspiring formal and informal social networks of caregiving, nurturance, and support.

The route to manly nurture is through doing it in the everyday way that women currently nurture in our society, the ways our mothers—and not usually our fathers—nurtured us. If mothers embody responsibility, care, and nurture, why would Bly suggest that our project is to reject mother and run away from her? Men need to heal the mother wound, to close the gap between the mother who cared for us and the mother we have tried to leave behind as we struggled to get free of her grasp. What we've lost in that process is precisely what we are currently searching for. Healing the mother wound would allow men to feel that their manhood was not inextricably linked to repudiating mother and all she stands for, but rather in reclaiming, as men, a positive connection to the pre-Oedipal mother, the mother who represented to us all those emotions we currently seek: connectedness, interdependence, nurture, and love.

In a distorted way, this is what's at the core of all the pseudo-rituals in the "men's movement." Isn't this what getting in touch with the earth is all about? When workshop leaders encourage men to smear dirt on themselves or take off their shoes and feel the earth under their feet (even when they happen to be in a carpeted meeting room), they hook into a fierce longing for reconnection with the earth and with our mothers who physically embodied our most visceral connection with life and its origins.

Anthropological Androcentrism

The desire to heal men's wounds leads the men's movement to a survey of initiation rituals and rites of passage, as the mechanisms by which traditional cultures established manhood as praxis. But here is one of the chief failings of the movement. Even the most cursory glance at the same myths, archetypes, and anthropological borrowings reveals that all the cultures so celebrated by the men's movement as facilitating deep manhood have been precisely those cultures in which women's status was lowest. As male domination is not a category of thought to the movement, it needn't be a category of history. But its absence creates a major analytic and strategic problem.

Bly and the others wander through anthropological literature like post-modern tourists, as if the world's cultures were an enormous shopping mall filled with ritual boutiques. After trying them on, they take several home to make an interesting outfit—part Asian, part African, part Native American. Moore and Gillette snatch theories from Native American cosmology, Jungian archetypes, and images from ancient Egypt, 7th century Tibet, Aztecs, Incas, and Sumerians. All are totally decontextualized. But can these rituals be ripped from their larger cultural contexts, or are they not deeply embedded in the cultures of which they are a part, expressing important unstated psychological and metaphysical assumptions about both the males and females of the culture as well as reflecting the social and economic realities of life, including structures of hierarchy and domination?

Bly argues that these men's rituals helped men achieve stable and secure senses of themselves as men, and that these rituals had nothing to do with the hierarchical relations between women and men. In fact, he hints that where men are secure in their gender identity, life is actually better for women. But what we actually learn from non-industrial cultures—as opposed to what we might wish we had learned—is that these initiation ceremonies, rituals, and separate spheres have everything to do with women's inequality. One survey of over 100 non-industrial cultures found that societies with separate men's huts are those in which women have the least power. Those cultures in which men sleep separately from women are those in which women's status is lowest. "Societies with men's huts are those in which women have the least power," writes geographer Daphne Spain.[11] In short, "institutionalized spatial segregation reinforces prevailing male advantages." Anthropologist Thomas Gregor agrees; men's clubs of all kinds are "associated with strongly patriarchal societies."[12]

Gregor's work on the Mehinaku of central Brazil illustrates the selectivity in the men's movement's mythic anthropology. The Mehinaku have well institutionalized men's houses where tribal secrets are kept and ritual instruments played and stored. Spatial segregation is strictly enforced. As one man told Gregor: "This house is only for men. Women may not see anything in here. If a woman comes in, then all the men take her into the woods and she is raped. It has always been that way" (p. 27).

The men's movement is quite selective about which societies and which of their customs they should appropriate. The initiation rituals were ones through which men symbolically appropriated women's power of reproduction and childbirth. Such rituals had a central place in early patriarchal cultures. After all, how could men possibly claim to be all-powerful when it was women who had the ultimate power of bringing life into the world? Men thus devalued women's power of reproduction and asserted that only men could give birth to men, symbolized in elaborate rebirthing rituals to bring men into the world.

If our goal was not to reassert male power but to ensure gender equality, then the best approach is not to champion the initiation of men into separate mythic spheres:

> When men take care of young children and women control property, boys are apt to grow up with fewer needs to define themselves in opposition to women, and men are less inclined toward antagonistic displays of superiority. When wives are not required to defer to husbands, and men are not encouraged to boast and display fierce hostility, then cultural ideologies are unlikely to portray men as superior and women as inferior.[13]

Interestingly, the interpretations of the myths themselves are asserted to be unambiguous, always leading men away from the home and from women, off into the company of other men. But to take but one example of the dozens of ambiguous readings which might emerge from a confrontation with the original texts, we are reminded that throughout the Odyssey, Odysseus spends his time yearning to be home with his wife and child, looking longingly out at the sea and weeping every night he is away. In Book 11, he returns home, following his prophecy to stop wandering. He takes his oar to a place where men do not salt their food (inland) and where they do not recognize the oar (mistaking it for a thresher), and there he plants the oar in the ground and offers a sacrifice. Then his wanderings will be at an end, and he will be at peace. To us, the quest is, like E.T. said, to go home.

What's more, the evocations of some mythic figures as unambiguous heroes is also problematic. While some mythopoetic leaders advocate the retrieval of Zeus energy, they willfully forget that Zeus was "an incessant rapist, molesting both mortal women and ancient goddesses," whose reign ushered in a terrible era for women, according to Robert Graves—"the hitherto intellectually dominant Greek woman degenerated into the unpaid worker and breeder of children wherever Zeus and Apollo were the ruling gods."[14] Loading up on "Zeus juice" may make compelling myth, but it makes for bad gender politics.

These rituals also have consequences for race relations that their purveyors either ignore or disguise as "respect for traditional cultures." To see a group of middle-class white men appropriating "Indian" rituals, wearing "war paint," drumming and chanting, and taking on totemic animal names is more than silly play, more, even, than "a bunch of boys playing games with the cultures of people they don't know how to live next door to."[15] It is politically objectionable, similar to the "Tomahawk Chop" of Atlanta Braves baseball fans. But then again, how wise is the storyteller who asserts, as Bly does, that golden hair is a universal sign of beauty? Perhaps, as Braves fans asserted, participants believe that their behavior honors these Native American traditions. In the post-modern, New Age supermarket of the mythopoetic men's movement, though, it feels more like boys playing cowboys and Indians, and letting the Indians win for a change.

There is another, deeper level at which the racism of the new men's movement is even more deeply troubling. Here, we will make a brief historical analogy. During the late 19th century, minstrel shows were enormously popular among white working class men. These shows were particularly popular with young Irish men, and later, in the first decades of the 20th century, among young Jewish men. Performers in "blackface" would imitate black men, singing and dancing in racial sendups. But what did these blackface performers sing about? They sang of their nostalgia, their longing for home, for the comforts of family, especially Mammy. In a sense, as historians understand it now, these young Irish and Jewish performers and audiences projected their own anxieties and longings—the ones that they could not express for fear of feminization—and projected them onto newly freed black migrants to the cities. Blackface was more about the longings of white immigrants than about the real lives of black people.

Of course, today, blackface would be immediately transparent as racist. So men's movement leaders encourage what we might call "redface,"—the appropriation of Native American rituals and symbols—the drum, chants of "ho," warpaint, animal names, etc. And they imagine that these Native cultures expressed a deep spirituality, an abiding love and respect for nature, and a palpable sense of brotherhood. What they are really doing, we believe, is projecting onto these cultures their own longings and their own needs. Such a project relies upon racial, and racist, stereotypes.

Some of the faux-religious iconography of the mythopoetic men's movement gets pretty silly. Moore and Gillette suggest a small crystal pyramid be carried around as "a useful portable icon," and that the soundtrack albums for *Spartacus* or *Ben Hur* provide good background music to access the inner King, since they are "particularly evocative of King energy" (1992, pp. 215 and 217). As Joseph Conwell wrote, in *Manhood's Morning*, a turn of the century advice manual for how to grow up and be a real man, "[r]ot is rot, and it is never more rotten than when it is sandwiched between religious quotations and antiquated poetry."[16]

Historical Hokum

This brief historical analogy of racist tropes in ritual appropriation leads to a larger historical contextualization of the mythopoetic quest. Bly and his followers claim that the current male malaise is the result of the confluence of several factors that has produced the overdominance of women and absence of fathers in a young man's life. The mythic search is initiated in a historically unique situation where routine forms of male bonding have been delegitimated or disappeared. Only men can validate other men's manhood, but the possibilities for this are limited. Thus, they claim, the search for the authentic male represents a step forward, into historically uncharted waters, where men will come face to face with our grief and our pain. On the contrary, we believe that the mythopoetic men's movement is a step backward in two distinct temporal senses—historical and developmental. It augurs a social return to turn of the century masculinist efforts to retrieve manhood and a personal effort to recreate a mythic boyhood. These two temporal retreats, we believe, require a spatial retreat from women's equality, to which we shall turn in the next section.

The concern that modern culture feminizes men, turning the heroic warrior into a desk-bound nerd, is not a very new idea at all. The late 19th century witnessed an equally potent critique of the enervation of modern manhood and the sources of feminization. Then, as now, the causal sequence of this enervation was seen as a consequence of the Industrial Revolution, which demanded more and more of men's time away from home. This father absence left a void in a young boy's life, which mothers rushed to fill. Thus mothers, and later women in general, as public school and Sunday school teachers, became the validators of manhood. When fathers did return to the home in the evening, they found an utterly feminized domestic sphere, against which they chafed as they squirmed to find some deep bonding with other men.

Such diagnoses echoed across the country in a variety of settings. Here's the dashing Basil Ransome's indictment of the age in Henry James's *The Bostonians*, a sentiment that could have been written by Robert Bly today:

> The whole generation is womanized; the masculine tone is passing out of the world; it's a feminine, a nervous, hysterical, chattering, canting age, an age of hollow phrases and false delicacy and exaggerated solicitudes and coddled sensibilities, which, if we don't soon look out, will usher in the reign of mediocrity, of the feeblest and flattest and the most pretentious that has ever been. The masculine character, the ability to dare and endure, to know and yet not

fear reality, to look the world in the face and take it for what it is . . . that is what I want to preserve, or rather, as I may say, to recover; and I must tell you that I don't in the least care what becomes of you ladies while I make the attempt![17]

From pulpits to editorial pages, from gymnasiums to classrooms, men appeared concerned about the feminization of American culture and sought remedies that would cure men of their culturally induced enervation.

Structurally, the traditional definitions of masculinity were rapidly eroding at the turn of the century. The closing of the frontier meant that no longer would men have that literal-geographic space to test their mettle against nature and other men. The rapid industrialization of American manufacturing meant that individual men were no longer the owners or proprietors of their own labor. As noted earlier, at the time of the Civil War, 90% of men in the United States were independent farmers or self-employed businessmen or artisans. By 1870, that number had dropped to two of three, and by 1910, less than one-third of U.S. men were economically autonomous. At the same time, the northward migration of newly freed slaves, the dramatic immigration of swarthy Southern Europeans, and the emergence of visible homosexual enclaves in major cities all signalled new competitors for white, middle class men's power in the public domain. What's more, women were demanding equality in the public sphere in unprecedented ways. Not only in the ballot box or the classroom, but women were demanding equality in the workplace and in the bedroom, as social "feminists" argued for the right to birth control and "sex rights."

Suddenly men felt themselves to be on the defensive, and launched a multi-faceted critique of turn of the century culture. A health and fitness craze swept over the country, as more and more men sought the tonic freshness of the outdoors to offset the daily routine of "brain work." Bernarr Macfadden and other promoters of "physical culture" rode a wave of interest that saw dramatic increases in sports such as boxing, football, and weightlifting as methods to develop real manhood.

Child rearing manuals promoted a dichotomous separation of little boys and little girls. Parents were instructed to dress boys and girls differently from birth, and to follow that separation through to youth, where boys were to be encouraged to do certain activities (sports, rough play) and prevented from doing others (reading, sleeping on feather beds, going to parties) for fear of possible contamination by feminizing influences. Separate child rearing continued into the schoolroom. Coeducation was feared because women would sap the virility of male students. By adolescence, "boy culture" was to be organized and disciplined under male supervision, but strict separation of the sexes was to be maintained to insure that boys would grow up to be real men. The reorganization of the Young Men's Christian Association in the 1880s, and the organization of the Boy's Brigades and Knights of King Arthur in the 1880s, and 90s, indicated an effort to provide young boys with adult male role models, simultaneously disciplining and controlling boy culture and demarcating male space from female space in a highly ritualized and mythopoetic setting. The founding of Boy Scouts of America in 1910 by Ernest Thompson Seton provides a graphic indictment of contemporary manhood. Women, he argued, were turning "robust, manly, self-reliant boyhood into a lot of flat chested cigarette smokers with shaky nerves and doubtful vitality."[18]

Cultural feminization was challenged by religious leaders, who sought to reinvest the cultural images of Jesus with virile manhood. The Muscular Christianity movement sought to transform religious iconography, which often portrayed Jesus as soft and gentle. Jesus was "no dough-faced, little spittle proposition," proclaimed evangelist Billy Sunday, but "the greatest scrapper who ever lived." "Lord save us from off-handed, flabby cheeked, brittle boned, weak-kneed, thin-skinned, pliable, plastic, spineless, effeminate, ossified, three carat Christianity" Sunday pleaded.[19]

And adult men had their fraternal lodges to retreat to. Fraternal orders were enormously popular at the turn of the century; slightly less than one of four American men belonged to an order.[20] The lodge was a homosocial preserve, celebrating a purified, nurturant masculinity. James Laird of the Nebraska Grand Lodge endorsed a Masonic war against "destructive effeminacy" in 1876. "What Masons want, what the world wants, is not sympathy, not cooperation, not reform, not redemption, but strength."[21]

These fraternal orders are the turn of the century precursor to contemporary mythopoetic retreats. Here, men's initiation rituals took on a systematic, routinized character: with up to fifty different levels of status, one could be reasonably certain that an initiation was going to take place at each meeting. Such rituals followed a similar appropriation of tradition. The profane man, the man born of woman, is symbolically killed, and reborn into the band of equal brothers, imitating what these men knew of initiation in non-western cultures. (Like baptismal priests, the fraternal elders often wore long robes and aprons—literally appropriating women's dresses as they symbolically appropriated women's reproductive power.)

There is one interesting difference in the images of these turn-of-the-century men from their 1990's progeny. The earlier movement reflected the 19th century fascination with the classical era—mythical views of ancient Egypt, Greece, and Rome provided the icons. Bly and the mythopoetic men's movement fall very much within the New Age iconography: the classical past is no longer in vogue. Rather there is a retreat to an even-more distant mythical past, that of repackaged images of native societies.

The masculinist efforts to retrieve authentic manly adventure resonated in American literature as well. Following that Freudian axiom that the objects that give meaning to life that we lose in reality we recreate in fantasy, writers sought to recreate what we had already lost. The first "western," Owen Wister's *The Virginian* (1902), Jack London's *The Call of the Wild* (1903), and Edgar Rice Burrough's Tarzan series returned men to the frontier and the jungle, even as they receded from men's grasp. Wrenched from effete civilized life, Tarzan and Buck hear the call of their primitive instincts and return to become, respectively, apes and wolves. Mythic heroes who stood for untamed manhood, capable of beating back rapid industrialization and feminization, abounded in artisanal heroes like Paul Bunyon (collected 1914–1916), John Henry (ca. 1873), and Casey Jones (1900).

Most troubling of all these masculinist efforts to revive a recharged manhood is the turn of the century cult of the warrior, embedded within the new militarism that contributed to the Spanish American War in 1898. The soldier was seen as a moral exemplar, none more than Theodore Roosevelt, whose triumph over youthful frailty and illness and subsequent robust aggression served as a template for a revitalized social character. Roosevelt fused compulsive masculinity (the strenuous life) with military adventurism (imperialist intervention) into a powerful synthesis. Evocations of the warrior in the era of Operation Desert Storm clearly made Robert Bly uneasy; he attempted, unsuccessfully, to organize a group of writers against the war in the Gulf, just as he earlier had worked to organize writers against the Vietnam war. But many of his followers uncritically embrace warrior images, without any trace of discomfort.

The weekend warriors join a host of contemporary masculinists who search for the masculine primitive among the shards of advanced industrial culture.[22] One Yale senior waxed nostalgic about his years as a member of Skull and Bones:

> I mean, it's a damn shame it's got to end. The fraternity and everything. Someday we should build us all a fraternity house that wouldn't end. And we could initiate all our friends and go off and drink like freshmen and never graduate.

Hell! Why build a fraternity house? Let's build one gigantic fraternity system! —
Graduating senior, age twenty-one.

How different are they from the wealthy members of the Bohemian Club in
San Francisco who go off to Bohemian Grove retreats every summer —
retreats that are drenched with ritualized male bonding, dancing partially
naked in front of campfires, "full of schmaltz and nostalgia" — with corporate
CEOs and legislators (and presidents), and other members of the American
ruling class,[23] or take part in the occasional Wild Man retreat if he felt the
creeping enervation of having to deal with adult women on an equal basis.
But in case the impact on women is lost to our dreaming Yalie, let him hear
the voice of one of his brothers, another member of Yale's Skull and Bones
club. "I would predict an increase in date rape," he prophesied, should the
club be forced to admit women.[24]

Boys' Town

The image of the eternal fraternity reveals a partially hidden longing that
lies just beneath the surface of Bly's appeal. The search for the deep masculine is actually a search for lost boyhood, that homosocial innocence of pre-
adolescence, at once rough and tumble and sweetly naive. It is an effort to
turn back the clock to that time before work and family responsibilities
yanked men away from their buddies, from a world of fun. Leslie Fiedler
noticed this nostalgic yearning for lost boyhood, a world of homosocial intimacy as the dominant theme in American literature. Unlike European literature, in which the action revolved around adult men and women in domestic
entanglements, the American novel allows the young man to escape domesticity by being kidnapped, running away, enlisting in the army, or being ship-
wrecked. The American romantic couple is Natty Bumppo and Chingachgook, Ishmael and Queequeg, Huck Finn and Jim, the Lone Ranger and
Tonto. These couples "proffer a chaste male love as the ultimate emotional
experience" revealing an "implacable nostalgia for the infantile, at once
wrong headed and somehow admirable," he writes. The authors' "self con-
gratulatory buddy-buddiness" also reveals an "astonishing naivete."[25] "I
reckon I gotta light out for the territory," says Huck, "cuz Aunt Sally, she's
gonna civilise me, and I can't stand it."

The mythopoetic men's retreats recall the clubhouse with the sign reading
"No Girls Allowed" or the movie *Stand By Me* that captures that last summer
before junior high school, before having to posture to impress girls will for-

ever distort the relationships among the boys. What Kenneth Keniston calls the "fallacy of romantic regression" appeals not to men who want to be men, but rather men who want to re-become boys; thus their antipathy towards women and work is so easily displaced onto mothers who have not been part of their lives for decades. "No one is going to catch me lady and make me a man. I want always to be a little boy and to have fun." So said Peter Pan. So say the men at wildman retreats.

This search for lost boyhood as the search for the authentic masculine helps explain several of the paradoxes that emerge at the men's retreats. The men's movement speaks to men not as fathers but as sons searching for their fathers. But curiously, the attendees at the workshops are middle-aged men, many of whom are, themselves, fathers. They rarely speak of their own children (and when they do, it's almost exclusively their sons; it's as if daughters do not exist in this world). They speak as sons, of their pain as sons estranged from fathers. That is, they would rather complain about something they can barely change than work towards transforming something that they can: their relationships with their own children and the structured inequalities of power between men and women, adults and children, and one man and another.

However, at the retreats, they are also asked to honor the elders, the older men at the weekend retreats, who are seen to embody a certain deeply male wisdom. Leaders invite us to admire the wisdom of older men, to listen to their stories, learn from the wisdom they have gained through the years. But wait, are these not the same elder men (fathers) who abandoned us? Thus when Bly or his followers speak as fathers, they criticize contemporary men as having followed mother, having been dutiful little boys (having been feminized). But when they speak as sons, they are angry and hurt by fathers who behaved exactly as they have.

How do we explain this shift in focus? "I'm not sure why they want to be back in the good old days," observed a woman therapist in 1967. "Do they want to be back there as the father, or do they want to be back there as the child?"[26] When we speak as sons, we are angry and wounded by our fathers. When we speak as fathers, we expect veneration and admiration from sons. We are thus going to have it both ways, particularly, whichever way allows us to feel like the innocent victim of other people's disempowering behavior, the victim of what others (fathers or sons) have done to us. This is again the lost (false) innocence of mythic boyhood.

But it is also more than that—it is staking a claim for victimhood and entitlement at the same time. This is what explains the emphasis on the role of the little prince in the Iron John story, and explains the way that these men, feeling like boys, want to claim their inner King. The prince is actually not the central figure in Iron John's story; it is Iron John himself, who is liberated by the young boy's quest. As the title indicates, he is the star. But male readers see themselves as the king's son, the prince, and not as Iron John.

But who is the prince? The prince is the rightful heir to power; he will be the King. He is literally *entitled* to power, but he is not yet ready for it. So too, for manhood. Men's movement participants believe themselves entitled to that power, the power that comes from being a man, the power we might call patriarchy, or male privilege. They do not feel that power yet—but they want to, and they feel themselves entitled to it. This is why the men at the mythopoetic retreats find it so much easier to imagine themselves as sons, to call themselves "adult children"—as if the word "adult" was an adjective, modifying the word "child"—rather than as fully adult, responsible to others, and refusing to claim their privileged inheritance.[27]

Whispers of the Heart

We believe that the mythopoetic quest is misguided, because it reproduces masculinity as a power relation—the power of men over women and the power of some men over other men. But there is no reason to doubt Bly or his followers' sincerity, or their desire to recreate a world of gender certainty. The appeal of this message is in response to feminism, but not only in the negative sense we have been describing. It is also an indication that millions of men have been forced to grapple with what it means to be a man. Men are searching, looking for a new sense of meaning. That they've been looking under every possible stone and crystal is no surprise, nor is it a surprise that the most popular solution so far is one that offers a quick and comfortable fix. While the mythopoetic solution may not bring real change, the enthusiasm with which he has been greeted represents, at least in part, part of a process of change.

A key aspect of that process, a progressive whisper within a reactive structure, is that mythopoetic groups and gatherings can be means for men to break their isolation from other men. Part of patriarchy's interpersonal cement is an isolation that keeps each man fearful of his own masculinity and forces him to go to lengths to prove to the other guys that he's a real man. By breaking the isolation, by setting up opportunities for men to express a range of feelings among themselves and to talk about their fears and loves and challenges, men can take steps towards disassociating manhood and domination and reestablishing it on the basis of connection and harmony with those around us.[28]

This activity of redefinition is seen in the nostalgia for boyhood. We've talked about the regressive side of this nostalgia, but we also must ask why this nostalgia is so powerful. Perhaps it is part of what Barbara Ehrenreich described as men's flight from commitment symbolized by the magazine that extolled a male inhabiting an adult body but acting like a boy at play, literally a Play-boy.[29] But there's more: It is a longing for what men have given up in order to fit into the tight pants of masculinity. Becoming a man required a suppression of a range of human capacities, capabilities, and emotions. But these capacities maintain a nagging presence in our own lives. Few of us completely or effortlessly fit into the dictates of male gender power, particularly in a society where women have demanded equality and have challenged men to examine our own lives. As we attempt to expand our emotional repertoire, as we learn to reach out to our brothers, sisters, and children, it reawakens a childhood voice that has long been buried. Playing in the woods recalls the days when we were less preoccupied with maintaining our gender barriers, when we felt more at home with the bodies and the tears of other males, and when we felt more at home with ourselves. It isn't that any moment of our lives we were completely free of the rigors of gender acquisition, but rather that gender demands did not yet so completely overwhelm a range of other human characteristics and possibilities. Of course, part of the yearning for the past is a nostalgia for a past that did not completely exist.[30]

The alternative is not to reject personal change and personal growth. It is not for men to start a political movement in the image of other political movements: Alright men, let's get out there and get this job done no matter what the cost. It is to hear what women have been telling us for the past two and one-half decades—that personal change is an indispensable element of, and tool for, social change, and that structural social change is an indispensable element for personal change.

It is a personal vision of political change and a political vision of personal change that we propose as an alternative to the men's movement that will allow men's wild and progressive impulses to blossom.

The Flight from Feminism

What keeps Bly and his followers from taking this radical course of personal and social change are his protests that his work has nothing to do with women or feminism. Bly writes that his book "does not constitute a challenge to the women's movement" that he "does not seek to turn men against women, nor to return men to their domineering mode that has led to repression of women and their values for centuries" (1990, p. x). But such claims are disingenuous.

Though Bly is careful to hedge his comments, the book is full of inferences that reveal how he embraces traditional gender roles:

> A mother's job is, after all, to civilize the boy. (P. 11)

or

> A man who cannot defend his own space cannot defend women and children. (P. 156)

or:

> As more and more mothers work out of the house, and cannot show their daughters what they produce, similar emotions may develop in the daughter's psyche, with a consequent suspicion of grown women. (P. 96)

Alone with other men, Bly gives this anti-feminist tendency fuller play. Journalists Steve Chapple and David Talbot describe an encounter between Bly and his campers at a retreat: "Robert, when we tell women our desires, they tell us we're wrong," shouts out one camper. "So," says Bly, "then you bust them in the mouth because no one has the right to tell another person what their true desires are."[31]

And if Bly sidesteps the issue, his followers do not. One leader of retreats to heal the father wound argues:

> A lot of men feel hung out to dry by the women's movement. A lot of men feel that they, personally, are being held responsible for everything that's macho and wrong in the world today: rape, wife-beating, war. They've been feeling very bad about themselves, and so they're overjoyed to recover their maleness and feel proud about themselves as men. (cited in Chapple and Talbot, 195)

Ray Raphael celebrates men's ability to do anything women can:

> At a time when an enlightened feminism has taken away many of our traditional props, at a time when many of our manly roles have become virtually obsolete, at a time when we have been placed on the defensive in what we perceive as a never-ending competition between the sexes, we have countered by aggressively usurping the roles once played by women.[32]

And journalist Trip Gabriel reports from the gender front that "more than the men's movement cares to admit, it is a reaction to the decades of feminism, a reclaiming of prerogatives that men have long been made to feel defensive about."[33]

Note how each of these men couches the reaction against feminism in terms of men's defensiveness. Men have been made to feel badly about traditional masculinity, about men's violence, rape, pornography, battery and a litany of other feminist accusations. Their response is not to enlist in the feminist struggle against these excesses of manly behavior but to declare themselves tired of listening.

The retreat to find a revitalized and recharged manhood, embodied in the new men's movement, is most definitely a retreat. It is a retreat from the mother, who embodies, in the practices of mothering, precisely the positive qualities of caring and nurturing that men are running away from her to find. It is a retreat from the historical specificity of the present era, a retreat from political responsibilities to confront male excesses that daily manifest themselves on our streets, in our schools, in our workplaces, in our bedrooms, excesses such as rape, violence, spouse abuse, gay bashing, high risk sexual behavior, drunk driving. It is a retreat to a highly selective anthropological world of rituals that reproduce men's cultural power over women and that are now used to facilitate a deeper nostalgic retreat to the lost world of innocent boyhood. It is thus a retreat from women, from adult men's responsibilities to embrace women's equality and struggle against those obstacles that continue to lie in the path of gender equality. Male bonding, hailed as the positive outcome of these weekend retreats, is double sided. Bonding implies connection with others, and also implies constraints, responsibilities. The deep masculine will never be retrieved by running away from women. Only by fighting for equality, side by side, as equals, can we realize the best of what it means to be a man.

NOTES

1. William Whyte, *The Organization Man* (New York: Anchor, 1956), 356.
2. Robert Bly, *Iron John* (Reading, Mass.: Addison-Wesley, 1990).
3. Robert Bly, "What Men Really Want," in *New Age Journal* (May 1982): 31–51.
4. Robert Moore and Douglas Gillette, *The King Within: Accessing the King in the Male Psyche* (New York: William Morrow, 1992), 49; Bly, *Iron John*, p. 230.
5. George Gilder, *Naked Nomads* (New York: Quadrangle, 1974).

6. Mircea Eliade, *The Sacred and the Profane* (Chicago: University of Chicago Press, 1962), 73.

7. Max Weber, *Economy and Society*, 2 vols. (Berkeley: University of California Press, 1978), 1144.

8. Gayle Rubin, "The Traffic in Women" in *Toward an Anthropology of Women*, ed. by Rayna R. Reiter (New York: Monthly Review Press, 1974).

9. Nancy Chodorow, *The Reproduction of Mothering* (Berkeley: University of California Press, 1978); Dorothy Dinnerstein, *The Mermaid and the Minotaur* (New York: Harper and Row, 1976); Gayle Rubin; and Jessica Benjamin, *The Bonds of Love* (New York: Pantheon, 1985); Lillian Rubin, *Intimate Strangers* (New York: Harper and Row, 1982).

10. R. W. Connell, *Gender and Power* (Stanford: Stanford University Press, 1988).

11. Daphne Spain, *Gendered Spaces* (Chapel Hill: University of North Carolina Press, 1992), 76.

12. Thomas Gregor, "No Girls Allowed," *Science* 82 (December 1982): 27.

13. Scott Coltrane, *Family Man* (unpublished ms.), p. 41.

14. Cited in Jane Caputi and Gurdene O. Mackenzie, "Pumping *Iron John*," in *Women Respond to the Men's Movement*, ed. Kay Leigh Hagan (San Francisco: Harper-Collins, 1992), 72. See also Harry Brod, "Reply to Bly," *AHP Perspective* (April 1985).

15. Hattie Gossett, "min's movement??? a page drama," in *Women Respond to the Men's Movement*, ed. Kay Leigh Hagan (San Francisco: HarperCollins, 1992), 21.

16. Joseph Alfred Conwell, *Manhood's Morning; or, "Go it while You're Young": A Book for Young Men Between 14 and 28 Years of Age* (Wineland, N.J.: The Hominis Book Company, 1896), 155.

17. Henry James, *The Bostonians* (1885; reprint, New York: Signet, 1966), 293. The material in this section is drawn primarily from Kimmel's *Manhood in America: A Cultural History* (New York: The Free Press, in press).

18. Cited in David Macleod, *Building Character in the American Boy* (Madison: University of Wisconsin Press, 1983), 49.

19. Cited in William McLaughlin, *Billy Sunday Was His Real Name* (Chicago: University of Chicago Press, 1955), 175, 179.

20. W. S. Harwood, "Secret Societies in America," *The North American Review* 164 (May 1897): 620–23.

21. Cited in Mark C. Carnes, *Secret Ritual and Manhood in Victorian America* (New Haven: Yale University Press, 1989), 141.

22. Masculinists, as distinct from either pro-feminist men or self-conscious anti-feminists, are more concerned with what they see as the feminization of men than the feminism of women. In response to this fear of feminization, they attempt to carve out homosocial environments in both the public and private spheres in order to celebrate male bonding and fantasies of escape from women. See Michael Kimmel, "Men's Responses to Feminism at the Turn of the Century," *Gender & Society*

1 (1987). Yale student cited in William F. Buckley, "The Clubhouse" in *About Men*, ed. D. Erickson (New York: Poseiden Press, 1987), 257.

23. See, for example, G. William Domhoff, *The Bohemian Grove and Other Ruling Class Retreats* (New York: Harper and Row, 1974).

24. Cited in *Newsweek*, 23 September 1991.

25. Leslie Fiedler, *Love and Death in the American Novel* (New York: Stein and Day, 1966), 144.

26. Cited in Myron Brenton, *The American Male* (London: George Allen and Unwin, 1967), 107.

27. It's also been suggested that movement participants are princes because there can only be one King, Bly himself, the symbolic "good" father who facilitates, through traditional analytic transference, the healing of the father wound. But we believe that the mythopoetic men's movement is more than Freudian psychoanalysis on a mass scale; it is also political and ideological.

28. An alternative approach to breaking this isolation but within a profeminist perspective, is addressed in Kaufman's *Cracking the Armour: Power, Pain, and the Lives of Men* (Toronto: Viking Canada, 1993).

29. Barbara Ehrenreich, *The Hearts of Men* (New York: Anchor, 1983).

30. Our thanks to Harry Brod for suggesting this final point, the sense of nostalgia for something that did not fully exist.

31. Cited in Steve Chapple and David Talbot, *Burning Desires* (New York: Simon and Schuster, 1990), 196.

32. Ray Raphael, *The Men From the Boys: Rites of Passage in Male America* (Lincoln: University of Nebraska Press, 1988), 172.

33. Trip Gabriel, "In Touch with the Tool Belt Chromosome," *The New York Times*, 22 September 1991, 31.

Mythopoetic Foundations
and New Age Patriarchy

KEN CLATTERBAUGH

As soon as war is declared it will be impossible to hold the poets back. Rhyme is still the most effective drum.

Jean Giraudoux, *Duel of Angels*, Act I

THE DEBATE

The poet Robert Bly has fired a salvo in what has been called "the longest war."[1] Some think he may even have started a small war of his own with the publication of *Iron John* and the innumerable men's gatherings he has hosted. Bly's ideas are almost universally rejected by feminist women and their male allies as patriarchal or at least as patriarchy friendly.[2] Bly himself acknowledges this hostility but seems to believe that he is contributing to rather than detracting from the long-term goals of the women's movement. "I want to make clear that this book [*Iron John*] does not seek . . . to return men to the domineering mode that has led to repression of women . . ." (Bly 1990, x).[3] He envisions a future when men and women will meet as true spiritual equals and he seems to welcome changing roles (Bly 1990, 60–61; Bly 1982, 51). How can such a vision be patriarchal or anti-feminist? Why do feminist critics find the mythopoetic movement problematic? This controversy has made Bly increasingly distrustful of how his message is being received and escalated the war of words between mythopoetic men and feminist critics.[4]

Feminist women are not uninformed about the several men's movements. Feminist women welcome the pro-feminist men's movement of the early 1970s. Books such as Warren Farrell's *The Liberated Man*[5] and Marc Feigen Fasteau's *The Male Machine*[6] featured endorsements by prominent feminists such as Wilma Scott Heide, president of the National Organization for Women, 1971–1974, and Gloria Steinem. Men's work was the other side of the coin. If women were to achieve a new set of choices, men would both lose privilege and gain choices for themselves. But only men could decide for themselves to go in a direction compatible with contemporary feminism. Thus, Gloria Steinem wrote in the introduction to *The Male Machine:* "This book is a complement to the feminist revolution, yet it is one no woman could write. It is the revolution's other half" (p. xv). Yet, Steinem's introduction to *Women Respond to the Men's Movement* typifies many feminists' view of the mythopoetic movement. While she openly respects male "allies in a shared struggle toward a new future," she denounces "the atavistic masculine" values proposed by Robert Bly in *Iron John* (Hagan 1992, viii).

Much is at stake in this debate. If feminist critics are right, then the mythopoetic movement threatens the revolution begun in the 1960s. Men pulled into the movement will find themselves embracing the values, attitudes, and behaviors that create and maintain the traditional roles that feminism seeks to remove. Such a regression not only harms the cause of feminism, but also puts men at risk, since they would lose the gains of a more equal society. On the other hand, if Bly is right, the mythopoetic movement is a means to the future equality sought by feminists. Men who reach down and find the deep masculine, will be better able to reject the immature men who become patriarchs. Of course, both could be wrong. But both cannot be right.

In this essay I argue that, independently of Bly's hopes or intentions, the mythopoetic men's movement is unlikely to go in any direction other than toward some version of patriarchy. The reasons for this misdirection lie in the very foundations of mythopoetic thought. And, these foundational beliefs can be easily gleaned from basic writings, such as *Iron John* and its progenitors, and Moore and Gillette's *King, Warrior, Magician, Lover.*[7] (Of course, one needs to supplement these sources with tapes, remarks at gatherings, interviews, and other incidental pieces.) Thus, my first conclusion is that the mythopoetic movement is indeed an obstacle to an egalitarian future. But my second conclusion is that the mythopoetic movement may not be a very serious obstacle. I am inclined to reject both Bly's claims of the compatibility of feminist goals with mythopoetic tendencies and feminist concerns that the mythopoetic movement may greatly extend the life of patriarchal society.

Patriarchal structures are not quite invisible, but they can be hard to discern. The point of men's and women's consciousness raising sessions in the 1970s was to detect such insidious structures and find ways to dissolve them.

Structures might be personal such as a woman being left out of a conversation in the classroom, or facts like the near absence of women in the U.S. congress and other places of political and corporate power. Part of the reason for the near invisibility of these structures is that they have been in place for so long that we are acculturated to see them as natural or inevitable. Institutionalized male power is just the way things are.

Many of these structures have deep roots in how we think about women and men, what attributes we give them, what science has concluded about male nature and female nature, and what religions tell us about the male and female. A few years ago a major university faced severe budget cuts; they believed they had to eliminate or reduce certain programs. Their selection of programs focused almost exclusively on those that had traditionally provided career opportunities for women, such as nutrition, textiles, dental hygiene, and nursing. They valued these programs less than engineering, physics, or mathematics. When it was pointed out that they were devaluing what was traditionally of value to women, they were surprised. Their answer was that they had valued certain areas more than others and not thought about the impact on women (even though closures dramatically dropped the percentage of women faculty). Patriarchy requires valuing what is traditionally male and devaluing what is traditionally female. Such deep roots make patriarchy hard to eradicate.

Devaluing what women do typically accompanies denying women access to what is traditionally male. Alleged essential differences between men and women often are the underpinnings of both devaluation and denial of access. Men are by "nature" active, creative, leaders, suited for certain arenas, while women are essentially passive, nurturing, followers of the male lead, and best suited for other arenas. Messages that reflect these underpinnings are common in the various instruments of ideology, namely, literature, film, and advertising. Thus, feminism must combat not only the messages of patriarchy but also the vehicles that convey these messages.

The accumulated denial of access for women shows itself clearly in the "men's clubs": Congress, the Supreme Court, the Federal Reserve, executive offices, colleges and universities, corporate boards, and spiritual institutions. These are where collective male power is institutionalized. To hold power is crudely to be able to make someone act, think, or feel in ways that person would not act, think, or feel if the power holder did not act. A market created by advertising is an act of power, as is passing a law or making a spiritual pronouncement. Another aspect of patriarchy is that being male in clearly recognized ways is a norm against which others are compared; men are centered in patriarchal discourse.[8] Being competent means being assertive, articulate, and efficient in a style that has evolved and is perceived as masculine. Women were and are excluded from certain athletic events, medicine, law, political office, and the military precisely because no one could imagine them living up to even minimal patriarchal definitions of ability. The fact that there is change today, a nibbling at the edges of patriarchy, does not mean that patriarchal society has been abandoned. Insidious and deeply layered power and definition remain characteristics of contemporary patriarchy.

My reasons for making these obvious points is that they make it clear how someone could overlook patriarchal ideas. What is hidden and deep-rooted may easily reappear in a new form, if patriarchal foundations are not noticed. Deep-rooted structures such as racism have continually taken new guises in the United States over the past 225 years. Sometimes these guises are intentionally cultivated; often they are not. Even liberal feminism with its inclusive message often accepts a patriarchal norm by arguing that women can be just as tough, competitive, efficient, and, if necessary, ruthless as men in holding power. Thus, the process of eradicating patriarchy is continuous and never easy. It is a series of mistakes from which we can hopefully discern the right direction.

I think something like this regenerated patriarchy is what has happened with the mythopoetic men's movement. Bly has knocked down the foliage of the old age version of patriarchy, dug up some roots, replanted them, and is harvesting a "new age patriarchy" for his efforts. I do not seek to pass judgment on Robert Bly, himself. There is plenty of evidence that he does not intend to recreate patriarchal themes or institutions. There is also evidence that he should have been more vigilant in his gatherings and writings. In any case, I argue that his foundational ideas are at their core patriarchal. But even well-intentioned failures can be highly instructive.

THE PATRIARCHAL FOUNDATIONS OF THE MYTHOPOETIC MOVEMENT

The Vehicle: The Grimm Fairy Tale of Iron Hans

The mythopoetic movement is fond of telling stories. The purpose of looking at stories, especially legends, mythology, and folk tales is to uncover repeated behavior patterns that count as archetypal or universal. These patterns are the "crystalline underpinning to the soul water" (Bly 1990, 229–30). Stories reveal the collective unconscious and the collective unconscious houses the scripts which must be understood (Bly 1990, 55).

There are a great many stories in all cultures at different historical moments, and Bly frequently alludes to African, Celtic, and Native American stories.[9] But his preferred vehicle is the Grimms' fairy tale "Iron Hans," which Bly tells as the story of Iron John. Bly says very little about the story except that it may be ten or twenty thousand years old (Bly 1990, 5 cf. Pelka). Older tales in the folk tradition are particularly important for picking up the primordial images which are housed in the unconscious.

Yet, even a most cursory look at the folklorist writings reveals that it is extremely doubtful that these tales can credibly be claimed as folk tales in an oral tradition. They are literary devices intended to convey rigid gender roles. Thus, John M. Ellis writes:

> The changes introduced by the Grimms were far more than mere stylistic matters, and the facts of their editorial procedures, taken together with the evidence as to their sources, are sufficient completely to undermine any notion that the Grimms' fairy tales are of folk, or peasant, or even German origin. And the facts also show the Grimms' attempts to foster these illusions.[10]

Even more significant are the blatantly sexist messages of the Grimms' tales. In *Grimm's Bad Girls and Bold Boys*, a title that neatly captures the gender messages of these tales, Ruth Bottigheimer notes two dominant patriarchal themes in these stories, namely, boys are active while girls are passive and girls need to be punished more severely for transgressions than boys.[11] The first theme is identified by almost every folklorist who has worked with the Grimm brothers' collection:

> [The] heroine [is] a pure virgin who becomes the well deserved prize for a courageous hero who had overcome the . . . enemy by a vigorous and determined fight. She was his reward. . . .[12]

> The male hero is the adventurer, the doer, and the rescuer, whereas the female protagonist is generally passive if not comatose. Moreover the Grimm . . . tales often conserve a medieval notion of "might makes right" along with typical "bourgeois myths" of industriousness, cleanliness, and truthfulness as holiness.[13]

Bottigheimer's second theme is clearly illustrated by comparing the two Grimm brothers' stories "Our Lady's Child" and "Iron Hans." In "Iron Hans" the boy breaks a minor rule and acquires a gold finger, but he is still allowed to travel the world and find fame and fortune. Marienkind in "Our Lady's Child" also breaks a minor rule and acquires a gold finger; her punishment is to sit alone, living off roots and berries while her clothes rot and fall off in a freezing rain (Bottigheimer, 91).

The patriarchal themes of the Grimm brothers' folk tale may have appealed to Prussian conservatives and Nazi conservatives; in fact the Allies banned the Grimms' tales for a brief time in 1945 out of fear of their fascist message. And, these stories, except for the magic they portray, also fit the images sought by the Christian right—masculine dominant and female submissive. One can hardly expect feminist critics, who must be concerned with the vehicles used to present gender roles, to rejoice in such "neatly fulfilling patriarchal roles and expectations" as those depicted in *Iron John*.[14]

ESSENTIALISM AND ITS IMPLICATIONS

Essentialism is the view that social differences such as those between men and women, people of different races, or social classes are due to intrinsic biological or psychic differences between the members of the different groups. Strong essentialism believes that social differences can be more fully explained by these innate differences than by social learning or the influence of social institutions. A consequence of essentialism is that given that people have these real inner differences, they will not be happy if they deny the expression of these differences. Thus, in the conservative thinking of George Gilder, men will never be fulfilled by staying at home taking care of the children and women will similarly be frustrated if they try to go against their nature and do what is traditionally masculine.[15] Essentialism plays a central role in historical patriarchal ideology. Bad things are bound to happen if change is introduced that goes against essential natures. Women are women and men are men and what men and women traditionally have done reflects their real natures—unhappiness, and possible social chaos, is the price of trying to alter gender roles.

Essentialism has enjoyed a revival in recent years with the development of sociobiology, which argues that because certain behaviors and attitudes have been useful as mechanisms for the perpetuation of genetic material, they have been encoded in our genes. We are, therefore, left with a set of male behavior patterns and female behavior patterns that are hard wired, built into us as genetic predispositions. Many who embrace this sociobiological theory do not see any point in trying to dramatically change male and female behaviors for the simple reason that either it will not work or the costs to society and individuals will be too high if we try to go against nature.[16]

The mythopoetic movement is as deeply essentialist as the classical or even religious conservative. Moore and Gillette in their foundational work, *King, Warrior, Magician, Lover*, are unashamedly essentialist. "It is our experience that deep within every man are blueprints, what we can also call 'hard wiring,' for the calm and positive mature masculine. Jungians refer to these masculine potentials as archetypes, or 'primordial images'" (p. 9). Bly is more metaphorical. He notes that although only 3 percent of the DNA in men and women is different, it exists in every cell in the body (Bly 1990, 234). Elsewhere, he seems to opt directly for the sociobiological alternative: "The ancient practice of initiation then—still very much alive in our genetic structure . . ." (Bly 1990, 36).

Bly's wild man is that essential male energy which men must tap in order to be fulfilled (Bly 1990, 55). Men today are unhappy because they have lost touch with and been denied this essential maleness. These men are feminized, in touch with the feminine but out of touch with the deep masculine (cf. Moore and Gillette, p. xviii). Bly believes that there was a better time when men were more in touch with their masculine side. But like many conservatives, Bly believes that "the United States has undergone an unmistakable decline since 1950 . . ." (Bly 1990, 35; also Bly 1982, 32).

In addition to unhappiness, a further consequence of Bly's essentialism is that no woman can ever initiate a boy into manhood (Bly 1982, 36; Bly 1990, 99). This consequence makes Bly very critical of single mothers; like his conservative counterparts, he finds women-headed families the major source of social disintegration (Bly 1985; Bly 1990, 17, 32).

Essentialism also plays a critical causal role in the mythopoetic concept of *shame*. A man is ashamed when his essential maleness is put down or denied to him (Bly 1990, 147, 18–19; cf. Bly and Tannen 1992, 92; Moore and Gillette, p. xviii). Men have been shamed into losing touch with the masculine side, thus becoming soft, feminine, and passive (Bly 1990, 2–5). Ending the shame and getting in touch with the wild man are very much the same accomplishment, and for Bly the solution is to steal the key from under the *mother's* pillow (Bly 1990, 10–11, 32–33). Shame and essentialism contribute to Bly's fondness for blaming mothers—it is the mother's role to raise the child, so a boy grows up with a feminine (inappropriate) view of his maleness. Women cannot help, given their natures, but shame the son (Bly 1990, 24–25). Women misinform sons about their fathers and themselves: "You're not going to get a straight picture of your father out of your mother. Instead, all the inadequacies of the father are well pointed out" (Bly 1982, 51). A wise woman turns the son over to other men. Similarly, feminist women cannot help but shame men because they too speak from their essentially female side; they cannot know the masculine and how it is needed by men (Bly 1982, 37; Bly 1990, 63).

These ancient patriarchal themes suggest that men have been misinformed by the women who raised them and that men can learn the truth only by going to other men (Moore and Gillette, p. xviii). Thus, the essentialism promotes a kind of separatism and distrust, a separatism that suggests that only men can heal men, that men are deeply wounded by women, that men need to be alone together in order to get it straight. Unlike contemporary psychology in which a person can be both masculine and feminine, mythopoetics see the masculine and feminine as opposite, "defenders" and "attackers" (Bly 1990, 174–75). In this essentialism, men have little or nothing to gain from women's teachings (feminism) and even need to defend themselves from female disinformation.

Both Bly's vehicle and mythopoetic essentialism are deep roots of patriarchy. Put them together and we have a story of an adventurous boy who comes to greatness by overcoming his mother's misinformation about himself and winning a princess for his prize. This is hardly the stuff of feminist dreams for a new and gender-equal future.

INTELLECTUAL AND MORAL AMBIGUITIES

Mythopoetic essentialism and its favored vehicles push the movement in an overtly patriarchal direction. But there is another root of patriarchy in this movement which allows it to covertly slide in a patriarchal direction. The neo-Jungian underpinnings of the mythopoetic movement leave behind a vacuous and morally sterile vision of masculinity. This vacuity and sterility together with its essentialist categories encourages a kind of patriarchal drift. Simply stated, unless patriarchal paths are firmly blocked within the foundations of a belief system operating in a patriarchy, patriarchal paths will remain open and attractive to believers. The mythopoetic movement does not challenge patriarchal beliefs and values; if anything it serves its members as a refuge from feminist critique.

How does this vacuity and permissiveness arise? The foundational concept within the neo-Jungian mythopoetic movement is that of an archetype. Bly himself prefers to talk of such things metaphorically. Thus, he refers to "old familiar energies, the seven figures or beings of luminous powers" (Bly 1990, 229–30). Or Bly talks about the "crystalline underpinning to the soul water" (Bly 1990, 229–30). Moore and Gillette, as we have noted, are more explicit in talking about archetypes or primordial images hard wired into the psyche. Pascal, in *Jung to Live By*, offers a capsule definition of archetype: "psychological realities of a biological, psycho-biological or image producing character that are typical, stereotypical, and universal."[17] Examples of archetypes include suckling in infants, frowning, crying, mating games, and repeated behaviors of any kind. Clearly, the concept is used ambiguously, as it was in Jung, to include behaviors, some of which are instinctual and some of which are learned. The ambiguity causes confusion about what men are since what is learned can often be unlearned; what is instinctual or biological must often simply be lived with. Bly's message is a dual one; it promises both change and permanence without offering any way to tell which is which.

The male psyche in the neo-Jungian description becomes a rather crowded city divided into four quadrants, represented by the archetypes of king, warrior, magician, and lover. These archetypes have a mature and an immature form (Moore and Gillette, p. 52). The trickster, a frequent visitor to the pages of the mythopoetic literature, is an immature archetype of the magician. Moore and Gillette identify the trickster as: "that immature masculine energy that plays tricks, of a more or less serious nature, in one's own life and on others. He is expert at creating appearances, and then "selling" us on those appearances. He seduces people into believing him, and then he pulls the rug out from under them" (Moore and Gillette, p. 28). Bly makes a very similar pronouncement in *Iron John* (Bly 1990, 228). In sum, the trickster is that part of us that plays tricks, the king is that part of us that acts kingly, the warrior is that part of us that makes us defend ourselves, the lover is that part of us that makes us sensuous.

The game that is being played out in these uninformative explications of the main archetypes is very old and very tired. Gould, in *The Mismeasure of Man*, calls it "reification."[18] The game of reification is easy to play. Find a human behavior, label it, invent a psychic thing that is said to cause that behavior, name it or find a metaphor for it, and pretend you have an explanation of the behavior in terms of the psychic thing you posited. Sociobiologists play it when they note that humans behave spitefully and then posit a spite gene to explain spiteful behavior. The game is endless and obviously explains nothing. It is an utterly circular exercise. We explain behavior of a certain kind by whatever it is in the psyche that causes that behavior. Of course, there is no evidence that such a psychic thing exists or even that the behavior is caused by the psyche. Obviously, since there are an indefinite number of human behaviors, archetypes can multiply indefinitely. A recent issue of *Wingspan* discusses the "archetype of the Green Man," an archetype that makes us act in an ecologically responsible manner.[19]

A similar game goes on in the mythopoetic movement when moral issues are raised. There is a tendency to identify immoral behavior as that behavior that is produced by immature archetypes. If the ego does not access the mature archetypes a number of nasty characters emerge: wife beaters, rapists, tyrants, flying boys, egotists, etc. "Patriarchy expresses what we are calling boy psychology. It is not an expression of mature masculine potentials in their essence . . ." (Moore and Gillette, pp. xvii, 13–42). Thus, we have encountered a circle of another kind, and it, too, is a dead end. Bad archetypes produce bad behavior. This sterile vision offers little information about what men should be except mature—whatever that means.

There is more than silly circularity at stake in these games. Not only do such reifications not explain why we behave as we do, they block more accurate and useful explanations. Let me illustrate with an analogy. Slave owners noticed that African slaves tended to run away. They posited a psychic factor that caused that behavior, a *love-of-running-away*. They then explained the running away by that psychic factor instead of the fact that slaves were human beings kept under inhuman conditions for the purposes of exploitation by their owners. Of course, one does not expect slave owners to have this much insight into the self-serving power relations of their own society, but the convenience of positing a tendency to run is too obvious.

Men, too, live in relations of power. Wife battering is one such relation. For centuries, many men got what they wanted from their wives by battering or threatening to batter them; it is still epidemic today. The fact is, that wife battering was and too often is a socially accepted way for men to control their wives. To neglect the gains from such power, to neglect the institutions which permit power to be gained in this way, and to attribute such behavior to immature archetypes or inadequate contact with real male energy seems at best socially irresponsible. Perhaps patriarchs, like slave owners, prefer to ignore social institutions, since, if the real causes of abuse are not addressed, men can more easily hang onto aggressive and controlling behaviors.

Similarly, vague admonitions to grow up—to move from an immature to a mature archetype—offer little moral guidance. Jack Straton's essay "Where Are the Ethics in Men's Spirituality" brings out the moral permissiveness of the mythopoetic movement.[20] In contrasting this movement with the pro-feminist movement to end male violence, Straton is able to note the absence of any clear vision within the mythopoetic movement, whereas the pro-feminist men's movement has a reasonably clear analysis of why violence happens, what are the different kinds of violence, and what needs to be done to stop it.

Bly's essentialism blends into his moral permissiveness in such a way that he sometimes suggests that violence against women is justified and inevitable given the deeper male essence—which is aggression.

> And women today complain that men are too aggressive, but if we hadn't been aggressive 30,000 years ago, the tigers would have devoured all the women (cited in Straton, 10).

At another gathering a camper asked Bly what to do: "when we tell women our desires, they tell us we're wrong," Bly answered "So, then you bust them in the mouth because no one has the right to tell another person what their true desires are."[21] Ignoring the fact that in some contexts it is very appropriate to tell someone what they want or that they are wrong to want something, physical assault is never the appropriate response to such verbal criticism.

Bly claims that pro-feminist men doing antiviolence work are doing something important, but his message is blurred by other statements he makes. For example, in one of his earliest interviews on what men really want, Bly tells a story about a mother who gets knocked across the kitchen by her teenage son for no other reason than that she is a woman. But she does not take it personally, she just realizes he needs more masculine energy and she sends him off to his father (Bly 1982, 37). Thus, the mythopoetic moral message gets murkier and murkier.

The vacuous explanations and permissive moral vision of the mythopoetic movement totally fail to address issues of male power, privilege, and patriarchal supremacy. It looks in the wrong direction, and it does not seem to care. And, to the extent that some of the nasty archetypal behaviors are hardwired, it suggests that there is very little that can be done about them.

THE MEN'S RIGHTS CONNECTION

Anyone who is even casually familiar with both the men's rights movement and the mythopoetic movement will notice the natural alliance between them. Many publications such as *Man!*, *Men Talk*, *Seattle M.E.N.*, and *Wingspan* carry both men's rights and mythopoetic articles side by side. Authors

like Jed Diamond deftly weave men's rights and mythopoetic thought together. Rarely, if ever, do pro-feminist articles appear along with men's
rights or mythopoetic articles. As Bly has noted the pro-feminist movement
is generally hostile to both the mythopoetic and men's rights perspectives
(Walters, p. 62). The bridges that make the men's rights connection are easy
to find.

From Guilt to Shame

Antony Astrachan, in 1986, called the men's rights movement the no guilt
movement, because the role of guilt, presumably dumped on men by women
and society, is so prominent in the thinking of this movement (cf. Clatterbaugh 1990, 61–83). This guilt keeps men in their traditional and self-destructive roles. A man who feels guilty because he does not bring home
enough income will work overtime. A man whose spouse always portrays
him as the heavy will feel guilty and not stand up for himself. Shame plays
an analogous role in the mythopoetic movement. The man who is made
ashamed of his deep masculinity does not defend it; he becomes the wimp
or the savage man. His warrior archetype is not strong enough to defend
him against the shame dumped on him by his parents, especially his mother,
feminists, and women whose essence is so different they cannot appreciate
his deep masculinity (Bly 1990, 146). Women want men to be nice, but deep
masculinity is not nice (Bly 1990, 8). Shame as it is used by the mythopoetics
is the direct ancestor of guilt as used by men's rights advocates.

Fathers

Bly's essentialism leads him to declare that the father or some central male
figure is necessary in the raising of sons. As we have noted, Bly has harsh
words for women who are "sperm stealers" or who, even through good intentions, try to go it alone (Bly 1985). The men's rights literature—like Dan
Quayle's speeches—is filled with the dismal statistics of what happens to
children raised by single women. Of course, men's rights and mythopoetic
literature—like conservative literature—never explore the possibility that low
income or failure of the father to visit or pay support is a major cause of
troubles that beset children in single parent homes. While the men's rights
perspective sees men as alienated from the family because of guilt and "male
bashing," Bly sees men as alienated from the family by male shaming.

Wounds and Harms

A striking similarity between men's rights literature and that of the mythopo-etic movement is the listing of wounds or harms that serve as evidence of how tough it is to be a man. The favorite list of the men's rights movement includes the shorter life expectancy of men, male death in combat, male bashing, higher successful suicide rates, and anger at women who think they are spiritually or morally superior to men. Bly, too, lists many wounds that afflict men. Father wounds, mother wounds, wounds from not being initi-ated by men and from feminist shaming (Bly 1985). Bly's central message is to get down into the deep masculine and heal the wound (Bly 1985; Bly and Tannen, p. 33). The men's rights perspective seeks limits on women's power over men by requiring joint custody in divorce, setting up men's commis-sions, and ending male bashing; mythopoetics pursue the exclusion of women from male initiations so that men can heal wounds, many of them caused by women, and an end to the shaming of men.

Denial of Patriarchy

Both the mythopoetic and men's rights perspectives tend to deny the exis-tence of patriarchy. Bly thinks that there are some fossilized remnants of patriarchy serving in Congress. But, he thinks that patriarchy is failing fast (Bly and Tannen, p. 33). If anything, he sees men as disadvantaged in society because of the successful women's movement, which has unleashed energy for women, but tends to make men into soft nice boys. The men's rights perspective also denies the existence of patriarchy; in fact, they deny the existence of male privilege and power.[22] Some men's rights advocates hold that patriarchy never existed, others hold with Bly that it once existed but that the women's movement created choices for women but none for men. So that men are now the new victims of sexism and oppression.

An interesting variation within the mythopoetic movement is Moore and Gillette's view that patriarchy equally shames both men and women (p. xviii). This view of patriarchy, while artfully dodging the institutionalized power of men, is highly reminiscent of the men's rights view that men and women are equally discriminated against; men are success objects and women are sex objects.[23] Thus, patriarchy is transformed into a system equally bad for men and women without noting that men primarily benefit and women suffer the greatest harms.

As a consequence of their views on patriarchy, neither the mythopoetic perspective nor the men's rights perspective look at male privilege and institutionalized power as a source of the harms that come from the masculine role. Whereas it is standard fare in pro-feminist perspectives to explore the injuries to men from having to be the best, to take control, to be the powerful dominant member in a relationship, to have institutionalized social and political power, these get no mention as likely or even possible causes of the costs of masculinity. Perhaps the most glaring example within the men's rights perspective is the fact that in support of male oppression they note that almost all political assassinations are of men. *Surely*, political assassination is a consequence of patriarchal political power, not an indicator of the powerlessness or oppression of men.[24]

Male Positive Permissiveness

A frequent defense of the mythopoetic movement is that it is "male positive," it encourages men to come together and express their feelings. Men's rights perspectives also make this claim. Such a defense does not go very far, however, once such expressions are put into context—the denial of male privilege and power, the assertion of female power, the lack of specific antipatriarchal guiding principles, the focusing on the wounds, and the ever present suggestion that women have very little to teach men. In this context, male expressions become either self-pitying complaints about male hurts or unchallenged and unguided expression of anger toward women. Mike Dash, a pro-feminist who sometimes attends mythopoetic gatherings, notes that when he talks about an experience informed by feminist analysis, he is accused of injecting politics into the discussion. But, when someone gets up and expresses an experience that is informed by men's rights analysis, it is accepted as nonpolitical and male positive. Being male positive within mythopoetic and men's rights circles has become, like being pro-white in David Duke's campaigns, a code word for being antifeminist.

A New Age, Old Time Religion

Bly does not hesitate to suggest that he is trying to bring back a sense of religion, in the old sense (Bly 1982, 51). It is helpful to take a hint from Bly's remark and see the religious aspects of the mythopoetic movement. Mythopoetic gatherings frequently remind me of a trip to a fundamentalist church; there is a lot of "witnessing." Men stand up and talk about their wounds and how they have found Robert Bly. The mythopoetic movement also has the essential ingredients of religion; they have charismatic leaders (evangelists) in James Hillman, Robert Bly, Robert Moore, and Michael Meade to name some of the first generation figures. They have sacred texts in *Iron John* and *King, Warrior, Magician, Lover*. Religions typically support the values of the society that surrounds them, in this case, patriarchal values. Religions build by formulating a special language by which to talk about experiences, for example, God showed me something through a certain sign. The mythopoetic movement, as we have noted, uses the special language of archetypes and shame as explanatory. And, finally, mythopoetry provides a refuge from feminism; mythopoetic gatherings are closed to feminist critique; men are re-established as the focal point. Every religion needs to protect its members from evil, and the greatest evil for mythopoetics is the shaming of male nature (feminist critique).[25]

Bly may have succeeded beyond his wildest dreams in establishing a religion in the old sense. His emphasis on the wounds to men, the need to be deeply masculine, valuing traditional masculinity and father figures, excluding feminist critique, and finding guidance in traditional myths and stories has enormous appeal to politically active evangelical Christians. The 1990s has seen the emergence of a large Christian movement, the Promisekeepers, committed to a literal interpretation of the Bible and focusing on making men better traditional fathers and husbands. Robert Hicks, one spokesman for this movement, in *The Masculine Journey* has discovered the "Book of Bly" and interprets the message of the *Bible* as a story of men becoming kings, warriors, and lovers in order to overcome their wounds *a la* Bly.[26] Hicks' references in his book are almost exclusively to the writings of Robert Bly (mythopoetic), George Gilder (conservative), and Warren Farrell (men's rights). Bly, himself, qualifies as a zaken (sage), the most mature form of being a man, surpassing immature forms such as Hugh Hefner (phallic stage), Oliver North (warrior stage), and Jim Bakker and the Iran Contra indictees (wounded warriors). The warmth with which this movement embraces Bly's teaching says more about the traditional patriarchal roots of the mythopoetic movement than many pages of analysis.

DANGEROUS CONSEQUENCES

The dangers of a movement that holds onto the old patriarchy with new language and metaphors are obvious. The essays in *Women Respond to the Men's Movement* reiterate the concerns of feminist women that mythopoetic men will simply return to standard patriarchal roles now justified by deep masculine archetypes. These women express fear that many men are finding the mythopoetic movement attractive precisely because it avoids issues of power or challenges to men as the norm, and because it requires nothing from men except to articulate their hurts, many of which are blamed on women. They fear, quite rightly, a return to misogyny.

Pro-feminist men, too, find these dangers in the mythopoetic movement. But the mythopoetic movement may also be a disaster to the men who are caught up in it. If the above analysis is accurate, mythopoetic men are not looking in even approximately right direction for the cause of their wounds. Certainly some injuries come from personal relationships and from parents. But even these injuries are often embedded in a social and institutional context. The boy who is beaten because his father or mother accepts certain stereotypes about male behavior is also being harmed by widely held social stereotypes. If he is punished to bring him up to standards demanded by male leadership, the deeper cause of his harm is the power and privilege which he is supposed to inherit.

Men who refuse to see their collective and institutionalized power are more likely to mistake the cause of their concerns. For example, men who hold positions of enormous power over women, as landlords, supervisors, and bosses often complain that these women do not like men. If such men extend their attitude into their relationships outside of work, which they frequently do, they may conclude that all or many women do not like men. They say this despite the knowledge that many women are happily married or have close male friends. What these women do not like is the *power* this individual holds over them and the arrogance that too frequently accompanies power. But a man who sees only the hostility and denies that he has real power will assume that it is because he is male—he will never make the connection that that hostility is due to the power which he exercises. He will never understand that the end of his power and how it shapes him are the remedy for his hurt. Men who misidentify the cause of their wounds are doomed to never heal.

IT DOES NOT HAVE TO BE THIS WAY

There is much that the leadership of the mythopoetic movement could have done to thwart the patriarchal drift of the movement. There could have been a clear rejection of the men's rights perspective. There could have been a clear appreciation of the fact that the stories used are blatantly sexist and that other stories need to be found or invented. There could have been more consciousness of the language that is used by the movement and that is disturbing to feminists. Bly himself seems to be of two minds about this language. On one hand, he suggests that words like "warrior" and "wild man" not be used outside the movement or apart from the context of the Grimm fairy tales, precisely because it will be misunderstood (Craig 1991). On the other hand, in a letter dated the same year he argues against *not* using "warrior" or "wild man" because he wants to force the listener to look at the positive side of these ideas (Bly 1991, 4).

Most importantly, there could have been an acknowledgment of the social reality of patriarchy. Probably nothing causes more feminist scrutiny than the mythopoetic denial of patriarchy and the accompanying denial of institutionalized male power.

Finally, the looseness of language and thought alarms feminists and their allies—"bust her in the chops"/the wild man is not dangerous/aggression is deeply masculine/stories are only to uncover the archetypes/the stories are sexist/don't blame women/steal the key from under your mother's pillow/ mothers lie about their husbands to their sons. Of course, Bly is a poet, not a philosopher or a scientist, but as a poet who has license to use metaphors and tell stories, he of all people should be aware of the power of language to harm and frighten.

Mythopoetic men are increasingly occupied with counterattacking feminist critics. Instead of allowing that patriarchal roots are deep and that we all succumb to them in some ways, they seek to deflect *all* feminist criticism. Consider the following responses to *Women Respond to the Men's Movement:*

> The essays make me ask whether feminism, as it exists today, is part of a progressive agenda. The essays are filled with a reflex negative view of men, dogmatic preaching, ready-made judgements, endless fault-finding, and a rigid blinding ideology that makes men wrong no matter what. . . . The mythopoetic movement provided much-needed food for our weary souls (Smethurst, 2).

> Mythopoetics is not a feminist movement, and this is seen as a major failing by these women. . . . Outraged that men have needs not focused on women, needs met by turning toward male energy instead of toward the mother, these feminists angrily twist upon the . . . truths they have themselves discovered, and which men have taken to heart.[27]

These responses show a pervasive blindness to the patriarchal notions of their own movement; it is not that feminist women are upset that men have needs or that feminist women are simply angry at a men's movement; it is that feminist writers see much more clearly than mythopoetic devotees the exposed patriarchal roots of the movement. These feminist writers have every reason to be concerned.

There is no immunity for anyone in a patriarchal society which contains a strong feminist movement. Ironically, adopting a defensive stance toward feminist criticism only increases feminist scrutiny.

The mythopoetic movement may be the largest of the various men's movements. Still, it is not very large. Most men drawn into it seem to come from a particular generation, a generation who rejected their fathers or who lost their fathers through divorce or death. The average age at a gathering is 40–42.[28] These men came of age during the new and vigorous feminist movements. Many are simply casualties of that gender revolution. Few men in their twenties and thirties are being drawn into the movement; they are more acculturated to a feminist presence.

In fact the mythopoetic movement may be short-lived. Its religious aspect makes it doubtful that the movement will survive much beyond the loss of its founding patriarchs. Furthermore, in a society which remains strongly patriarchal there are plenty of vents for the rage of men who feel like they have been displaced. There is the men's rights movement, the religious right's efforts to restore patriarchy, and politically conservative groups. There is growing empirical evidence that the movement is shrinking. Several major publications, *Man!*, *Wingspan*, *Men Talk*, have either suspended publication (*Man!* and *Wingspan*) or curtailed circulation. Attendance at conferences is also declining—the Austin men's conference declined from 700 men three years ago to under 200 at the last conference.

If I were to make one prediction about the future of the mythopoetic movement as presently constituted, it is that a substantial part of it will be captured by the men's rights movement. There is too much common ground between the two perspectives and the necessary ongoing feminist critique will lead to tighter nonfeminist and antifeminist alliances. Such a capture will drive out many men who are attracted to the mythopoetic movement precisely because it seems nonpolitical. The men's rights movement, on the other hand, is fighting a hopeless battle—claiming men are the real victims—based on a gross distortion of social reality and fanatical antifeminism (Clatterbaugh 1992).

Hopefully, that part of the mythopoetic movement that is not merged with the men's rights movement will be open to looking into the deep masculine, seizing the patriarchal archetype, and hoisting him out. Of course that would require acknowledging the male privilege and power embedded in the traditional masculinity. Such an exorcism would be more truly healing, and the good news is that more and more men are doing just that.

ACKNOWLEDGMENT

Many of the ideas in this paper are the result of discussions with Mike Dash. In this case I take responsibility for their formation.

NOTES

1. Carol Tavris and Carole Wade. *The Longest War, Sex Differences in Perspective*, 2nd ed. (New York: Harcourt Brace Jovanovich, 1986).

2. Kay Leigh Hagan, ed., *Women Respond to the Men's Movement* (San Francisco: Harper Collins, 1992).

3. Works by Robert Bly referred to in this paper include "What Men Really Want: A New Age Interview with Robert Bly by Keith Thompson," *New Age Journal* (May 1982): 30–37, 50–51; "Men and the Wound," Audiotape (Minneapolis: Ally Press, 1985); "The Wild Man," *American Health* (January/February 1989); *Iron John: A Book about Men* (New York: Addison-Wesley, 1990); "Bending Over Backwards: A Letter from Robert Bly," *Seattle M.E.N.* (November 1991): 4; and Robert Bly and Deborah Tannen, "Where are Women and Men Today," *New Age Journal* (February 1992): 32–33, 92–97.

4. See, for example, John Craig, "Money, Media, Men Mulled in Minneapolis," *Wingspan* (December 1990–March 1991): 3; Fred Pelka, "Robert Bly and Iron John," *On the Issues* (Summer 1991): 17–19; Jon Cohen, "Feminist Allies or Anti-Feminist Backlash: Analyzing (the) Men's Movement," *Nonviolent Activist* 9 (March 1992): 7–9; James Smethurst, "From the Executive Director," *Seattle M.E.N.* (August 1992): 2; and Marianne Walters, "The Codependent Cinderella and Iron John," *The Family Therapy Networker* (March/April 1993): 60–65.

5. Warren Farrell, *The Liberated Man* (New York: Bantam, 1975).

6. Marc Feigen Fasteau, *The Male Machine* (New York: McGraw-Hill, 1974).

7. Robert Moore and Douglas Gillette, *King, Warrior, Magician, Lover: Rediscovering the Archetypes of the Mature Masculine* (San Francisco: Harper Collins, 1991).

8. Carol Tavris, *The Mismeasure of Woman* (New York: Simon & Schuster, 1992).

9. Cf. Ward Churchill, "Indians are Us?" in *Indians Are Us? Culture and Genocide in Native North America* (Monroe, Maine: Common Courage Press, 1994), 207–72.

10. John M. Ellis, *One Fairy Story Too Many: The Brothers Grimm and Their Tales*

(Chicago: University of Chicago Press, 1983), 12. Cf. also Maria Tartar, *The Hard Facts of the Grimms' Fairy Tales* (Princeton: Princeton University Press, 1987), 32.

11. Ruth B. Bottigheimer, *Grimms' Bad Girls and Bold Boys* (New Haven: Yale University Press, 1989).

12. Christa Kamenetsky, *Children's Literature in Hitler's Germany: The Cultural Policy of National Socialism* (Columbus: Ohio University Press, 1984), 79.

13. Jack Zipes, ed. and trans., *Fairy Tales and Fables from Weimar Days* (Hanover, N.H.: University Press of New England), 10–11.

14. Jane Caputy and Gordene O. MacKenzie, "Pumping Iron John," in *Women Respond to the Men's Movement*, Kay Leigh Hagan, ed. (San Francisco: HarperCollins, 1992), 69–81.

15. George Gilder, *Men and Marriage* (Gretna, La.: Pelican Publishing Co., 1986); also cf. Kenneth Clatterbaugh, *Contemporary Perspectives on Masculinity, Men, Women, and Politics in Modern Society* (Boulder, Colo.: Westview, 1990).

16. David P. Barash, *The Whispering Within* (New York: Elsevier, 1979). Also, cf. Clatterbaugh 1990, 20–36.

17. Eugene Pascal, *Jung to Live By* (New York: Time Warner, 1992), 79–80.

18. Stephen Jay Gould, *The Mismeasure of Man* (New York: Norton, 1981).

19. Aaron R. Kipnis, "The Green Man Reawakens," *Wingspan* (October–December 1991): 1, 4.

20. Jack Straton, "Where Are the Ethics in Men's Spirituality," *Changing Men* (Fall/Winter 1991): 10–12.

21. Steve Chappel and David Talbot, *Burning Desires* (New York: Simon and Schuster, 1990), 196.

22. See Herb Goldberg, *The Hazards of Being Male: Surviving the Myth of Masculine Privilege* (New York: Signet, 1976); and Warren Farrell, *The Myth of Male Power: Why Men Are the Disposable Sex* (New York: Simon and Schuster, 1993).

23. David A. Ault, "Let's Ratify a Gender-Inclusive Equal Rights Amendment," *Seattle M.E.N.* (January 1992): 3, 11; cf. Clatterbaugh (1990, 74).

24. Jack Krammer, " 'Male' is not a Four Letter Word," in *Wingspan: Inside the Men's Movement*, ed. Christopher Harding (New York: St. Martin's Press, 1992), 70.

25. Carol Bly, "The Charismatic Men's Movement: Warrior Wannabes, Unconscious Deals, and Psychological Booty," *Omni* (March 1991): 6.

26. Robert Hicks, *The Masculine Journey: Understanding the Six Stages of Manhood* (Colorado Springs: Navpress, 1993).

27. Dan Raphael, "Women Respond to the Men's Movement," *Seattle M.E.N.* (August 1992): 4, 14.

28. Michael Meade, "Are We Going in the Right Direction?" *Wingspan* (December 1990–March 1991): 5.

Gazing into Men's Middles: *Fire in the Belly* and the Men's Movement

DON SABO

SOMEONE ONCE SAID THAT, "The fish are the last ones to discover the ocean." And so it is with men and patriarchy. Despite patriarchy's historical longevity and societal pervasiveness, men have failed to reckon with the fundamental realities of male dominance and social grouping by sex. Women have been trying to get our attention for more than a century. Lately, however, some men are beginning to hear the din of women's heady protests, anger, political and cultural dreams, and messages from the heart. Indeed, some men have begun to think about, feel about, and talk about themselves in new ways.

Sam Keen's book is an expression of the emerging critical dialogue around men and masculinity in American culture. I say "critical" in the sense that Keen isn't just flapping and yapping about male identity, male socialization, and the male experience because it's somehow become an academically correct discourse. Keen is problematizing men and masculinity. This means that, for Keen, there's something rotten in the ways that manhood has been defined, the ways that men spend their lives, the ways that men relate to one another and to women and to the planet. Right now, at this point in history, Keen says that men are part of the problem, not part of the solution. Men need to rethink their identities, their sexuality, their lives. Men need to change themselves and to reweave the latticework of their relationships. Keen knows that patriarchy has been a problem for women, but he also senses that patriarchy is messing up men's lives as well.

Keen's insights and basic arguments, and those of Robert Bly, the pied piper of the mythopoetic men's movement, are not new. Betty Friedan published *The Feminine Mystique* in 1963. Along with Simone de Beauvoir's *The*

Second Sex, which was published in the late '50s, these works signalled the beginning of modern women's critique of gender. In 1966, Myron Brenton published *The American Male*, a probing and critical analysis of men's changing lives and identities. Indeed, there have probably always been male critics of the patriarchal status quo who, one way or another, allied themselves with women and/or feminism. Frederick Douglass, for example, advocated for women's rights as well as abolition during the 1850s and 1860s. I suspect that the voices of these pro-feminist men were silenced in much the same ways that women's voices were silenced.

Keen's book is best seen, therefore, as an extension of critical dialogue around what might be called "men's critique of gender" or, in general, "the critique of patriarchy." It is important to see Keen's book as one voice in an emerging choir of male critics of gender issues for two reasons. First, it helps highlight some of the strengths of Keen's message. Second, by placing Keen's book in the wider flow of gender analysis and politics, we can begin to see some of its weaknesses.

GENDER IDENTITY AS SOCIAL CONSTRUCTION

Keen builds nicely on the fundamental insight that gender is a social construction.

Many of the characteristics that have traditionally been considered 'masculine'—aggression, rationality—are not innate or biological components of maleness but are products of a historical era in which men have been socially assigned the chief roles in warfare and economic order.[1]

There is a great deal of evidence that men's behavior and identity are not somehow standardized by biological determinants. Male domination of women, for example, is far from being culturally universal. There have been societies in which parity and respect existed between the sexes. We have also become aware that, within any culture, there is a variety of "masculinities" that comprise the tapestry of men's lives—some soft, some aggressive, some stoic, some expressive, some playful, some militaristic.

In his "brief history of manhood," he ponders "Man as Hunter," "Man as Planter," "Man as Warrior," "Scientific-Technological Man," "Self-made Man," and "Post-modern Man." Though Keen's quasi-historical, evolutionary taxonomy of manly types is guilty of oversimplicity and over-generalization, it does highlight the recognition that masculinity is not so much biologically ordained as it is socially and historically constructed.

THE POLITICS OF MASCULINITIES

Keen also does an excellent job of bringing home the observation that there is no such thing as masculinity—only masculinities. "Masculinity" is best viewed as a multifaceted mosaic and not a cultural monolith. Keen is helping us to realize not so much that the proverbial emperor has no clothes, but that there are a helluva lot of outfits in the wardrobe. There is much more going on here than cultural diversity. There is an obvious political relationship between the various models of masculinity that comprise the gender order. The prevailing forms of masculinity (i.e., hegemonic masculinity) reflect and reinforce traditional, patriarchal beliefs and social practices, thus reinforcing the status quo. Other kinds of more culturally and politically marginalized masculinities are geared to protesting, resisting, and transforming the realities of gender order. Today more and more men are engaged in struggles *inside* and *outside* themselves, which ultimately are serving to redefine and reconstruct their lives. The lines between personal and political are increasingly blurred in men's minds and, as a result, the gender politics that have always shaped so much of our lives are becoming more visible.

WHERE ARE THE WOMEN?

As I read through Keen's book, enjoying the clipped tenor and sometimes passionate warmth of its prose, I began nestling into self-preoccupation. I contemplated my masculine navel—though I never really did manage to fan the flames of a fire in my belly! I basked in manly self-reflexivity. By about page 150 or so, however, I began to sense that something was missing from Keen's textual landscape. There was a silence forming, and eventually it screamed loud enough for me to hear it. Where are the women? Listen to Keen's vision of manhood:

> At the center of my vision of manhood there is no lone man standing tall against the sunset, but a blended figure composed of a grandfather, a father, and a son. The boundaries between them are porous, and strong impulses of care, wisdom, and delight pass across the synapses of the generations. Good and heroic men are generations in the making—cradles in the hearts and initiated in the arms of fathers who were cradled in the hearts and initiated in the arms of their fathers (p. 185).

The absence of women from Keen's gender landscape first dawned on me for scholarly reasons. (Scholars read titles first and then footnotes.) Keen quotes, among others, T. S. Elliot, Dylan Thomas, Sigmund Freud, Albert Camus, Soren Kierkegaard, Aristotle, Karl Jaspers, Socrates, Herman Hesse, Paul Tillich, Reinhold Niehbur, and Jean-Paul Sartre. At times I felt I was listening to the roll call for a course in an all-male university called NEW AGE DISCOURSE 101. Where are the women? Has Keen read any of the thousands of books and articles by women that gave birth to the current rethinking around gender issues? Wasn't it women who initiated the dialogue around gender identity and the social and emotional costs of sex inequality? Does Keen owe any conscious debt to his feminist foremothers? And, if he does, why doesn't he recognize them? Why does he continue to reside in the intellectual long house of Western Androcentric Thought?

Take this line of thinking one step further. Let's depersonalize Keen the man and Keen the book. Why is it that the two bestselling books on men and masculinity (*Fire in the Belly* and Robert Bly's *Iron John*) present mainly men's ideas, men's words, men's existential rallying cries? I think that at least part of the answer for the stunning success of these books is the very fact that they leave women out of the emerging pictures of "now and future manhood" that are crystalizing men's heads. There is a strange contradiction at work here. On one hand, Keen and Bly do represent a sincere effort on the part of men to change themselves and their relationships with men and women. Yet, on the other hand, the silencing of women's voices and the slighting of feminist theory and practice speak of and reinforce gender separatism and male supremacy. Men historically and hysterically have loved patriarchal pageantry, the rituals of male bonding, and the blaring of masculine cultural trumpets, especially when men's voices drone out those of women.

There is yet one other indication of where women fit into the belly of Keen's thoughts and feelings. In the early stages of the book he argues that men are "unconsciously bonded to women." He then cloaks women in some rather grandiose abstractions: i.e., "WOMAN as goddess and creatrix," "WOMAN as Erotic-Spiritual Power." The problem with these kinds of mythic-proportion portrayals is that I don't recognize any real-life women in them. Keen is into some heavy intellectual air-brushing here. Even if I buy into the categories as intellectual constructs, I am not sure what to do with them, uncertain how they are going to help me live in a society in which 53% of the people are women.

Finally, after about 190 pages, in chapter 13, Keen does get around to dealing with the feminist critique. He describes feminist thought as a "kaleidoscope"; a good image that speaks to the diversity of feminist thought and practice. But then, within a page or so, he takes the kaleidoscope and conveniently and simplistically splits it into two pieces; on one side there is "prophetic feminism," on the other side there is "ideological feminism." He defines "prophetic feminism (as) a model for the changes men are beginning to experience" (p. 195). He defines "ideological feminism (as) a continuation of a pattern of genderal enmity and scapegoating that men have traditionally practiced against women" (p. 195). Gee, that's odd, I thought feminism was an ideology and practice that was designed to expose, analyze, and seek to eliminate sexism, sex inequality, men's enmity and scapegoating of women. If you are confused, take comfort. Look at how Keen distinguishes between the two feminisms. "The distinction between prophetic and ideological feminism is largely a matter of mood, tone of voice, focus, emphasis, feeling-tone" (p. 195). Say what!?

Keen's commentary on feminism is the weakest part of the book. He oversimplifies, deals with 3 or 4 pieces of outdated feminist writing, has virtually no inkling of what feminist analysis is, where it has been, where it is, and where it is going. He just hasn't taken the time to do his homework. Also, when he is talking about the "ideological feminists," I noticed that his "tone" and "mood" are definitely angry. I wonder why.

JOURNEYING INWARD: NEW VISION OR OLD STORY?

Keen is right in arguing that men need to look inward and change themselves. He outlines a list of "heroic virtues" that can help men move from the "'me' to the 'we', from the solitary self to community, from therapy to action in the everyday world." Men, he ably asserts, need to wonder more about being and becoming in the world. Men would do well to learn the skills of empathy, to develop a "heartfelt mind" that links thoughts with feelings, to be morally outraged by other people's suffering and to endeavor to do something about it, to enjoy life, to value friendships, to get back to the wilds of nature. With these virtues in head and heart, Keen indicates, the "now and future hero" is ready to complete Joseph Campbell's mythic journey in which "The hero comes back from (the) mysterious adventure with the power to bestow boons on his fellow men" (p. 152).

With Keen, I believe that men will need these virtues in order to face and solve the problems and inequities of the post-modern disorder. Men will need to tap what has been best in traditional culture in order to transform themselves and future culture. However, I have a small problem with Keen's list of virtues, which he sees as being essentially masculine in character and domain. I see them as being basically human mores and values that can be shared by or aspired to by women and men without ruminations about gender.

I have a much more serious problem with Keen's analytic rap and recipe for gender change. Too often, he seems to fall "down the well" of psychological reductionism, that the change process begins in or emanates from within the fires in men's bellies or the deep recesses of men's psyches. Human psychology is mainly a cultural phenomenon, a social construction. Men's psyches grow up in and out of the culture, society, and the political order: identity and behavior are less informed by myths than the product of political and economic circumstances. Any look inward into the minds and hearts of men, therefore, has got to recognize the interdependencies between psychic life, gender identity, culture, and social structure.

Because our culture is patriarchal in its historical origins and blueprints, and because our social structure is characterized by class, race, and gender hierarchies, this means that it is an illusion to separate personal change from institutional change. This is the dialectical insight contained in the feminist phrase, "The personal is political." Because the prevailing definitions of masculinity are collectively defined in ways that reflect and reproduce structured sex inequality, men who want to change their heads and hearts need to seek to change their institutional circumstances as well.

Keen counsels men to become "psychonauts" as he waxes and wanes about the inner journey of masculine rebirth. (As you read the following quotation, imagine a Gustav Mahler symphony is playing in the background, or perhaps the soundtrack from "Apocalypse Now.") Keen writes:

> The way of the psychonaut leads into the jungle of the psyche, into the heart of darkness. It is no less fearsome or fraught with perils than the outer path. . . . Because they have not dared to wrestle with anxiety, fear, hate, anger, pride, greed, longing, grief, loneliness, despair, impotence, and ambivalence, many extroverts bow obediently to authority and established opinion and never claim the territory of their psyche for themselves. . . . (T)he psychonaut must confront . . . nothing less than our fear of suffering and death and our attachment to pleasure.

Hey, Sam, lighten up a bit. I grew up worshipping a man in excruciating pain hanging on a cross; I don't want to be crucified myself in order to attain gender salvation. I feel like I have got to become some neo-Freudian Indiana

Jones, a New Age "raider of the Lost Ark" of manhood in order to get through to the metaphorical "other side" of the gender jungle.

The task of re-envisioning men and masculinity and changing men's lives has got to be more than a therapeutic exercise, getting in touch with one's feelings, or going off to the forest to beat drums with the guys. If men really want to climb outside their roles as the pimps of patriarchal history, we need to move beyond mythopoetic pomp and link with one another and with women in ways that substantially change the way we live and not just who we imagine we are.

WHAT CAN MEN REALLY DO FOR CHANGE?

Any realistic agenda for the transformation of gender relations has got to go beyond therapeutic vision and practice. Yes, we need personal change but, without changing the political, economic, and ideological structures of the gender order, the subjective gains and insights forged within individuals will erode and fade away. Personal change needs to be rooted in structure, and buoyed up by institutional realities. Without a raft or boat or some structure to hang on to, even the best swimmer will tire and slip beneath the waves. Within a framework that recognizes the structural as well as psychological interdependency of gender relations, Bob Connell (1991) has set up a modest platform for mustering countersexist action. I have added a few planks myself.[2]

1. Share the care of babies and young children equally between women and men. Change hours of work and promotion rules to make this practical.
2. Work for equal opportunity, affirmative action, and the election of women, until women occupy at least 50% of decision-making positions in both public and private organizations.
3. Support women's control over their own bodies, and contest the assertion of men's ownership of "their" women. Contest misogyny and homophobia in media and popular culture. Contest sexual harassment in the workplace.
4. Work for pay equity and women's employment rights, until women's earnings are at least equal to men's.
5. Support the redistribution of wealth and the creation of a universal social security system.

6. Talk among men to make domestic violence, gay-bashing, and sexual assault discreditable. Work positively to create a culture that is safe for women and for gays of both sexes.

7. Organize political and economic support for women's refuges, rape crisis centers, and domestic violence intervention.

8. Work to make the lives of marginalized groups of men better; e.g., gay men, poor men, homeless men, unemployed men, men in prison, men with AIDS, men who have been battered by (rather than profiting from) the war experience. These men have been economically and politically disenfranchised within the intermale dominance hierarchies that comprise the American gender order. Their individual and collective plight, at some level, perpetuates the privileges of male elites.

9. Take steps to rethink and stop male violence against men. Empathize with male victims of male violence. Stop the bar brawling and fraternity hazing. Don't sit back and let coaches put your kid at risk for acute injury. Don't let neighborhood gangsters and drug dealers steal your children's dreams and futures. Don't let the thugs in gray suits send your children off to Central America in order to protect "American interests." Recognize and seek to ameliorate the economic violence against minority men.

10. Work to heal the victimizers. Work with men who batter men, child molesters, prison rapists, and murderers. If they cannot be healed, then lock them up and try again through rehabilitative programs.

Fire in the Belly helped me understand a great irony that permeates much thinking and writing about the "new men's movement," especially the thinking that receives a lot of attention from the popular media. I mean the talk show stuff. It is ironic that Keen and Bly, the two leading proponents of the new men's agenda of the 1990s, recapitulate what is a traditional patriarchal refrain of maximizing men's identity with men via separation from women.

The real issue, I believe, is not that men need bonding with one another. It is that their traditional separation from women in patriarchal society has kept them from truly "bonding" with anyone—with men *and* with women. The separatist strategies for change that Keen lays out are at best good therapeutic advice and, at worst, a vehicle for perpetuating structured gender inequality, sexism, and the oppression of women, children, and marginal men. The chances of men going off together by themselves and then coming back and changing gender relations are about as slim as if all the white people in South Africa or South Boston went off together in order to figure out how to end racism. They would come up with some new and powerful insights, there would be lots of new stirrings in their brains and bellies, but, in the end, alas ... Personal change and political change are inextricably related. As men begin to take off their royal robes, they will do well to get both men's and women's advice on what to wear to the 21st century.

NOTES

1. Sam Keen, *Fire in the Belly: On Being a Man* (New York: Bantam, 1991), 65.
2. I am much indebted to Bob Connell's work on gender order and gender politics. Many of his ideas about Keen and Bly, and the state of the men's movement, are reflected in this review. Items 1 through 7 in the list are excerpted verbatim from his essay, "Men at Bay: The 'Men's Movement' and Its New Bestsellers." For detailed discussion of men and the "gender order," see Robert Connell, *Gender and Power: Society, The Person, and Sexual Politics* (Stanford, Calif.: Stanford University Press, 1987).

II

THE PERSONAL IS POLITICAL: THE MYTHOPOETIC MEN'S MOVEMENT AS A SOCIAL MOVEMENT

Men at Bay: The 'Men's Movement' and Its Newest Best-Sellers

BOB CONNELL

BOOKS ABOUT MASCULINITY on the best-seller lists. Satirical cartoon strips in the newspapers. Hundreds of men heading off into the woods to thump drums and wave spears. Primitive masculine rituals revived. Talk-show appearances. Strong men weeping about their fathers, their love lives, their lost sense of self . . .

Something is going on here; something odd, but possibly important. The underlying issues certainly do matter.

WHAT IT'S ABOUT: FEMINISM AND MEN

The 'men's movement' and its Books About Men (a distinct genre of publishing now) are basically a response to the new feminism. To understand them one must start with what feminists have been saying about men over the past two decades. Feminist critics have pointed to inequalities of power, to exploitation, to violence and sexual abuse on a massive scale. The picture of men is not pretty.

Men do hold most of the power in society. Men generally control governments, armies, corporations, professions, political parties, and social movements. The evidence is easy to find. A few years ago I collected the figures on men's and women's participation in a range of national legislatures, militaries and judiciaries. The statistics are remarkably consistent. Men make up 95 percent to 100 percent senior office holders in these power structures, in all parts of the world.

Power is exerted in private life too. Men attempt to control women's sexuality in a wide range of ways. They generally claim authority in families. The phrase 'head of household' was meant to apply to men; so was 'breadwinner.' Put these points about public life and domestic life together, and a general pattern emerges, where men hold most of the power and women are controlled.

It is not surprising, then, that there are massive economic advantages in being a man. More men than women have paid jobs. Among people with paid jobs, men, on average, get higher wages than women. Men control the large concentrations of wealth (look at any list of billionaires). In countries like the United States the majority of people with no income, or very low income, are women. In the 1980s researchers began to speak of 'the feminisation of poverty.' But in a basic sense women's economic disadvantage had been there all along.

On top of economic and political inequality there is extensive violence against women. Rape, often in the past dismissed as a consequence of sexual provocation by promiscuous women, has now been shown to be mainly about men asserting power. Research on domestic violence in the 1970s and 1980s uncovered a huge volume of assault by husbands on wives, traditionally ignored by police and condoned by public opinion. Street intimidation, workplace harassment, sex trades, pornography, misogynist advertising can all be seen as part of a pattern of men's abuse of women's bodies.

This adds up to a fairly tough indictment. The emerging picture of men was so uninviting that by the late 1970s many feminists had begun to emphasise women's difference from men. They argued that women should separate themselves from men as far as possible, and put all their energies into supporting other women.

Other feminists, however, saw a more complex picture. Gay men are aligned with women on some issues (though not all). Charges of rape against black men function as a means of racial oppression, which has its impact on black women too; this after all was the purpose of lynchings. A privileged minority of women benefit from their wealthy families' class advantages, and lead more secure and more comfortable lives than any working-class men.

As Lynne Segal shows in her excellent book about masculinity, *Slow Motion*, the divisions of race, class, and sexuality don't obliterate the basic feminist points about men. But they make the politics of masculinity much more complex than they might seem at first.

During the last two decades, large numbers of men in the U.S. and similar countries have become aware that they are under some kind of challenge. Often their idea of feminism is extremely vague, no more than a blurred media image of bra-burning 'libbers.' But some men, especially middle-class men with higher education, became aware of the details, and learned that what feminists say about men is not just an invitation to loosen their sex roles and slip into something more comfortable.

Some of the men who have caught the message during the past two decades experienced a paralyzing guilt. Rather more men responded with complete denial. Others again have tried to work out better ways of relating to women; and from these attempts came the media image of the 'new man.'

THE 'NEW MAN' IN AMERICA: A SHORT HISTORY

Some of the first feminist Consciousness-Raising groups in the late 1960s had both women and men as members. When the Women's Liberation movement developed its emphasis on autonomy, mixed groups were abandoned. But some CR groups for men started up in 1970–71. For the next few years a small feminist movement among heterosexual men existed in the United States. Its members were supporters of feminism, often partners of feminist women. They took up issues about 'sexism', and tried to eliminate sexist attitudes and practices from their own lives. Some accepted the Gay Liberation analysis of the oppression of homosexual people, and tried to do something about homophobia too.

From this starting-point several streams emerged. Academic researchers, mainly psychologists, interpreted patriarchy as a question of 'sex roles' and set about researching the 'male sex role.' This research showed the existence of popular stereotypes about proper masculinity. It did not show very much else. But it provided a language for talking about men which avoided the tougher parts of the feminist indictment. The language of 'sex roles' suggests men and women are in parallel, not unequal, positions, and that men suffer from restrictive sex roles just as much.

Several authors in the mid-1970s began to create a popular literature about masculinity which suggested change in this 'role' was both easy and desirable. Books like *Men's Liberation* and *The Liberated Man* proposed that feminist ideas would benefit men. By abandoning their restrictive sex role, men would have fuller emotional lives, more inventive sex lives, closer relations with women and children, even better health.

If men were psychologically injured by their sex role, psychotherapy might be the answer. Through the 1970s another movement developed which I can only describe as 'masculinity therapy.' It consisted of a network of therapeutic groups, workshops and individual therapists, and it gave rise to a small industry of books with titles like *The Hazards of Being Male: Surviving the Myth of Masculine Privilege.* As this subtitle suggests, the therapy attempted to assuage the guilt set up by the feminist indictment.

This seems to have been a popular enterprise. A stream of masculinity-therapy books continued through the 1980s. The 'mythopoetic men's movement' has its roots in this milieu, and offers a kind of group therapy and a complete denial of guilt.

The idea of 'men's issues,' created as a mirror-image of 'women's issues' in the 1970s, soon turned into a defence of men's *interests* against women's. By the late 1970s a number of 'men's rights' groups had formed to oppose women in divorce and custody cases. Such activism turned to opposing women over jobs (against affirmative action), and over abortion rights (claiming father's rights over the fetus). Through the 1980s, heterosexual men's activism on issues of sexual politics increasingly showed an anti-feminist face.

The feminist impulse among men was not completely lost. Indeed, in some settings it had become very firmly established. Among younger intellectuals, for instance, shared child care and support for feminist principles are common. There is some very interesting U.S. research on the way these issues have been negotiated inside families and households—with some success, though unavoidable tension given the oppressive gender arrangements of the society as a whole.

Various men's groups and individuals have also become involved in more formal counter-sexist projects. They include opposing sexual harassment in the workplace, through union action; publicising the issue of domestic violence, and working with batterers to end their attacks on women; teaching men about gender issues through college courses; developing curricula and teaching strategies for schools; supporting women's defence of reproductive rights; providing support for gay community action around AIDS prevention and care.

The list is substantial, and indicates the range of possibilities for action by straight men. But it has to be said that most of these projects have remained small-scale, and they have attracted little media attention or public discussion. Given the political swing to the Right in the 1980s, this counter-sexist position has had little support from public policy, and often feels like an embattled minority response as much as it feels like the wave of the future.

The 'new man' is not quite a myth, but is certainly not a widely established reality. What is a reality is a new politics of masculinity, in which men's involvement in sexual politics is openly debated. Enter, on the stage thus prepared, a poet with a message for troubled men.

FANTASY POLITICS: ROBERT BLY

Bly is a well-known American poet, white, married, presumably heterosexual. For the last ten years or so he has been giving lectures and leading workshops at which he has expounded a view of masculinity, its troubles and how to heal them. A definite movement has grown up around him. Bly has now put his ideas together in a book, *Iron John: A Book About Men*, which has become a non-fiction best-seller.

The book's framework is provided by a tale from the Grimms' early 19th century collection of Germanic folklore. 'Iron John' is a hairy wild man discovered at the bottom of a pool. The story tells of his relations with a prince who sets him free from a cage, goes into exile, fails certain tests, has his hair turned gold, and after other adventures marries a princess with the magical help of the Wild Man, who turns out to have been a king under an enchantment.

Bly discovers, in this little-noticed tale, a mighty allegory of masculinity and masculine initiation. Each chapter of his book picks up a few elements from the Grimm story. With the aid of Bly's personal reading of world history, anthropology, poetry and anecdotes of modern American experience, each element is expounded as a source of deep wisdom about men.

The themes Bly expounds are the loss of true manliness in modern culture; the need for men to be 'initiated' into manliness by other men, their symbolic or actual fathers; the need to separate from women, and revive ancient masculine rituals; the need to reclaim and celebrate the lost elements of masculinity such as the Warrior, the King, the Magician, and of course the Wild Man.

It is clear that Bly's story has a strong *emotional* appeal for a particular group of men, and it is important to consider why. There are two main clues. One is the texture and territory of the book. When you strip away the 'mythopoetic' superstructure, the central themes of *Iron John* are difficulties in emotional relations within the family, especially in boys' relationships with their mothers and fathers. This is, of course, the classic territory of psychoanalysis, and is currently the territory of a kaleidoscope of therapeutic movements and cults. Bly's movement, at a practical level, is simply the most ably marketed of a string of masculinity therapies that have appeared since the early 1970s. It uses many of the techniques of group therapy, jazzed up with freshly-minted myth and ritual that invoke the primitive and celebrate masculine fierceness.

The second clue is the historical moment in which movement and book appear. They appear in a period of deepening political conservatism, *but* among the group of men—white, middle-class, heterosexual North Americans—who have been most impacted by the new feminism. Many men in this group are troubled about sexual politics, especially by the feminist indictment. Bly calls them, in effect, to stop feeling guilty about their privileges, to celebrate masculinity—and to get clear from women.

That point is the emotional key. Bly's reading of emotions in the family, which highlights fear of engulfment by the mother, fuels his central prescription for reform: build a separate men's culture. (His proposals are, ironically, a mirror-image of the separatist feminism of the late 1970s, which also discovered a mythic past and proposed to build a separate future.) True masculinity, Bly insists, is developed only by links between men. One of his most effective appeals is to his followers' feelings that they were let down by, or emotionally blocked off from, their fathers. The movement's emphasis on 'initiation' is very much about finding substitute fathers.

Getting clear from women is not only an emotional resolution, it is a political resolution for two problems at the same time. One is the feminist indictment. Men, Bly insists, are very different from women, and the difference should be emphasised and celebrated. Bly's story about the 'Wild Man,' his insistence on the importance of fierce, untamed emotion and bold action, his rhetoric about warriors and swords (and some of his followers' rhetoric about spears) must be read in the light of the feminist indictment of male violence. Bly clearly thinks that feminism has unmanned men, and he wants to de-wimp them. He is smart enough not to present himself as openly anti-feminist; the doctrine of separate spheres is his way around the problem.

At the same time this addresses another problem that has become acute for North American middle-class men in the last decade. The familiar rhetoric of American individualism has been worked up, by the ascendant Right, into a public celebration of aggressive individualism. The entrepreneur, the competitor, the self-made man, are trumpeted.

The problem is that this rhetoric corresponds very little to the realities of most white-collar working lives. (Even less for blue-collar workers of course; but working-class communities, both white and black, have some collectivist traditions that produce scepticism about this rhetoric.) Some time ago the German sociologist Claus Offe demonstrated, in a classic piece of social

science, that in the highly-organised, large-scale production systems characteristic of modern economies, it is impossible to get a rational measure of
any individual's productive worth. The massive contradiction between the
public exhortation to aggressive individualism, and a reality where most
white-collar workers are unavoidably cogs in the economic machine, is neatly
resolved by displacing the scene of action into a mystic cult of masculinity.
We can't all be Donald Trumps, but, by God, we can be equally fierce in
our hearts.

So much for Bly's emotional appeal. But where is this Pied Piper leading
his troop? Given that Bly is now so much referred to as the last word on
masculinity, we have to put some tough questions to him. Especially—is
what he says 'about men' actually true?

IS BLY RIGHT?

There is, now, a body of research against which we can check his ideas. The
result of the check is unequivocal: Bly is massively wrong. Four points about
the book stand out.

First, Bly's level of argument is abysmal. For those of us who have been
trying to get questions about masculinity on the intellectual agenda, it is
deeply embarrassing to see such material publicised as the latest word
about men.

It is not just that *Iron John* is a little cavalier with the facts. By any intellectual standards the book is appallingly bad: over-generalised, under-re-
searched, incoherent (and at times self-contradictory). The text is packed
with sweeping statements about what 'men' are, feel or need. Most of them
have no basis in evidence or argument at all. Bly routinely ignores counter-
vailing evidence (e.g., evidence of cultural diversity). He routinely distorts
material from mythology, history, anthropology, even other people's poetry,
to suit what he wants to believe.

It is difficult to document this without going on at tedious length. But for
sheer verve it is hard to improve on claims like these:

> Hermes is the god of the interior nervous system. His presence amounts to
> heavenly wit.[1]

> We could say that a third of each person's brain is a warrior brain; a third of
> the instincts carried by our DNA relate to warrior behavior; a third of our

thoughts—whether we like it or not—are warrior thoughts. This is a sobering idea. (P. 150)

Robert Frost ate a lot of his shadow, which is certainly a part of his greatness. (P. 206)

More trickster energy seems to be stored in the North American soil than in any continent in the world. (P. 228)

Powerful sociological and religious forces have acted in the West to favor the trimmed, the sleek, the cerebral, the noninstinctive, and the bald. (Pp. 247–48)

Powerful stuff. (Bly, according to the photo on the dustjacket, is definitely not bald.) When Bly gets to talking about the world most of us live in, he consistently distorts the facts. Let me quote just two examples, from hundreds that could be used. The first comes in a chapter entitled 'The Hunger for the King in a Time with No Father':

Kings as leaders of huge cities and empires, holding broad powers, are first noticed during the second millenium BC, in the city-states of Mesopotamia. No-one is sure if the Sun King in China preceded or followed the Mesopotamian king. The political king merges heavenly sun power and earthly authority . . . The Sun King and his Moon Queen . . . held societies together for about four thousand years. As principles of order, they began to fail in the eighteenth and nineteenth centuries in Europe.

As a matter of cold fact, kingship emerged before the 2nd millenium; the relative chronology of Mesopotamia and China is quite well known, e.g., from carbon-14 dating (Bly didn't bother to look it up); the idea of universal sun monarchy (incidentally based in Egypt not Mesopotamia) was discredited as long ago as the 1920s; in many cultures kingship was not identified with the sun; many 'societies' existed between 2000 BC and the 18th century without kings of any sort (among them such obscure cases as Athenian democracy, the Roman republic, Venice . . .); and the mystique of European kingship was challenged before the 18th century (remember Machiavelli? Cromwell?). The passage is a farrago of error and misinterpretation; and this is typical of Bly's excursions into history. Here is what he does with anthropology:

To judge by men's lives in New Guinea, Kenya, North Africa, the pygmy territories, Zulu lands, and in the Arab and Persian culture flavored by Sufi communities, men have lived together in heart unions and soul connections for hundreds of thousands of years.

The mind boggles. None of the cultures listed has lasted for 'hundreds of thousands of years.'

Bly isn't interested in the truth of what he says; he is interested only in its emotional effect. The effect of passages like this is to create a sense of continuity between his readers/hearers and an imagined stream of forefathers stretching back into the mists of the past.

To create this kind of effect, however, *requires* intellectual confusion, and this is the second point to be made about the book. To produce his myth of an over-arching male culture, Bly muddles together bits and pieces from different periods of history, different cultures, different modes of experience. He grabs a sun-king from China, an initiation ritual from Aboriginal Australia, a poem from Ireland, and throws them all into the blender. The resulting language, as the quotes show, is cloudy and abstracted, sustaining a prophetic tone at the expense of meaning.

At one point Bly invokes, and distorts, Yeats. (I resent this, Yeats being my favourite poet.) The contrast is telling. Yeats at his most prophetic still struggled for precision (think of those crystalline images in *Byzantium*). Bly settles for muddiness. His ambition is to talk, in Jungian terms, about recurrent masculine archetypes. Jungian cultural analysis is difficult, and needs a delicate touch to avoid stereotyping. Bly has all the delicacy of a beer truck. He never gets out of stereotypes, because he has no interest in the realities of the world.

The third point follows from this. The whole presentation rests on a stereotyped, outdated and now untenable concept of what masculinity is. Bly's underlying idea is that there is one basic masculinity, one pattern of true masculine rituals, one set of male psychological needs. At times he asserts that this masculinity is genetically determined (see, e.g., the Warrior Brain above).

The notion of a single masculine template is ethnographic and historical nonsense. Abundant evidence shows that cultural representations of masculinity, and men's actual ways of life, vary widely between cultures. They change in history, and they are diverse within any one culture at a given point of time.

Bly is dimly aware that there is a struggle going on over cultural definitions of desirable forms of masculinity. But he manages to ignore homophobia — a central feature of hegemonic masculinity in his own culture, as routine news reports of gay-bashing and AIDS hysteria illustrate. He manages to ignore the differences in men's lives produced by their class situations and by racial oppression, let alone colonialism. He therefore misses most of the interesting issues about masculinity that have been raised in the last thirty years.

Bly assumes that the masculine template exists independently of women; that 'male values,' 'male initiation,' etc are *separate* from women's affairs; so in healing their wounds men must follow a separate path. There is, in fact, convincing evidence from ethnographic and life history research that masculinities are constructed in *interaction* with women. It is not just that cultural images of 'masculinity' are always defined in relation to images of 'femininity.' Real women, real women's work (in child care, housework, emotional support work, etc.), are intimately involved in making and re-making men's characters.

Fourth, to cap it all, the perspective is racist. Here I don't particularly have in mind Bly's explicit appeal to 'the Indo-European race' and its warrior heritage (p. 150); nor his astonishing stuff about the glory of golden hair, and gold symbolising genius and spirituality (p. 39, etc.) while black stands for evil, death and crude matter (p. 201).

I am more concerned with something central to the whole 'mythopoetic men's movement,' the invocation of a contrast between primitive and civilized peoples. The 'ancient' male rituals are supposed to have survived better among the former. Bly loves to cite snippets of anthropology to prove this. In the course of this, *all* non-western cultures get thrown into the 'primitive' basket, as we saw in the passage about pygmies and Sufis quoted above.

One would be more impressed with Bly's appeal to non-western cultures if he respected them enough to learn the details of their ways of life. He hasn't. The text is riddled with crude errors. Again, lots of examples could be given. As I come from Australia, I am particularly jarred by what he says about Aboriginal Australians. On p. 28, for instance, he says that 'the aborigines of Australia' (all of them men, apparently) follow a certain initiatory ritual, tell a story about 'the first man, Darwalla,' and knock out a tooth from each boy. Bly didn't take the trouble to find out the first fact about Aboriginal Australia, which is that there are hundreds of languages (700 different languages and dialects, by one linguist's estimate), and an equal diversity of rituals. On p. 165 he equips the Aboriginal initiators with swords, which have an edge that 'cuts clinging away from love, cuts boyish bravado away from manly firmness, and cuts passive-aggression away from fierceness.' Stirring words. A pity that Aboriginal Australian cultures were actually based on neolithic hunter-gatherer technology, and had no metal tools at all . . .

Basically, Aboriginal men are not real people to Bly, worth getting acquainted with on their own terms. Like Zulus, Arabs and the rest, they are cyphers that fit into a particular slot in his imagination. When Bly's followers go into the woods to beat on drums, they are not respecting real African or American Indian traditions. They are enacting a stereotyped, basically racist, notion of the primitive.

Bly's muddled fantasy of masculinity might seem laughable, if all it led to was middle-class men sitting under pine trees and pretending to be bears. But I think it is more dangerous than that. Racist, myth-mongering, warrior cults of masculinity have existed before: in Germany in the 1920s, for instance. The mainstream Right is different now from what it was then, but its leaders can still find such ideas useful. President Bush recently came out in support of sex-segregated schools for black boys—a policy which if followed is certain to divide black communities and worsen problems of sexual politics, mainly at the expense of black women and girls. This diversion from the real problems of mass unemployment and racism is neatly legitimated by a discourse of masculinity that declares the key problem for young men is their lack of male mentors.

Bly is quite right on one major point, the key to his success. His readers are worried about sexual politics, and lack a language for talking about them. They lack this language precisely to the extent that they have refused to listen to the uncomfortable truths told by feminism and gay liberation. In the final analysis, *Iron John* and the 'mythopoetic men's movement' are a massive evasion of reality. Bly is selling fantasy solutions to real problems. What's worrying is that this evasion so easily opens space for far-right politics.

THERAPEUTIC POLITICS: SAM KEEN

Sam Keen has listened to feminists, and to gays, and has accordingly written a better book. *Fire in the Belly: On Being a Man* is much more literate and consequent than *Iron John*. Keen has some concern about offering evidence, and has some sensitivity to social conditions. He has heard about racism, homophobia, global inequality, and environmental issues. The book has some good passages of social and cultural criticism. He has practical experience in a men's group that has worked unpretentiously on consciousness-raising and sexual politics.

A Book About Men with these qualities is rare in the literature. I would rejoice over it, if it were not for the parts about masculinity.

Here, Keen's account is surprisingly close to Bly's. The basic territory is the same: the emotional needs of men and emotional relations in the family. Keen uses much the same method: speculative generalisation spiced with snippets of history, anthropology, and contemporary anecdotes. Keen constructs a speculative and ethnocentric 'history of manhood' from the Stone Age to Postmodernism which is nearly as thin as anything in Bly—though to his credit Keen recognises the fact of continuing historical change.

Like Bly he draws on Jungian notions of male and female archetypes. Like Bly he argues that modern men lack initiation rituals, and proceeds to invent some to fill the gap. Like Bly he insists that men need to separate from women to do their healing; though some of the time he specifies that this applies to the archetype of Woman and not to actual women in the flesh.

However Keen departs from Bly about the form of separation. Rather than an all-male cult, Keen makes it an individual psychic quest, a 'pilgrimage.' Here he shows his closer relationship with growth movement ego-psychology. The political agenda Keen recommends is basically a therapeutic one: healing the male psyche, healing relations between men and women, healing the planet.

Using his practical experience in counselling and psychotherapy, Keen has some useful suggestions for the first step in this agenda. For instance he offers some sound practical tips on running a men's group. (Not very different, however, from what Farrell and Tolson were saying in Books About Men in the mid-1970s; the genre has little sense of its own history.)

But the impulse seems to run out at the second step. Keen doesn't carry us much beyond face-to-face relations towards the institutions and social structures that shape personal life. He doesn't have much sense of practical politics, nor useful advice about the grubby business of actually changing public policy about child care or housing, pay equity or the environment.

This disappointing ending is, in a sense, built into his analysis from the start. Keen draws on psychological traditions which have little room for what is now called 'the social construction of emotion,' the production of emotions (and emotional problems) by social structures and culture. One must ask, indeed, what 'healing' of masculinity is possible through the kind of individual psychic quest he advocates.

In my view it is very limited. Therapy of course has value for dealing with situations of crisis and despair. In less dramatic situations it often helps with sheer survival. But to *transform* emotional relationships, and a complex emotional structure like 'masculinity,' is inherently a collective project not an individual one. It must involve large numbers of people; it must deal with the institutions (e.g. the labor market, the State) which regulate men's lives; it therefore must centrally involve social action.

'Healing' is a metaphorical language for human relationships that has only limited reach. To grasp adequately the project of changing masculinity we also need a language of 'justice' and 'equality.'

A PRACTICAL POLITICS OF GENDER FOR HETEROSEXUAL MEN

Bly, Keen and others in the genre are talking about real issues, however limited or mystifying the language they use. What would be an adequate, non-mystifying response to these issues?

The starting point has to be this: you cannot solve emotional problems about gender by ignoring the social conditions that give rise to them. Psycho-analytic researchers, from Jessica Benjamin and Dorothy Dinnerstein right back to Freud and Adler at the turn of the century, have shown in great detail how emotional tensions in masculinity grow out of the social arrangements that define a particular form of the family, and specify particular social positions for women and men.

What from one point of view is a feminist indictment of men, from another is a description of the social inequalities which have to be dismantled before either women or men can be 'healed.' This defines the central task for heterosexual men who want to do something constructive about masculinity.

Specifically, they have to go to work on each of the structures of inequality outlined at the start of this essay. Here is a modest agenda, building on existing activities of countersexist men in various parts of the United States:

1. Share the care of babies and young children equally between women and men. Change hours of work and promotion rules to make this practical.
2. Work for equal opportunity, affirmative action, and the election of women, until women occupy at least 50% of decision-making positions in both public and private organizations.
3. Support women's control over their own bodies, and contest the assertion of men's ownership of "their" women. Contest misogyny and homophobia in media and popular culture. Contest sexual harassment in the workplace.
4. Work for pay equity and women's employment rights, until women's earnings are at least equal to men's.
5. Support the redistribution of wealth and the creation of a universal social security system.
6. Talk among men to make domestic violence, gay-bashing, and sexual assault discreditable. Work positively to create a culture that is safe for women and for gays and lesbians.

7. Organize political and economic support for women's refuges, rape crisis centres, and domestic violence intervention.

This 'agenda,' obviously enough, involves work in other forums than the therapeutic men's groups preferred by Bly and Keen. It involves politics in the workplace and in the public realm. In other countries one of the most important forums for such work is the unions. The union movement is so weak in the United States that it is hardly ever noticed in discussions of masculinity; it is nevertheless important, not least because of its working-class base. Many prescriptions for 'changing men' come unstuck over issues of class, appearing as a middle-class guilt trip laid on working-class men. A realistic approach will recognise the importance of exploitation and powerlessness in working-class life, without wishing away the misogyny and violence that often go with them. The kind of agenda just outlined doesn't call on working-class men to add guilt to their other burdens. It calls on them to do positive things in the name of equality, which will benefit working-class women.

This is far from being the only program that could be drawn up; but it illustrates what might be involved in getting to the source of the problems. It is not an agenda for the nervous. There are problems here that are tough enough to engage the energy, fierceness, and creativity of a goodly number of men. Maybe some of the Warriors would care to come down from the hills and lend a hand in the cause of social justice.

This suggestion is not entirely a jest. A political agenda such as this, though it works to resolve emotional contradictions in the long run, is highly stressful in the short run. Quite frankly it requires heterosexual men to act against their own immediate interests. Activists will have to negotiate internal guilt and fatigue, suspicion from women, outright hostility from powerful men, and sometimes physical threat.

In these conditions, the techniques of emotional support worked out in the 'men's movement' might be very helpful for personal survival, and for sustaining a campaign. It would be nice to see these methods, and all this enthusiasm, put to better use.

NOTE

1. Robert Bly, *Iron John: A Book About Men* (Reading, Mass.: Addison-Wesley, 1990), 143.

This essay is an expanded version of the article "Drumming Up the Wrong Tree" (TIKKUN, vol. 7, no. 1). Reprinted from TIKKUN MAGAZINE, A BI-MONTHLY JEWISH CRITIQUE OF POLITICS, CULTURE, AND SOCIETY. Subscriptions are $31.00 per year from TIKKUN, 251 West 100th Street, 5th floor, New York, NY 10025.

The Politics of the Mythopoetic Men's Movement

HARRY BROD

In those days people shall no longer say: "The fathers have eaten sour grapes, and the children's teeth are set on edge."
  Jeremiah 31:29

ROBERT BLY'S *Iron John* was on the syllabus of a course I taught recently on "Men and Masculinities." In my most cynical mood I found myself telling my students that reading this felt to me like reading one's daily horoscope in the newspaper. It was written in *such* abstract terms, with such leaping poetic imagery, that everyone can project so much of their own experience into it that, after reading it, they leave with the feeling, "My God, this is talking *exactly* about me."

I know this is unfair to Bly. I am both by professional training and personal temperament a philosopher, and what you may be hearing is another enactment of the age-old quarrel between the philosopher and the poet, as I play Plato to Bly's Homer. The philosopher wants everything spelled out in neat linear arguments; the poet resists. I find much of value in Bly's work. Men respond to him enthusiastically because he talks about things men feel a crying need to talk about—things no one else is discussing, at least not in a way most men can hear—and which have no airing in our culture. He answers real needs—for men to reach out across generations, for men to honor their fathers (though I confess I find myself nostalgic for the Biblical formulation, which at least told us to honor our fathers *and mothers*), for men to have a positive, assertive sense of self, for men to heal their grief.

The virtues of Bly's approach have been lauded elsewhere and often. In this essay I critique Bly's work and the practices of the movement which claims him as at least a primary, and at times the preeminent, guiding light. I largely skirt the difficult question of the extent to which leaders must be held accountable for what followers make of their work. When I attended a workshop led by Bly and Michael Meade in 1988, I felt very uncomfortable, much more than I did with Bly himself. He told a number of "jokes," some at women's expense and some at men's. I found myself feeling a degree of tolerance for him personally, even while finding his sexist remarks intolerable. His comments seemed without personal animus, spoken in the tone of the poet sardonically commenting on the human condition. The all male audience laughed too much at the jokes about women, and too little at the jokes about men. I felt very much in the midst of misogynist male bonding.

Who are the men who are attracted to this movement? One segment responding to wild man and warrior imagery in the 90s consists of white, middle-class men who overdosed on sensitivity training in the previous decades. If these men have stopped contemplating their navels and have now reached down to their hairy feet, we may hope that eventually they will reach the ground and cease being "flying boys," as our mythopoets put it. This does seem a positive step. On a similarly positive note, I recall that, before the mythopoetic movement captured the public imagination, the phrase "men's movement," if it meant anything at all to most people, probably suggested the explicitly backlash "men's rights" movement. Whatever one thinks of the mythopoetic movement, it seems clear enough to me that they are better than *that*.

One phenomenon that has been insufficiently analyzed in understanding what attracts some men rather than others to mythopoetic gatherings is the large number of men who are veterans of various recovery and 12-step groups. (Michael Kimmel estimated the number to be about half at a large conference he attended.)[1] What accounts for this? Is it just that these men emerge from a therapeutic discourse which makes them more susceptible to the appeal of such gatherings? Should we look for some common set of underlying circumstances or personality traits that makes both movements attractive to certain men? Is our culture's gendered equation between (female) emotionality and powerlessness so great that men must lay claim to an identity of victimization before they feel it legitimate or safe to emote? Perhaps the many men who identify specifically as children of alcoholics or survivors of child abuse learned as boys certain skills of emotional sensitivity usually reserved for females. Has disillusionment with their own fathers stoked the fires of the search for the mythic father? These questions require further investigation.

One aspect of the mythopoetic appeal involves the issue of class. The movement attracts not only middle-class men, for obvious reasons relating to access to the time and money required for participation, but, more specifically, a high proportion of middle-class sons of working-class fathers.[2] Upward mobility requires that we turn our backs on our roots, that we psychically disown our families of origin and the work of our fathers. Much of the quest for the mythic father seems fueled by guilt over this venal betrayal of the real fathers, the banishing from sight, sound, and sense of their work and sacrifices, their accents, and their smells, in order for the next generation to "make it" and "pass" in these WASP, nonclass-conscious United States. The elder Minnesota farmer, Robert Bly, understands in his gut what these middle-aged urban professionals are missing from their lives as he takes them on weekend camping trips into the woods.

This is not the first time we have seen such a response from men who feel themselves under siege by what they perceive as an increasing and increasingly threatening feminization of their world. Michael Kimmel has analyzed what he calls the masculinist response to feminism a century ago in the United States. Men flocked to fraternal organizations: lodges, fraternities, clubs, and sent their sons to the Boy Scouts: "The reassertion of traditional masculinity resonated with antiurbanism and the reactivated martial ideal that characterized a strain of antimodernist sensibility at the turn of the century."[3] Sometimes one gets the feeling that there really is very little new under the sun.

Various aspects of mythopoetic practice need to be addressed. We are told that the key issue is the lack of personal initiation rites into masculinity. Other older and wiser cultures had such initiations, but we lack them. Hence, our problems. A number of things must be said about this. First, we need to look at history through a different lens than the one Bly offers. The history of masculinities, the history of men in families, at work, with each other, must be told as the history of patriarchy, or it is not truly being told at all. Without that perspective, we are in the presence of myth as falsehood, rather than myth as deep truth. I find an awareness of patriarchy utterly lacking in the story of our past which Bly and the mythopoetic movement tell us.

Yes, industrialization separated men from their families. And yes, we miss them. But industrialization was part of another process as well, the institutionalization of patriarchy. In preindustrial societies, patriarchs are men who hold and embody in their own person political, legal, social, economic, and religious power over the other members of their families. But with the shift from preindustrial or precapitalist to capitalist patriarchy, this power is taken out of scattered individual male hands and centralized in more controllable and controlling collective institutions: the state, the market, the military. Theorists have developed various ways of describing this shift—some speak of it as a transition from private to public patriarchy.[4] We might speak not of patriarchy as the rule of the fathers, but of fratriarchy, the rule of the brothers, whose sibling rivalry is a form of competitive bonding that keeps things in the family of men.[5]

So why do men no longer receive personal initiation into manhood in modern societies? Why will there never be such rituals in modern societies, no matter how many devotees of mythopoetic practices clamor for them? Because individual manhood is no longer the fundamental site of the exercise of male power. Initiation is always initiation into authority. Today, the most important game in town, the club worth joining, is the depersonalized, institutional recognition of one's manhood. To those men who feel a lack of personal empowerment and who are looking for a male initiation rite to bestow it, I would say that this quest cannot be successful unless participation in personal rituals is combined with participation in a political movement to overthrow the capitalist patriarchal state, which is taking your power from you only to use it against you.[6]

Something else follows from this analysis of the institutionalization and depersonalization of male power under modern patriarchy. When those of us committed to feminist activism approach men with a statement like, "What you need to realize is that you are a powerful patriarch," they respond with, "Well, then how come I sure don't feel like one? How come I don't seem to have this authority over my own life, let alone anyone else's, that you're telling me I have?" There's something profoundly right in what they tell us, something many of us usually don't hear. Given the classical, preindustrial image most people have of the authority of real patriarchs, according to which a man is the king of his castle, these men are right—they *aren't* personally patriarchs in that sense, though institutional patriarchy and male power remain as powerful as ever. There *is* today a disjunction in men's experience, a contradiction between the facts of their power—of which we as a profeminist men's movement are aware but which are often not visible to men—and the feelings that men *are* aware of, those acute feelings of personal disempowerment. We serve no one, we advance no just causes if the only message we bring is that these men are simply wrong about their experience of power, or that they're not being honest, or that they suffer false consciousness. None of the standard, arrogant, elitist responses put forth by those who think they're more enlightened works to persuade those they think are less enlightened. Similarly, we do no good if we tell men who say they have been helped personally by mythopoetic practices that they are somehow deluded or misguided about their own well-being because we, with our heightened political consciousness, *know* that they could not *really* have been helped. Our job is, rather, to explain the connection between how men experience their powerlessness but not their power under advanced capitalist patriarchy, in order to enlist their help in overthrowing this system.

We need further to eliminate the class bias through which we experience and evaluate men. For example, stereotypes supposedly characterizing *really* sexist men target working-class men, while middle- and upper-class men appear to be more "sensitive." The reality is that working-class people have only their personal power, so they manifest their prejudices personally. But those who hold institutional power let the institutions do it for them. Those who often appear personally "kinder and gentler," then, are often those who in reality are exercising greater patriarchal power. Analogous racial bias is evident when the term "macho," which carries many positive connotations within Hispanic cultures, is used by Anglos as a synonym for sexist behavior or attitudes. This is a case of white men using white privilege to deflect the critique of male privilege.

The mythopoetic men's movement is itself often ambiguous or confused about its own politics. This was illustrated in a panel discussion involving myself and Wayne Liebman, a mythopoetic men's movement leader, entitled "The Mythopoetic and Profeminist Men's Movements: A Dialogue," which took place at the Seventeenth National Conference on Men and Mascu-linity, sponsored by the National Organization for Men Against Sexism (NOMAS), in Chicago in July 1992. Defending the mythopoetic men's movement against my political criticisms, Liebman argued that the move-ment *had* no politics, but was simply concerned with men's personal growth. When criticizing NOMAS's profeminist politics, however, he argued that the mythopoetic movement represented a *new kind* of politics. When I pointed out the contradiction he understood that he couldn't have it both ways. Liebman should not be personally faulted, but rather lauded for openly confronting a general lack of political awareness in the movement that he simply reflected.

Despite claims to be deeply rooted in the history of masculinity, the move-ment misses an opportunity to situate the contemporary father–son tensions that it is trying to heal in the context of our own recent history in the United States. In his essay, "The Vietnam War and the Erosion of Male Confi-

dence," Bly describes how the younger generation of men was deeply
wounded by the older generation's betrayal and abdication of moral responsibility, the continuing effect of which is evident in our moral and spiritual
decline.[7] The movement's neglect of this historical factor in its discourse is
particularly striking given Bly's own writing in this essay and elsewhere on
the impact of the war against Vietnam on intergenerational relations among
men in the United States. It is this younger generation, whose sensibilities
were formed during the Vietnam war, that now makes up a large percentage
of the mythopoetic movement in the United States. By participating in our
society's historical amnesia about Vietnam, the movement repudiates its own
awareness of the deadliness of denial. It makes healing more difficult by
prioritizing the honoring of the fathers over the healing of the sons.

The movement also often honors the fathers too much by placing the
burden of father–son reconciliation on the sons. I recall how struck I was
when I first read Bly's analysis of how sons collaborate with their mothers
against the fathers. It pushed all my guilt buttons about my relationship with
my father, and I was consequently about ready to sign on to this movement
when I caught myself. For me, blaming my childhood self or my mother for
the lack of closeness I felt with my father would have been blaming the
victim. The (my) father's abandonment of interpersonal relationships within
the family for the patriarchal rewards of the public sphere came before what
Bly calls the (my) "conspiracy" between mother and son against the father.
The misguided blaming of the victim denies the fathers' accountability, and
thereby makes a true reconciliation impossible. (As far as relationships between particular fathers and sons are concerned, different fathers and sons
will obviously bring different histories and resources to the encounter, providing different opportunities and responsibilities for each. Further, assign-
ment of responsibility to the fathers must of course be mitigated by their *own*
experiences as sons.)

While the mythopoetic men's movement criticizes the profeminist men's
movement for, ostensibly, being motivated by guilt towards women, the
mythopoetic movement recruits men into its quest for reconciliation with the
father precisely by exploiting the sons' guilt over their lack of closeness with
their own fathers. This from a movement that has supposedly moved beyond
what it calls "the politics of guilt." The charge that its adherents are motivated by guilt would be better turned back on the mythopoetic men's movement itself.

The abuse of history by mythopoets becomes even more acute as we move further back into the past, and ancient tribal rituals are invoked as models. Not all imitation is flattery. For example, I have reservations about appropriating Native American religious ceremonies for purposes quite foreign to their native use. When members of the dominant culture appropriate elements of a marginalized culture for their own purposes, it is quite different from appreciating that native culture in its own right—a distinction often lost on those who cite such appropriations to fend off criticisms of the whiteness of this movement.

Second, historical and anthropological evidence is invoked in a highly selective fashion. The brutality of many of these initiations, the way they demote women to secondary status, and the way many involve homosexuality are all ignored. Indeed, a key flaw in this movement is how much of its theoretical basis is derived from the dichotomous masculine and feminine gender archetypes it inherits from Jungian psychology that marginalize or eliminate gay perspectives. Further, its adherents sometimes cite the fact that, in their indigenous settings, women have certain supplemental roles in many of the initiatory rituals appropriated by the mythopoetic movement to demonstrate that their views are sympathetic to feminism. But these women's roles do not lessen the patriarchal structure of these practices. The subordinate always have *some* role in the system in which they are subordinated, but the system as a whole nonetheless serves the interests of the dominant group.

Finally, a more theoretical consideration. The archetypal psychology invoked by the mythopoetic men's movement often serves to make historically changing gender configurations seem static and eternal. This reification of gender contributes to the movement's political obtuseness, and its lack of sufficient attention to the issues I have raised above. My general interpretive framework for understanding gender is referred to in academic circles as social constructionist. Such a view holds that gender itself is artificial; the processes by which we become engendered are a function of manufactured difference being imposed on us. Any theory which tells us the solution lies either in a new, improved masculinity or in the recovery of some real or essential manhood cannot solve the problem, because that theory is itself part of the problem. It solidifies an idea of gender that needs to be dissolved. The question is not *how* we are to be men. Rather, the fundamental violation and violence done to all of us lie in the notion that men must *be* masculine, that masculinity is a goal to be attained.

NOTES

This essay originated in an opening keynote address delivered to the Sixteenth National Conference on Men and Masculinity, sponsored by the National Organization for Men Against Sexism and the Tucson Men's Cooperative in Tucson, Arizona, June 1991. I wish to thank NOMAS and the conference organizers for providing a forum for the exploration of these ideas. I also wish to thank Michael Kimmel for helpful comments. A briefer unauthorized version appeared in *Wingspan: A Guide to the Men's Movement*, ed. Christopher Harding (New York: St. Martin's Press, 1992).

1. See Michael Kimmel, "The Men's Movement and Me" in *brother*, 1992.

2. A local study by Michael L. Schwalbe of the Sociology Department at North Carolina State University confirms this. Personal communication to author, June 1991.

3. Michael S. Kimmel, "Men's Responses to Feminism at the Turn of the Century," *Gender & Society* 1, no. 3 (September 1987): 270–71.

4. Carol Brown, "Mothers, Fathers, and Children: From Private to Public Patriarchy," in *Women and Revolution: A Discussion of the Unhappy Marriage of Marxism and Feminism*, ed. Lydia Sargent (Boston: South End Press, 1981).

5. See my "Pornography and the Alienation of Male Sexuality," *Social Theory and Practice* 14, no. 3 (Fall 1988): 265–84.

6. An earlier version of this essay seemed to suggest that I saw personal and political activities as polar opposites, rather than being at least potentially complementary. I wish to thank Robert Bly for calling my attention to my oversimplification earlier.

7. Robert Bly, "The Vietnam War and the Erosion of Male Confidence," in *Unwinding the Vietnam War: From War into Peace*, ed. Reese Williams (Seattle: The Real Comet Press, 1987), 161–75.

"Changing Men" and Feminist Politics in the United States

MICHAEL A. MESSNER

IN RECENT YEARS, U.S. MEN HAVE RESPONDED TO—and at times initiated—changes in the personal and social relations of gender. There is an increasing cultural preoccupation with men's roles as fathers.[1] Gay liberationists and anti-sexist men are confronting heterosexism and male domination in society,[2] while some academic men contribute to the feminist challenge to phallocentric curricula.[3] Meanwhile, born-again Christians are subtly re-defining women's and men's "god-given roles,"[4] while conservative ministers hold popular seminars on "the meaning of man-hood,"[5] and angry men (mostly divorced fathers) organize for "men's rights."[6] And as I write, Robert Bly's book, *Iron John: A Book About Men*[7] enjoyed over half a year on the national top ten best-sellers list.

Clearly, the question is not "Can men change?" or "Will men change?" Men *are* changing, but not in any singular manner, and not necessarily in the directions that feminist women would like. Some of these changes support feminism, some express a backlash against feminism, and others (such as Bly's retreat to an idealized tribal mythology of male homosociality) appear to be attempts to avoid feminist issues altogether. One thing is clear: Although these changes by men are not all feminist, the growing concern with the "problem of masculinity" takes place within a social context that has been partially transformed by feminism. Like it or not, men today must deal, on some level, with gender as a problematic construct, rather than as a natural, taken-for-granted reality.[8]

Although men are currently changing in a multiplicity of directions, the popular—and to a great extent, social-scientific—view of contemporary masculinity in the United States is that we now have basically two types:

the emergent emotionally-expressive New Man, who is heavily involved in parenting, and the inexpressive, hypermasculine Traditional Man. One (very conventional and optimistic) view is that the New Man is the wave of the future, while the Traditional Man is an atavistic throwback. Another (radical feminist and pessimistic) view is that the New Man is more style than substance, that he is self-serving and no more egalitarian than the traditional man, and thus does not represent genuine feminist change.

Both of these views of changing men are overly simplistic, but they are understandable, especially in the United States, given our lack of a sophisticated theorization of masculinity. In this article, I draw from recent theoretical insights to examine some current expressions of U.S. masculinity that have received a great deal of attention in popular media. Two general questions guide my analysis: (1) How can we assess the meanings and significance of contemporary men's changes? and (2) To what extent do the dominant expressions of men's changes support a feminist project of social transformation?

THEORIZING CHANGING MASCULINITIES

Until very recently, even the best of U.S. theorization of masculinity has been uncritically predicated on a role theory that posits a traditional "male sex role" vs. an emergent "new" or "modern" masculinity.[9] Though some U.S. feminists have criticized the limits of role theory,[10] it is largely social theorists outside of the United States that have constructed a theory through which we can begin to assess the shifting meanings, styles, and structures of masculinity.[11] These theories make two points that represent a major break with role theory. First, masculinity and femininity are not fixed, static "roles" that individuals "have," but rather, they are dynamic relational processes. Masculinity and femininity are constantly re-constructing themselves in a context of unequal, but shifting, power relations. Second, there is no singular "masculine role." Rather, at any given time, there are a multiplicity of masculinities. Hegemonic masculinity—that form of masculinity that is currently ascendant and dominant—is constructed not only in relation to femininities, but also in relation to subordinated and marginalized masculinities.

My discussion below relies heavily on Lynne Segal's recent analysis of changing masculinities, aptly titled *Slow Motion*.[12] In taking power as the central dynamic in the construction of a multiplicity of gender identities and relations, Segal avoids the simplistic and overly-optimistic "men's liberationism" of the 1970s that viewed almost any changes by men as a sign that men were embracing feminism, and the pessimistic belief by many 1980s radical feminists that violence and domination are an expression of some natural male essence. Segal is realistic in that she recognizes the continued existence of men's multi-level oppression of women. But she is optimistic in that she refuses to view this oppression ahistorically or as fixed in men's and women's biological essence. Instead, she insists on viewing men's dominance and women's subordination as a historically grounded relational system, in which women continually contest men's power. Moreover, following Connell, she views masculinity and femininity not as singular, fixed, and dichotomous "sex roles," but rather as contradictory and paradoxical categories, internally fissured by class, sexual orientation, race, ethnicity, and other systems of inequality. The facts that women often contest men's power, and that some men oppress other men, create possibilities for change.

But how can we conceptualize "change"? In this article, I briefly examine three changes in U.S. masculinity that have received considerable attention in print journalism, television, and film: The New Fathering, the mythopoetic men's movement, and the increase in the prevalence of highly successful men weeping in public. I argue that these phenomena represent highly significant (but exaggerated) shifts in the cultural and personal styles of hegemonic masculinity, but these changes do not necessarily contribute to the undermining of conventional structures of men's power over women. Although "softer" and more "sensitive" styles of masculinity are developing among some privileged groups of men, this does not necessarily contribute to the emancipation of women; in fact, quite the contrary may be true.

NEW FATHERS AND CHANGING GENDER RELATIONS

In the early 1980s, Friedan announced the arrival of a "quiet revolution among men," and Goode cited what he saw as a "grudging acceptance" by men of more egalitarian gender relations.[13] Two interrelated phenomena fueled this optimism: First, public-opinion polls indicated that the majority of men were in favor of equal opportunities for women in public life, and increasing numbers of men—especially young men—expressed a desire for egalitarian relationships with women. And second, the 1970s and early 1980s saw the emergence of the cultural image of the New Father, a man who placed family relationships—especially the care and nurturance of children—ahead of career goals.

By the mid-to-late 1980s, evidence suggested that the view that men were embracing feminism may have been grounded more in shifts in what men *say*, rather than in what they actually *do*. Today, many young heterosexual men appear to be more inclined than were their fathers to "help out" with housework and childcare, but most of them still see these tasks as belonging to their wives or their future wives.[14] And despite the cultural image of the "new fatherhood," and some modest increase in participation by men, the vast majority of childcare, especially of infants, is still performed by women.[15]

How do we explain the gap between what many men say (that they are in favor of egalitarian families, that they want to be "involved fathers") and what they do? One possible explanation is that their publicly-stated opinions are inauthentic presentations-of-self that can be viewed as attempts to conform to an acceptable image of the New Father. Indeed, Eliasoph argues that opinions expressed in polls often tell us more about how people construct public selves than they do about people's genuinely held attitudes about public issues.[16] Along these same lines, some feminists today speculate that many men's publicly expressed egalitarian attitudes about gender issues might prove to be "a liberal 'gloss' on a generally more conventional outlook."[17] In this view, it may be in men's interests to change their words, but not to change their behaviors in any substantial manner.

It is probably true that some of the men's publicly-expressed gender egalitarianism is inauthentic, but evidence suggests that there is likely more to it than that. Recent research on fathering—much of which includes qualitative research in addition to opinion polls—indicates that many young men today truly desire greater involvement and connection with their children than they had with their own fathers.[18] But why, then, does this desire so rarely translate into substantially increased involvement? Segal argues that the fact that men's apparent attitudinal changes have not translated into widespread behavioral changes may be largely due to the fact men may (correctly) fear that increased parental involvement will translate into a loss of their power over women. But she also notes that men who truly desire to share parenting find that it is difficult to do because of the continued existence of ". . . external and social as well as internal and psychic factors."[19]

The "internal" constraints on increased paternal involvement include deeply-held psychological fears and ambivalences surrounding intimacy and nurturance.[20] But recent research on "men who mother" suggests that men's "psychological incapacity" to care for and nurture infants has been over-stated and may be as much a myth as women's "natural maternal instinct." Drawing from Russell's survey of "a host of relevant studies," Segal notes that "the most remarkable finding about reversed-role parenting with full-time fathers is how little difference it seems to make to the children, female or male, *which* parent parents."[21]

Although we should not minimize the extent to which women and men are still differentially prepared to parent, men's psychological and emotional constraints can apparently be overcome if social conditions are conducive to substantially increased paternal involvement and responsibility. Most important among the "external" structural constraints to men's increased parenting are the demands of men's wage labor. Men with young children are likely to work more irregular hours and more overtime hours, while the opposite is true of mothers.[22] This reality is reinforced by the facts that women earn substantially lower wages than men do, and that there is little (often no) childcare or parental leave provided by employers or by the state in the United States.[23]

Thus, although a small proportion of fathers today are choosing to parent equally with women, increased paternal involvement in childcare will not become a widespread reality unless and until the structural preconditions exist. Rosanna Hertz found in her study of upper-middle-class "dual career families" that egalitarian divisions of family labor did not develop because of a commitment to feminist ideologies, but rather, as a rational (and constantly negotiated) response to a need to maintain his career, her career, and the family.[24] In other words, career and pay equality for women was a structural precondition for the development of equality between husbands and wives in the family.

However, Hertz notes two reasons why this is a very limited and flawed "equality." First, Hertz's sample of dual career families where the woman and the man make roughly the same amount of money is still extremely atypical. In two-income families, the husband is far more likely to have the higher income. Women are far more likely than men to work part-time jobs, and among full-time workers, women still earn about 65 cents to the male dollar, and are commonly segregated in lower-paid, dead-end jobs.[25] Thus, most women are not in the structural position to be able to bargain with their husbands for more egalitarian divisions of labor in the home.[26]

Second, Hertz observes that the roughly egalitarian family division of labor among dual career couples is severely shaken when a child is born into the family. Initially, new mothers are more likely than fathers to put their careers "on hold." But eventually, many resume their careers, as the childcare and much of the home labor are performed by paid employees, almost always women, and often immigrant women or women of color. Thus, the construction of the dual career couple's "family equality" is premised on the continued existence of *social inequality,* as a pool of poor women performs domestic labor for relatively low wages. In other words, some of the upper-middle-class woman's gender oppression is, in effect, bought off with her class privilege, while the man is let off the hook from his obligation fully to participate in childcare and housework. The upper-middle-class father is likely to be more involved with his children today than his father was with him, and this will likely enrich his life. But, as Segal observes, given the fact that the day-to-day and moment-to-moment care and nurturance of his children is still likely to be performed by women (either his wife or a hired, lower-class woman), "the contemporary revalorisation of fatherhood has enabled many men to have the best of both worlds."[27]

ZEUS POWER AND THE NEW MAN

Just as with the New Father, the more general cultural image of the New Man is based almost entirely on the lives of white, middle-, and upper-class, heterosexual men. What we are witnessing is a shift in personal styles and lifestyles of privileged men that eliminate or at least mitigate many of the aspects of "traditional masculinity" that men have found unhealthful or emotionally constraining. At the same time, these shifts in styles of masculinity do little, if anything, to address issues of power and inequality raised by feminist women. For example, the "gatherings of men" organized by Robert Bly are based on the assumption that young males need to be "initiated into manhood" by other men in order to get in touch with "the deep masculine," an instinctual male essence. Echoing his masculinist predecessors at the turn of the century who also feared a "feminization of society,"[28] Bly states that "when women, even women with the best intentions, bring up a boy alone, he may in some way have no male face, or he may have no face at all. The old men initiators [in tribal societies], by contrast, . . . helped boys to see their genuine face or being."[29] Bly virtually ignores an entire generation of social-scientific research that demonstrates that masculinity is socially constructed.

It is important, but not too difficult, to criticize Bly's curious interpretations of mythology and his highly selective use of history, psychology, and anthropology as "bad social science."[30] Perhaps more needed than a critique of Bly's ideas is a sociological interpretation of why the "mythopoetic men's movement" has been so attractive to so many men in the United States over the past decade (thousands of men have attended Bly's "gatherings," and as mentioned above, his book is a national best seller). I speculate that Bly's movement attracts so many U.S. men *not* because it represents any sort of radical break from "traditional masculinity," but precisely because it is so congruent with shifts that are already taking place within current constructions of hegemonic masculinity. Many of the men who attend Bly's gatherings are already aware of some of the problems and limits of narrow conceptions of masculinity. A major preoccupation of the gatherings is the poverty of these men's relationships with their fathers and with other men in workplaces. These concerns are based on very real and often very painful experiences. Indeed, industrial capitalism undermined much of the structural basis of middle-class men's emotional bonds with each other, as wage labor, market competition, and instrumental rationality largely supplanted primogeniture, craft brotherhood, and intergenerational mentorhood.[31] Bly's "male initiation" rituals are intended to heal and reconstruct these masculine bonds, and they are thus, at least on the surface, probably experienced as largely irrelevant to men's relationships with women.

But in focussing on how myth and ritual can reconnect men with each other, and ultimately with their own "deep masculine" essences, Bly manages to sidestep the central point of the feminist critique—that men, as a group, benefit from a structure of power that oppresses women, as a group. In ignoring the social structure of power, Bly manages to convey a false symmetry between the feminist women's movement and his "men's movement." He assumes a natural dichotomization of "male values" and "female values," and states that feminism has been good for women, in allowing them to reassert "the feminine voice" that had been suppressed. But, Bly states (and he carefully avoids directly blaming feminism for this), "the masculine voice" has now been muted—men have become "passive . . . tamed . . . domesticated."[32] Men thus need a movement to reconnect with the "Zeus energy" that they have lost. And "Zeus energy is male authority accepted for the good of the community."[33]

The notion that men need to be empowered *as men* echoes the naiveté of some 1970s men's liberation activists who saw men and women as "equally oppressed" by sexism.[34] The view that everyone is oppressed by sexism strips the concept of "oppression" of its political meaning, and thus obscures the social relations of domination and subordination. "Oppression" is a concept that describes a relationship between social groups; for one group to be oppressed, there must be an oppressor group.[35] This is not to imply that an oppressive relationship between groups is absolute or static. To the contrary, oppression is characterized by a constant and complex state of play: oppressed groups both actively participate in their own domination and they actively resist that domination. The state of play of the contemporary gender order is characterized by men's individual and collective oppression of women.[36] Men continue to benefit from this oppression of women, but, significantly, in the past twenty years, women's compliance with masculine hegemony has been counterbalanced by active feminist resistance. Men, as a group, are not oppressed by gender, but some certainly feel threatened by women's challenge to their power. Men are also hurt by this system of power: we are often emotionally limited, and commonly suffer poor health and a lower life-expectancy than women. But these problems are more accurately viewed as the "costs of being on top."[37] In fact, the shifts in masculine styles that we see among relatively privileged men may be interpreted as a sign that these men would like to stop paying these "costs," but it does not necessarily signal a desire to cease being "on top."

In addition to obscuring the oppressive relations between the sexes, and thus positing a false symmetry between women's and men's "movements," Bly's workshops also apparently do not question or challenge hierarchies of intermale dominance based on class, race, or sexuality. It is predominantly white, middle-aged, middle- and upper-middle class, and heterosexual men who attend these men's gatherings. Indeed when, several years ago, I was invited to a meeting of "mythopoetic followers of Robert Bly," the man who invited me attempted to lure me by enthusiastically whispering to me that "these are all *very* successful men!" Clearly, Bly's "men's movement" is so popular among relatively privileged men because, on the one hand, it acknowledges and validates men's experiences of pain and grief while guiding them to connect with other men in ways that are both nurturing and mutually empowering. On the other hand, and unlike feminism, it does not confront men with the reality of how their own privileges are based on the continued subordination of women and other men. In short, Bly facilitates the reconstruction of a new hegemonic masculinity—a masculinity that is less self-destructive, that has re-valued and re-constructed men's bonds with each other, and has learned to feel good about its own "Zeus power."

THE POWER TO CRY IN PUBLIC

A large part of the naiveté about the emergent New Man is the belief that if boys and men can learn to "express their feelings," they will no longer feel a need to dominate women. The idea that men's "need" to dominate others is the result of an emotional deficit overly psychologizes a reality that is largely structural. It does seem that the specific kind of masculinity that was ascendant (hegemonic) during the rise of entrepreneurial capitalism was extremely instrumental, stoic, and emotionally inexpressive.[38] But there is growing evidence that, today, there is no longer a neat link between men's emotional inexpressivity and their willingness and ability to dominate others. For instance, shortly following the recent Gulf War, U.S. General Schwartzkopf was lauded by the media as an example of the New Man for his ability to show his compassion (he unapologetically shed a tear in public) for the U.S. men and women who were killed, wounded, or captured. But this "new" emotional expressivity did not supplant a very "old" style of violent, dominating masculinity: As he was showing his feelings for his troops, Schwartzkopf was unsuccessfully urging President Bush not to stop the war too early. Following his hero, the Carthaginian general Hannibal, Schwartzkopf argued that "we had them in a rout and we could have continued to reap great destruction on them. We could have completely closed the door and made it a battle of annihilation."[39]

In recent years there does appear to be an increase of powerful and successful men crying in public—Ronald Reagan shedding a tear at the funeral of slain U.S. soldiers, basketball player Michael Jordan openly weeping after winning the NBA championship. It might be, ironically, that crying in public (at situationally appropriate moments) is becoming a legitimizing sign of the New Man's power. On the other hand, public crying for women—for instance when U.S. Representative Patricia Schroeder shed tears during a press conference while announcing her decision not to run for President—is still viewed as a sign of women's "natural weakness."

The easy manner in which Schwartzkopf was enthusiastically lauded as a New Man for shedding a tear in public is indicative of the importance placed on *styles* of masculinity, rather than the institutional *position of power* that many men still enjoy. In fact, there is no necessary link between men's "emotional inexpressivity" and their tendency to dominate others.[40] Men can learn to be situationally expressive while still very efficiently administering the institutions from which they gain their power over others. Representative Schroeder, a member of the U.S. House of Representatives Armed Services Committee, tells the story of how when she regularly visits military bases to assess their needs, the generals and admirals privately tell her that their "number one need" is childcare facilities. But when these same generals and admirals address Congress, their stated needs are ships, planes, tanks, and weapons systems. Childcare disappears from the list. Powerful men's public performances, after all, are staged primarily for each other. And though shedding a public tear for one's fallen comrades in war may now be an accepted part of the public presentation of hegemonic masculinity, there is still very little willingness among powerful men to transform the social institutions within which they construct their power and privilege over others.

BEYOND STYLE TO POLITICS

Lynne Segal's theorization of masculinities challenges us to ". . . move beyond the methodological individualism of all psychological thinking . . . to see that the relative powers and privileges that most men may still take for granted are not reducible to any set of facts about individual men." The key question, she suggests, is "under what social and structural conditions will men be encouraged, induced, or forced to change in ways that support feminist goals of equality and justice?" Since it is highly unlikely that all men—or even the majority of men—will actively support feminism, I would state the question even more specifically: "Under what social and structural conditions will *particular groups of men* be encouraged, induced, or forced to change in ways that support feminist goals of equality and justice?" This is an inherently political question.

Segal identifies the state and the economy as two key sites of political struggle. State social-welfare policies, parental leave and childcare programs, workplaces transformed by affirmative action and comparable worth, and the creation of democratic working conditions are structural changes that are necessary both to empower women and to encourage (or force) men to change in ways that are consistent with women's emancipation. Segal and other socialist-feminists have observed that the United States has the most regressive state policies and workplace structures when compared with other industrialized nations, and thus women's quest for equality there has moved at a snail's pace.[41]

This raises an important (but certainly not a new) question: What does it mean to be in favor of socialist-feminist transformations of the state and the workplace in the United States, given the weakness of our unions and given the fact that we have virtually no socialist or feminist presence in our government (especially at the federal level)? One answer is that "change" in the United States takes place less in the conventional political realm that in the arenas of culture and personal lifestyles. This is particularly true when we examine the most visible forms of recent change in U.S. masculinity. I have suggested that middle-class New Fathers, Mythopoetic Wild Men, and weeping generals are real and significant changes (i.e., they are genuine responses to real limits and dangers that many men face). But these changes represent a shift in the style—not in the social position of power—of hegemonic masculinity. In fact, I have suggested that these shifts in style might in some cases serve as visible signs of men's continued position of power and privilege vis-à-vis women and less powerful men.

Does this mean that all of men's changes today are merely symbolic, and that they ultimately do not contribute to the kinds of changes in gender relations that feminists have called for? It may appear to be so, especially if social scientists continue to collude with this reality by theoretically framing shifts in styles of hegemonic masculinity as indicative of the arrival of a New Man, while framing marginalized men (especially poor black men, in the United States) as Other—as atavistic "traditional" men. Instead, a feminist analysis of changing masculinities in the United States might begin with a focus on the ways that marginalized and subordinated masculinities are changing.

This shift in focus would likely accomplish three things. First, it would remove hegemonic masculinity from center-stage, thus creating a view of masculinities that emerges from a different standpoint. Second, it would require the deployment of theoretical frameworks that examine the ways that the politics of social class, race, ethnicity, and sexuality interact with those of gender.[42] Third, a sociology of masculinities that starts from the experience of marginalized and subordinated men would be far more likely to have power and politics—rather than personal styles or lifestyles—at its center. This is because men of color, poor and working-class men, and gay men are often in very contradictory positions at the nexus of intersecting systems of domination and subordination.

Though it is beyond the purview of this article, I briefly suggest here some key questions that future studies of changing masculinities might begin with: To what extent are working-class men, when confronted with issues such as comparable worth, identifying not simply as "men," but with women as "workers?"[43] To what extent are Black, Chicana, and Asian women and men successfully linking feminism with struggles against racism?[44] We can ask similar questions about gay men's roles in feminist and sexual politics. Gay men—especially those who are white and middle class—often share much of men's institutional power and privilege, while at the same time undermining a key component (heterosexuality) of hegemonic masculinity. There is evidence that some gay men identify with conventional masculine power, and would simply like to incorporate homosexuality into the definition of hegemonic masculinity.[45] On the other hand, for the past twenty-plus years, gay men have been in the forefront of pro-feminist men's organizations that have supported feminist political struggles. For instance, gay men's recent active participation in the defense of women's abortion clinics against anti-choice demonstrators suggests a sophisticated political understanding of the mutually interlocking nature of gender and sexual oppression. It is precisely this sort of analysis and political practice that is necessary if today's changing masculinities are to contribute to the building of a more egalitarian and democratic world.

ACKNOWLEDGMENTS

Some of the ideas for this article were first delivered at the "Unraveling Masculinities" conference, University of California, Davis, February 1991. The paper was delivered at the American Sociological Association Meetings, Pittsburgh, August 1992. Thanks to Lois Banner, Pierrette Hondagneu-Sotelo, Michael Schwalbe, Don Sabo, and the reviewers for *Theory and Society* for helpful comments and suggestions on earlier versions of this article.

NOTES

1. R. La Rossa, "Fatherhood and Social Change," *Family Relations* 37 (1988): 451–457.

2. K. Clatterbaugh, *Contemporary Perspectives on Masculinity: Men, Women, and Politics in Modern Society* (Boulder: Westview Press, 1990); T. Edwards, "Beyond Sex and Gender: Masculinity, Homosexuality, and Social Theory," 110–123 in J. Hearn and D. Morgan, editors, *Men, Masculinities and Social Theory* (London: Unwin Hyman, 1990); M. Shiffman, "The Men's Movement: An Exploratory Empirical Investigation" in M. S. Kimmel, editor, *Changing Men: New Directions in Research on Men and Masculinity* (Newbury Park: Sage, 1987).

3. H. Brod, editor, *The Making of Masculinities: The New Men's Studies* (Boston: Allen & Unwin, 1987); J. Hearn and D. Morgan, editors, *Men, Masculinities and Social Theory* (London and Boston: Unwin Hyman, 1990); M. Kaufman, editor, *Beyond Patriarchy: Essays by Men on Pleasure, Power, and Change* (Toronto and New York: Oxford University, 1987); M. S. Kimmel, editor, *Changing Men: New Directions*

in Research on Men and Masculinity (Newbury Park: Sage, 1987); M. S. Kimmel and M. A. Messner, editors, *Men's Lives* (New York: Macmillan, second edition 1992).

4. J. Stacey, " 'We Are Not Doormats': The Influence of Feminism on Contemporary Evangelicals in the United States," in F. Ginsburg and A. Tsing, editors, *Negotiating Gender in American Culture* (Boston: Beacon Press, 1989).

5. See, for instance, E. L. Cole, *Maximized Manhood: A Guide to Family Survival* (Springdale, Penn.: Whitaker House, 1982).

6. For a representative "men's rights" text, see F. Baumli, editor, *Men Freeing Men: Exploding the Myth of the Traditional Male* (Jersey City: New Atlantis Press, 1985). For an analysis of the "men's rights movement," see K. Clatterbaugh, *Contemporary Perspectives on Masculinity.*

7. R. Bly, *Iron John: A Book About Men* (Reading, Mass.: Addison-Wesley, 1990).

8. R. W. Connell, "A Whole New World: Remaking Masculinity in the Context of the Environmental Movement," *Gender & Society* 4 (1990): 452–477; R. W. Connell, "An Iron Man: The Body and Some Contradictions of Hegemonic Masculinity," in M. A. Messner and D. F. Sabo, editors, *Sport, Men and the Gender Order: Critical Feminist Perspectives* (Champaign, Ill.: Human Kinetics Publishers, 1990).

9. For example, see J. H. Pleck, *The Myth of Masculinity* (Cambridge: MIT Press, 1982).

10. For instance, see J. Stacey and B. Thorne, "The Missing Feminist Revolution in Sociology," *Social Problems* 32 (1985): 301–316.

11. T. Carrigan, B. Connell, and J. Lee, "Toward a New Sociology of Masculinity," *Theory & Society* 14 (1985): 1–40; R. W. Connell, *Gender and Power* (Stanford: Stanford University Press, 1987); J. Hearn and D. Morgan, editors, *Men, Masculinities and Social Theory;* L. Segal, *Slow Motion: Changing Masculinities, Changing Men* (New Brunswick, N.J.: Rutgers University, 1990).

12. L. Segal, *Slow Motion.*

13. B. Friedan, *The Second Stage* (London: Michael Joseph, 1982); W. J. Goode, "Why Men Resist," in B. Thorne and M. Yalom, editors, *Rethinking the Family: Some Feminist Questions* (New York: Longman, 1982).

14. A. Machung, "Talking Career, Thinking Job: Gender Differences in Career and Family Expectations of Berkeley Seniors," *Feminist Studies* 15 (1989); R. Sidel, *On Her Own: Growing Up in the Shadow of the American Dream* (New York: Penguin, 1990).

15. A. Hochschild, *The Second Shift: Working Parents and the Revolution at Home* (New York: Viking, 1989); R. La Rossa, "Fatherhood and Social Change"; C. Lewis, *Becoming a Father* (Milton Keynes: Open University Press, 1986); G. Russell, *The Changing Role of Fathers* (London: University of Queensland, 1983).

16. N. Eliasoph, "Political Culture and the Presentation of a Political Self: A Study of the Public Sphere in the Spirit of Erving Goffman," *Theory & Society* 19 (1990): 465–494.

17. A. Thomas, "The Significance of Gender Politics in Men's Accounts of

Their 'Gender Identity,' " 143–159 in J. Hearn and D. Morgan, editors, *Men, Masculinity, and Social Theory*, 156.

18. R. La Rossa, "Fatherhood and Social Change"; S. Osherson, *Finding Our Fathers: How a Man's Life Is Shaped by his Relationship with His Father* (New York: Fawcett Columbine, 1987); J. H. Pleck, "American Fathering in Historical Perspective," 83–97 in M. S. Kimmel, editor, *Changing Men: New Directions in Research on Men and Masculinity* (Beverly Hills: Sage, 1987); E. A. Rotundo, "American Fatherhood: A Historical Perspective," *American Behavioral Scientist* 29 (1985): 7–25; L. B. Rubin, *Intimate Strangers: Men and Women Together* (New York: Harper & Row, 1983); G. Russell, "Problems in Role-Reversed Families," in C. Lewis and M. O'Brien, editors, *Reassessing Fatherhood* (London: Sage, 1987).

19. L. Segal, *Slow Motion*, 37.

20. N. Chodorow, *The Reproduction of Mothering* (Berkeley: University of California Press, 1978).

21. See G. Russell, "Problems in Role-reversed Families"; L. Segal, *Slow Motion*, 46.

22. L. McKee, "Fathers' Participation in Infant Care: A Critique," in L. McKee and M. O'Brien, editors, *The Father Figure* (Travistock: London, 1982); P. Moss and J. Brannon, "Fathers and Employment," in C. Lewis and M. O'Brien, editors, *Reassessing Fatherhood* (London: Sage, 1987).

23. R. Sidel, *Women and Children Last: The Plight of Poor Women in Affluent America* (New York: Viking Penguin Books, 1986).

24. R. Hertz, *More Equal Than Others: Woman and Men in Dual Career Marriages* (Berkeley: University of California, 1986).

25. L. Blum, *Between Feminism and Labor: The Significance of the Comparable Worth Movement* (Berkeley: University of California Press, 1991); B. F. Reskin and P. A. Roos, *Job Queues, Gender Queues: Explaining Women's Inroads into Male Occupations* (Philadelphia: Temple University Press, 1990).

26. A. Hochschild, *The Second Shift*.

27. L. Segal, *Slow Motion*, 58.

28. See M. S. Kimmel, "Men's Responses to Feminism at the Turn of the Century," *Gender & Society* 1 (1987): 517–530.

29. R. Bly, *Iron John*, 17.

30. For critiques of Bly, see R. W. Connell, "Drumming up the Wrong Tree," *Tikkun* 7/1 (1992): 517–530; M. S. Kimmel, "Reading Men: Men, Masculinity and Publishing," *Contemporary Sociology* 21 (1992): 162–171; F. Pelka, "Robert Bly Romanticizes History, Trivializes Sexist Oppression, and Lays the Blame for Men's 'Grief' on Women," *On the Issues* 19 (1991): 17–19, 39.

31. See M. A. Clawson, *Constructing Brotherhood: Class, Gender, and Fraternalism* (Princeton, N.J.: Princeton University Press, 1989); A. Tolson, *The Limits of Masculinity: Male Identity and Women's Liberation* (New York: Harper & Row, 1977).

32. Bly, *Iron John*, 61.

33. Ibid., 22.

34. See, for example, W. Farrell, *The Liberated Man* (New York: Bantam Books, 1975).

35. For an analysis of oppression as a relational concept, see P. Freire, *Pedagogy of the Oppressed* (New York: Herder & Herden, 1970).

36. See R. W. Connell, *Gender & Power*.

37. M. E. Kann, "The Costs of Being on Top," *Journal of the National Association for Women Deans, Administrators & Counselors* 49 (1986): 29–37.

38. See M. F. Winter and E. R. Robert, "Male Dominance, Late Capitalism, and the Growth of Instrumental Reason," *Berkeley Journal of Sociology* 25 (1980): 249–280.

39. "Schwartzkopf Says He Hoped for a Rout of Iraqi Forces, But Bush Chose to Halt War," *Los Angeles Times* (27 May 1991).

40. See J. W. Sattel, "The Inexpressive Male: Tragedy or Sexual Politics?" *Social Problems* 23 (1976).

41. See, for instance, R. Sidel, *Women and Children Last*.

42. M. Baca Zinn, L. Weber Cannon, E. Higgenbotham, and B. Thornton Dill, "The Costs of Exclusionary Practices in Women's Studies," *Signs: Journal of Women in Culture and Society* 11 (1986): 290–303; P. H. Collins, *Black Feminist Thought: Knowledge, Consciousness, and the Politics of Empowerment* (Boston: Unwin Hyman, 1990); S. Harding, *The Science Question in Feminism* (Ithaca: Cornell University Press, 1986); M. A. Messner, "Men Studying Masculinity: Some Epistemological Questions in Sport Sociology," *Sociology of Sport Journal* 7 (1990): 136–153.

43. L. Blum, *Between Feminism and Labor*.

44. See P. H. Collins, *Black Feminist Thought;* b. hooks, "Black Women and Men: Partnership in the 1990s," 203–214 in b. hooks, *Yearning: Race, Gender and Cultural Politics* (Boston: South End Press, 1990).

45. T. Edwards, "Beyond Sex and Gender."

III

THE PERSONAL
IS INTELLECTUAL:
HISTORICAL
AND ANALYTIC
CRITIQUES

"Born to Run": Nineteenth-Century Fantasies of Masculine Retreat and Re-creation (*or* The Historical Rust on Iron John)

MICHAEL S. KIMMEL

The man began to run: now he had not run far from his own door, when his wife and children, perceiving it, began to cry after him to return; but the man put his fingers in his ears, and ran on, crying Life, Life, eternal Life! So he looked not behind him, but fled towards the middle of the plain.

John Bunyon, *Pilgrim's Progress* (1678)

IN THE LAST LINES OF THE NOVEL that bears his name, Huckleberry Finn anxiously plans his escape. "I reckon I got to light out for the territory ahead of the rest, because Aunt Sally she's going to adopt me and sivilize me, and I can't stand it. I been there before." Since the early nineteenth century, the quest for manhood has revolved around a flight from women. The search for manhood has come to mean a relentless effort to avoid all behaviors that might remotely hint of the feminine. Women signified constraints on manhood—temperance, Christian piety, sober responsibility, sexual fidelity. Women set the tone of those institutions that restrained masculine excess—schoolroom, parlor, church. Women meant, first, mother, with her incessant efforts to curtail boyish rambunctiousness; and later, wife, with her incessant efforts to keep men in harness as responsible and respectable workers, fathers, and husbands. Thus women represented responsibility—marriage, fatherhood, workplace stability. It is from the perceived clutches of "woman," this collection of constraints and responsibilities, as much as real live women, that American men have been escaping for the past two hundred years. And American men have devised a rich and varied collection of escape hatches. Contemporary mythopoetic men may believe they have created these retreats from examining other cultures; a bit of historical perspective on their own culture might prove far more revealing.

In both real life and the dreams that populate American fiction, men have run away to join the army, been kidnapped or abandoned on desert islands, gone west, or, as today, run off to the woods for all-male retreats.

In this essay I want to discuss a few moments of masculinist retreat from feminization in nineteenth-century America. By feminization I refer both to real women, whose feminizing clutches—as teachers, mothers, and Sunday School teachers—was seen as threatening to turn robust boyhood into emasculated little pipsqueaks, and also to an increasingly urban and industrial culture, a culture that increasingly denied men the opportunities for manly adventure and a sense of connectedness with their work. At the end of the nineteenth century, this latter tendency was best expressed by Henry James, in *The Bostonians,* as the dashing Basil Ransome, displaced southern beau, rails against modern society (and suggests his position on women in the process):

> The whole generation is womanized; the masculine tone is passing out of the world; it's a feminine, nervous, hysterical, chattering, canting age, an age of hollow phrases and false delicacy and exaggerated solicitudes and coddled sensibilities, which, if we don't soon look out, will usher in the reign of mediocrity, of the feeblest and flattest and most pretentious that has ever been. The masculine character, the ability to dare and endure, to know and yet not fear reality, to look the world in the face and take it for what it is . . . that is what I want to preserve, or rather . . . recover; and I must tell you that I don't in the least care what becomes of you ladies while I make the attempt![1]

Here was the critique of the feminization of American culture in condensed form. Something had happened to American society that had led to a loss of cultural vitality, of national virility. And ever since the first few decades of the nineteenth century, men have been running away—off to the frontier, the mountains, the forests, the high seas, the battlegrounds, outer space—to retrieve what they feel they've lost—some deep, essential part of themselves, their identity, their manhood.

Part of the struggle was simply to get out of the house. The separation of spheres had transformed the nineteenth-century middle-class home into a virtual feminine theme park—where well-mannered and well-dressed children played quietly in heavily draped and carpeted parlors, and adults chatted amiably over tea served from porcelain services. This delightful contrast with the frantic and aggressive business world made men feel uneasy in their own homes, even as they felt themselves exiled from it. A man's house "is a prison, in which he finds himself oppressed and confined, not sheltered and protected," wrote Thoreau. "His muscles are never relaxed. It is rare that he overcomes the house, and learns to sit at home in it."[2]

Not only had the home itself become a feminine preserve, but domestic activities, especially the children's moral and religious instruction, were a woman's province. Women were not only domestic; they were domesticators, expected to turn their sons into virtuous Christian gentlemen, that is, dutiful, well-mannered and feminized. Orestes Brownson growled about "female religion" as well as male ministers who were the domesticated pets of widows and spinsters, "fit only to balance teacups and mouth platitudes." The increased roles of mothers and decreased role of absentee fathers in the early nineteenth century meant that it fell increasingly to women to teach their sons how to be men.[3]

Thus did the definition of manhood become the repudiation of the feminine, the resistance to mother's, and later the wife's, efforts to civilize men, to domesticate men. This resistance to feminization, whether in the form of real women (mothers and wives) or in terms of those cultural qualities of modern life that spell enervation and feminization (religion, education, workplace responsibilities, doing "brain work")—this resistance is what I call *masculinism*. Masculinism involves an effort to restore manly vigor and revirilize American men, by promoting separate homosocial preserves where men can be men without female interference. Some masculinist efforts involve the symbolic appropriation of women's reproductive power, by developing distinctively masculine forms of ritual initiation and nurture—initiations that displaced maternal care with manly validation.

Masculinism is, at its center, resistance to femininity, to the forces that turn hard men into soft, enervated nerds; it is by escape from women and resistance to femininity that masculinists hope to retrieve their manhood. In their view, men had to wriggle free of these feminine, feminizing, clutches—ironically, the very clutches that male insecurity had created to free the workplace of female competition and to make the home into a man's castle and thus preserve patriarchal authority. It was in the public sphere that men faced the greatest challenges to their manhood, where their sense of manhood was won or lost, and yet these anxieties were projected, instead, onto women as the bearers of enervating lassitude. Men were suddenly terrified of feminization in the very homes they had created, and now yearned to escape or at least more clearly demarcate themselves from women.

The fears of feminization reached a crescendo in the late 1840s through the 1850s. Beards and moustaches proliferated as masculine fashion, while critics lampooned feminized styles among urban men. Walt Whitman chastised the painted urban male who "looks like a doll," and a writer in *Harper's Monthly* described the human "poodles" who paraded in the cities with their "velvet tunics" and "long glossy locks." And Oliver Wendell Holmes foresaw the end of our race in 1858, convinced that a "set of black-coated, stiff-jointed, soft-muscled, paste-complexioned youth as we can boast from our Atlantic cities never before sprang from loins of Anglo-Saxon lineage."[4]

What was a real man to do? Get out of town. When Horace Greeley advised, in 1837, to "Go West, young man, and grow up with the country," men perked up their ears and followed in droves.[5] The west—both reality and idea—was the centerpiece of masculinist resistance. The west was a safety valve, siphoning off excess population, and providing an outlet for both the ambitious and the unsuccessful. As Frederick Jackson Turner, the historian who made the west the central theme of American history, put it:

> To the peasant and artisan of the Old World, bound by the chains of social class, as old as custom and as inevitable as fate, the West offered an exit into a free life and greater well-being among the bounties of nature, into the midst of resources that demanded manly exertion and that gave in return the chance for indefinite ascent in the scale of social advance.[6]

A more decidedly gendered tone is seen by literary critic David Leverenz, who writes that "[t]o be aggressive, rebellious, enraged, uncivilized; this is what the frontier could do for the European clones on the East Coast, still in thrall to a foreign tyranny of manners." Timothy Flint suggested, in 1831, that these "shrinking and effeminate spirits, the men of soft hands and fashionable life" ought to follow the pioneers, for "there is a kind of moral sublimity in the contemplation of the adventures and daring of such men" with their "manly hardihood." When young men read in Yale's president Timothy Dwight's four-volume *Travels in New England and New York* (1821–22) the author's regret that as the pioneer pushed further and further into the wilderness, he became "less and less a civilized man," or J. Hector St. John Crevecoeur's lament that on the frontier, men "degenerated altogether into the hunting state" and became, ultimately, "no better than carnivorous animals of a superior rank," they probably couldn't wait to get started.[7]

Reports from the field of this westward rush all celebrated the return to manly virtues. Francis Parkman's *The Oregon Trail: Sketches of Prairie and Rocky Mountain Life* (1849) was an immediate best-seller, as was his later *Discovery of the Great West* (1869). A scrawny, feeble-bodied, rich boy, Parkman saw his masculine salvation in the repudiation of all things civilized (much as did another ruling class weakling Richard Henry Dana, who penned another masculinist escape memoir, *Two Years Before the Mast* in 1840). Charles Webber's *Old Hicks, The Guide; or, Adventures in the Comanche Country in Search of a Gold Mine* (1848) also celebrated the "philosophy of the savage life."[8]

The rush westward reached its apotheosis with the California Gold Rush of 1849. Never before, or since, have men created such a homosocial preserve on such a scale. Between 1849 and 1850, 85,000 men came to California, composing 93 percent of the state's population—71 percent of whom were younger men, aged 20 to 40. They were lured by the exciting possibilities of sudden and exorbitant wealth, but money alone did not keep them there. It was the homosocial life, the life outside the conventional boundaries of civilization, the life away from wives. "There was no female society," wrote Rev. John Todd, "no homes to soften and restrain." "The condition of the mining population, especially their carelessness in regard to appearances, mode of life, and habits in general," observed C. W. Haskins, "showed conclusively that man, when alone, and deprived of that influence which the presence of woman only can produce, would in a short time degenerate into a savage and barbarous state." One doctor explained that in California, "all the *restrictive influence* of fair women is lost, and the ungoverned tempers of men run wild."[9]

And they looked and acted the part. Forty-niners cast off the cultural baggage they brought from the east, relinquishing evidence of their former civilized lives. They took new names, manly and rough, like Texas Jack, Whiskey Tom, French Flat Pete, Buckeye and Sawbones (a doctor), neither bathed nor changed their clothes, gambled, drank incessantly, swore, attended bare-knuckled prize fights more often than they attended church services. A deck of cards was called the "California prayer book." Thus did the Forty-niners find what they were really looking for in those gold mines; they retrieved their lost manhood, even if they didn't find any gold.[10]

Of course, one needn't go to all the trouble of traveling across the country to retrieve manhood by a confrontation with nature. One could find it in one's own backyard, the way that Henry David Thoreau did. Thoreau, too, rejected the enervated version of Marketplace Men, who led, in his famous phrase "lives of quiet desperation"—a man who is "in such desperate haste to succeed and in such desperate enterprises" that his life is "frittered away by detail." Urban businessmen were literally suffocating on the enervating tendencies of modern life, but working men lacked the leisure to develop their manly integrity: both, Thoreau believed, needed liberation.[11] "We should come home from far, from adventures, and perils, and discoveries every day, with new experience and character." In short, we need the "tonic of the wilderness," as an antidote to the lockstep inanity of the new marketplace.[12]

So Thoreau set out to live at Walden Pond in 1845, shunning the company of women in order to create himself, to become a self-made man in the wilderness. In a sense, Thoreau conducted his own initiation into a new version of manhood. First, he rejected as a model the old, aristocratic father, England. "I look on England today as an old gentleman who is travelling with a great deal of baggage, trumpery which has accumulated from long housekeeping, which he has not the courage to burn." Then, he baptized himself. "I got up early and bathed in the pond; that was a religious exercise, and one of the best things which I did." And, finally, he took communion, in a rather brutal fashion. "I caught a glimpse of a woodchuck stealing across my path, and felt a strange thrill of savage delight, and was strongly tempted to seize and devour him raw; not that I was hungry then, except for that wildness which he represented." Ingesting the wildness, Thoreau suggests, allows middle-class men to free themselves.[13]

If middle-class men were unable to venture to the west, or even to a local pond, the tonic virtues of the wilderness could be brought to their homes; they could escape through fantasy. In the first half of the century, two forms of fantasy were available: popular biographies of pioneers and backwoodsmen, elevated to the level of national myths, and popular fiction, both of which allowed men to escape through fantasies of identification. For example, although Kit Carson and Daniel Boone were both active in the first two decades of the century, and Davy Crockett active in the 1830s, all became mythic heroes in the 1840s and especially in the 1850s, when their biographies were rewritten as primitivist narratives of innate, instinctual manhood. All three were in constant retreat from advancing civilization.

Boone was the "natural man," disinterested in accumulation of wealth, always on the move, never weighted down. "Boone used to say to me," declared one backwoodsman, who claimed to be Boone's hunting buddy, "that when he could not fall the top of a tree near enough to his door for fire wood, it was time to move to a new place." Another legend held that when Boone heard that someone was clearing a farm 12 miles west of him, he declared the area "too thickly settled"—his version of "there goes the neighborhood"—and prepared his next move. Lionizing such misanthropic grumpiness seems to be a peculiarly American trait.[14]

Equally distinctive was the creation of the American myth of mobility, and especially the link between geographic mobility, social mobility, and self-recreation as men. The heroic artisan returns in the guise of the pioneer, the masculine primitive, but he is still humble and beholden to his origins. As Richard Slotkin, who has traced what he called the "frontier fable" as a dominant theme in American culture, writes:

> The protagonist is usually represented as having marginal connections to the Metropolis and its culture. He is a poor and uneducated borderer or an orphan lacking the parental tie to anchor him to the Metropolis and is generally disinclined to learn from book culture when the book of nature is free to read before him. His going to the wilderness breaks or attentuates the Metropolitan tie, but it gives him access to something far more important than anything the Metropolis contains—the wisdom, morality, power, and freedom of Nature in its pure wild form.[15]

Though the myth contains an irony invisible to its protagonists—that their very activity in moving west to escape civilization transforms them into its advance guard, as they tame the west for future settlement—it remains a most potent myth today. When one historian dared to debunk aspects of the myth about how and when Crockett died at the Alamo, he was berated by irate writers as a "wimp," fit for nothing better than the lowly profession of college teaching. In the 1992 presidential campaign, Republican challenger Pat Buchanan donned a coonskin cap as he campaigned in Crockett's native Tennessee.[16]

These real-life historical figures were transformed into mythic heroes within a decade or two of their deaths; the fictional creations of early nineteenth-century American novelists made them up as they went along. In their insightful books, *Love and Death in the American Novel* (1966), and *Manhood and the American Renaissance* (1988), literary critics Leslie Fiedler and David Leverenz, respectively, describe the two dominant, and related, themes in American literature: male bonding in the escape from women (Fiedler) and discomfort and resistance to the marketplace (Leverenz). Fiedler explains best those writers who embraced and articulated this vision most completely—Washington Irving, James Fenimore Cooper, Mark Twain; Leverenz focuses instead on those who were more ambivalent, like Ralph Waldo Emerson, Nathaniel Hawthorne, and Walt Whitman.[17]

To Fiedler, the classic American novel is entirely different from the classic European novel, in which the plot revolves around a heterosexual couple, struggling with issues of sexual fidelity, workplace responsibility, family and domestic concerns—as in, for example, *Madame Bovary, Tom Jones,* or *Jane Eyre.* American novels are marked by the absence of sexuality, the absence of marriage and families—the virtual absence of women entirely. The American novel is about "adventure and isolation plus an escape at one point or another, or a flight from society to an island, a woods, the underworld, a mountain fastness—some place, at least, where mothers do not come."[18]

Take Washington Irving's story "Rip Van Winkle" (1820). Alongside the surface treatment of progress—Van Winkle sleeps for twenty years and comes back to find everything changed—there is also the escape from his shrewish wife. "Morning, noon, and night her tongue was incessantly going, and everything he did or said was sure to produce a torrent of household eloquence." Usually, Rip simply "shrugged his shoulders, shook his head, and cast up his eyes" in response. But finally he had to get away. "Poor Rip was at last reduced almost to despair; and his only alternative, to escape from the labor of the farm and clamor of his wife, was to take gun in hand and stroll away into the woods." Rip's musket-laden stroll culminates in a twenty-year alcoholic reverie and confrontation with the homosocial world of the mountain trolls. Upon his return, Rip is most struck by the changes in the gender order that his absence, and his wife's death, has elicited:

> Rip, in fact, was no politician; the changes of states and empires made but little impression on him; but there was one species of despotism under which he had long groaned, and that was—petticoat government. Happily that was at an end; he had got his neck out of the yoke of matrimony, and could in and out whenever he pleased, without dreading the tyranny of Dame Van Winkle. Whenever her name was mentioned, however, he shook his head, shrugged his shoulders, and cast up his eyes; which might pass either for an expression of resignation to his fate, or joy at his deliverance.

The story's last line extends Irving's fable to the "common wish of all henpecked husbands in the neighborhood, when life hangs heavy on their hands, that they might have a quieting draught of Rip Van Winkle's flagon." Rip is the first of this fictional American archetype, the man in flight to avoid persecution—the fugitive, born to run.[19]

By the mid-nineteenth century, until today, this new American male hero also encounters another man, preferably a man of another race, as a sort of spirit guide to this world without women. From Natty Bumppo and Chingachgook, Huck and Jim, Ishmael and Queequeg, all the way to the Lone Ranger and Tonto, Captain Kirk and the Vulcan Mr. Spock, and Lt. John Dunbar and Kicking Bird in *Dances with Wolves,* and Murtaugh and Riggs in the *Lethal Weapon* series, American fiction has celebrated male bonding, "a love between males, more enduring and purer than any heterosexual passion," which culminates in an asexual counter-marriage "in which the white refugee from society and the dark skinned primitive are joined till death do them part." That a society so defined by racism and homophobia should place homoerotic union between two men of different races as its central theme is somewhat astonishing. Fiedler attributes this to a search for redemption in fantasy for white heterosexual guilt, but I believe it is also a way to present screens against which manhood is projected, played out, and defined.[20] Women and children, in their absence, offer such a screen; they do not even enter the arena of masculinity. The non-white male, then, stands in for them—as dependent child ("Nigger Jim"), male mother (Chingachgook, Tonto), spiritual guide and moral instructor (Queequeg, Chingachgook). Their homoerotic passion is never the passion of equals; the non-white is either the guide and exemplar or the Rousseauian "noble savage" who, in his childlike innocence, is more susceptible to the wiles of civilization.[21]

Sexuality—succumbing to the lustful temptations of the body—would ruin everything, just as carnal desires ruin men's ability to wriggle free of their connection with women. With women, sexuality leads to marriage and family; with men, transforming homo*erotic* bonding into homo*sexual* union would likewise destroy the charged but chaste basis for the bond.[22] Nowhere is this more clear than in the five-novel saga of the Leatherstocking Tales by James Fenimore Cooper, the most popular novelist of antebellum America. Cooper had earlier groped for a way to develop his critique of emerging marketplace manhood and his idealization of the natural man. In his 1821 novel *The Spy*, for example, his critique of one character, Harvey Birch, as a shrewd, acquisitive, Yankee peddlar whose "love of money is a stronger passion than love of his kin" is less effective without another masculine archetype to play off against.

In 1823, Cooper found him in Natty Bumppo, the hero of *The Pioneers* (1823), *The Last of the Mohicans* (1826), *The Prairie* (1827), *The Pathfinder* (1840), and *The Deerslayer* (1841). In Bumppo, Cooper created the prototype of masculinist flight into the wilderness and "showed how the solitary hunter, unencumbered by social responsibilities, utterly self-sufficient, uncultivated but endowed with a spontaneous appreciation of natural beauty could become the central figure in the great American romance of the West." "And Natty, what sort of man is he?" asked D. H. Lawrence. "Why, he is a man with a gun. He is a killer, a slayer. Patient and gentle, as he is, he is a slayer. Self-effacing . . . still he is a killer." No Marketplace Man, Bumppo is a traditional gentleman, naturally virtuous, in "flight from civilized unmanliness to Native-American traditions of patriarchal comrade-ship." Natty Bumppo is the first "last real man in America."[23]

When we first meet him, and his Indian companion Chingachgook, they are engaged in a debate about whether whites have any rights to take the Indians' land. At first, Natty says that whites are only doing to the Indians what the Indians used to do to each other, although he acknowledges that it does seem a bit unfair to be using bullets. But then Natty launches into a critique of feminization that seems to come out of nowhere. Modern white men no longer publicly shame the "cowardly" and applaud bravery; nowa-days, they "write in books" instead of telling their deed in the villages, "where the lie can be given to the face of a cowardly boaster, and the brave soldier can call on his comrades to witness for the truth of his words." As a result, "a man who is too conscientious to misspend his days among the women, in learning the names of black marks, may never hear of the deeds of his fathers, nor feel a pride in striving to outdo them."[24]

If books are agents of feminization, women are but helpless and frail crea-tures. Throughout the novel, men spend a lot of time in the forests, risking all manner of danger, to rescue women whom they believe cannot survive without male protection. Enemies are also feminized: "The Delawares are women!" exclaims Hawkeye. "The Yengeese, my foolish countrymen, have told them to take up the tomahawk, and strike their fathers in the Canada, and they have forgotten their sex. Does my brother wish to hear Le Cerf Agile ask for his petticoats, and see him weep before the Hurons, at the stake?"[25] Though Hawkeye delivers the masculinist attacks on effeminate Mama's boys and disdains women, it falls to Chingachgook, the Indian, to deliver the most stinging critique of Marketplace Manhood—in the guise of a critique of the white man:

> Some [The Great Spirit] made with faces paler than the ermine of the forests: and these he ordered to be traders; dogs to their women and wolves to their slaves. He gave this people the nature of the pigeon; wings that never tire: young, more plentiful than the leaves on the trees, and appetites to devour the earth. He gave them tongues like the false call of the wildcat; hearts like rabbits; the cunning of the hog . . . and arms to fight his battles; his cunning tells him how to get together the goods of the earth; and his arms inclose the land from the shore of the salt water to the islands of the great lake. His gluttony makes him sick. God gave him enough, and yet he wants all. Such are the palefaces.[26]

Such was the masculinity expressed by the urban entrepreneur, against which Cooper was rebelling, celebrating instead the return of the virtuous hunter, the Heroic Artisan in the wilderness.

Other antebellum writers were ambivalent about the triumph of Market-place Man. Some, like Horace Greeley, were concerned that unbridled marketplace competition caused corruption. "The relations instituted among men, by the present form of society, are those of individual Selfishness, which generates Indigence, Fraud, Oppression, War, Disease, and False and delusive Doctrines," which "cannot be prevented by any change short of a thorough social reorganization," he wrote in 1850.[27] Whitman celebrated the vital sensuality of the Heroic Artisan as a counterpoint to the stoic self-control of the self-made man, as in his homoerotic adulation of artisanal comradeship—both physical and spiritual:

> I will plant companionship thick as trees along the rivers of America, and along
>   the shores of the Great Lakes, and all over the prairies.
> I will make inseparable cities with their arms about each other's necks,
>   By the love of comrades
>   By the manly love of comrades.

More than any other work, Herman Melville's *Moby Dick* provides the most compelling analysis of the mid-century crisis of masculinity. Captain Ahab's "desperate narcissistic rage" and "mesmerizing coerciveness" are the marks of "a man obsessed with avenging his shattered manhood."[28] In Ahab, Melville provides a portrait of gendered madness, a blind rage fueled by sexualized obsession, the self-destruction of the self-made Marketplace Man. Here is a man driven to dominate, compulsively competitive, obsessively insecure—in short, the archetypal capitalist man, a nineteenth-century Type A powerbroker. His monomania, that obsession with domination that is the disease of the driven, is the nineteenth-century male version of hysteria.[29]

The great whale is both the more powerful man against which masculinity is measured and the archetypal woman—carnal, sexually insatiable, Other.[30] What are we to make, after all, of the fact that Ahab, who had lost his "leg" trying to plunge his "six inch blade" into the whale, is now engaged in a "crazed flight to prove his manhood"? *Moby Dick* is "the most extravagant projection of male penis envy" in American literature.[31] Ahab's inevitable failure is both economic and sexual; Marketplace Manhood is no match for the forces of nature, and so the relations are inverted, revealing the terror of being dominated that lies beneath the drive to dominate. Ahab is the male Dora, seducing and seduced, rapist and raped, willing to partake of the savage butchery of his entire crew to avoid humiliation at the hands of his rival. Like the real-life Andrew Jackson, the fictional Ahab is finally hysterically mute, incapable of speech. He dies strangled in the harpoon's ropes, choking, voiceless and terrified.

These violent passions provide a startling contrast to the tender artisanal homoeroticism between Ishmael and the harpoonist, Queequeg, who discover, as they lie asleep in bed, wrapped in each other's arms, that chaste yet eroticized homosociality that characterizes the purified male bond. To Melville, those bonds were impossible if one adopted the competitive drive of Marketplace Man; they were possible only in the homosocial fraternalism of the Heroic Artisan, all but one of whom is destroyed by Ahab's monomaniacal pursuit of the Leviathan.

TURN-OF-THE-CENTURY FANTASIES OF ESCAPE

By the turn of the century, the frontier was closed. What was a man to do? Well, for one thing, he could join the hundreds of organizations that had sprung up to answer his manly needs—institutions like local sports teams, Muscular Christian revival meetings, or fraternal orders, which boasted over 5.5 million members in 1897—out of an adult male population of slightly less than 19 million! And through the YMCA, Boy Scouts, single-sex schools, he could ensure that his sons received proper training in hardy manhood.[32] Or he could retrieve his deep manhood by fantasy. After all, it is a psychoanalytic axiom that what we lose in reality we recreate in fantasy. Why not gender identity?

For example, the exploits of Frank Merriwell at Yale found avid young male readers. Here was the embodiment of the strenuous ideal, excelling in every sport, always winning the big game for Yale when the chips were down—he could even throw a curve ball that curved twice!—without any compromise of his manly and moral virtues. Like Gilbert Patten (who wrote the Merriwell stories under the name Burt Standish), turn-of-the-century writers pursued male readers with fantasy tales of heroic adventure on the edges of civilization, scathing critiques of sedentary life, and offered their readers the possibility of escape. In fantasy, we re-enter the world of the independent virtuous artisan, our recurring fantasy role model, even up to the present day. In his most famous incarnation, he is the cowboy.

The cowboy occupies an important place in American cultural history—he is America's contribution to the world's stock of mythic heroes. What is most interesting is that the cowboy was not always a hero; he was invented. And he was invented, in a sense, after he had disappeared. In the 1860s and

1870s, the cowboy was called a "herder," and he appeared in public prints and writing as rough, uncouth, shaggy, and dirty; his behavior was violent, barbarous, and rowdy. He was the brutal outlaw, not the good guy. Writing in 1875, Laura Winthrop Johnson saw no glamour in these "rough men with shaggy hair and wild staring eyes, in butternut trousers stuffed into great rough boots." But around 1882, a cowboy named Buck Taylor at the First Wild West Show first captured the attention of a writer, Prentiss Ingraham. The Wild West Show was a conscious re-creation of the west, now tamed for mass consumption, into a traveling circus. Organized by Buffalo Bill Cody, the pre-eminent trader in mythic archetypes, the show depicted the conquest of the wild west, transforming it into an American allegory of expansion and marketplace success. In 1887, Ingraham wrote a fictional biography of Taylor, later expanded in a series of dime novels, and the new cowboy was invented.[33]

By 1887, the great cattle drives that were his home had ended, and the "Big Die-Up" of the winter of 1886–87 had bankrupted many cattle outfits, and so altered ranch life that the cowboy was "less a knight errant and more a hired man on horseback." The cowboy thus emerges in literature at the exact moment of his disappearance as independent artisan and his transformation into a wage worker in a new industry of cattle ranching. Though the cowboy was a worker, "a skilled technician hired to do the boring, and often dangerous business of 'working' cows," his iconic representation shows the possibility of the employee as hero.[34]

If the workaday world of the cowboy had been somewhat proletarianized in real life, in its fictional representation it was all guts and glory. The end of the century also witnessed the creation of the rodeo, a "celebration of the unique and daring sports indulged in and enjoyed by all the virile characters of the western frontier," as a promotional handbill for Cheyenne's Frontier Days put it. The first rodeo was held in 1883 in Pecos, Texas; five years later, folks in Prescott, Arizona, paid admission to see cowboys strut their cowpunching stuff in contained arenas. By the 1890s, rodeos had defined formats and rules which governed the major competitions—steer wrestling, bareback riding and bronco busting. Cheyenne's Frontier Days were inaugurated in 1897 as a self-conscious "annual resurrection of the west as it was, for the edification of the west as it is." One magazine writer explained the significance of Frontier Days in 1909:

> Civilization is pushing everything before it: thriving cities and well kept farms are taking the place of the cattle upon a thousand hills. But the pioneer still

clings with a pathetic tenacity to the old customs . . . a pathetic but vigorous desire . . . to prove that strong arms and courageous hearts still existed on the range.[35]

Organizers had no doubts that it was rugged western manliness that was also being resurrected. Individual acts were extolled for their "peril to life and limb"; commentators were awed by the "sheer nerve" of the bareback rider, and one waxed poetic about broncos—"murderers that plunge with homicidal fury beneath the cinches of leather of a bucking saddle." For the participants, the rodeo gave the "feeling of being part of the frontier that still lives in the professional rodeo arena. A cowboy on a bronc symbolizes the rugged individuality of the Western man and beast." For the spectators, the rodeo was a "true taste of the wild and wooly."[36] The rodeo pen preserved the frontier as gladiatorial arena; its competitors, participants in a blood sport.

As a mythic creation, the cowboy was fierce and brave, willing to venture into unknown territory, a "negligent, irrepressible wilderness," and tame it for its less-than-masculine inhabitants. As soon as the environment is subdued, he must move on, unconstrained by the demands of civilized life, unhampered by clinging women and whining children and uncaring bosses and managers.[37] His is a freedom that cannot be "bounded by the fences of a too weak and timid conventionalism," as Harold Wright put it in his western novel, *When a Man's a Man* (1916).[38] He is a man of impeccable ethics, whose faith in natural law and natural right is eclipsed only by the astonishing fury with which he demands rigid adherence to them. He is a man of action—"grim [and] lean, . . . of few topics, and not many words concerning these." He moves in a world of men, in which daring, bravery, and skill are his constant companions. He lives by physical strength and rational calculation; his compassion is social and generalized, but he forms no lasting emotional bonds with any single person. He lives alone, a "hermited horseman" out on the range, settling the west.[39]

And, of course, he doesn't really exist, except in the pages of the western, the literary genre heralded by the publication of Owen Wister's novel *The Virginian* in 1902.[40] Wister is not only the creator of the genre, but one of its biggest boosters and celebrators. Born into an aristocratic Philadelphia family, Wister's first love was music, and he went to Harvard to study composition. When it became clear that he would never become a truly great composer, his father insisted that he return home to a position at Boston's largest brokerage house. Within a few months, Wister had a nervous breakdown and developed Bells palsy (a paralysis of the face). He consulted S. Weir Mitchell, who diagnosed Wister's problem as neurasthenia and prescribed a trip to a Wyoming dude ranch for a cure. At the ranch, Wister slept outdoors in a tent, bathed in an icy creek each morning, spent hours in the saddle, hunted, fished, and worked in the roundup, and helped brand calves, castrate bulls, and deliver foals. "I am beginning to be able to feel I'm something of an animal and not a stinking brain alone" he wrote from the ranch in 1885. In three weeks, Wister believed himself to be completely cured.[41]

And he was completely converted to western life, which he was now devoted to celebrating. The western was his creation, a vehicle for "an upper class composer-short-story-writer with doubts about his independence to claim a robust masculinity," according to literary critic Jane Tompkins.[42] As a genre, the western represented the apotheosis of masculinist fantasy, a revolt not against women but against feminization. The vast prairie is the domain of male liberation from workplace humiliation, cultural feminization, and domestic emasculation. The western provides men with alternative institutions and experiences—the saloon replaces the church, the men sitting around the campfire is the equivalent of the Victorian parlor, the range replaces the factory floor. The western is a purified, pristine male domain, the world that contemporary middle class men believed was once populated by free, independent artisans of the west.[43]

What are the traits of such a mythic figure? Of course, he is manly.[44] He was a natural aristocrat—a "natural nobleman, formed not by civilization and its institutions but the spontaneous influence of the land working on an innate goodness." Like Natty Bumppo or Davy Crockett before him, the Virginian, as the narrator first meets him, finds a "handsome, ungrammatical son of the soil"; "here in flesh and blood was a truth which I had long believed in words, but never met before. The creature we call a *gentleman* lies deep in the hearts of thousands that are born without a chance to master the outward graces of the type."[45] Having served his apprenticeship he is now a master of his craft of riding, roping, and killing. His virtues are artisanal virtues: "self-discipline, unswerving purpose; the exercise of knowledge, skill, ingenuity, and excellent judgement; and a capacity to continue in the face of total exhaustion and overwhelming odds." He is free, in a free country, embodying republican virtue and autonomy.[46]

And he is white. To Wister, the west was "manly, egalitarian, self-reliant, and Aryan"; it was the "true" America, far from the feminizing, immigrant-infested cities, where voracious blacks and masculine women devoured white men's chances to demonstrate manhood. A 1902 review of *The Virginian* in

The World's Work saw this deeper theme in the western at the moment of its origins:

> To catch the deeper meaning of our life, one's path must be toward that West-
> ern verge of the continent where all white men are American born, because
> there only are the culture and conservatism of the East, the chivalrism and the
> fire-eating spirit of the South, and the broad, unhampered gambler's view of
> life native to raw Western soil, all transmuted into a democracy of no distinc-
> tions.[47]

Perhaps most important, the cowboy hero of the western was an anachro-
nism, obsolete at the moment of his creation, a conscious effort to recreate
in fantasy what America had lost in reality. As Wister wrote in an editorial
preface to the book:

> What has become of the horseman, the cow-puncher, the last romantic figure
> upon our soil? For he was romantic. Whatever he did, he did with his might.
> The bread that he earned was earned hard, the wages that he squandered were
> squandered hard . . . Well, he will be among us always, invisible, waiting his
> chance to live and play as he would like. His wild kind has been among us
> always, since the beginning, a young man with his temptations, a hero without
> wings.

No western writer of the era managed to cover all these themes as powerfully as Wister, but several writers plied a similar trade. Like Wister, Zane
Grey came from a wealthy Philadelphia family, but abandoned his career as
a dentist to write westerns. In his first, and most famous, work, *Riders of the
Purple Sage* (1912), the hero, Bern Venters, represents the nineteenth-century men who "have been enfeebled by the doctrines of a feminized Christianity," embodied by Jane Witherspoon, who has symbolically emasculated
him in the opening pages by taking his guns away from him. Through his
transformation, "American men are taking their manhood back from the
Christian women who have been holding it in thrall." "Harness the cave
man—yes!" wrote Grey in 1924, "but do not kill him. Something of the wild
and primitive should remain instinctive in the human race."[48]

Some real men were turned into western heroes, whose skill, bravery, or
cunning allowed them to live outside the law or defeat the engines of the
bureaucratic machine. Jesse James, for example, developed armed robbery
into an artisanal skill. "Highway robbery as a fine art has been cultivated
only in a way that has tended to bring it into disrespect," observed a writer
in *The Republic* in 1874, until the James gang "burst upon us, and revealed a
new field of worthy labor." The mythical James and the real James were

difficult to distinguish, in part because he fueled the myth himself. James embodied the republican virtue of the Heroic Artisan, promoting "the traditional world in which loyalty to family and friends took precedence over the greed and secularism the railroads had unleashed." Like Dick Turpin or Robin Hood (whose names he used when he signed letters, as if to claim a legacy with them), he "sought to reunite the community and reassert tradition by making the reluctant rich and powerful support the weak and defenseless."[49] The mythic figure of George Armstrong Custer was also seen as "the incarnation of the heroic, virile, self-restrained and tough minded American." Dashing, debonair and dutiful, Custer was also ruthless and monomaniacal in his pursuit of his manhood through the conquest of Indians. His carefully constructed persona was part flamboyant aristocrat, part cold sober professional, and part wild savage hunter.[50]

While Custer and James were real men who participated willingly in the cultivation of their mythic sides, Casey Jones (1900), John Henry (ca. 1873), and Paul Bunyan (collected 1912–1914) were mythic representations of the Heroic Artisanal triumphs in the very arenas and against the same forces that had defeated him in reality. Jones's track skills are necessary to keep the Illinois Central trains running; John Henry outperforms a steam drill in a masterpiece of suicidal craftsmanship, dying "with the hammer in his hand," and the giant logger, Paul Bunyan, out cuts the most technically developed chainsaws with his mighty ax. They were "heroes of an industrial world" projected back to the moment of the artisan's demise.[51]

Just as some masculinists called for war for regenerative manhood, so too did novelists celebrate the battlefield as masculine testing ground. Stephen Crane's *The Red Badge of Courage* (1896) is perhaps the most famous such novel.[52] When Henry Fleming first sees the enemy, he is "not a man, but a member" of the army, because he "felt the subtle battle-brotherhood more potent even than the cause for which they were fighting." His experience is less about virtue than about the fear of shame, humiliation, and disgrace. His trial, his initiation, is really the substitution of one form of fear—the fear of social humiliation in front of other men—for an earlier, childlike fear, the fear of death. Crane's novel has a similar trajectory to the "Iron John" myth. Fleming tries to "measure himself by his comrades," and falls short. Following his shameful inability to prove his manhood in battle, he was "amid wounds," feeling that his shame "could be viewed." He "wished that he, too, had a wound." But eventually he rediscovers his inner warrior, and his shame and humiliation lead him to fight like a "barbarian, a beast," a "pagan who defends his religion," so that, ultimately, he was a "hero," like other "proved men." As we leave Henry Fleming we see him now in the possession of

> a quiet manhood, nonassertive, but a sturdy and strong blood. He knew that he
> would no more quail before his guides wherever they should point. He had
> been to touch the great death, and found that, after all, it was but the great
> death. He was a man.[53]

Finally, one could go back—way back—to our earliest natures, to reunite with our Darwinian ancestors, and retrieve our pure masculinity by shedding all the trappings of modernity. Wrenched from effete, civilized life, or born into the life of the primitive, Buck and Tarzan hear the call of their primitive instincts and return to become wolves and apes. When we first meet Buck, in Jack London's *Call of the Wild* (1903), he is a relatively tame house pet in California, dognapped by an impoverished gardener and sold to a Klondike expedition. There, in the wild, he learns quickly the "law of club and fang" and becomes the strongest and most successful and ferocious sled dog. He has a multitude of adventures, including a deep love for the man who saves him from a savage beating and then treats him kindly—a deep, manly love, not the love of a tame animal. But even that love could not "civilize" the "strain of the primitive":

> Deep in the forest a call was sounding, and as often as he heard this call,
> mysteriously thrilling and luring, he felt compelled to turn his back upon the
> fire and the beaten earth around it, and to plunge into the forest.[54]

To which he eventually succumbs, in a masterful regression that is at once revolutionary and developmental.[55] London revels in Buck's muscular power and brute ferocity and provides a potent antidote to overcivilization. Here's London at his most eloquent:

> There is an ecstacy that marks the summit of life, and beyond which life cannot
> rise. And such is the paradox of living, this ecstacy comes when one is most
> alive, and it comes as a complete forgetfulness of living, comes to the artist,
> caught up and out of himself in a sheet of flame; it comes to the soldier, war-
> mad on a stricken field and refusing quarter; and it came to Buck, leading the
> pack, sounding the old wolf-cry, straining after the food that was alive and that
> fled swiftly before him through the moonlight. He was sounding the deeps of
> his nature, and of the parts of his nature that were deeper than he, going back
> into the womb of Time. He was mastered by the sheer surging of life, the tidal
> wave of being, the perfect joy of each separate muscle, joint, and sinew and that
> it was everything that was not death, that it was aglow and rampant, expressing

itself in movement, flying exultantly under the stars and over the face of dead matter that did not move.[56]

This contrast of civilization and animality is the bedrock of Edgar Rice Burroughs's *Tarzan of the Apes* (1912) and the subsequent series of Tarzan books that saw him have every manly adventure known to Burroughs, including returning to the old west, and rocketing off to outer space! Tarzan is the personification, Burroughs writes, "of the primitive man, the hunter, the warrior," the Rousseauian innocent, the "naked savage" who is also, it turns out, a blue-blooded English nobleman. In his dramatic and steamy encounters with Jane, we fully understand the power of the primitive.[57] Tarzan embodies the mythic heroism of the "avenging hero, half animal and half human, fusing beast and patrician, descend into an evil underclass to save a helpless bourgeois civilization." Thus portrayed, Tarzan reasserts white supremacy also, the dominance of nature over nurture; after all, Tarzan "has a man's figure and a man's brain, but he was an ape by training and environment." At the climax of this Darwinian nightmare, in which descending the evolutionary ladder is the only mechanism to retrieve manhood, Tarzan tells Jane that he has "come across the ages out of the dim and distant past from the lair of the primeval man to claim you—for your sake I have become a civilized man—for your sake I have crossed oceans and continents—for your sake I will be whatever you will me to be." Tarzan's triumph is that he will be civilized by a woman.[58]

From Tarzan's aristocratic birth to the natural aristocracy of the cowboy avenger and the primitive nobility of the reborn animal in Buck, the myth expressed a paradox of a middle class that is collectively empowered, but in which individual men feel personally powerless and unmanly, in the workplace and at home.

TR, THE STRENUOUS LIFE AND BULLY MANHOOD

The fin-de-siècle masculinist mission to thwart feminization and revirilize American men reached its symbolic apotheosis in the emergence of Theodore Roosevelt as masculine archetype. TR symbolized turn-of-the-century masculinism, embodying the triumph over effeminacy and the enthusiastic promotion of the strenuous life. Roosevelt "epitomized manly zest for the new imperial nation in part because of his jaunty energy, but also because his image brought together both aspects of the new myth: the top rung of the ladder of social aspiration and the gladiatorial animal arena sensed at the bottom." Perhaps no American has ever so perfectly embodied the contradictions of masculinism. TR was America's self-proclaimed and self-constructed "real man."[59]

Roosevelt's self-creation begins, as they all seem to, with triumph over the body. He was, he recalled in his autobiography, "a sickly and delicate boy, suffered much from asthma, and frequently had to be taken away on trips to find a place where I could breathe." (On one of those trips, to Europe, he was seasick most of the time and rarely came on deck.) Here was a "shy and timid boy, frail in body . . . thin, pale, asthmatic, outwardly the typical 'city feller,'" as the *Boy's Life of Theodore Roosevelt* put it. "Teedie," his family affectionately called him, was a childhood wimp; his father constantly exhorted him to "make your body."[60]

Making his body was also a strategy to make his political image. Entering politics in the early 1880s, TR was called "Young Squirt" and "Jane Dandy" by the local press, and the *New York Star* threw in a little gay-baiting calling him "our own Oscar Wilde." Roosevelt needed "to attain a state of manliness, and attempt to exorcise through exercise his effeminizing sickness, and at the same time . . . attempt to masculinize and thereby strengthen his political position."[61] And where would a wimpy upperclass sissy go to make his body and thereby remake his political image? Go west young man!

Roosevelt arrived in the Dakota territory in April 1885, determined to try his hand at ranching in the rapidly disappearing old west. Like Owen Wister, Frederic Remington, and other eastern boys, Roosevelt had journeyed west to stake a claim on his manhood. On his arrival, a reporter from the Pittsburgh *Dispatch* observed "a pale, slim young man with a thin piping voice and a general look of dyspepsia about him . . . boyish looking . . . with a slight lisp, short red moustache and eye glasses"—in short, the "typical New York dude." A local railroad man recalled "a slim, anemic-looking young fellow dressed in the exaggerated style which newcomers on the frontier affected, and which was considered indisputable evidence of the rank tenderfoot." Locals found him initially a laughingstock, calling him "Roosenfelder" and "Four Eyes" and "the Eastern punkin-lily." When he first mounted his horse, he tapped it and said meekly, "Hasten forward quickly there," which made local cowboys double over with laughter, and the phrase soon became part of Badlands lore.[62]

But TR persevered, and eventually triumphed over his effete dude-ism, becoming the embodiment of "strength, self-reliance, determination"—the three terms that defined his vision of manhood. He became a booster of the western cure, claiming that he owed "more than I could ever express to the west" because the frontier brings out manly virtues—mutuality, honor, self-respect—not the "emasculated milk-and-water moralities" of the eastern elite.[63] And what became his personal credo for his self-making became the basis for a moral and political philosophy.

Using himself as the example, Roosevelt expressed fears that "overcivilization was sapping the strength of the civilized few, who therefore needed remedial training in barbarism, violence, and appropriation."[64] In two speeches, "The Strenuous Life" (1899) and "The Pioneer Spirit and American Problems" (1900), Roosevelt railed against "the cloistered life which saps the hardy virtues," the "flabbiness" and "slothful ease" and trumpeted the call for the "strenuous life." Roosevelt used his fears of feminization—of men with "small feet and receding chins"—as the springboard to promote a full-scale imperialist adventurism:

> We cannot avoid the responsibilities that confront us in Hawaii, Cuba, Puerto Rico, and the Philippines. All we can decide is whether we shall meet them in a way that will redound to the national credit, or whether we shall make of our dealings with these new problems a dark and shameful page in our history. . . . The timid man, the lazy man, the man who distrusts his country, the overcivilized man, who has lost the great fighting masterful virtues, the ignorant man, and the man of dull mind, whose soul is incapable of feeling the mighty lift that thrills 'stern men with empires in their brains'—all these, of course, shrink from seeing the nation undertake its new duties; shrink from seeing us build a navy and an army adequate to our needs; shrink from seeing us do our share of the world's work, by bringing order out of chaos in the great, fair, tropic islands from which the valor of our soldiers and sailors has driven the Spanish flag. . . .
>
> I preach to you, then, my countrymen, that our country calls not for the life of ease, but for the life of strenuous endeavor. The twentieth century looms before us big with the fate of many nations. If we stand idly by, if we seek merely swollen, slothful ease and ignoble peace, if we shrink from the hard contests where men must win at hazard of their lives and at the risk of all they hold dear, then the bolder and stronger peoples will pass us by, and will win for themselves the domination of the world.[65]

With that speech, Roosevelt catapulted to the head of a long list of American presidents, from Andrew Jackson to George Bush, who sought to prove their manhood through imperial aggression against smaller and weaker countries or cultures. From the Seminoles to the Philippines, from Panama (twice) to Grenada, the best strategy to promote war is to question the President's manhood.[66]

Theodore Roosevelt massaged this epidemic fear of the overcivilized effeminacy of the American upper class into his crowning moment of symbolic manhood, the Rough Riders. The Rough Riders consisted of twelve troops, all but one of which came from the western territories. But this last, K troop, came from "New York and the Eastern states," and was widely believed to be a collection of "swells," who had left their upper-class men's clubs, dress suit in their hands, to follow Roosevelt up San Juan Hill and into the national mythology. The Rough Riders were the symbolic meeting place of the eastern establishment and western manhood—as soldiers. Some may have worn "the broad brim hat and had the bronze cheek of the plains" while others "bore the unmistakable stamp of the student and club man," one reporter wrote, but all "mingled with easy good fellowship." The Denver *Post* reported (21 May 1898) in verse the western men's perspective:

We was somewhat disappointed, I'll acknowledge, fur to see
Such a husky lot o' fellers as the dandies proved to be,
An' the free an' easy manner in their bearin' that they had
Sort o' started the impression that they mightn't be so bad.
There was absence of eye-glasses, an' of center parted hair,
An' in social conversation they was expert on the swear,
An' the way they hit the grub pile sort o' led us to reflect
That our previous impressions mightn't prove so damn correct.

To which the Chicago *Tribune* (12 July 1898) responded two months later with the easterners' perspective:

They scoffed when we lined up with Teddy,
    They said we were dudes and all that;
They imagined that "Cholly" and "Fweddie"
    Would faint at the drop of a hat.
But let them look there in the ditches,
    Blood-stained by the swells in the van,
And know that a chap may have riches,
    And still be a man![67]

TR used the presidency as a "bully pulpit" to promote the strenuous life for individuals and as a grounding for the American Empire. Politically, he opposed policies he chastised as "half-and-half, boneless," and railed against opponents he called spineless sissies. He promoted work as heroic, moralizing and masculinizing, and saw big capital and finance as emasculating effeminacy, chastising the "moneyed and semi-cultivated classes" for "producing a flabby, timid type of character which eats away at the great

fighting qualities of our race." He prescribed sports to develop a hardy masculinity—but only "the true sports for a manly race," like running, rowing,
playing football and baseball, boxing and wrestling, shooting, riding and
mountain climbing." No president before or since has been a bigger pro-
moter of exercise and sporting life—and no number of photos of George
Bush sailing or fishing, or of Dan Quayle golfing, could make the point as
emphatically as one photograph of TR in full hunting gear. Sport was the
vehicle for the self-made and self-constructed manhood of the new century.
In a 1900 essay, "The American Boy," TR echoed the same sentiments as
Muscular Christians and body-builders:

> Forty or fifty years ago the writer on American morals was sure to deplore the
> effeminacy and luxury of young Americans who were born of rich parents. The
> boy who was well off then . . . lived too luxuriously, took to billiards as his chief
> innocent recreation, and felt shame in his inability to take part in rough pas-
> times and field sports. Nowadays, whatever other faults the son of rich parents
> may tend to develop, he is at least forced . . . to bear himself well in manly
> exercises and to develop his body—and therefore, to a certain extent, his char-
> acter—in the rough sports which call for pluck, endurance, and physical ad-
> dress.

Roosevelt celebrated the outdoors, creating five national parks, sixteen
national monuments, and fifty-one wildlife refuges in America's wilderness,
and founding the Boone and Crockett Club to promote the strenuous life
for young boys.[68] He sought personal refuge in the wilderness. As late as
1912, after the failure of the Bull Moose crusade, a 53-year-old Roosevelt
joined an expedition to probe the unknown regions of the Amazon. Encoun-
tering a river never before seen by a white man, Roosevelt was ecstatic, even
though the expedition cost the life of one of the explorers, and nearly all of
them. (The river was named Rio Roosevelt by the Brazilian government.)
Asked why he risked his life for such a venture, he replied that he "had to
go. It was my last chance to be a boy." As one of the founders of the American Museum of Natural History, Roosevelt linked Darwinian evolution, eu-
genics, and racism into a potent blend that historian of science Donna Haraway ingeniously calls "Teddy Bear Patriarchy."[69]

Roosevelt also rehearsed the stock in trade of American masculinism—
racism, anti-feminism, and nativism—as rhetorical themes and political
strategies for reconstituting American manhood and the world dominion of
the American nation. Man-making required the separation of boys and girls;
TR consistently opposed coeducation, and praised G. Stanley Hall's efforts

to stem the tide of feminization. Although he supported woman suffrage "tepidly," he was more fervent in his support of women as mothers, and furious at college-educated women who delayed childbearing or did not bear children altogether. Accusing them of race suicide, TR suggested that women who did not bear at least four children be tried as traitors to America, much the same way as soldiers who refused to fight. A woman who "shirks her duty as wife and mother is . . . heartily to be condemned," he commented in an address to the Congress of Mothers in 1908. "We despise her as we despise and condemn the soldier who flinches in battle." Soldiers and mothers—this was the way TR saw the fulfillment of patriotic duty. If the "process of race decay continued in the United States and the British Empire, the future of the white race would rest in the hands of the German and the Slav."[70]

Thus did TR's sexism merge with his racism and nativism. He consistently sounded the alarm about the Yellow Peril, calling the Chinese "an ancient and effete civilization" and attempting to limit immigration at the same time as his overseas military adventures. In his last speech before he died, Roosevelt sounded the post–World War warning that America not slink back to its former effeminacy—in terms that resound against the contemporary debate about multiculturalism and hyphenated Americans:

There must be no sagging back in the fight for Americanism merely because the war is over. Any man who says he is an American, but something else also, isn't an American at all. We have room for but one flag, the American flag, and this excludes the red flag, which symbolizes all wars against liberty and civilization, just as much as it excludes any foreign flag of a nation to which we are hostile. We have room for but one language here, and that is the English language, for we intend to see that the crucible turns our people out as Americans, of American nationality, and not as dwellers in a polyglot boardinghouse; and we have room for but one soul loyalty, and that is loyalty to the American people.[71]

Here, then, was a real man for twentieth-century America—rebuilt, recharged, and revirilized for new opportunities in the new century. The materials for his self-construction relied on traditional themes of racial, ethnic and gender exclusion, but more on what men did outside of their work lives than what they did for a living. Though TR paid less attention to reclaiming home life, by the end of World War I, it was clear that the self-construction of American masculinity depended as much on one's consumption as on one's activity in production.

As G. Stanley Hall had identified adolescence as a fragile stage requiring special attention to a rite of passage, so too did Roosevelt offer an adolescent nation the initiation rites to a new manhood. TR was the perfect embodiment of American-as-adolescent boy-man. His definition of manhood was reactive, defensive, an effort to repudiate a sickly childhood and his over-dependence on his mother. To accomplish this, Roosevelt engaged in a frenzied effort to appear a man in every possible guise, "changing frenetically from cowboy costume to safari suit to Rough Rider garb, Roosevelt shot more animals, rode more dusty trails, and risked his neck in combat" more than any American before John Wayne.[72] TR wore every conceivable hat—warrior, statesman, pioneer, cowboy, Rough Rider, president, father, historian, hunter, husband, naturalist, diplomat, and preacher—the first "protean man" of the century, able to shift roles depending on external circumstances, a flexible, yet hardened manly presentation of self. In the coming decades this sense of manhood would be sorely tested, as the Depression and another world war threatened to emasculate men as breadwinners and frightened unfit soldiers. What Theodore Roosevelt made clear, by creating a national legend out of his own personal triumph, is that masculinity is a constant test, relentless, unprovable, and evident in every place that men go.

CONCLUSION

Fantasies of western adventure, testing and proving manhood on the battle-field, celebrating the manly in literature, even going native in a Darwinian devolution to pure animality—these were the dominant themes of masculinist literature through the nineteenth century. But escape—from wives, partners, children, work, from adult responsibilities in general—has never provided the stable grounding for gender identity its promoters have promised. From Rip Van Winkle and Natty Bumppo to Iron John and today's "weekend warriors," men have sought the homosocial solace of the wilderness, the frontier, the west. Here, they have found a temporary respite from the feminizing clutches of women and from enervating workplace lives. But the respite has only been temporary, and either must be constantly renewed in ever more bizarre ritual appropriations, or they lapse into the same politics of resentment and exclusion of anti-feminism and racism. Men will be free, D. H. Lawrence wrote, "when they are in a living homeland, not when they are escaping to some wild west."[73] We profeminist men are still waiting for the weekend warriors to come home, and to fight alongside women, alongside gay men and lesbians, alongside people of color in what will be the most challenging battle of their lives: to create a democratic manhood, a manhood based on equality, a manhood that is at home with itself inside the house as it is off in the woods.

NOTES

1. Henry James, *The Bostonians* [1885] (New York: Modern Library, 1984), 293.
2. Henry David Thoreau, *Walden* [1846] (New York: New American Library, 1960).
3. Brownson converted to Catholicism because he felt it to be more manly and patriarchal. Brownson, cited in Barbara Welter, "The Feminization of American Religion, 1800–1860" in *Clio's Consciousness Raised*, ed. Mary Hartman and Lois Banner (New York: Harper and Row, 1974), 139. See also Rotundo, "Learning About Manhood," p. 47.
4. Whitman and *Harper's Monthly*, cited in William Leach, *True Love and Perfect Union: The Feminist Reform of Sex and Society* (New York: Basic Books, 1980), 217. Oliver Wendell Holmes, "The Autocrat at the Breakfast Table" in *Atlantic Monthly*, 1 May 1858, p. 881. An 1851 issue of *Scientific American* celebrated the practicality of the American genius, as against the ornateness and luxury of European inventions. See John Kasson, *Civilizing the Machine: Technology and Republican Values in America, 1776–1900* (New York: Grossman, 1976), 151. A wave of anti-European sentiment was fueled in part by masculine panic about feminization.
5. Although I will treat only the west in any detail here, there were other forms of masculinist resistance to cultural feminization. For example, much of the early nineteenth-century commune movement, from Fourierist phalanxes to Oneida, Brook Farm, and New Harmony, were efforts to restore manly dignity to men's work, to return men to the land, from which all integrity sprang. Idealizing the rapidly disappearing Heroic Artisan and yeoman farmer, these communes were, in this sense, reactionary and conservative efforts to retrieve and restore artisanal virtue as the artisan and yeoman were themselves being proletarianized. It is interesting that many of those efforts to restore the manly dignity of the Heroic Artisan did not do so at the expense of women, since many communal leaders actually supported women's equality. Masculinism could be a flight from a feminized *culture*, and still promote women's equality. See Kimmel and Mosmiller, eds., *Against the Tide* (documents by John Humphrey Noyes, Robert Dale Owen). See also Moses Harmon, Ezra Heywood, and other "sex radicals" in the latter half of the century.
6. Turner, *The Frontier in American History*, p. 92. See also Meyer, *The Jacksonian Persuasion*, p. 139. In 1836, a Massachusetts House Committee saw the choice before young artisans and farmers as "the alternative of becoming essentially a manufactur-

ing people, or of bidding adieu to their native hills . . . and following the rising glories of the west." Cited in Schlesinger, *The Age of Jackson*, p. 148.

7. Leverenz, "The Last Real Man in America," p. 763; Flint, cited in Adams, *The Great Adventure*, p. 25; Timothy Dwight, *Travels in New England and New York*, 4 volumes (New Haven, 1821), vol. 2, p. 441; Crevecoeur, cited in Roderick Nash, *Wilderness and the American Mind* (New Haven: Yale University Press, 1967), 30.

8. Webber wrote that "[t]he primitive virtues of a heroic manhood are all sufficient, and they care nothing for reverences, forms, duties, etc., as civilization has them, but respect each other's rights and recognize the awful presence of a benignant God in the still grandeur of mountain, forest, valley, plain, and river, through, among, and over which they pass." Such men, Webber wrote, "do not look back to society except with disgust." Charles Webber, *Old Hicks, The Guide; or Adventures in the Comanche Country in Search of a Gold Mine*, 2 volumes (New York, 1855), vol. 1, p. 311.

9. Richard Stott, "The Geography of Gender in Nineteenth Century America: Youth, Masculinity, and the California Gold Rush," paper presented at the 1991 Annual Meeting of the Organization of American Historians, esp. p. 6; Rev. John Todd, 1871, pp. 44–45; C. W. Haskins, *The Argonauts of California* (New York: 1890), 73. Elisabeth Margo, *Taming the Forty-Niner* (New York, 1855), 8.

10. Stott, "The Geography of Gender," pp. 6, 8, 11.

11. Henry David Thoreau, *Walden*, pp. 10, 216, 66. Businessmen "come tamely home at night only from the next field or street, where their household echoes haunt, and their life pines because it breathes its own breath over again," he wrote, while workers "are so occupied with the factitious care and superfluously coarse labors of life that its finer fruits cannot be plucked by them." As a result, "[t]he laboring man has not the leisure for a true integrity day by day; he cannot afford to sustain the manliest relations to men; his labor would be depreciated in the market. He has no time to be anything but a machine" (pp. 142, 9).

12. Thoreau, *Walden*, pp. 142, 211.

13. That today, thousands of men troop off to the woods to follow men's movement leader Robert Bly in a similarly stylized initiation process, is, of course, part of the story I am telling. No wonder Bly calls Thoreau one of his heroes. In a recent poem, Bly praises Thoreau for living so "extravagantly alone . . . keeping company with his handsome language." Robert Bly, "The Insatiable Soul," poetry reading at Scottish Rite Temple, San Francisco, 30 January 1993.

14. See Henry Nash Smith, 1950; Turner, *The Frontier in American History;* John Mack Faragher, *Daniel Boone: The Life and Legend of an American Pioneer* (New York: Henry Holt, 1992), esp. pp. 6, 29, 66, 327–28. Recall, also, the words of Stephen Vincent Binet's poem:

When Daniel Boone goes by at night,
The phantom deer arise
And all lost, wild America
Is burning in their eyes

(Benet, *Selected Works,* volume I, p. 402.) In that phantom retreat, was also rebellion; Boone sought to escape the fate of most men who become, as his biographer Gilbert Imlay put it, "mere machines of the state." All three men were, as Yale President Theodore Dwight wrote, "impatient of the restraints of law, religion, and morality;" the pioneer despises the "dull uniformity and monotony" of civilized life when "compared in his mind with the stirring scenes of wild western adventure" wrote David Coyner, in his fictionalized 1847 biography of Carson, *The Lost Trappers,* cited in Turner, *The Frontier in American History,* p. 251. All were fiercely anti-intellectual; Boone, for example, "rather eschewed books, parchment deeds, and clerky contrivances as forms of evil," as his biographer Timothy Flint put it; cited in Dubbert, *A Man's Place,* p. 35. And all were virtuous, embodying the hardiness and simplicity that characterized the Heroic Artisan, "drawing from association with uncultivated nature, not the rudeness and sensualism of the savage, but genuine simplicity and truthfulness of disposition, and generosity, bravery, single heartedness, to a degree rarely found in society" as one popular biographer portrayed Kit Carson in the *Rough and Ready Annual* of 1847; cited in Slotkin, *The Fatal Environment,* p. 204.

15. Slotkin, *The Fatal Environment,* p. 374.

16. Michael A. Lofaro, "Riprorious Shemales: Legendary Women in the Tall Tale World of the Davy Crockett Almanacs" in *Davy Crockett at Two Hundred,* ed. Michael Lofaro and Joe Cummings (Knoxville: University of Tennessee Press, 1989), 26.

17. Leslie Fiedler, *Love and Death in the American Novel* (New York: Stein and Day, 1966) and David Leverenz, *Manhood in the American Renaissance* (Ithaca: Cornell University Press, 1989). Though both authors also discuss Herman Melville, I find neither as convincing as Michael Rogin's *Subversive Genealogy* (New York: Knopf, 1983).

18. Fiedler, *Love and Death,* p. 181.

19. Washington Irving, "Rip Van Winkle" (1820), in *Collected Stories of Washington Irving* (New York: Signet, 1963), 43–57. Ever since Rip, writes Leslie Fiedler, "the typical male protagonist of our fiction has been a man on the run, harried into the forest or out to sea, down the river or into combat—anywhere to avoid 'civilization' which is to say, the confrontation of a man and woman which leads to the fall to sex, marriage and responsibility." Fiedler, *Love and Death,* p. 26.

20. See Fiedler, *Love and Death,* pp. 214, 211, et passim.

21. Recent versions of this cross-race male bonding require the absence of any hint of sexual contact between the two men, and so one of them—usually the white man—is transformed into an overtly sexualized—and heterosexual—character. Thus do the movies like *Last of the Mohicans, Lethal Weapon,* and *Dances with Wolves* stress Natty's, Riggs's, and Lt. Dunbar's love interests. The man of color as spirit guide remains relatively desexualized.

22. "The existence of overt homosexuality threatens to compromise an essential aspect of American sentimental life: the camaraderies of the locker room and ball

park, the good fellowship of the poker game and fishing trip, a kind of passionless passion, at once gross and delicate, homoerotic in the boy's sense, possessing an innocence above suspicion." Fiedler, *Love and Death*, p. 143.

23. Christopher Lasch, *The True and Only Heaven*, p. 94. D. H. Lawrence, *Studies in Classic American Literature* (New York: Grove Press, 1967), 59. David Leverenz, "The Last Real Man in America," p. 754, et passim. See also Henry Nash Smith, *Wilderness*, p. 256; Cawelti, *Apostles of the Self Made Man*, p. 78.

24. Cooper, *Last of the Mohicans*, p. 26. Bumppo returns to this theme of anti-intellectualism, and the feminizing qualities of women throughout the novel:

"Book!" repeated Hawkeye, with singular and ill-concealed disdain. "Do you take me for a whimpering boy at the apron string of one of your old gals; and this good rifle on my knee for the feather of a goose's wing, my ox's horn for a bottle of ink, and my leathern pouch for a cross-barred handkercher to carry my dinner? Book! What have such as I, who am a warrior of the wilderness, though a man without a cross, to do with books? I never read but in one, and the words that are written there are too simple and too plain to need much schooling; though I may boast that of forty long and hard-working years. (P. 132)

25. Cooper, *Last of the Mohicans*, p. 318. But Hawkeye's escape requires that he exchange clothes with David, the bespectacled bookworm and with the golden song. "Are you much given to cowardice?" Hawkeye asks him. "My pursuits are peaceful, and my temper, I humbly trust, is greatly given to mercy and love," David responds, "a little nettled," Cooper tells us, "at so direct an attack on his manhood," p. 323.

26. Cooper, *Last of the Mohicans*, p. 356.

27. Cited in Burns, 1876, p. 89.

28. Leverenz, *Manhood and the American Renaissance*, pp. 279, 281. This is the same unconscious obsession, Leverenz argues, that fueled Melville's rage at the capitalist Leviathan that had consumed his own father, driven by marketplace failures to bankruptcy, insanity, and eventually suicide.

29. Like its female counterpart, this insanity is based not on gender nonconformity, but an *over*conformity to crazed behavioral norms.

30. "The monsters of antebellum politics, like Jackson's Bank and Ahab's whale, were centers of hidden power, which explained the bourgeois's failure to master the world," writes Michael Rogin. "They have the power he wants, and the sensual materiality he experiences as resisting his will, and so he makes war against them." Rogin, *Subversive Genealogy*, p. 126.

31. Leverenz, *Manhood and the American Renaissance*, pp. 290, 294.

32. These fin-de-siècle institutional mechanisms to retrieve manhood are discussed at greater length in Chapter 6 of *Manhood in America: A Cultural History* (New York: The Free Press, 1995).

33. Johnson is cited in Henry Nash Smith, *The Virgin Land*, p. 122.

34. Wallace Stegner, cited in Ben Merchant Vorpahl, *My Dear Wister: The Frederic*

Remington-Owen Wister Letters (Palo Alto: American West Publishing Co., 1972), ix. James Robertson, "Horatio Alger, Andrew Carnegie, Abraham Lincoln and the Cowboy" in *Midwest Quarterly*, 20 (1979): 253.

35. Frontier Days handbill and program, American Heritage Center, University of Wyoming Library, Laramie, W994-t-ch-fd, 1925. E. M. Bond, "The Cowmen's Carnival," in *Sunset*, 23, no. 2 (August 1909): 173. The Union Pacific Railroad was equally boosterish, and with good reason—the railroad was an early sponsor of the rodeos, and offered special package tours for Easterners to Frontier Days:

> Here one may still see the real West of more than a quarter of a century ago— not a weak imitation after the manner of the tented Wild West Show known to the Easterner, but a realistic reproduction in which the actors play but once a year, and that for blood and the glory of a world's championship. It is no tamed Wild West Show under canvas, repeated day by day by tired performers. It is the "real thing," as the Cheyennes boastfully term it—and the increasing crowds from the East each year attest to its realism. It is the biggest show of its kind in all the world, and the only one in which the visitor may comfortably view the spectacular reproduction of the West as it was.

Such authenticity included tableaux of Sioux warriors in full regalia during the inter-missions between the events of the rodeo competition. Union Pacific Program to 14th Annual Cheyenne Frontier Days, 1910, in American Heritage Center, University of Wyoming, Laramie, W994-t-ch-d.

36. Bond, "The Cowmen's Carnival," p. 176; Jimmy Walker, "Rodeo Killers" in *True West*, 1958; article in scrapbook at American Heritage Center, University of Wyoming, Laramie, Ro 614. See also *The Saturday Evening Post*, 29 November 1919.

37. The cowboy is a man "in flight from his ancestors, from his immediate family, and from everything that tied him down and limited his freedom of movement," writes cultural critic Christopher Lasch, *The True and Only Heaven: Progress and Its Critics* (New York: Norton, 1991), 39. To the cowboy, as Wallace Stegner puts it, civilization "meant responsibility, meant law, meant fences and homesteads, and wa-ter rights and fee simple land ownership, meant women" (Stegner cited in Ben Merchant Vorpahl, *My Dear Wister*, p. ix).

38. Wright is cited in Mark Gerzon, *A Choice of Heroes* (Boston: Houghton Mifflin, 1983), 77.

39. The unattributed quotations above are all from Owen Wister's letters to his friend Frederic Remington, and an essay "The Evolution of the Cow Puncher" (1893) all in Ben Merchant Vorpahl, *My Dear Wister*, pp. xi, 81, 93, 94, et passim.

40. Owen Wister, *The Virginian* [1902] (New York: New American Library, 1979).

41. Cited in G. Edward White, *The Eastern Establishment and the Western Experience* (New Haven: Yale University Press, 1968), 124.

42. Jane Tompkins, *West of Everything: The Inner Life of Westerns* (New York: Oxford University Press, 1992), 136.

43. It was also an eroticized world, which has not escaped the notice of contemporary cultural critics. Robert K. Martin, for example, calls the western a "homoerotic cowboy romance" in which cowboys "gallop 'side by side' in furious flight from an increasingly feminine world in which they fear they will have no place; their search is ultimately for an imagined past before the civilizing entry of women." Robert K. Martin, "Knight Errant and Gothic Seducers: Representations of Male Friendship in Nineteenth century America" in *Hidden From History: Reclaiming the Gay and Lesbian Past*, ed. M. B. Duberman, M. Vicinus, and G. Chauncey (New York: New American Library, 1989), 174. Of course, it was not only male camaraderie that was eroticized on the range; in the absence of women, several other props—like guns and horses—also carried that erotic charge.

44. "It is this note of manliness which is dominant through the writings of Mr. Wister," wrote Theodore Roosevelt in 1895:

> Beauty, refinement, grace, are excellent qualities in a man, as in a nation, but they come second . . . to the great virile virtues—the virtues of courage, energy, and daring: the virtues which beseem a masterful race—a race fit to fell the forests, to build roads, to found commonwealths, to conquer continents, to overthrow armed enemies. (Roosevelt, cited in G. Edward White, *The Eastern Establishment and the Western Experience*, p. 197)

On this point, all reviewers agreed. William Dean Howells called it "a man's book throughout," and Morton Payne hailed it as "a man's book with not one touch of sickly sentiment." Frederic Taber Cooper notes it as a "thoroughly virile book." Morton Payne, review of *The Virginian* in *The Dial*, 33, 1902, p. 242; Theodore Roosevelt, "A Teller of Tales of Strong Men" (a review of *Red Men and White* by Owen Wister) in *Harper's Weekly*, 39, 1895, p. 1216; William Dean Howells, review of *Red Men and White* in *Harper's Weekly*, 39, 1895, p. 2032; Frederic Taber Cooper, *Some American Story Tellers* [1911] (New York: Avon, 1968), 379. See also Sanford E. Marovitz, "Testament of a Patriot: *The Virginian*, the Tenderfoot, and Owen Wister" in *Texas Studies in Literature and Language*, 15, 1973, pp. 551–75. To contemporary feminist literary critic Madonne Miner, *The Virginian* is a "panegyric to American manhood" that ultimately fails—"a terrified, and decidedly unsuccessful, response to processes undermining traditional modes of manhood." Miner, "Manhood on the Make: Owen Wister's *Virginian*" in *Men's Studies Review*, 8(4), 1991, p. 15. See also her "Documenting the Demise of Manly Love: Owen Wister's *Virginian*," in *Journal of Men's Studies*, 1(1), 1992. I am grateful to Madonne Miner for her help in thinking through this section.

45. Donald Worster, *Under Western Skies: Nature and History in the American West* (New York: Oxford University Press, 1992), 80; Will J. Wright, *Six Gun Society* (Berkeley: University of California Press, 1975), 152; Robert Murray Davis, *Playing Cowboys: Low Culture and High Art in the Western* (Norman: University of Oklahoma Press, 1992), 13. In Wister's fiction, as in many westerns, a tenderfoot narrator serves to bring the eastern reader into the western setting, and we see the west through his admiring and less-manly eyes.

46. The western hero is the living repudiation of Marketplace Masculinity. Wister writes that the cowboy scorned the traveling salesman's "being too soon with everybody, the celluloid good fellowship that passes for ivory with nine in ten of the city crowd. But not so with the sons of the sage brush. They live nearer nature, and they know better." Wister, *The Virginian*, p. 16. Wister rededicated the novel in 1911 to Theodore Roosevelt.

Of course, the cowboy rides a horse, just as modern men's lives were increasingly dominated by steam and gasoline powered modes of transportation. The horse, literary critic Jane Tompkins aptly notes, represented "everything the bureaucratic, machine-run, rule bound modern world would deprive them of—spontaneity, beauty, freedom from rules and routines, and the right to enjoy life" (Tompkins, *West of Everything*, pp. 12, 102). By contrast, the automobile suppressed manhood, demanding a sobriety and attention that precluded rambunctious animation. As Henry Adams saw it in 1906:

> The typical American man had his hand on a lever and his eye on a curve in the road; his living depended on keeping up an average speed of forty miles an hour, tending always to become sixty, eighty or a hundred, and he could not emit emotions of anxieties or subconscious distractions, more than he could admit whiskey or drugs without breaking his neck. (Adams, cited in Diane Johnson, "Something for the Boys" in *New York Review of Books*, 16 January 1992, p. 17)

47. Interestingly, Wister's western egalitarianism halted before inequality based on race, gender, or even class. There are really two classes in America, he claimed, the "quality and the equality." "It was through the Declaration of Independence that we Americans acknowledged the *eternal; inequality* of man . . . [and] gave freedom to true aristocracy, saying 'Let the best man win, whoever he is' . . . That is true democracy. And true democracy and true aristocracy are one and the same thing" (cited in Robert Murray Davis, *Playing Cowboys*, p. 14).

48. Cited in Jane Tompkins, *West of Everything*, pp. 167, 33.

49. David Thelen, *Paths of Resistance: Tradition and Dignity in Industrializing Missouri* (New York: Oxford University Press, 1986), 74, 75. When the gang robbed a train in 1874, they examined the hands of all male passengers, because they did not want to rob workingmen, but only the "plug hat gentlemen."

50. Richard Slotkin, *The Fatal Environment*, p. 363.

51. James Robertson, "Horatio Alger, Andrew Carnegie . . ." p. 251.

52. Stephen Crane, *The Red Badge of Courage* [1895] (New York: Penguin, 1983). When more than 100 historians, novelists and journalists were asked by *American Heritage* magazine to name their favorite historical novel in U.S. history, *The Red Badge of Courage* was the most often mentioned—an amazing feat for a work of fiction in which virtually no women appear, the only exception being Henry Fleming's mother, and she only in his memory. (*Gone with the Wind*, *The Scarlet Letter* and *War and Peace* were tied for second, another astonishing result, since those surveyed were specifically asked about *American* novels. *USA Today*, September 30, 1992.)

53. In his famous short story, "The Open Boat" (1896), Crane presents an allegory of baptism by fire, immersion and regeneration, only after the ordeal of survival in a lifeboat can the men who did survive "then be interpreters" of life. Overcoming the first fear, the fear of death, the fear born of woman, is the masculine project, so that action can be motivated by the second—homosocial—fear is Crane's version of the transition to adult manhood.

54. Jack London, *The Call of the Wild* [1903] (New York: Signet, 1975), 75.

55. In the last line of the book, Buck becomes both wolf and boy, so that now "he may be seen running at the head of the pack through the pale moonlight or glimmering borealis, leaping gigantic above his fellows, his great throat a-bellow, as he sings a song of the younger world, which is the song of the pack" (p. 102). I'm afraid I had precisely the opposite reaction to this book when I first read it at about age 13. I was heartbroken when Buck was dognapped, and the only conclusion that would have pleased me, since I could only imagine this happening to my own little beagle puppy, was if Buck returned to his *real* family back in the garden in California, who were probably worried sick about him. Even in rereading the book, I was dismayed that once dognapped, we never again hear anything about the bereft family Buck leaves behind.

56. No wonder critics raved. "Such a primitive story, in the atmosphere of decadence and over-civilization which enveloped the turn-of-the-century years, came to its readers as a bracing wind," writes one critic, while another assesses London's popularity as due to

> the great elan and vigor that are properly associated with this country and its people emerge from his pages. Europe drained dry of such faculties, it is understandable that London's people, their concerns and their virtues, should have a nostalgic appeal that Europeans might even read of them as more credulous generations read of such heroic figures as Roland and Hector. (Harry Sylvester in *The New York Times*, 19 August 1951)

Contemporary literary critic David Leverenz adds that "London unambivalently contrasts Buck's natural leadership with the degeneracy of [feminized] men. Nevertheless, ideal manliness thrives in Buck only because he becomes less and less human, more and more wild, while his admiring narrator—like Cooper—writes a 'wild' book about him for boy-men readers who feel trapped in the maturation and long for exotic virility" (David Leverenz, "The Last Real Man in America: From Natty Bumppo to Batman" in *American Literary History*, 3, 1991, p. 761).

57. Edgar Rice Burroughs, *Tarzan of the Apes* [1912] (New York: Signet, 1966). When Jane first sees him, she is a captive of a great ape, and Tarzan swings in on a vine to her rescue. Jane's "lithe young form flattened against the trunk of a great tree, her hands pressed against her rising and falling bosom, and her eyes wide with mingled horror, fascination, fear, and admiration—watched the primordial age battle with the primeval man for possession of a woman—for her" (pp. 155–56). When Tarzan has slain his foe, he grabs Jane's arm and she rebuffs him. "And then Tarzan

of the Apes did just what his first ancestor would have done. He took his woman in his arms and carried her into the jungle" (p. 157).

58. Burroughs, *Tarzan*, p. 243. See also David Leverenz, "The Last Real Man in America," p. 759.

59. David Leverenz, "The Last Real Man in America: From Natty Bumppo to Batman" in *American Literary History*, 3, 1991, p. 763. "Probably no finer illustration of American manhood has ever occupied the office of the presidency than Theodore Roosevelt" was how one contemporary observer put it. John Brisben Walker, "A Working Man in the Presidency" in *The Cosmopolitan*, 32, 1901, p. 25. I have also relied on several contemporary accounts of Roosevelt, including Kathleen Dalton, "Theodore Roosevelt: Morality and Manliness in the Progressive Era," unpublished manuscript, 1979 and "Why America Loved Teddy Roosevelt," in *Our Selves/Our Past: Psychological Approaches to American History*, ed. Robert J. Brugger (Baltimore: The Johns Hopkins University Press, 1981); William Davison Johnson, *TR: Champion of the Strenuous Life* (New York: Theodore Roosevelt Association, 1958).

Of course, TR himself was a frequent contributor to his own mythology. I have relied here on *Addresses and Papers of Theodore Roosevelt*, ed. W. F. Johnson (New York: The Unit Book Publishing Co., 1909); *The Works of Theodore Roosevelt*, 20 vols. (New York: Charles Scribner's, 1926); *Autobiography* [1913] (New York: Charles Scribner's, 1958); *The New Nationalism* (New York: The Outlook Company, 1910); *The Letters of Theodore Roosevelt*, ed. Elting Morrison (Cambridge: Harvard University Press, 1951).

60. Herman Hagedorn, *A Boy's Life of Theodore Roosevelt* (New York: Harper, 1918). One of the best selling boys' books of all time, Hagedorn made Roosevelt's journey a template for twentieth-century American men.

61. Tom Lutz, *American Nervousness, 1903*, p. 79.

62. Roosevelt, himself, thought he looked smashing in his "sombrero, silk neckerchief, fringed buckskin shirt, sealskin chaparajos or riding trousers, and alligator hide boots" and with his "pearl-hilted revolver and beautifully finished Winchester rifle," he felt "able to face anything," as he wrote to his sister, cited in Donald Day, ed, *The Hunting and Exploring Adventures of Theodore Roosevelt* (New York: Dial, 1955), 47. See also G. Edward White, *The Eastern Establishment and the Western Experience*, p. 83, and John Eliot, "TR's Wilderness Legacy" in *National Geographic*, September 1982, p. 344.

63. *Autobiography*, p. 76. The west, he wrote, "is no place for men who lack the ruder, coarser virtues and physical qualities, no matter how intellectual or how refined and delicate their sensibilities" (*Ranch Life and the Hunting Trail*, 1888, p. 56, 10).

64. Tom Lutz, *American Nervousness, 1903*, p. 28.

65. Theodore Roosevelt, *The Works of Theodore Roosevelt*, volume 13, pp. 322–23, 331.

66. Of course, this concern was particularly salient at the turn of the century; as

one California newspaper editorialized in the 1890s, "the ardor and strength of prime manhood is a much needed quality in American government, especially at this time, when all things political and all things social are in the transition stage." Cited in Bruce Curtis, "The Wimp Factor" in *American Heritage*, November 1989, p. 44. Masculinist themes resounded across the political spectrum, as the campaigns for James Garfield—"the workingman's best friend; Ignoring fop and dandy"—or that between Benjamin Harrison, "the man who captured flags in battle's blazing track," and Grover Cleveland, "the cringing craven who would give them back" would attest (*Songbooks*, pp. 139, 140). Senator Roscoe Conkling continually characterized his opponents as "the man-milliners, the dilettanti and carpet knights of politics," whose stock in trade is "rancid canting, self-righteousness," and who "forget that parties are not built up by deportment, or by ladies magazines, or by gush." See Roscoe Conkling, *The Life and Letters of Roscoe Conkling*, ed. Alfred Conkling (New York: Webster, 1889), 540, 541. Even Woodrow Wilson eventually had to assert his manhood, since his early bookishness as president of Princeton did not outfit him for the manly heroism of the Presidency of the nation. One article praised his transformation from the rarefied realm of Princeton, where he was "bulwarked by books," into a "boss wrecker of corrupt machine, and militant master of his party." See *Munsey's*, October 1911, p. 3.

67. See "Muster Out Roll," reprinted in Roosevelt, *The Rough Riders*, pp. 238–69. Santa Fe *New Mexican*, 11 May 1898. These journalistic reports are cited in G. Edward White, *The Eastern Establishment*, p. 155.

68. His boys' books, *The Wilderness Hunter* (1894), *American Big Game Hunting* (1894), and *Hunting in Many Lands* (1896), were written for the Boone and Crockett Club, and became part of boy culture in the early twentieth century.

69. William Davison Johnson, *TR: Champion of the Strenuous Life*, p. 138, 126–27; Donna Haraway, *Private Visions: Gender, Race and Nature in the World of Modern Science* (New York: Routledge, 1989), Chapter 3.

I admit to a very personal relationship to Teddy Bear Patriarchy. My great uncle, Morris Michtom, was one of those Americans who was completely mesmerized by this big-game hunting rough and rowdy image of the President. An immigrant candy store owner and part-time tailor on the Lower East Side, Morris read about TR's hunting exploits and was particularly struck by a story of how TR refrained from killing a bear because he suddenly saw her small cub. Piecing together a little model of the bear cub, he sent it to TR in the White House, where the President was so pleased with his trophy that he displayed it in a magazine photograph. Within days, Uncle Morris was deluged by Washington's political elite with requests for copies, and soon Morris had hired a collection of local neighborhood boys to manufacture these "Teddy Bears." Morris Michtom founded the Ideal Toy Corporation the next year.

I also admit to having been completely taken in by TR's image in my youth. After devouring *The Boys' Life of Theodore Roosevelt*, I vividly recall a family outing to Sagamore Hill, TR's home and retreat on Long Island. His study was the manliest room I've ever encountered: animal rugs on the floor, deep rich leather chairs and book bindings, animal heads covering the dark brown wood paneling, and, most impressive to me, a chair made entirely from elephant tusks and covered with zebra skin. For years, I kept a postcard of the room on the bulletin board at my desk and fantasized about the life that must have been lived in order to collect such trophies.

70. Roosevelt, *Addresses and Papers*, p. 433; German and Slav quote cited in Richard Hofstadter, *Social Darwinism in American Thought* (Boston: Beacon Press, 1955), 189. Roosevelt also opposed women's working, believing that it would work "change and disturbance" in American life, especially since it also produced the "decrease" in marriage and especially in the birth rate." See *Addresses and Papers*, p. 275.

71. Cited in *Boys Life of Theodore Roosevelt*, pp. 384–85.

72. See Kathleen Dalton, "Theodore Roosevelt," p. 11. Dalton argues that even as he charged up San Juan Hill, TR "could not murder his invalid self" (p. 12).

73. D. H. Lawrence, *Studies in Classic American Literature* (New York: Thomas Selzer, 1923), 9.

Deep Masculinity as Social Control: Foucault, Bly, and Masculinity

TIMOTHY BENEKE

We are often reminded of the countless procedures which Christianity once employed to make us detest the body; but let us ponder all the ruses that were employed for centuries to make us love sex, to make the knowledge of it desirable and everything said about it precious. Let us consider the strategems by which we were induced to apply all our skills to discovering its secrets, by which *we were attached to the obligation to draw out its truth* . . . we need to consider the possibility that one day, perhaps in a different economy of bodies and pleasures, people will no longer quite understand how the ruses of sexuality, and the power that sustains its organization, were able to subject us to that austere monarchy of sex, so that *we became dedicated to the endless task of forcing its secret,* exacting the truest of confessions from a shadow.

The irony of this deployment is in having us believe that our "liberation" is in the balance.
Michel Foucault, *The History of Sexuality: An Introduction*[1]

FOUCAULT

The later writings of Michel Foucault offer an unsettling perception: increasingly, it is through seeking a deep, presumptively liberating truth about ourselves—formulated and established by authority—that we are likely to cast aside our freedom. Power works less as an external force which constrains us, and more by giving us a self-interpretation which implicitly, even urgently, dictates action within the context of institutions under the guise of liberation.

I want to apply this notion to Robert Bly's *Iron John* and the contemporary mythopoetic men's movement's search for the "deep masculine." I am less concerned with the accuracy of my interpretation of what is a small part of Foucault, than with the usefulness of its appropriation.[2] Finally, I will offer some remarks about the political implications of the concept of masculinity.

FOUCAULT

Following Foucault, we can distinguish two notions of power which I will call "external power" and "power/knowledge." External power is what we traditionally understand as power; one separate external entity or force exerts power over another entity or force. This model appears to be grounded in the workings of the physical world where one object exerts physical pressure against another. Master and slave, jailer and prisoner, occupier and occupied, owner of the means of production and worker, society's dicta and repressed self, censorer and censored are thought to be in this relation of power. Power in this sense is negative: it represses, denies, prohibits and constrains.

On this model, power is resisted through the pursuit, expression and application of truth, which is believed to unmask and delegitimize power and provide strategies for its undoing. The power of tyrants will be overcome by perceiving their moral illegitimacy; Marxist truth will free workers of their chains and establish a classless society; Freudian truth will unleash repression caused by societal taboo and enable a freer negotiation with society's oppression; Jungian truth will connect the self to collective archetypes which will deepen the meaning of existence and free one from social repression. From the standpoint of those attempting to resist external power, it is necessary to subjectively cultivate a demystifying grasp of the workings of power in order to subvert its authority. The oppressed self is separate from and at odds with authority, and must understand how authority dominates it. Truth on this model is seen to be intrinsically opposed to power and to play a liberating role in relation to it: the truth will set us free.

The Foucaultean notion of power/knowledge turns external power on its head. Power/knowledge functions by the internalization and pursuit of truth—one is in fact precisely controlled by power through the pursuit of a deep truth about the self. On this model power is not something separate from truth, but operates *through* truth, specifically the truth of the social sciences and religion. Power/knowledge functions to interpret us to ourselves. In trying to know ourselves by way of theory provided by authority, we are placed invisibly under the sway of power.

Power/knowledge is "positive" and productive: it produces discourses, self and societal interpretation, liberatory projects; it constructs psychological, social, and political reality. The great Foucaultean irony is that power/knowledge, in its purest form, functions through masking itself as liberation from power, conceived as external power.

With the advent of Christianity, Foucault believes, humankind took a wrong turn, and gave *knowing* the self priority over *caring* for the self. A certain enduring structure solidified itself. An authority, the priesthood, had privileged access to truth about the self and its relation to the cosmos, and offered a practice—confession and expiation—which could interpret and redeem the self. The early Christians learned to scrutinize their consciousness for evidence that the devil was tempting them; then they would confess the results of their scrutiny, along with sins of behavior, to a priest, who, possessing privileged knowledge and theory, would offer techniques of remediation. In seeking to free oneself through knowledge of the self one was under the sway of institutional power.

This relation among authority, theory, institutions, and self understanding, constituted a misguided and dangerous conjunction: as the pursuit of knowledge of the self took hold, an endless multiplication of discourses became possible, each of which committed to exfoliating deep truths about the self. For Foucault this was dangerous because there is in truth no human nature, no deep truth about the self, no human essence. There exist selves and subjectivity constructed by the discourses of culture, that with the advent of Christianity, became subject to certain tendencies: the establishment of institutions and expertise which could construct the self and self knowledge and provide standards of normality that would become grounded in science; the obsessive examination of consciousness in the pursuit of truth.

The tendency—inherent in the pursuit of knowledge and the eventual hegemony of scientific thinking—to form comprehensive, coherent, generalizing, totalizing theories resulted in the construction of the "dubious disciplines": the so-called sciences of man which have turned out to be unstable circulators of power/knowledge, and instruments of normalization. For Foucault, in the social sciences, unlike the physical, there is no real progress, no rough accumulation of a body of truths; there is merely one story after another, each grounded in degrees of plausibility and likely to be instruments of power and normalization, and each attempting to explain away any anomalies of human nature.

The most vivid manifestation of power/knowledge is in the domain of sexuality and psychoanalysis, where sexuality has been constructed as a deep truth which must be endlessly inspected. But for Foucault it is all a ruse; there is no such thing as "sexuality": only bodies and pleasures. For Foucault, "sexuality" is something that we create, not something that possesses deep truth which we must discover through self inspection.

Psychoanalysis and the whole post-modern therapeutic culture have clearly exemplified the relation between theory, authority, institutions, the deep self, liberation, and power/knowledge. Freud's genius crystalized a preexistent tendency and opened a wider door for the persistent pursuit of deep truth about the self. Theories of the self became more elaborate, intellectually "deeper," more arcane, and held in trust by the privileged, initiated few who alone possessed the time and the ability to grasp them. The freeing of repressed feeling from the constraints of society became a fetish; everything generated by the psyche became fodder for theory; every motive suspect. A deep distrust of the self conjoined with the necessity of liberating the self to establish a therapeutic culture bent on liberation, but really under the sway of power/knowledge.

BLY

From the outset, let me be clear: I do not find *Iron John* sufficiently rigorous, scholarly, or downright serious enough to merit much attention. But as a social phenomenon which has riveted American men, and as the apparent source of new liberatory institutions, it deserves scrutiny. I am as much interested in Bly's relation to power and liberation as in the content of his ideas, which as others have shown, fail to withstand examination.[3]

Bly's basic story is that an array of forces have brought men to a state of malaise and identity crisis: the most recent wave of feminism which has softened men excessively; the loss of connection between sons and fathers brought on by the industrial revolution, which relocated places of work outside the home, and which has resulted in the loss of male wisdom, and connection to the "deep masculine," which can only be passed on from older men to youths; the deadening effects of contemporary work; the general loss of connection with myths and initiation rites. Bly's discourse takes place in the general context of the American therapeutic culture which rather vaguely sees modern life as enervating, stressful, and soul destroying.

He offers a solution in a lost deep truth about masculinity which can only be reclaimed by following some kind of initiation, perfected by pristine cultures of the past, and alive in a few such "primitive" cultures today. The particular initiation he advocates centers around the reclamation of grief over one's lack of connection with one's father, and rituals which enable men to feel their "wildness" and recover their capacity for nurturance. "Deep masculinity" is a pan-cultural, transhistorical essence, built into the male psyche and (presumably) biology, which is men's true, "deepest" identity. It seems vaguely modeled on traditional Asian mysticism, eg., the relation of identity between the atman, the deep self in the individual, and the brahman, the deep self or energy from which the manifest universe emanates in Hinduism; or the "original face" or Buddha nature, which underlies the phenomenal self in parts of Buddhism.

Bly's "deep masculine" is said to be approached in more pristine cultures through aggressive initiation where boys endure physical pain and injury in the presence of older men. This somehow connects boys to psychic pain and enables them to become men and ready to mate with women.[4] He uses a myth from Grimms' fairy tales, "Iron Hans," as a device to illumine men's psychospiritual condition.

It is striking the degree to which his descriptions of reality carry with them implicit incitements for men to change. Consider a few:[5]

> Eventually a man needs *to throw off all indoctrination* and begin to *discover for himself* what the father is and what *masculinity is*. For that task, ancient stories are a good help, because they are free of modern psychological prejudices, because they have endured the scrutiny of generations of women and men. . . . (P. 25 emphasis added)

> The ancient practice of initiation then—still very much *alive in our genetic structure*—offers a third way through, between the two "natural" roads of manic excitement and victim excitement. (P. 36, emphasis added)

> Having abandoned initiation, our society has difficulty in leading boys toward manhood . . . we have so many boys and so few men. The main reason I think is our own ignorance of initiation, and our dismissal of its value. (P. 182)

> . . . the *structure* at the *bottom* of the male psyche is still as firm as it was twenty thousand years ago. A contemporary man simply has very little help in getting down to it. (P. 230, emphasis added)

Contrary to his rhetoric, Bly's basic conception of manhood is conservative—he supports the prevailing cultural notion that masculinity is an achievement. One earns, discovers, gains deep knowledge of, one's quasimystical manhood. Bly is only a step away from the edict that manhood is something one proves through taking distress "like a man." Otherwise, one is not a "real" man. Whoever and whatever you are as a man, you are not enough, unless you have been initiated into the deep masculine. Since few have been, almost all are made to once again feel inadequate about their status as men. The uninitiated are characterized as possessing an array of negative features—too superficial, wimpish, lost, brutal, too out of touch with the "feminine," too in touch with the "feminine," too repressive of grief, too indulgent of grief. Contemporary American manhood, for Bly, is not something that you *are* "naturally" but something which, through arduous struggle, you discover at the core of your being under the guidance of older "real" men. Or, to put it differently, it's something that *is* your true natural self but which you have lost touch with and must now recover.

Arguably, Bly has taken a traditional model of American manhood, which involves proving masculinity through enduring external distress and conquering the wilds, and refocused it inward. If you can face your grief and your *internal* wildness and demons, and endure initiation, you may discover your true hidden (and virtually divine) masculine self. Bly's success can in part be attributed to the fact that his view of men is, at once, consonant with, and ennobling of, reigning conceptions of masculinity: what you have been as a man is inadequate, but who you truly are underneath is a god.[6]

Bly's persona is that of a psychic revolutionary preaching individual transformation. He positions himself against the forces of repression on behalf of deep truth. His model of power is reminiscent of the Freud of *Civilization and Its Discontents,* only following Jung, he is more sanguine about the possibility of achieving some kind of peace in the face of necessary repression. Bly sees himself as fighting external powers which in modern industrial societies keep men from their true identities. He presents himself as at odds with the forces of external power and "indoctrination."

In an important sense this is true. White, middle-aged, middle- and upper-middle-class men giving vent to their grief over their painful relationships with their fathers, and offering each other support, is surely an attempt to throw off social conditioning which denies men's ability to feel vulnerable and invigorating emotions, and support each other.[7]

But this is only a small part of the story. Bly exemplifies Foucault's structures of power/knowledge: Bly, an authority, tells men that there is a deep truth about ourselves that we are out of touch with, and that constitutes our true identity. Through age old initiatory wisdom "alive in our genetic structure" we can see our "genuine face or being" and recapture our "true radiant energy" in the "magnetic field of the deep masculine." We can thus gain knowledge of "male spirit and soul." To do this we "need to throw off all indoctrination and discover for ourselves who our father is and what masculinity is." So we have an authority with privileged access to theory, disseminating a view of the self which offers liberation through initiatory methods to be provided by the authority.

Men are asked to internalize this self-interpretation and seek liberation in terms of it and its institutions. This is where Bly becomes insidious. It is a commonplace in moral philosophy that we often simultaneously evaluate by describing and prescribe by evaluating. Bly's descriptions of reality not only evaluate and prescribe: they incite. If one really believes his account, one is inexorably tied to his institutions, and panic would be a not unreasonable emotion. It is only because men at this point in history are in such extreme confusion that they need someone to sell them identity.

It is here worth noting that *Iron John* grew out of Bly's public talks and presentations and is inseparable from the evolving institutions of the mythopoetic men's movement where men, let us not forget, pay money to search for their identities. *Iron John* came along when the politics of identity, with all their moral complexity, blossomed; when patriarchal assumptions have slowly become dismantled, and as manhood has become decentered, men have become visible to themselves as men, bringing with it enormous identity confusion, and a need to form their own enclave. Just at a historical moment when feminism seems to be attempting to engage men, Bly has come on the scene preaching the existence of a quasi-divine ontological essence which men can only recapture through going off with other men and grieving over their fathers. It is tempting to view the mythopoetic men's movement as a neurotic symptom: the forming of a grandiose self image and flight into longing for the father as a defense against the anxieties brought about by women's entry into the work force and feminism's engagement of men.[8]

Bly represents yet another twist in the search for deep knowledge of the self. Masculinity, or more broadly, gender is now the source of deepest truth; not sexuality or manifestations of the devil. Notice what Bly does not say: he does not merely say that, "Well, we men are confused and depressed these days, and almost all of us feel sad about what happened with our fathers. It might be valuable for us to get together to express our feelings and talk about it. Maybe we can beat on some drums and dance and find a way to be strong without being oppressive or brutal. This might shake some of our depression." Instead he sacralizes masculinity and calls upon the romantic authority of the past and "primitive" men to legitimize himself as a kind of priest.

But what of the specific "self" generating technologies which are used in the mythopoetic men's movement? Sociologist Michael Kimmel, describing his experience at a mythopoetic weekend retreat, makes several interesting observations. He notes that workshop leader Shepherd Bliss uses a particular locution as he guides men to retrieve a "sacred masculine space" through ritual incantation and guided fantasy:

Bliss leads the group by suggesting what some of us might *feel* like doing . . .

'Some of you might want to get on all fours and explore the ground with your hands' he mentions. All the men drop to their hands and knees to feel the earth tilled by their ancestors.

'Some of you might feel some noises coming into your throats, the noises of male animals,' he mentions. Everyone immediately starts growling, snorting. A few howls.

'Some of you might feel like moving around the room, getting in touch with other animals,' Bliss predicts. Everyone is now moving slowly around the room, growling and snorting, occasionally bumping into one another.

'Some of you might even feel yourselves recalling that most repressed sense, our sense of smell and begin sniffing.' Suddenly men are sniffing one another as they move through the room on all fours . . .[9]

Soon Bliss tells them they might find themselves feeling like "that most masculine of animals the billy-goat. Billy-goats are very rambunctious and playful and they love to butt heads." Kimmel observes that the men play "human bumper cars" for a while. Bliss appears to generate emotions by telling these men "what they might find themselves feeling like doing." Notice: it is the language of self discovery Bliss is applying. He is telling them what they might "*find* themselves feeling like doing." But it is clear they are expected to "find themselves feeling" what he suggests. And the men are eager and willing to do so. Again notice: he does not say, "Everyone start screaming like a pig," or "Everyone start sniffing each other." Instead he persuades.

A few minutes later, the lights are turned down and the men are taken through a guided fantasy in which they encounter their fathers, and say and hear things they always wanted to say and hear but never could. Suddenly the men are overflowing with grief over their lost intimacy with their fathers. Kimmel hears sobs coming from around the room. What most astonishes him is the sudden shift of emotions; no more than three minutes before, they were butting heads and growling and sniffing each other like rutting billy goats. Kimmel finds it remarkable that they are able to retrieve the appropriate emotion at will.

Their emotions are scripted and cued; they seem to be following what Arlie Hochschild calls "feeling rules." They are expected to feel spontaneously—and "authentically"—what they are encouraged to feel. Most of the men have been to these workshops before and know what is expected of them. Bliss is like a father guiding them to the right emotions. They support each other as they move quickly from exhilarating "deep masculine wildness" to "deep father grief."

Can such emotions be real? Is there such a thing as a real emotion? Emotions, as any actor knows, can be easily evoked and triggered and maintained with a little help. Bliss would doubtless insist that he is applying the technology of modern psychology to enable these men to discover the deep truth of their masculinity. But is this truth discovered or constructed? Are the emotions heartfelt or generated? Or is there any such distinction? The men who go to these retreats would most likely see themselves as overcoming the forces in their lives that keep them from feeling vital, in touch and close to other men—a fact that ought not be analyzed away or dismissed.

Is it too glib to argue that just as confession and expiation expel genuine guilt and restore psychic equilibrium, so too does organized, scripted catharsis release real pain? But how much of the grief that is contacted and released is a matter of "good boy" tears, tears shed in the spirit of approval seeking or praise from authority? How much of it is white middle- and upper-middle-class men being high achievers in a different realm? No single answer can or should be given. But the questions are worth pondering. It is one thing for men to begin to painfully acknowledge what's inadequate about their lives; quite another to absorb a whole narrowly focused political ideology which confers and romanticizes identity, and scripts emotions.

Following Foucault I would argue that, just as there is no such thing as "sexuality," but only bodies and pleasures, there is no such thing as "deep masculinity" because there is no such thing as masculinity. There are only humans with certain primary and secondary sex characteristics and cultures which, for reasons often unclear, rather invidiously generate certain modes of experience, being and behavior according to sex characteristics.

It is an open question to what degree the genetic makeup of human males and females offers a kind of "governing causality" which structurally constrains the range of possible variables of being, behavior and experience for each sex. Obviously in matters such as physical size and strength and childbearing, the constraints are bracing.

We need neither a new "masculinity" nor an old one, but none whatsoever. Otherwise we will be endlessly pursuing a mirage generated by power/knowledge. Men certainly need to change, but not under the banner of masculinity.

"MASCULINITY"

All definitions are motivated. We can define more or less descriptively, by simply showing how a concept is used: "Bly uses masculine to mean . . ."

We can define in order to prescribe how we ought to use a word and how we ought to live, often by invoking putative essences: "Real masculinity is that powerful yet gentle force at the center of the psyche." We can define ascriptively for purposes of clear communication: "I will define masculinity as . . ."

But is there a morally legitimate use for the word "masculine"? Can it do anything but oppress us? Can we safely use the word masculine "merely" to describe? Can we think of the "masculine" or "feminine" without evoking and legitimating a whole cluster of associations which reconstitute oppressive conceptions of men and women?[10] These questions demand a separate essay; here I will only make a few points.

Certain uses are destructive and ought to be eliminated. From *Iron John:*

> Our obligation . . . is to describe *masculine* in such a way that it does not exclude the masculine in women and yet hits a resonant string in the man's heart . . .
> Our obligation is to describe the *feminine* in such a way that does not exclude the feminine in men but makes a large string resonate in the woman's heart. (Pp. 235–36)

These uses invoke and tacitly legitimate male and female essences, which is precisely what oppress us. By describing essences one implicitly prescribes appropriateness; one cannot speak of the "masculine in women" or the "feminine in men" without implying that there exists a set of features which do, and therefore, *should* characteristically belong to men or women. I believe it is preferable that men and women feel free to embody a wide range of qualities which are important for humans to possess. To refer to any human quality as masculine or feminine is to perpetuate an artificial association between that quality and men and women.[11] Such an association can only be based upon the distorted notions of humanity that gender has thus far given us. Thus it perpetuates the problem.

The same point holds for the following, which identifies masculinity and femininity in terms of cosmic principles. "Fire manifests the masculine principle in the cosmos; water the feminine." Again, to speak of "masculine" and "feminine" aspects of the cosmos grandiosely legitimates the association between certain qualities and actual men and women. The gendered division of labor may well cause us to differentially distinguish certain qualities as characteristically "masculine" or "feminine" but this is something we ought to take pains to avoid.

A useful principle might be: to use "masculine" or "feminine" without either explicitly or by context denying the legitimacy of an association be-

tween "masculine and feminine" qualities and men and women is to perpetuate sexism and the oppressiveness of gender. This is because we ordinarily
tacitly assume that it is desirable for men to be "masculine" and women to
be "feminine" unless otherwise stated or implied.

But what about "simple description"? It is tempting to counter this point
by saying that we can innocently say, "Pete Rose is very masculine," and
know that we merely mean that Pete Rose has characteristics that we normally associate with men, which does not mean we *should* make this association.

But we are *never simply describing.* Linguistic context commits us to background assumptions which if not abjured, will be assumed. It is likely that in
attempting to avoid destructive assumptions in talking about men and
women, we will for a long time be mired in messy circumlocution. If I don't
distance myself from my language by putting "masculine" in quotes or saying "stereotypically masculine" I legitimate the notion that men are and
should be like Pete Rose.

It is not clear to me that there exist any desirable, "earnest" uses of
"masculine" or "feminine." Attempts to ennoble men and women often call
upon notions of "the masculine" or "the feminine," but again, these offer
prescriptive identifications on the basis of sex. To "metaphysicalize" gender
may encourage momentary identities which correct against social repression—"I am in touch with the 'deep masculine' and able to be wild"—but,
ultimately, such efforts serve only to constrain us.

NOTES

1. Michel Foucault, *The History of Sexuality: An Introduction* (New York: Random
House, 1978), 159, emphasis added.

2. Interpreting Foucault is something of an industry. The ideas from Foucault in
this essay derive from *The History of Sexuality, An Introduction* and *Power/Knowledge:
Selected Interviews and Other Writings 1972–1977,* ed. C. Gordon (New York: Pantheon,
1980). By far the most useful secondary source is H. Dreyfus and P. Rabinow's
Michel Foucault: Beyond Structuralism and Hermeneutics (Chicago: University of Chicago, 1983). The problems of interpretation are legion.

3. I have found Michael S. Kimmel and Michael Kaufman's "Weekend Warriors" quite clarifying, as well as R. W. Connell's essay "Drumming Up the Wrong
Tree," both reprinted here. Bly's anthropology, psychohistory, and psychoanalytic
theory, aside from being intellectually wrong, all seem to me to mask and legitimate
a backlash against women.

4. It seems to me that Bly's idea that the widespread practice of initiating boys through forcing them to endure physical pain and distress without losing composure is a way of connecting them with, and healing *psychic* wounds, has it backwards. Bly believes that the initiation "tells men what to do with wounds." The initiation is much more likely to be training in the art of resisting the impulse to regress and demand nurturance when distressed. It strikes me as an attempt to force a traumatic identification with manhood through learning the art of repressing "weak" feelings that would demand that one seek nurturance and identification with mother. It isn't wisdom about wounds that such rituals teach, but flight into repression in the service of resisting regression.

5. Quotations are from Robert Bly, *Iron John* (Reading, Mass.: Addison-Wesley, 1990).

6. This seems to be a basic therapeutic move among Jungians: to encourage us to see ourselves as "participating" in quasi-divine archetypes. It strikes me as the fundamental way that "vulgar" religion makes people happy: by interpreting the self and world as "better" than they are. In depression, one "distorts downward" and poisons one's mood by making the self and world seem worse than they are. Religious and Jungian cosmologies uplift the self and one's mood by instilling "positive" beliefs which can't be confirmed or denied.

7. It may be that the mythopoetic men's movement is valuable for reasons peripheral to its intellectual claims. It may provide a sense of community and support and may create a space for men to reflect upon their identities in constructive ways. But this has nothing to do with the movement per se. It could do this and possess a completely different intellectual content.

8. I am indebted to sociologist Chuck Stephen for this formulation. Stephen also persuasively argues that with entrenched multicultural interests, along with feminism, beginning to decenter white middle-class masculinity, the mythopoetic men's movement can be usefully understood as attempting to establish itself as an ethnic group, with its own rituals, a glorified past, and a discrete cultural identity. From such a standpoint it can gain political and personal strength.

9. From Michael S. Kimmel, "The Men's Movement and Me: A Weekend At The First International Men's Conference" in *Brother: The Newsletter of the National Organization for Men Against Sexism* (Fall 1992): 2.

10. "Masculine and feminine" are not parallel in usage. "Femininity" has become part of what radical feminists have attacked as destructive to women: the cultural compulsion to be "feminine"—soft, afraid of bald truths, nurturant, incapable of earthiness or lust. Feminists have attempted to retrieve and exalt what's valuable in the "feminine" but so far as I am aware, they have not attempted to exalt "femininity" in the traditional sense.

11. It seems to be that "man" and "woman" are themselves oppressive words because to even think them is to evoke and therefore legitimize stereotypes. Our ways of categorizing the world necessarily commit us to prototypes from which individual

members of a category may vary. Such prototypes themselves ride upon idealized cognitive models, so it may be impossible to categorize human males and females without calling upon implicit models of gender, which will be as oppressive and sexist as the culture they dwell in. Still a certain fluidity and watchfulness and irony may be useful when thinking and speaking "man" or "woman." For more on categories see George Lakoff, *Woman, Fire, and Dangerous Things* (Chicago: University of Chicago Press, 1987).

A Woman for Every Wild Man: Robert Bly and His Reaffirmation of Masculinity

DAVID S. GUTTERMAN

IN DECEMBER OF 1991, I AND HUNDREDS of other men attended a retreat in Chapel Hill, North Carolina, led principally by Robert Bly and Robert Moore, entitled "Making a Small Hole in Denial: Grief, Courage and Beauty in Male Soul." Among the remarkable assertions made by Bly and Moore was the following statement by Robert Bly. Bly is discussing images of women in the 1950s and the impossibility of women merging completely with a man "à la Doris Day." Wondering what options are available to women, Bly declares:

> Well one thing you can do is to go to the opposite side and say "I will depend on nothing from a man. I'm going to have nothing to do with a man. I'm going to become a lesbian and forget the whole thing. *And I don't become a lesbian out of joy, I become one out of anger.* And the decision that I can live completely separately from any man and that I'll never be dependent on any man again."
>
> But I was thinking about that. How isolated it makes these women, is that right? Part of the loneliness of men is this feeling that thousands, millions of women have made this decision. And they don't want to give anything to a man, nor receive anything from a man. And we know that somewhere, we know that somewhere in our bodies.
>
> And then I happened to pick up this poem of D. H. Lawrence. And what is the trouble with that idea? The trouble with the idea that since I can't merge with a man, I'm going to have nothing to do with him at all? (Audience member says, "It's the denial of the masculine side." And Bly says,) "Yes, that's quite right. It's also a complete inability to understand what it's like to be *completely isolated.* Terrifying, it's probably more terrifying than being Doris Day. But the feminist movement has not warned them of what it's like when you are in your

room by yourself and don't have any friends and no man or anybody to fight with.

But D. H. Lawrence looks at it differently and he took me by surprise. He says that what's happened is that they have forgotten the "Third." They are thinking of the man and the woman and they are forgetting the Third. And this is where Lawrence says it:

"As we live we are transmitters of life and when we fail to transmit life, life fails to flow through us. That is a part of the mystery of sex. It's a flow onwards. *Sexless people transmit nothing.*"[1]

I have quoted this passage at length, for it powerfully demonstrates a series of fundamental problems with Bly's efforts to reassess masculinity. I believe that it is critical to recognize that the definition of masculinity (at least in the United States today) is based on the entanglement of normative male gender behavior and normative heterosexual behavior. Bly's assessment of masculinity focuses only on the component of male gender and neglects to critically examine the constitution of sexuality. As a result, his critique of contemporary American manhood is dangerously deficient.

Let's take a brief look at how Bly addresses the question of sexuality in this passage in order to indicate an elementary problem with his analysis. In particular, I want to highlight that in Bly's vision, heterosexuality serves as the core of the natural order essential to the health and well-being of society. Homosexuality—in this case lesbianism—is the aberrant result of irrational anger which leads to isolation, terror, and "lifelessness." There is no joy, no community, no sexuality, and no sexual pleasure, in Bly's conception of lesbianism. Rather these "angry women" inhabit a bleak and barren world isolated from men. Beyond the gloominess of this world, these women are also responsible for betraying men, leaving the males, who in Bly's heterosexual ideal would be the partners of these women, aching with loneliness deep in their bodies. Bly somehow cannot imagine that women can survive and thrive without men, that women don't need to depend on men for friendship, for sex, or for life itself. Nor does Bly have room in his world for men who don't long for these lost women, but who instead long for each other.

Indeed, Bly's central concern in this passage seems to be with the preservation of a society composed of heterosexual pairs. In fact, Bly's entire framework rigidly divides the world into opposite genders and fixes heterosexuality as the "natural" state of being. This uncritical reaffirmation of the heterosexual matrix which underwrites our social order is a central problem in Bly's examination of masculinity. I want to offer some thoughts on how to rethink this heterosexual matrix through the use of feminist theory, queer theory and postmodernist philosophy. I will then return to Bly and the mythopoetic men's movement to further discuss the importance of critically addressing the heterosexual matrix.

In the United States today, a great deal of attention is focused on reexamining questions of sexuality and gender, including issues of how individual identity and behavior are shaped by society. The recent and current efforts of the American feminist and "gay liberation" movements (including their academic arms in Women's Studies and Gay and Lesbian Studies) have been instrumental in raising these concerns. As John D'Emilio and Estelle Freedman assert in *Intimate Matters: A History of Sexuality in America,* "Both movements focused national attention on issues of sexuality, sharply challenging common assumptions about the 'naturalness' of gender and sexuality."[2]

These efforts to critically explore the social construction of sexuality and gender are further reinforced by postmodern philosophy's attempts to deconstruct the transcendental nature of humans common to Enlightenment philosophy. In short, postmodernism focuses on the ways social forces constitute human subjects. Rather than viewing people as coming before culture and creating society through their actions which are rooted in "Reason," such a notion of the transcendental subject is dramatically rewritten.[3] For example, a leading figure in the postmodern philosophic tradition, Michel Foucault, instructs us that social subjects are discursively "produced" by "relations of power."[4] By perceiving a subject in relation to a variety of social discourses (for example: race, class, education, religious belief, body type, etc.) it becomes clear that subjects are multiply constituted.[5] In other words, an individual's identity is produced by the intersection of cultural discourses of race, gender, sexuality, etc. Moreover, one cannot simply "add" race to gender to sexuality and thereby understand (or "get") a person's identity, but rather must explore how race, gender, sexuality and other cultural discourses, are mutually constitutive. (For Bly, as we will see, this multiplicitous constitution is dismissed in favor of an essential mythical core within all individuals.) For now, I want to simply focus on the inter-relationship between discourses of sexuality and gender.

The modernist or Enlightenment tradition which has largely governed cultural discourse in the West is rooted in dualistic formulations. Binarisms such as male/female, self/other, heterosexual/homosexual, black/white, same/different, etc., represent a series of either/or categories within which individuals are expected to exist. Moreover, each identifier is associated with another series of dualisms (i.e., male/female, public/private, culture/nature, active/passive, mind/body, etc.).[6] The hazards of perceiving identity within this absolutist binary framework are manifold, particularly with regard to the perception of difference. William Connolly asserts:

> An identity is established in relation to a series of differences that have become socially recognized. These differences are essential to its being . . . Identity requires difference in order to be, and converts difference into otherness in order to secure its own self-certainty.[7]

For example, the axis which serves as the fundamental basis of gender identity in the West clearly functions along this organization of same/different. That is, the perception that men and women are "opposite sexes" (with accompanying "genders"—masculine/feminine) creates the expectation that one is either a man or a woman and that these two categories are essentially disparate. This sense of difference then becomes the demarcation of otherness when gradations of value are placed upon the two distinct domains. In our culture, of course, that which is usually associated with men (Activity, Culture, Reason) is usually held in higher esteem than that which is associated with women (Passivity, Nature, Emotion).[8]

Accordingly, as Jeffrey Weeks has illustrated, the social construction of masculinity provides a striking demonstration of the ways the "drive to convert difference to otherness" has functioned. Weeks states:

> Masculinity or the male identity is achieved by the constant process of warding off threats to it. It is precariously achieved by the rejection of femininity and homosexuality.[9]

Implicit in this notion is the recognition that masculinity is contingent and unstable. It must be constantly reaffirmed by establishing and maintaining the barriers between normative standards for men and women and heterosexual and homosexual. This concept of rigid demarcations serves as a framework of the heterosexual matrix. Drawing from the work of Monique Wittig and Adrienne Rich, Judith Butler defines the "heterosexual matrix" as:

> [A] hegemonic discursive/epistemic model of gender intelligibility that assumes that for bodies to cohere and make sense there must be a stable sex expressed through a stable gender (masculine expresses male, feminine expresses female) that is oppositionally and hierarchically defined through the compulsory practice of heterosexuality.[10]

168 : DAVID S. GUTTERMAN

In other words, the cultural demand for heterosexuality creates the need for clear markers of gender so that sexual partners can be "correctly" chosen. In this way discourses of (hetero)sexuality establish the categories of gender, and these categories enable the perpetuation of that system of sexuality. Because this system is "oppositionally and hierarchically defined" any aberration from either the categories of gender or normative heterosexuality is met with efforts to silence, change or destroy the differences. This process illustrates how gender is used to maintain heterosexuality which is itself a "contingency branded into" men and women in our culture (Connolly, p. 176).

If we can conceive of the heterosexual matrix which governs in our culture as contingent rather than "natural," institutions and cultural values which sustain the sexist and homophobic state of our culture can be challenged more readily. For example, we can critically assess Bly's conception that lesbians (and presumably gay men) are "sex-less" people who do not "transmit," or produce, "life." Within the heterosexual matrix which has been naturalized in our culture, sexual behavior is supposed to be between a man and a woman (i.e., "opposite" genders) and is intended for, or at least bound up with, reproduction. However, if the relationship between sexuality and (re)production is denaturalized, the role of heterosexuals as reproducers of life becomes unstable. The political implications of this recognition are manifold—not the least of the potential outcomes is the proliferation of "non-normative heterosexual" parental and familial structures.

Another potential result of perceiving the heterosexual matrix as contingent is the freeing of sexuality from binaristic formulations. That is, as Samira Kawash points out, if, as the heterosexual matrix dictates, the gender of a person's sexual object choice is perceived as the defining element of one's sexuality, cultural notions of sexuality will revolve around the axis of the heterosexual/homosexual binary.[11] One ramification of this configuration of sexuality is the way:

> It delegitimates non-gender-exclusive desires. Current struggles over the 'authenticity' of bisexuality illustrate this effect: if the world is divided into 'same' and 'different,' 'homo' and 'hetero,' then bisexuality is something which cannot exist, and individuals claiming a bisexual identity are confused or in a state of transition. (Kawash, p. 28)

Efforts to destabilize the heterosexual matrix thus will enable bisexuality and other forms of sexuality which do not conform neatly to governing categories to be culturally perceived as "authentic." In *Epistemology of the Closet*, Eve Sedgwick offers a brief list of alternate ways of conceiving sexuality that illuminates the possibilities opened by freeing sexuality from the dualisms of the heterosexual matrix. Included in this list are: "To some people, the nimbus of 'the sexual' seems scarcely to extend beyond the boundaries of discrete genital acts; to others, it enfolds them loosely or floats virtually free of them. Many people have their richest mental/emotional involvement with sexual acts that they don't do, or even don't want to do [i.e., fantasy]."[12] Ultimately rethinking the relationship and the distinctions between sexuality and gender enables a reimagination of sexuality which is open to a cornucopia of contingent, shifting, identifying "axes."

The recognition of the contingent quality of sexuality and gender also enables a critical exploration of masculinity. One illustration of how the governing definition of masculinity, established by the heterosexual matrix, is being interrogated is the way gay men challenge definitions of normative male gender identity. For example, some gay men adopt what Jeffrey Weeks calls a "macho-style" (Weeks, p. 191). As Richard Dyer explains:

> By taking the signs of masculinity and eroticising them in a blatantly homosexual context, much mischief is done to the security with which "men" are defined in society, and by which their power is secured. If that bearded, muscular beer drinker turns out to be a pansy, how ever are they going to know the "real" men any more? (Dyer, as quoted in Weeks, p. 191)

Clearly, this is a case where standards of normative masculinity exhibit a slippage from the supposed "state of nature" of the heterosexual matrix.

The mythopoetic men's movement and its most prominent leader, Robert Bly, also proclaim that they are undertaking a major revision of contemporary American masculinity. Bly begins *Iron John: A Book About Men*, by stating, "We are living at an important and fruitful moment now, for it is clear to men that the images of adult manhood given by the popular culture are worn out; a man can no longer depend on them."[13] The emphasis on emotions (from grief to joy), the critique of definitions of "success" and the militaristic attitudes prevalent among men in our culture, and the prominent use of poetry in Bly's efforts, provide hope that a fundamental reassessment of masculinity is being entertained. Unfortunately, Bly's approach is incomplete. While he is willing to challenge male gender role behavior in his search for the "Eternal Masculine," he fails to examine the social construction of male sexuality.

Indeed, Bly's position on sexuality varies from reaffirming the heterosexual matrix to silencing homosexuality's challenge to his conception of masculinity. As Don Shewey, in a 1992 article in the *Village Voice* suggests, part of the mythopoetic movement's homophobia comes from the need to prove their own manhood, surrounded as they are by poetry which has been "feminized" in our culture. Shewey also believes that, "Bly and [another mythopoetic leader Michael] Meade purposely want to limit the amount of gay expression at their events for fear that too strong a gay presence will drive away straight men. . . ."[14] As a result, the role played by homophobia in the construction of normative masculinity in our culture is never examined. The more challenging step of questioning the naturalness of heterosexuality is far from being entertained.

Instead, Bly's ideas concerning gay men are conspicuously absent—he simply maintains that he is speaking to men and that whatever he says about heterosexual men applies to gay men as well. This is clear in the introduction to *Iron John,* where Bly writes, "Most of the language in this book speaks to heterosexual men but does not exclude homosexual men. It wasn't until the eighteenth century that people ever used the term homosexual; before that time gay men were understood simply as part of the large community of men. The mythology as I see it does not make a big distinction between homosexual and heterosexual men" (Bly, p. x). Gay men were mentioned by the facilitators twice during the day-long retreat I attended, both times simply to assert that whatever was being said about heterosexual relationship applied to "them" as well. Given that the subject of the retreat was male denial and courage, it is disturbingly ironic that Bly and Robert Moore couldn't find the courage to confront society's—or their own—homophobia.

Indeed, I believe that this silencing of questions concerning sexuality is no mere accident. Rather the preservation of the heterosexual matrix and the "naturalness" of heterosexuality is essential to Bly's theories. In order to discover the "Eternal Masculine" which purportedly lies within every man, Bly needs to reaffirm and accentuate the differences between men and women. To preserve this dualistic heterosexual order, Bly, in turn, needs to either ignore homosexuality, or frame homosexuality as an irrational, unnatural aberration. Thus while Bly is willing to challenge contemporary male gender behavior, he neglects questions of sexuality—the deeply entwined and complementary component of normative masculinity. As a result, Bly's re-vision of contemporary American manhood is not just incomplete, but fundamentally, and, in light of Bly's popularity, even tragically, flawed.

ACKNOWLEDGMENTS

I am indebted to Andrew Gutterman, Phil Poley, Warren Hedges, Vivian Robinson, Miriam Peskowitz, Jean O'Barr, Michael Kimmel, and Jennifer

Johns for their valuable insights, support, and patience during the writing of this paper.

NOTES

1. Robert Bly and Robert Moore, "Making a Small Hole in Denial: Grief Courage and Beauty in Male Soul" (Audiotape: Sound Horizons, 1991); emphasis added.

2. John D'Emilio and Estelle B. Freedman, *Intimate Matters: A History of Sexuality in America* (New York: Harper & Row, 1988), xii.

3. Postmodernism, in many ways, can be traced to Nietzsche's pronouncement in *On the Genealogy of Morals and Ecce Homo* that, "There is no 'being' behind doing, effecting, becoming; 'the doer' is merely a fiction added to the deed—the deed is everything" (trans. Walter Kaufman and R. J. Hollingdale [New York: Vintage Books, 1967], 45). The subject is thus perceived as being constituted by the event.

4. Michel Foucault, *Politics, Philosophy, Culture: Interviews and Other Writings, 1977–1984*, ed. Lawrence D. Kritzman (New York: Routledge, 1988), 118.

5. The historic conflicts between African-American and white women within the feminist movement provide an illustration of the way in which the cultural constructions of women in our society vary due to other cultural discourses like race and class.

6. For further discussion of binary logic, see Barbara Herrnstein Smith, *Contingencies of Value: Alternative Perspectives for Critical Theory* (Cambridge: Harvard University Press, 1988).

7. William E. Connolly, *Identity/Difference: Democratic Negotiations of Political Paradox* (Ithaca: Cornell University Press, 1991), 64.

8. I say "usually" here for I want to suggest that within broad cultural paradigms there are often localized situations where gendered attributes can be reversed. This inversion transpires both in terms of identity (i.e., women who compel men to attend the opera are sometimes seen as the bearers of culture) and of value (i.e., when male aggressiveness intersects with the racial identity of African-Americans in our society, the assertive, forceful qualities of those men are demonized rather than valorized by portions of the larger American population.)

In negotiating the obstacles to opening closed binary systems (grounded on difference as otherness), it is crucial to remember that not only are cultural norms socially constructed but so too are the values and roles attached to those norms (see Smith, especially chap. 3.).

9. Jeffrey Weeks, *Sexuality and Its Discontents: Meanings, Myths & Modern Sexualities* (London: Routledge and Kegan Paul, 1985), 190.

10. Judith Butler, *Gender Trouble: Feminism and the Subversion of Identity* (New York: Routledge, 1990), 151.

11. Samira Kawash, "Feminism, Desire and the Problem of Sexual Identity," in

Proceedings from "Engendering Knowledge/Engendering Power: Feminism as Theory and Practice," ed. Cynthia W. Baker (Durham: Duke University Women's Studies Program, 1993), 28.

12. Eve Kosofsky Sedgwick, *Epistemology of the Closet* (Berkeley: University of California Press, 1990), 25–26.

13. Robert Bly, *Iron John: A Book About Men* (Reading, Mass.: Addison-Wesley, 1990), ix.

14. Don Shewey, "Town Meeting in the Hearts of Men," *The Village Voice*, vol. XXXVII, no. 6 (11 February 1992): 45.

Renewal as Retreat: The Battle for Men's Souls

TIMOTHY NONN

THE MEN'S MOVEMENT AND THE CHURCH

The contemporary search for a male soul by religious conservatives and mythopoetics appears to have a certain affinity with Christian spirituality. Perhaps this explains a recent proliferation of articles on the men's movement within Christian journals. But there are other reasons for the mainstream Christian embrace of the concept of a male soul that derive from resistance to the political struggles of women, gays and people of color. Although the men's movement is politically diverse, the perspectives of religious conservatives and mythopoetics on masculinity dominate Christian journals. Significant differences exist between religious conservatives and mythopoetics but their interests converge in a two-pronged offensive: opposition to feminism and valorization of masculinity. In brief, "masculine spirituality" is offered as an antidote to the supposed feminization of the church.[1]

The religious conservative and mythopoetic branches have been contrasted with the profeminist branch of the men's movement.[2] Kimmel divides the men's movement among profeminists, antifeminists, and masculinists.[3] In this analysis, I use the term "Masculine Renewal" to refer to antifeminist elements of the men's movement in the church. Masculine Renewal represents a quasi-religious quest for an essential meaning to masculinity. Historically, Masculine Renewal is part of a larger social project whose purpose is the continued subordination of women, gays and people of color. The valorization of masculinity—"renewal" denotes belief in an essential masculine identity—includes blaming feminists, gays, and other groups for men's confusion and pain over shifting gender roles and a blurring of gender identities.

Three basic claims unite mythopoetics and religious conservatives under the banner of Masculine Renewal: (1) Men are victims of oppression, either directly by newly empowered social groups (feminists, gays), or indirectly by an indifferent social order. Men are the victims of reverse discrimination, Moore argues, because "sexism is a two-way street" (p. 114). (2) Men must gather together in spiritual retreats to rediscover their authentic masculine identity. (3) Men must unite under male leadership in order to preserve and protect the natural gender order and Western civilization. Masculine Renewal frequently relates arguments about spirituality, soul, and male essence to Biblical figures.[4] Yet when their claims are compared with the lives and teachings of Moses and Jesus, an inseparable gulf divides Masculine Renewal and Christian faith. In their responses to the cries of the oppressed, Moses and Jesus may actually be seen as early "profeminist" men.

THE VICTIMIZED MALE

The first claim of Masculine Renewal is that men have been emasculated by feminists and gays. Men have lost touch with their eternal masculinity—hence, the quest for a male soul (Trippe, p. 120).[5] *Newsweek* characterizes men's response to social turmoil over race, gender, and sexuality as "white male paranoia."[6] But Masculine Renewal interprets the crisis of male identity as a source of social chaos and destructiveness. Men must rediscover their masculine nature to restore social and metaphysical harmony. In *Iron John*, Robert Bly claims that "soft men" are products of dominant mothers and lovers.[7] Mythopoetics worry that the "male soul" is endangered because only wimps and women occupy the pews of a "feminized" church (O'Malley, p. 405). Patrick Arnold asserts that misandry (hatred of men) has driven men from a "dominantly feminine" church.[8] Religious conservatives attack feminists for disputing that God's "masculinity is essential."[9]

Attacks on feminists and gays proliferate in the rhetoric of Masculine Renewal. Arnold claims that the ultimate goal of feminists is male castration (p. 7). Compromise is impossible, antifeminist author Donna Steichen argues, because feminism is a "deadly disease" attacking all women: "[F]eminism is a continuum: it is a single disease that progresses from incipient rebellion to raving lunacy. If we think of it as the moral equivalent of AIDS, even those in the early stage could be seen as HIV positive, and predictably doomed."[10] Masculine Renewal claims that men are severely constrained in a feminized society. Bly notes a widespread lack of male energy. Moore echoes that "warrior energies" are repressed in a society dominated by women. Masculine Renewal advocates men's retreats as a means to regain male power through ritualized practices. But power is relational; masculinity is constructed in the context of historical relations of gender, class and race. Masculine Renewal has alienated various groups of men—specifically, gays and men of color—by myopically relating masculinity to the white European history of conquest and domination.

Masculine Renewal structures its response to feminism around a claim of male victimization. Men feel defeated. Toxic hostility toward expression of genuine masculinity has condemned men to desperate, empty lives. Religious conservatives and mythopoetics fault "radical feminists" for a decline of manhood and morals. Charles Colson, convicted Watergate conspirator and right-wing evangelist, says that legislation supported by militant feminists dehumanizes men. Since witnessing a prison scene in which a female guard intruded upon a male inmate in a toilet, Colson argues that antidiscrimination laws demand unnatural gender integration.[11] Leon Podles warns that liberal social engineering in pursuit of gender equality undermines masculinity because it obscures the "deep structures of human nature" that divide men from women and heterosexuals from homosexuals.[12] The religious rhetoric of Masculine Renewal blames feminists for unleashing demonic forces upon society. Robert Moore, a popular mythopoetic writer, says: "One of the things we have to get the churches to do, both Protestant and Catholic, is not continue getting aboard this bandwagon of demonization of the masculine gender that has become so popular among some radical feminists, though by no means all" (p. 114). Others describe Christian feminists as "witches," "spiritual termites," "women of rage," "pagan," and "heretics." There is no room for dialogue, conservatives argue, since "angry" feminists seek total victory: "This rage is unappeasable except by annihilation of the Church and complete supremacy of radical religious feminism."[13]

Masculine Renewal inadvertently highlights the centrality of power in gender relations by linking a "revealed" masculinity to political opposition to feminism. It is untenable to argue that middle-class heterosexual white men are victimized in a society where they exercise power and privilege; masculine identity, a product of gender relations, is socially constructed through men's collective power. Masculine identity conceived through the marginalization of women, gays, and people of color is destabilized by the resistance of subjugated groups to domination.[14] Hence, Masculine Renewal signifies the mobilization of a privileged class of men determined to maintain position and power in church and society. Kimmel documents cycles of anti-feminism in American history.[15] Beverly Harrison, a leading Christian feminist, points out that the core of misogyny "is the reaction that occurs when women's concrete power is manifest." She advocates a relational view of "mutual" power in contrast to a zero-sum view. Through a relational approach, men and women are mutually empowered and attain human dignity. Harrison argues that anger leads women from victimization to moral agency: "The deepest danger to our cause is that our anger will turn inward and lead us to portray ourselves and other women chiefly as victims rather than those who have struggled for the gift of life against incredible odds. The creative power of anger is shaped by owning this great strength of women and others who have struggled for the full gift of life against structures of oppression."[16]

Religious conservatives and mythopoetics, instead, portray feminists' anger as the root of men's victimization. Colson warns that scattered skirmishes between men and women will lead to "all-out gender wars" (p. 72). In Masculine Renewal, the experience of victimization is the basis for an ideological offense against feminism. In striking contrast, the lives of Moses and Jesus demonstrate that personal failure—decline in social status and power—may lead to a new consciousness in which an awareness of suffering and an identification with the oppressed provide a foundation for collective liberation.

Two related stories in the second chapter of Exodus reveal the character and destiny of Moses. Moses grew up in the Egyptian royal household. He had everything obtainable through power and privilege. But after murdering an Egyptian overseer who was beating a Hebrew slave, he was forced to flee. In Exodus 2:16–17, Moses was destitute when he spotted seven young women at a well in the Midian desert: "They came to draw water, and filled the troughs to water their father's flock. But some shepherds came and drove them away. Moses got up and came to their defense and watered their flock." Both stories show that Moses hated injustice. They also reveal his compassion for the exploited and powerless. We see the seeds of a personality that became identified with God's liberating power in history: Moses, the liberator, became a great religious figure only because Moses, the person, responded to the cries of the oppressed.

The character and destiny of Jesus are similarly revealed in his response to society's victims. Jesus acted with compassion toward the poor and oppressed but, like Moses, became a fugitive from a corrupt and paranoid ruling elite. In Luke 10:38–42, Jesus praised Mary for pursuing religious contemplation instead of household duties. Women were not allowed to become rabbis, or study and discuss holy scripture. Despite public disapproval and institutional opposition, Jesus supported Mary's decision to become his disciple. He accepted the stigma of "gender traitor" out of a deep commitment to social justice. In Mark 7:27–29, Jesus rebuffed a woman's plea for her ailing daughter because she was from Syrophoenicia, and not Israel: "He said to her, 'Let the children be fed first, for it is not fair to take the children's food and throw it to the dogs.' But she answered him, 'Lord, even the dogs under the table eat the children's crumbs.' Then he said to her, 'For saying that, you may go—the demon has left your daughter.' " It took someone from the bottom of society—an impoverished woman from an alienated social group—to teach Jesus the true meaning of his mission. After this encounter, Jesus reached out to the lowly and persecuted of every religious and cultural background. Jesus was open to a universal vision of justice only after experiencing hardship and persecution. The Syrophoenician woman helped Jesus move from chauvinism to solidarity.

These Biblical stories highlight the relationship between failure and the development of empathy for the oppressed. Similarly, a decline in social status and power in contemporary society need not lead to a "valorization of victimization" or "a kind of chauvinistic particularism" but divulges our "mutual dependence and vulnerability."[17] Masculine Renewal distorts the Christian message of compassion and solidarity through its call to entrenchment and division. A focus on men's victimization privileges men's experience of pain and confusion while denying the malleability of gender roles and identity. The claim of victim status for men is detrimental to faith and community because it seeks to replace the vital dialogue of women, gays and people of color with the worn-out monologue of white middle-class heterosexual men. Victimization is not a privileged status but a beginning point in the process of creating just social relations. Religious conservatives and mythopoetics evidently find it difficult to join a dialogue of equals and a process of coalition-building. Consequently, Masculine Renewal fails to guide men of faith along paths of personal or social transformation and, instead, leads them to a dead end of distortion, confrontation, and separatism.

MEN IN RETREAT: THE EXCLUSIVE MALE SOUL

The second claim in Masculine Renewal is that men must retreat from women to recover their masculine identity. Popular Christian writers draw on the tradition of spiritual retreat in support of Masculine Renewal. In the wilderness, it is argued, men will find the elusive male soul. Catholics and Protestants writing about masculine spirituality concur that the male soul is discovered in separation from women (O'Malley, pp. 405–6; Trippe, p. 118).[18]

Separation from women presumably allows men to free masculine "energies" (Moore, p. 113); but the new age mythopoetic man bears a suspicious resemblance to the traditional man of religious conservatives. Masculine Renewal emphasizes an heroic masculinity in which the male soul is identified with violence, power and conquest personified by the "warrior" archetype (Thompson). Some differences emerge between mythopoetics and conservatives on the warrior's image. On the one hand, mythopoetics envision a more benign type of warrior. Trippe supports a "hero's journey" in which sensitive men "listen first to our own souls and to each other" (p. 118). Moore argues that "warrior energies" must be used discriminately, in a mature and responsible manner, to create a better society (p. 113). O'Malley venerates the crusading warrior: "The male soul thrives on challenge, the heroic, the wild, the individuated — qualities not expected in Catholic males, in pew or in the pulpit At work, a man is expected to be a stallion; at Mass, to metamorphose into a gelding. That temporary neutering is not possible. What Catholic males need to regain is our sense of pilgrimage, of the bloodless crusade: the Grail quest" (pp. 405–6).

Religious conservatives, on the other hand, favor a violent hero at war with a hostile world. Kreeft argues that we live in an era of "spiritual warfare" between pagan feminists and authentic Christians (p. 28). Podles writes that men's violence is an expression of a militant Christian faith: "The hero is the ultimate pattern of maleness. He goes forth from ordinary life to confront the powers of evil, to battle with them, to be wounded and scarred by them, and only then to take his place as King . . . Sacred violence is the ultimate meaning of masculinity."[19] Contemporary religious images of men's violence, widespread in Masculine Renewal, are reminiscent of Christian patriarchal warfare against women and non-Christians: the Crusades, the Spanish Inquisition, witch hunts, and, today, Serbian rape-camps for Muslim women. Podles believes that "sacred violence is the ultimate meaning of masculinity" (1991, p. 8) and that "masculinity is, at heart, a willingness to sacrifice oneself even unto violent, bloody death for the other" (1993, p. 39). Despite variations, the prominence of the warrior motif in Masculine Renewal springs from a culture of terror in which masculinity is the organizing principle for the subordination of women: violence creates men. Walter

Wink argues that "the myth of redemptive violence" is used to adversely condition boys in our society in an arbitrary use of violence. He writes that violence assumes a quasi-religious form: "Redemptive violence gives way to violence as an end in itself—not a religion that uses violence in the pursuit of order and salvation, but a religion in which violence has become the ultimate elixir, sheer titillation, an addictive high, a substitute for relationships."[20]

The stories of Moses and Jesus provide an alternative understanding of violence and power. Violence is not an essential aspect of masculinity; it is associated with institutionalized domination. Power is not interpreted as a self-interested possession; it is the shared responsibility of the community. Power is the process by which a just society is maintained. Moses and Jesus did not retreat into the wilderness to tap into an inner resource of supernatural power that would allow them to exercise extraordinary abilities or violently assert their will over others. Instead, in retreat, they discovered their own humanness—a profound relatedness to all Being. They experienced a sacred sense of the unity, not division, of humanity. Elie Wiesel writes that Moses, the greatest figure in Jewish tradition, identified with the whole community: "Moses was a humanist in all things. Even his courage, his generosity were human virtues; all his qualities and all his flaws were human. He had no supernatural powers, no talent for the occult. Everything he did, he conceived in human terms, concerned not with his own 'individual salvation' but with the well-being of the community."[21]

Moses and Jesus accepted an individual loss of power in pursuit of the liberation of an oppressed people. Their understanding of leadership did not consist of an identity that set them apart from others but evolved from their identification with the struggle of the oppressed for justice. James Nelson says that Jesus "mediates God's vulnerability and weakness, thereby eliciting our own. In our mutual need we are, for the moment, bonded in life-giving communion."[22] Jesus confronted his own vulnerability and, thereby, discovered the relational power that makes collective liberation an historical possibility. Harrison writes that the transcendence of self-interest is vital in the struggle for justice: "The genuine experience of transcendence arises in the ecstatic power emergent between those who have connected with each other, intimately engaged with God, in emancipatory praxis" (p. 263). The renunciation of self-interested power and manifestation of relational power marks the radical nature of spiritual retreat. Moses and Jesus emerged from retreat with a commitment to the liberation of the oppressed. They had not discovered their inward nature so much as their social role. Franciscan spirituality reflects this tradition of social responsibility. The prayer of St. Francis begins: "Lord, make me an instrument of thy peace." The Christian tradition of spiritual retreat provides a basis for addressing unequal social relations. It is not a military tactic for reorganizing the troops. The claim in Masculine Renewal that men must separate from women in order to discover genuine masculinity obscures both the actual origin of masculinity in gender relations and the path to gender justice.

MASCULINE RENEWAL AND MALE POWER

The third claim in Masculine Renewal is that men must unite under male leadership in order to preserve and protect the natural gender order and Western civilization. Stu Weber, a conservative Christian minister, relies on mythopoetic authors Robert Bly and Robert Moore to construct a Christian model of masculinity. Weber, in opposing feminism, argues that men are destined to rule over women. Like Moore (p. 113), he believes that masculine "hardwiring" preconditions men for the roles of "king" and "warrior."[23] The Christian right has adopted the language of mythopoetics in an antifeminist media campaign. Weber used an appearance on "Beverly LaHaye Live" (June 23, 1994) to attack feminists, claiming "men feel beat up." LaHaye, president of Christian Women of America, agreed that "the antics of the radical feminist movement" victimize men.

Masculine Renewal is flowering under the tender care of religious conservatives who find in mythopoetic rhetoric about masculinity a basis for mobilizing Christians against feminist and gay liberation movements. There are, of course, significant differences between religious conservatives and mythopoetics; but accessibility of mythopoetic concepts and terminology by religious conservatives suggest that, in both cases, we are witnessing a reinscription of white heterosexual masculinity under the guise of belief in a male soul. The experience of women, gays, and men of color is marginalized. For instance, Dittes assures men that the mythopoetic "men's movement is about becoming more manly, not less; it is not about becoming more feminine or more androgynous" (p. 589). O'Malley clarifies that "a man is not a woman and a woman is not a man" (p. 403). Religious conservatives, with thinly-veiled racism, argue that white heterosexual men regard the "ethos of manhood" as an ideal not shared by men who live in "mild climates" (Podles, 1993, p. 37). Whatever tension exists between religious conservatives and mythopoetics is visible only in conflict over political strategy. On the one hand, conservatives support open, direct confrontation with feminists and gays. Feminism is described as "a radically different religion from Christianity" (Kreeft, p. 25). Non-whites and the poor are also targets. Podles writes: "Inner-city blacks, the underclass, the lumpenproletariat of America, have a vicious and destructive ethos of pseudo-masculinity" (1993, p. 40). On the other hand, mythopoetics argue that the men's movement must reach out to gays and men of color. George Trippe writes: "Further, our sense of "together" must expand as never before to include all men, especially those who were oppressed or excluded in patriarchal structures. We men need to take up the task together—men of all races and ethnic groups, men of all sexual orientations, men in all our sorts and conditions" (p. 121). White middle-class mythopoetics have already set the agenda for the recovery of male power. It is not surprising that gays and men of color feel excluded and resent the appropriation of their cultural traditions. A Native American writer quips: "White men can't drum!"[24]

The concept of male liberation also differentiates mythopoetics from religious conservatives (Dittes, p. 589). But, in accord with Masculine Renewal, male liberation rests on an interpretation of men as victims. In fact, men are viewed as the most oppressed sector in society because they carry "the burden of civilization, law and order, government, and culture throughout history" (Arnold, p. 51). Schurman argues that supporters of male liberation are white, well-educated, middle-class men in search of individualistic emotional fulfillment rather than social change.[25] The illusory search for the male soul is a symptom of social pathology nourished by therapists and clergy who would rather comfort the besieged male than challenge a sexist society. Male liberation, favored by mythopoetics, converges with the reactionary politics of religious conservatives in scapegoating women and gays for shifting gender roles. Both groups are united around the reassertion of male power, one consciously, the other, perhaps, unwittingly.

At the heart of Masculine Renewal is a litany of rituals designed for boys (Moore, p. 113). O'Malley says "the distinctively male soul" requires that boys be initiated into manhood through ritual practices to prepare them for positions of power in the church (p. 406). Others, in the tradition of Billy Sunday, offer Jesus as a model of masculinity for boys. Arnold, a mythopoetic, writes: "Jesus was himself a very manly figure, and the biblical metaphors for God in the ancient Judeo-Christian traditions are charged with masculine archetypal energy" (p. 68). Kreeft, a conservative, argues that Roman Catholic female priests would be flawed role models because Jesus will "forever be a male body" (p. 22).

Through their focus on male powerlessness, the conservative and mytho-poetic branches of the men's movement fail to help men change. There is no place for gender justice within Masculine Renewal because religious conservatives do not recognize the basic right of women and gay men to organize collectively for social equality, Mythopoetic essentialism also prob-lematizes women. First, by arguing that destructive masculinity is related to an undiscovered universal male nature, mythopoetics evade historical re-sponsibility for patriarchal social structures that privilege men. While pro-moting the "warrior" archetype, Moore blames the arms race on "a lot of emotionally and spiritually immature boys living in grown-up men's bodies (p. 113). Others attempt to distinguish negative "masculine energy" from authentic masculinity which will usher in "a postpatriarchal era" (Trippe, p. 118). Second, the individualistic essentialist perspective undermines ac-countability to the women's movement since only men are able to discover their true masculine nature. Women have nothing men need because "a men's movement is about men" (Dittes, p. 589).

Perhaps most ominous are demands for purges of feminists in social and educational institutions—beginning with the church. In Arnold's attack on Christian feminists, traces of antisemitism are evident as he rallies men to battle: "Males need to know when someone is poisoning their wells, whether in the media, at school, or at work" (p. 63). Masculine Renewal has also spread its net in the moderate waters of mainstream Christian evangelism. Charles Colson writes in Billy Graham's *Christianity Today* that feminists are undermining American society: "The fundamental pillar of our society, the family, has been under assault for years, and its crumbling has long been of vital concern to Christians. But do not miss the progression. The artillery salvos are escalating against something even more fundamental: the very notion of what it means to be a man and what it means to be a woman" (p. 72).

Feminists have evaluated reactionary elements in the men's movements with humor, suspicion, and alarm. Caputi and MacKenzie argue that the mythopoetic "movement for liberation is actually a manifestation of an au-thoritarian backlash and joins the political and religious right" in opposition to the women's movement.[26] Moore attempts to deflect feminist critique of the men's movement by distinguishing between "mature" and "immature" forms of masculinity (p. 113). But Rosemary Radford Ruether finds that certain basic claims, such as male victimization, are absurd. She relates mythopoetic rhetoric to the hypothetical rise of a "white people's movement":

We are told that white people are deeply wounded by the lack of positive white role models, exacerbated by the 'vicious' criticism of white people that took place in the civil rights and the anti-apartheid movements. What is needed is to restore white people's confidence in whiteness as a manifestation of strong and positive psychic traits. Journeys to regions of pure white sands and skies are recommended in which white people, dressed in white sheets, can dance around a birch wood fire, brandishing symbols of white power . . . Perhaps David Duke might become the cultural hero of such a white men's movement.[27]

Religious feminists, like Ruether and Mary Daly, are under assault in the church for challenging traditional male images of God. Kreeft warns that Daly is attempting to castrate "God the Father" (p. 28). The attack against a "feminized" church, articulated in Masculine Renewal, has led to a state of crisis in several religious denominations. Participants at an international Christian feminist conference "found the use of Sophia as a name for God to be liberating." But the conference was "denounced as blasphemous" by conservatives who fear that "change in church teachings on sexuality or language about God are driven by contemporary political causes."[28]

The claim that men are oppressed, and, therefore, must unite to achieve liberation, cannot be effectively supported by appeals to Biblical authority. Moses and Jesus drew a sharp division between oppressed and oppressor; their lives demonstrate a downward movement from privilege to marginalization. Moses lived many years in the Egyptian court before he finally committed a single act of solidarity with the Hebrew slaves. He must have listened to their cries of anguish for many years before he acted; it was not easy to change. Jesus was unwilling to assist the Syrophoenician woman because he regarded her as inferior. Only after the woman humbled herself did Jesus modify his understanding of liberation. He also found it difficult to change. Moses and Jesus were blind to their own privilege and power until the cries of the oppressed penetrated the dominant consciousness that formed their identities as men. Their greatness lies in their capacity to respond to the oppressed. While it is difficult for men to change, Moses and Jesus demonstrate that personal and social transformation—even gender justice—is an historical possibility. Moses and Jesus learned, through their experiences of downfall and retreat, to identify with the weak and powerless. They put aside individual self-interest to work for the well-being of the whole community. Religious conservatives and mythopoetics have not yet confronted their own social privilege and power. Instead, they retreat to a place where the genuine voices of the oppressed are drummed into silence. In the mythopoetic scenario, Moses and Jesus would retreat into the wilderness merely to obtain self-awareness through ecstatic spiritual awakening—probably in a sweatlodge! Moses and Jesus pleaded with God not to compel them to leave their safe havens because they feared for their lives. Moses had a good life in the Midian desert raising goats. If he returned to help the Hebrew slaves, he faced death at the hands of Pharaoh. Jesus faced crucifixion by a Roman occupation army for assisting the poor and oppressed.

Middle-class, white men who discovered their "masculine energy" face no real danger. Their battle for men's souls is not an occasion for persecution but an opportunity to persecute. Moses and Jesus demonstrate the hazards and opportunities of risk-taking: their individual sacrifice brought forth collective liberation. Contemporary men have found change to be a laborious and painful process. They have found it easier to defend the old than risk the new. Masculine Renewal is a reactionary movement leading men down a path of confrontation with feminists, gays, and people of color in defense of men's privilege and power. The renunciation of power by a privileged social group requires a visionary spirit rooted in the Biblical mandates of service and justice. The lives of Moses and Jesus reveal compassion culminating in justice and justice rooted in compassion. Today, heterosexual white men must learn to put aside their masculine privilege and join together with women, gays, and men of color in the struggle for gender justice. The new man will be born when we discover our identity—not as leaders, but as servants.

NOTES

1. Robert Moore, "Helping Men Discover the Spirit Within," *The Catholic World* 235 (1992): 113.

2. Kenneth Clatterbaugh, *Contemporary Perspectives on Masculinity, Men, Women, and Politics in Modern Society* (Boulder, Colo.: Westview, 1990).

3. Michael S. Kimmel and Thomas E. Mosmiller, *Against the Tide: Pro-Feminist Men in the United States, 1776–1990* (Boston: Beacon, 1992), 9.

4. George E. Trippe, "Between the Wimp and the Rambo: Finding New Models in a Post-Patriarchal Age," *The Catholic World* 235 (1992): 120. See also William G. Thompson, "Men and the Gospels," *The Catholic World* 235 (1992): 105–10.

5. See also William J. O'Malley, "The Grail Quest: Male Spirituality," *America* 166 (1992): 402–6.

6. David Gates, "White Male Paranoia," *Newsweek* (29 March 1993): 48.

7. Robert Bly, *Iron John* (Reading, Mass.: Addison-Wesley, 1990).

8. Patrick Arnold, *Wildmen, Warriors, and Kings: Masculine Spirituality and the Bible* (New York: Crossroad, 1991), 19.

9. Peter Kreeft, "Gender and the Will of God," *Crisis* 11 (1993): 23.

10. Donna Steichen, "Are We All Feminists Now?" *Social Justice Review* 84 (1993): 13.

11. Charles Colson, "The Thomas Hearings and the New Gender Wars," *Christianity Today* 35 (1991): 72.

12. Leon Podles, "Masculinity and the Military: Love in the Trenches," *Crisis* 11 (1993): 20.

13. E. W. O'Brien, "Which is Witch?" *Crisis* 9 (1991): 47.

14. R. W. Connell, *Gender and Power* (Stanford: Stanford University, 1987), 52–53.

15. Michael S. Kimmel, "The Contemporary 'Crisis' of Masculinity in Historical Perspective," in *The Making of Masculinities: The New Men's Studies*, ed. Harry Brod (New York: Routledge, 1987), 143–49.

16. Beverly W. Harrison, *Making the Connections: Essays in Feminist Social Ethics*, ed. Carol S. Robb (Boston: Beacon, 1985), 5.

17. Michael Lerner, "Strategies for Healing and Repair," *Tikkun* (1994): 36–38.

18. See also James E. Dittes, "A Men's Movement for the Church?" *The Christian Century* 108 (1991): 590.

19. Leon J. Podles, "Men Not Wanted: A Controversial Protest against the Feminization of the Church," *Crisis* 9 (1991): 19.

20. Walter Wink, "The Myth of Redemptive Violence: Exposing the Roots of 'Might Makes Right,'" *Sojourners* 21 (1992): 35.

21. Elie Wiesel, *Messengers of God: Biblical Portraits and Legends* (New York: Summit, 1976), 202.

22. James B. Nelson, *Body Theology* (Louisville: Westminster, 1992), 109.

23. Stu Weber, *The Tender Warrior* (Sisters, Ore.: Multnomah, 1993).

24. Sherman Alexie, "White Men Can't Drum!" *The New York Times Magazine* (4 October 1992): 30.

25. Paul Schurman, "Male Liberation," *Pastoral Psychology* 35 (1987): 191.

26. Jane Caputi and Gordene O. MacKenzie, "Pumping Iron John," in *Women Respond to the Men's Movement*, ed. Kay Leigh Hagan (San Francisco: HarperCollins, 1992), 72.

27. Rosemary Radford Ruether, "Patriarchy and the Men's Movement: Part of the Problem or Part of the Solution?" in *Women Respond to the Men's Movement*, ed. Kay Leigh Hagan (San Francisco: HarperCollins, 1992), 16–17.

28. Peter Steinfels, "Presbyterians Try to Resolve Long Dispute," *The New York Times* (17 June 1994): A9.

Mythopoetic Men's Work as a Search for Communitas

MICHAEL SCHWALBE

IN THE LATE 1980S AND EARLY 1990S, the commercial media discovered the mythopoetic men's movement. Newspapers, magazines, and television reported that thousands of middle-aged, middle-class white men were retreating to rustic settings to share their feelings, to cry, hug, drum, dance, tell poems and fairy tales, and enact primitive rituals. The men were supposedly trying to get in touch with the inner "wildman" and other masculine archetypes, as urged by movement leader Robert Bly, a famous poet and author of the 1991 bestseller *Iron John*.[1] Mythopoetic activity was covered because it was offbeat and so, not surprisingly, most stories played up its odd trappings. The serious side of the movement—its implicit critique of men's lives in American society—was not examined.

While most observers thought mythopoetic activity was harmless and silly, others saw it as dangerous. Feminist critics accused Bly and the mythopoetic men of nefarious doings at their all-male retreats: whining about men's relatively minor psychological troubles while ignoring the much greater oppression of other groups, especially women; "modernizing" rather than truly changing masculinity; retreating from tough political realities into boyish play; unfairly blaming mothers and wives for men's troubles; and reproducing sexism by using fairy tales and rituals from patriarchal cultures. Critics thus saw the mythopoetic movement as part of an anti-feminist backlash or as a New Age maneuver in the battle of the sexes.[2]

Much of the criticism of the movement was based on the same superficial stories fed to the public. More responsible critics at least read Bly's book, saw his 1990 PBS interview ("A Gathering of Men") with Bill Moyers, attended a retreat, or read other pieces of mythopoetic literature.[3] Even so, almost none of the criticism was based on firsthand knowledge of what the men involved in mythopoetic activity were thinking, feeling, and doing together. The men themselves either disappeared behind the inflated image of Bly, or critics presumed that there was no need to distinguish them from Bly. But while Bly was indeed the chief public figure of the movement and a main source of its philosophy, mythopoetic activity or, as the men themselves called it, "mythopoetic men's work," was much more than Robert Bly.

In the fall of 1990, before Bly's *Iron John* raised the visibility of the mythopoetic movement, I began a participant-observation study of a group of men, associated with a local men's center, who were engaged in mythopoetic activity. I wanted to find out how the men began doing "men's work" and how it was affecting them. I was especially interested in how it affected the meanings they gave to their identities as men. So from September 1990 to June 1993, I attended 128 meetings of various kinds; observed and participated in all manner of mythopoetic activities; attended events led by the movement's prominent teachers; read the movement's major texts and many smaller publications; and interviewed 21 of the local men at length. The full account of my study appears elsewhere.[4]

Two points may aid understanding of the mythopoetic men. One is that, while they held Robert Bly in high esteem, they did not see him as an infallible guru. Most of the men knew that Bly could be obnoxious, that he tended to exaggerate, and that he liked to be the center of attention. It would be fair to say that the men saw him as wise, entertaining, charismatic, and challenging—but hardly without fault. Many of the men had equally high regard for other teachers in the mythopoetic movement, especially the Jungian psychologist James Hillman and the drumming storyteller Michael Meade. Even so, the mythopoetic men were wary of leaders and did not want to be dependent on them. They believed that men could and should learn to do men's work on their own.

The second point is that many of the men rejected the label "movement" for what they were doing, since to them this implied central organization, the imposition of a doctrine, and political goals. It's true that mythopoetic activity was not centrally coordinated, overtly oriented to political goals, or restricted to those who swore allegiance to a particular set of beliefs. There was, however, an underlying philosophy (derived in large part from Jungian psychology), a circuit-riding group of teachers, a body of inspirational literature, nationally circulated publications, and many similarities of practice among the mythopoetic men's groups that had sprung up around the country. So to add this up and call it a movement is a legitimate convenience.

Many of the men also shared certain goals which they sought to achieve through mythopoetic work. As individuals they sought the therapeutic goals of self-acceptance, greater self-confidence, and better knowledge of themselves as emotional beings. As a group they sought to revalue 'man' as a moral identity; that is, they collectively sought to define 'man' as an identity that implied positive moral qualities. Identity work of this kind, which was partly a response to feminist criticism of men's behavior, was accomplished through talk at gatherings and through the movement's literature. Much of what the men sought to accomplish thus had to do with their feelings about themselves as men.

It's important to see, however, that mythopoetic men's work was not just about sharing feelings, as if the men knew what they were feeling and then met to talk about it. Things were not so simple. Often the work itself aroused feelings that surprised the men. And these feelings were not always pleasant. But even unpleasant feelings were resources for fashioning a special kind of collective experience. It was this experience, which the anthropologist Victor Turner calls "communitas," that the men sought to create at their gatherings. This was a rare and seductive experience for men in a highly bureaucratized society such as ours.

COMMUNITY AND COMMUNITAS

Most of the mythopoetic men were between the ages of 35 and 60. Nearly all were white, self-identified as heterosexual, and college educated. Most had good jobs, owned homes, and helped maintain families. They were, by and large, successful in conventional middle-class terms. Yet the men said that living out this conventional script had left them, at midlife, feeling empty and dissatisfied. They found that the external trappings of success were not spiritually fulfilling. What's more, many of the men felt isolated, cut off from other men, except for competitive contexts, such as the workplace. Hence many described mythopoetic activity as part of an effort to create a community where they could interact with other men in a supportive, non-competitive way.

But it was not exactly community that these men created through mythopoetic work. Although they sometimes established serious friendships and networks of support, the men did not enter into relations of material dependence upon each other, live in close proximity to each other, work together, or interact on a daily basis. The men who met at gatherings and in support groups usually went home to their separate lives. Thus, strictly speaking, it was not a true community they created. What the mythopoetic men sought, and tried to create at their gatherings, was both more and less than community. It was communitas.

Victor Turner, an anthropologist who studied tribal rituals, describes communitas as both a shared feeling-state and a way of relating. To create communitas people must relate to each other outside the constraints of formally defined roles and statuses. As Turner describes it:

> Essentially, communitas is a relationship between concrete, historical, idiosyncratic individuals. These individuals are not segmentalized into roles and statuses but confront one another rather in the manner of Martin Buber's 'I and Thou'. Along with this direct, immediate, and total confirmation of human identities, there tends to go a model of society as a homogeneous, unstructured communitas, whose boundaries are ideally coterminous with those of the human species.[5]

Communitas, as Turner says, can happen when the force of roles and statuses is suspended; that is, when individuals in a group feel themselves to be equals and there are no other significant differences to impede feelings of communality. Although the mythopoetic men did not use the term communitas, they sought to relate to each other in the way that Turner describes as characteristic of communitas. At gatherings they tried to engage each other in a way that was unmediated by the roles they played in their everyday work lives. The men tried to practice this kind of relating by talking about the feelings they had which they believed arose out of their common experiences as men.

Turner distinguishes three types of communitas: normative, ideological, and spontaneous or existential. Of these, it is spontaneous or existential communitas that the mythopoetic men sought to create. Turner says that spontaneous communitas is "richly charged with affects, mainly pleasurable ones," that it "has something 'magical' about it," and that in it there is "the feeling of endless power."[6] He compares hippies and tribesmen in a passage that could also apply to the mythopoetic men:

> The kind of communitas desired by tribesmen in their rites and by hippies in their 'happenings' is not the pleasurable and effortless comradeship that can arise between friends, coworkers, or professional colleagues any day. What they seek is a transformative experience that goes to the root of each person's being and finds in that root something profoundly communal and shared.[7]

There are several ways in which Turner's description of spontaneous communitas fits mythopoetic activity. First, the men sought personal growth through their experiences of "connection," as they called it, at mythopoetic gatherings. A connection was a feeling of emotional communion with another man or group of men. Such connections were made when a story, poem, dance, ritual, or psychodramatic enactment brought up strong feelings in one or more men, and this in turn induced emotional responses in others. In these moments the men learned about their own complexity as emotional beings. The changes they sought were greater awareness of their feelings, more clarity about them, and better ability to use those feelings constructively.

The mythopoetic men also presumed it was possible to establish deep emotional connections with each other because they were all, at root, men. This presumption grew out of the Jungian psychology that informed mythopoetic activity. The idea was that all men possessed the same set of masculine archetypes that predisposed them to think, feel, and act in similar ways.[8] In Jungian terms, these masculine archetypes are parts of the collective unconscious, to which we are all linked by our common humanity. Thus all men, simply by virtue of being male, were presumed to possess similar masculine energies and masculine ways of feeling. Mythopoetic activities were aimed at bringing out or tapping into these energies and feelings so that men could connect based on them and thereby mutually reinvigorate themselves.

Turner's references to pleasurable affects and mysterious feelings of power are echoed in how the mythopoetic men described their experiences. Mythopoetic activity was enjoyable, the men said, because "It's just being with men in a way that's very deep and powerful"; "There's a tremendous energy that grows out of men getting together and connecting emotionally"; and "It just feels great to be there connecting with other men in a noncompetitive way." And indeed the feelings were often intense. As one man said during a talking circle at the end of a weekend retreat, "I feel there's so much love in this room right now it hurts." Men also said that going back to their ordinary lives after a gathering meant "coming down from an emotional high." I, too, experienced this transition from the warm, open, supportive, emotionally-charged atmosphere of a gathering to the relatively chilly atmosphere of a large research university.

The success of a gathering was measured by the intensity of the emotion it evoked and the connections thereby established. A less successful gathering was one where the emotional intensity was low and the men did not make strong connections. At a small two-day gathering, one man commented somewhat sadly, "We've had some good sharing, but only once did I feel much happening to me. That was when B. was talking. I felt tears welling up. So there's a deeper level we could get to." This was said at the start of the final talking circle, in hopes of prompting a more emotional discussion before the gathering was over. In addition to showing the desire for communitas, this statement also shows that it took effort to achieve. Spontaneous communitas did not happen spontaneously.

CREATING SPONTANEOUS COMMUNITAS

Mythopoetic men's work was in large part the conversation work required to create spontaneous communitas. I'll explain here how this work was done, through talk and other means. It should be understood that not all gatherings were aimed as intently at creating the same degree of communitas. Some gatherings were more "heady," in that they were devoted to discussion of a topic, such as fathering or men's health or men's friendships. Often there were moments of communitas at these kinds of meetings; but it was at the retreats—those which had an explicit mythopoetic or "inner work" theme— where the greatest efforts were made to produce communitas. Talk, ritual, and drumming were the chief means for doing this.

Forms of Talk

At mythopoetic gatherings men often made personal statements that revealed something shameful, tragic, or emotionally disturbing about their lives. Such statements might be made by each man in turn at the beginning of a retreat, as part of saying why he was there, what he was feeling, and what he hoped to accomplish at the retreat. Before any statements were made, the leader of the retreat or gathering would remind the men of the rules to follow in making statements: speak briefly, speak from the heart (i.e., focus on feelings), and speak to the other men—who were supposed to listen intently, make no judgments, and give no advice. The idea was that the statements should bring the unrehearsed truth up from a man's gut, since this would stir feelings in him and move other men to speak their "belly truth."

A great deal of feeling was stirred up as men talked about troubled relationships with fathers; being sexually abused as children; struggling to overcome addictions; repressed anger over past hurts and betrayals; grief and sadness over irreplaceable losses; efforts to be better fathers to their children. When men choked up, wept, shook with fear, or raged as they spoke it induced strong feelings in other men in the group. At one gathering a man, after hearing several moving personal statements, said to the group as a whole, "Your stories give me life. They make me feel more alive."

The sequence in which personal statements were made amplified this effect. Men would often begin their remarks by saying, "What that [the previous statement] brings up for me is . . . ," or "I really identify with what _____ said, because . . ." The more disclosing, expressive, and moving a man's statement, the more likely it was to evoke from the other men heavy sighs, sympathetic "mmmms," or a loud chorus of "Ho!" (supposedly a Native American way of affirming that a man's statement has been heard and felt). If a statement seemed inauthentic or insufficiently revealing it might evoke little or no reaction. The men thus reinforced a norm of making risky, revealing, and evocative statements.

The men were thus not only sharing feelings but, by virtue of how they talked, knitting those feelings together into a group mood. In this way they were also creating communitas. It is important, too, that the settings in which these statements were made were defined as "safe," meaning that, by agreement, the men were not there to compete with or judge each other, but to listen and provide support. Even so, there was an element of risk and a degree of anxiety associated with making personal statements, since the mythopoetic men, like most men in American society, were unused to sharing feelings of hurt and vulnerability with other men. This anxiety aided the achievement of communitas because it created a higher-than-usual level of emotional arousal to begin with. It also allowed the men immediately to identify with one another over being anxious. As Turner likewise noted: "danger is one of the chief ingredients in the production of spontaneous communitas."[9]

In making personal statements, and in their general conversation at gatherings, the men could not help but refer to people, events, and circumstances outside themselves that evoked the feelings they had. In doing this, the men were careful to add to their statements the disclaimer "for me," as in "For *me*, the Gulf War was very depressing." This disclaimer signified that the man speaking was talking about *his* feelings based on *his* perceptions of things, and he was making no presumptions about how other men should feel. The use of this disclaimer helped the men maintain the fellow-feeling they sought by avoiding arguments about what was true of the external world. The mythopoetic men wanted their feelings validated, not challenged. As long as each man spoke the truth from his heart, no one could say he was wrong.

Talk about fathers was another way the men achieved communitas. It worked because almost every man had a father to talk about, and those few who didn't could talk about not having fathers. So every man could participate. Father talk also worked because it brought up feelings of sadness and anger for many of the men, and thus created the necessary emotional charge. Because many of the men experienced their fathers as physically or emotionally absent, or in some way abusive, the men could identify with each other based on these common experiences. Father talk may have helped them to reach insights about their relationships to their fathers. But father talk went on to the extent it did because it was so useful for creating communitas.

Poems and fairy tales were also a staple part of mythopoetic activity.[10] Most of the time no commentary or discussion followed the reading or reciting of a poem. The men would just steep in the feelings the poems evoked. An especially stirring poem, like a moving personal statement, would elicit deep sighs, "mmmmm," "yeah," sometimes "Ho!", and often calls for the reader to "read it again!" And as with the personal statements, these responses, which were signs of shared feelings, served to turn the individual feelings into a collective mood, and thus helped to create communitas. When fairy tales were told there usually was commentary and discussion, in a form that also encouraged communitas.

When a story was told the storyteller would usually instruct the men to look for an image that evoked strong feelings. That image, it was said, would be a man's "doorway into the story"—his way of discovering what the story could tell him about his life as a man. This is consistent with Turner's observation that the "concrete, personal, imagist mode of thinking is highly characteristic of those in love with existential [or spontaneous] communitas, with the direct relation between man and man, and man and nature. Abstractions appear as hostile to live contact."[11] In the case of the mythopoetics, the emphasis on specific images grew out of Jungian psychology, according to which the psyche was best explored by working with emotionally evocative images.

After a story or part of a story was told, men would talk about the images that struck them and the feelings these images evoked. In a large group of men many different images might be mentioned. Sometimes men reacted strongly to the same image. Talking about the stories in this way created more chances for men to express feelings and to find that they shared feelings and experiences with other men. This was in part how feelings of isolation were overcome and connections were made. Again, the stories may have helped the men to better understand their lives. But it was *how* the stories were talked about that helped the men to experience the good feelings and mysterious power of communitas.

Ritual

Ritual is different from routine. Routine is the repetition of a behavioral pattern, like brushing one's teeth every night before bed. Ritual involves the symbolic enactment of values, beliefs, or feelings. It is a way of making external, visible, and public things that are normally internal, invisible, and private. By doing this, members of a community create a shared reality, reaffirm their common embrace of certain beliefs and values, and thereby keep the community alive. Ritual can also be a way of acknowledging changes in community members or of actually inducing such changes. The mythopoetic men used ritual for the same purposes: to call up, express, and share their otherwise private feelings, and to make changes in themselves.

Not all gatherings were ritual gatherings, though most included some ritual elements. Those gatherings where an explicit attempt was made to create "ritual space" or "sacred space" usually began with a symbolic act of separation from the ordinary world. For example, sometimes men would dip their hands into a large bowl of water to symbolize a washing off of concerns and distractions linked to the outside world. Other times at the outset of gatherings the "spirits of the four directions" (and sometimes of the earth and sky, too) would be invoked and asked to bring the men strength and wisdom. Still other times the men would dance their way into the space where the meeting was to be held, while the men already inside drummed and chanted. The point was to perform some collective act to mark a boundary between outside life and the ritual space.

The scene of a gathering also had to be properly set. Ritual gatherings were often held at rustic lodges where various objects—candles, bird feathers, masks, antlers, strangely shaped driftwood, animal skulls—might be set up around the main meeting area. Sage was often burned (a practice called "smudging") to make the air pungent and to cleanse the ritual space for the action that was going to take place. Usually the leader or leaders of the gathering made sure these things were done. Again, the idea was to heighten the sense of separation from ordinary reality, to make the physical space where the gatherings would take place seem special, and to draw the men together. This preparation was talked about in terms of "creating a container" that could safely hold the psychic energies about to be unleashed.

The separation from ordinary reality also helped the men let go of the concerns for status and power that influenced their interactions with other men in everyday life. In the ritual space the men were supposed to be "present for each other" in a direct and immediate way, as equals, as "brothers," and not as inferiors and superiors. Defining the situation as one in which feelings and other psychic matters were the proper focus of attention and activity helped to create and sustain this sense of equality. Thus the men seldom talked about their jobs, except to describe job-related troubles (and sometimes triumphs) in general terms. Too much talk about occupations would have introduced status concerns which in turn would have corroded the sense of equality and brotherhood that fostered feelings of communitas.

Two examples can help show more concretely how the mythopoetic men used ritual to create communitas. One example is from a six-day gathering of about 120 men in a remote rural setting. At this gathering the men were divided into three clans: Trout, Ravens, and Lions. During the week each clan worked with a dance teacher to develop a dance of its own, a dance that would symbolize the spirit of the men in the clan. At the carnivale on the last night of the gathering, each clan was to share its dance with the rest of the men. One clan would drum while another danced and the third clan "witnessed."

The carnivale was held in a large, dimly lit lodge built of rough cut logs. Many of the men wore the wildly decorated masks they had made earlier in the week. When their turn came, the 40 men in the Trout clan moved to the center of the room and formed a circle. The men stood for a few moments and then hunched down, extended their arms with their hands together in front of them, and began to dip and sway like fish swimming. Then half the men began moving to their right and half to their left, creating two flowing, interweaving circles. The Trout men also carried small stones, which they clicked together as they moved. About 30 men drummed as the Trout men danced. The rest of the men watched.

After a while the Trout men stopped and stood again, holding hands in a circle inside the larger circle of witnesses. They began a sweet and mournful African chant that they said was used to honor the passing away of loved ones. One by one each of the Trout men moved to the center of their circle and put down the stones he was carrying. As he did so, he called out the name of a person or people whose passing he wished to honor. Another of the Trout men walked along the row of men standing in the outer ring and said, "We invite you to join us by putting a stone in the center of the circle to honor your dead." The drumming and chanting continued all the while.

At first a few, then more and more of the Raven and Lion men stepped outside to get stones. Each man as he returned went to the center of the circle, called the name of the dead he was honoring, put down a stone, and then stepped back. There was sadness in the men's voices as they spoke. This lent gravity to their acts and drew everyone into the ritual. By now all the men had picked up the chant and joined hands in one large circle. The sound filled the lodge. After about 20 minutes the chanting reached a lull— and then one man began to sing "Amazing Grace." Soon all the men joined in and again their voices rose in chorus and filled the lodge. When we finished singing we stood silent, looking at all the stones between us.

This example shows how a great deal of work went into creating spontaneous communitas. The dance was carefully choreographed and the stage was elaborately set (one could say that the five days leading up to the carnivale were part of the stage setting). But later I talked to Trout men who said that they had planned the dance only up to the point of asking the other men to honor their dead. They were surprised by what happened after that, by how quickly and powerfully the other men were drawn in. No one had expected the surge of emotion and fellow-feeling that the ritual induced, especially when the men began to sing "Amazing Grace." Several men I talked to later cited this ritual as one of the most moving experiences they had had at a mythopoetic gathering.

Another example comes from a sweat lodge ritual modeled on a traditional Native American practice.[12] In this case the lodge was tiny, consisting of a framework of saplings, held together with twine, upon which were draped several layers of old blankets and tarps. Before the frame was built a fire pit was dug in the center of the spot on which the lodge stood. Although a lodge could be made bigger, here it was about ten feet in diameter and four feet high—big enough for a dozen men to squeeze in. From the outside it looked like a miniature domed stadium.

It was a drizzly 45-degree morning on the second day of a teacher-led weekend retreat. I was in the second group of 12 men who would go into the lodge together. This was the first "sweat" for all of us. The men in this group were almost giddy as we walked from the cabins to the shore of a small lake where the sweat lodge had been built. When we got there the men from the previous group had just finished.

The scene stopped us abruptly. Next to the lodge a large rock-rimmed fire was burning. A fierce, black-haired man with a beard stood by the fire, a five-foot staff in his hand. Some of the men who had just finished their sweat were standing waist-deep in the lake. Others were on shore hugging, their naked bodies still steaming in the cool air. Our moment of stunned silence ended when the leader of the retreat said to us, matter of factly, "Get undressed, stay quiet, keep your humility." We undressed and stashed our clothes under the nearby pine trees, out of the rain.

Before we entered the lodge the teacher urged us to reflect on the specialness of the occasion and to approach it with seriousness. Upon entering the lodge through a small entry flap each man was to say, "all my relations," to remind himself of his connections to the earth, to his ancestors, and to the other men. Once we were inside, the teacher called for the fire tender to bring us fresh, red-hot rocks. As each rock was placed by shovel into the fire pit, we said in unison, "welcome grandfather," again as symbolic acknowledgement of our connection to the earth. Now the teacher burned sage on the rocks to scent the air. When he poured water on the rocks the lodge became a sauna. The space was tightly packed, lit only by the glow of the rocks, and very hot. We were to do three sessions of ten to fifteen minutes each. Because of the intensity of the heat, a few men could not do all three sessions.

During one of the sessions the teacher urged us to call upon the spirits of our ancestors from whom we wanted blessings. In the cacophony of voices it was hard to make out what was being said. Some men were calling the names of people not present. A few were doing what sounded like a Native American Indian chant learned from the movies. The man on my right was gobbling like a turkey. At first this all struck me as ridiculous. I looked around the lodge for signs of similar bemusement in other men's faces. Surely they couldn't be taking this seriously. But those whose faces I could see appeared absorbed in the experience. Some men seemed oddly distant, as if they were engaged in a conversation going on elsewhere.

Although I was still put off by the bogus chanting and baffled by the gobbling, I too began to feel drawn in. I found myself wanting to suspend disbelief and find some meaning in the ritual, no matter how culturally foreign it was. In large part this was because the teacher and the other men seemed to be taking it seriously. I certainly didn't want to ruin the experience for them by showing any sign of cynicism. These were men who had taken my feelings seriously during the retreat. I felt I owed them the same consideration in the sweat lodge.

In both examples, a carefully crafted set of appearances made communitas likely to happen. The physical props, the words and actions of the ritual leaders, and the sincere words and actions of some men evoked real feelings in others and drew them in.[13] Because it seemed that there were genuine emotions at stake, it would have taken a hard heart to show any sign of cynicism during the Trout dance or the sweat lodge. To do so would have risked hurting other men's feelings and dimming the glow of communitas. It would also have cut the cynic himself off from the good feelings and mysterious power being generated by these occasions. Whether or not everyone "really believed" in what was happening didn't matter. Appearances made it seem so, and to achieve the communitas they desired, all the men needed to do was to act on these appearances.

Another dynamic was at work in the case of the sweat lodge. On the face of it, the idea of late 20th-century white men enacting a Native American sweat lodge ritual was absurd. And for most of these men, the idea of squatting naked, haunch to haunch, with other men would have been—within an everyday frame of reference—embarrassing and threatening to their identities as heterosexuals. Thus to avoid feeling ridiculous, threatened, or embarrassed the men had to stay focused on the form of the ritual and show no sign of doubting its content or propriety. Because there was such a gap between their everyday frame of reference and the ritual, the men had to exaggerate their absorption in the ritual reality just to keep a grip on it. In so doing the men truly did create a common focus and, again, the appearance that a serious, collective spiritual activity was going on.

The sweat lodge example also illustrated how the creation of communitas was aided by literally stripping men of signs of their differences. In the sweat lodge, men were only men—as symbolized by their nakedness. They were thus also equals. When a small group of us spoke afterwards about the experience, one man said, "The closeness and physicality, and especially being naked, are what make it work. Everyone is just a man in there. You can't wear any merit badges."

Drumming

Next to Bly, the most widely recognized icon of the mythopoetic movement was the drum. Drumming was indeed an important part of mythopoetic activity. Some mythopoetic groups held gatherings just to drum, although the group I studied was more likely to mix drumming with other activities. Not all of the men drummed. A few didn't care for it; others preferred to use rattles or tambourines during drumming sessions. The most enthusiastic men had congas, African-styled djembes, or hand-held shaman's drums, though all manner of large and small folk drums appeared at gatherings. On one occasion a man used a five-gallon plastic pail turned upside down.

Why did the mythopoetic men drum? Some of the men in the local group said that they began drumming after a visit by Michael Meade, a prominent teacher in the mythopoetic movement, who was skilled at using drumming to accompany his telling of folk tales. This is what inspired one man I interviewed:

> Bly came and told his "Iron John" story and that was my first introduction to using stories as a way of illuminating dilemmas or emotional situations in your life. Michael Meade came the following year in the spring and introduced some drumming at that weekend. I just loved the energy of that right away. It just really opened me up. After drumming I felt wonderful. I liked the feeling of it and felt a connection with the mythopoetic ever since then, more to the drumming than to anything else.

But on only a few occasions did any of the local men use drumming as accompaniment to story telling. Most of the drumming was done in groups, which varied in size from six to forty. And while the men who were better drummers might lead the group into a complex rhythm, often something samba-like, the drumming was usually freeform, leaderless, and simple.

The appeal of this activity had little to do with acquiring virtuosity at drumming. Rather, much of the appeal stemmed from the fact that the men could be bad drummers and still participate. It was, most importantly, another means to achieve communitas. Victor Turner notes that simple musical instruments are often used this way: "It is . . . fascinating to consider how expressions of communitas are culturally linked with simple wind instruments (flutes and harmonicas). Perhaps, in addition to their ready portability, it is their capacity to convey in music the quality of spontaneous human communitas that is responsible for this."[14] This was equally true of drums, which were also readily portable and required even less skill to play.

What the mythopoetic men say about their experiences drumming tells much about not only drumming, but about the communitas it helped create and about the mythopoetic experience in general. In an interview another man, a 48-year-old salesman, spoke of drumming as both ordinary and special at the same time:

> You can kind of lose yourself in it. It's like any hobby—fishing or playing ball or whatever. There is something that happens. You go into an altered state almost, hearing that music. At this national meeting in Minnesota a month ago the common thing was the drums. You could hear the beating of that drum. At break people would drum and we would dance. So it's this common bond.

Put another way, drumming was an activity that gave men who were strangers a way to quickly feel comfortable and familiar with each other. Some of the mythopoetic men believed that men in general had a special facility for connecting with each other via non-verbal means. The way that men were able to quickly bond via drumming was seen as evidence of this.

Although the men were aware that drumming was not an activity limited to men, some clearly felt that it held a special appeal for them. Another man, a 33-year-old technical writer, said in an interview:

> Drumming does something—connects me with men in ways that I can't understand, in the same way I've observed women who have babies connecting with each other. There's something in it that I don't participate in emotionally. In the same way, the drumming—society with other men—is emotionally important to men in ways that women don't understand. They can't.

Some of the mythopoetic men's ideas about gender are evident in this statement. Many of them believed that women, no matter how empathic they might be, could not know what it was like to be a man, just as men could not know what it was like to be a woman. Hence men needed the understanding and support that could come only from other men, just as women needed the same things from other women.

For other men drumming was both a communal and, sometimes, a personal, spiritual experience. In an interview a 42-year-old therapist told me:

> There was one point where I was really deeply entranced just drumming and then all of a sudden I had this real powerful experience where I felt like I was on a hill, on some mountainside or some mountaintop, in some land far far away, in some time that was all time. And I was in the middle of all my men, who were my brothers, who were all men. It was one of those powerful mystical experiences where all of a sudden I felt planted in the community of men. And that changed my life, because I felt like I was a man among men in the community of men and we were drumming and the drum was in my bones and it was in my heartbeat and it was good.

This statement captures in spirit, tone, and rhythm the experience that many of the men found in drumming. Even if they didn't report such flights of imagination, others said that drumming provided a similar sense of communality, of connection, which I have been calling communitas.

My own experience corroborates this. I found that when I could pick up a beat and help sustain it without thinking, the sense of being part of the group was strong. It was as if the sound testified to the reality of the group and the rhythm testified to our connection. By drumming in synch each man attached himself to the group and to the other men in it. The men valued this also because the attachment was created by physical action rather than by talk, and because it seemed to happen at a non-rational level. Drumming thus helped the men do two other things that mythopoetic philosophy called for: getting out of their heads and into feeling their bodies; and bypassing the rational ego that kept a lid on the archetypal masculine energies the men sought to tap.

COMMUNITAS AND POLITICS

My point has been to show that much mythopoetic activity can be understood as a search for communitas. This experience was rare in these men's lives and precious on the occasions when it occurred. Sometimes the men talked about the activities at their gatherings as "inviting the sacred to happen." Particular forms of talk, the orchestration of ritual, and drumming were means to this end. Because communitas was so valuable to the men, there were also things they *avoided* doing to make communitas more likely to happen. One thing they avoided was serious talk about politics.

This is not to say that the men were apolitical. Most of the men I studied were well informed on social issues and supported progressive causes. They were also critical of the rapacious greed of big corporations, the duplicity and brutal militarism of Reagan and Bush, and the general oppressiveness of large bureaucracies. But there were two revealing ironies in the politics of the mythopoetic men. First, while they were critical of the behavior of corporations and government, they avoided saying that these institutions were run by men. Usually it was an unspecified, genderless "they" who were said to be responsible for destroying the environment or for turning all culture into mass marketable schlock. And second, while many of the men saw corporate power and greed as root problems in U.S. society, they were uninterested in collective action to address these problems. This is as one might expect, since the white, middle-class mythopoetic men did not do so badly in reaping the material benefits of the economic system they occasionally criticized.

In other words, the men were selectively apolitical. They did not want to see that it was other *men* who were responsible for many of the social problems they witnessed and were sometimes affected by. To do so, and to talk about it, would have shattered the illusion of universal brotherhood among men that helped sustain feelings of communitas. Talk about power, politics, and inequality in the external world was incompatible with the search for communitas, because it would have led to arguments, or at least to intellectual discussions, rather than to warm emotional communion. When discussions at mythopoetic gatherings inadvertently turned political, disagreements surfaced, and tensions arose, someone would usually say, "We're getting away from the important work here." Or as one man said in trying to stop a conversation that was becoming an argument, "I think we're losing the power of the drums."

The mythopoetic men believed that engaging in political or sociological analysis would have led them away from their goals of self-acceptance, self-knowledge, emotional authenticity, and communitas. The men wanted to feel better about themselves as men, to learn about the feelings and psychic energies that churned within them, to live fuller and more authentic emotional lives, and to experience the pleasure and mysterious power of communitas. They did not want to compete over whose interpretation of social reality was correct. They wanted untroubled brotherhood in which their feelings were validated by other men, and in which their identities as men could be infused with new value.

Here can be seen both the power and limits of mythopoetic men's work. Through this work some men have begun to free themselves from the debilitating repression of emotion that was part of their socialization into traditional masculinity. Feminism provided the intellectual basis and political impetus for this critique of traditional masculinity, though the mythopoetics have difficulty appreciating this. Yet they deserve credit for developing a method that allows some men to explore and express more of the emotions that make them human. Mythopoetic men's work has also helped men to see how these emotions can be the basis for connections to men they might otherwise have feared, mistrusted, or felt compelled to compete with. And to the extent that men begin to see that they don't have to live out traditional masculinity, and can even cooperate to heal the damage it causes, mythopoetic men's work has progressive potential.

One problem is that the progressive potential of mythopoetic men's work is limited because it leads men to think about gender and gender inequality in psychological or, at best, cultural terms. Mythopoetic men's work may open men to seeing things in themselves, and help them make connections with each other, but it also blinds them to seeing important connections between themselves and society. For example, the mythopoetic men do not see that, in a male-supremacist society, there can be no innocent celebration of masculinity. In such a society the celebration of manhood and of masculinity—even if it is a supposedly "deep" or "authentic" and thus a more fully human version of masculinity—reaffirms the lesser value of women, whether this is intended or not. The therapeutic focus of mythopoetic men's work—as done by a largely homogeneous group of middle-class white males—also blinds them to matters of class inequality and to the exploitation of working-class people and people of color by the elite white *men* who run the economy.

Yet mythopoetic men's work is a form of resistance to domination. It's not just an entertaining form of group therapy, or collective whining over imagined wounds, or retrograde male bonding. These middle-class white men, who are not the ruling elites, are responding to the alienation and isolation that stem from living in a capitalist society that encourages people to be greedy, selfish, and predatory. Their goal of trying to awaken the human sensibilities that have been benumbed by an exploitive economy is subversive. But to get to the root of the problem men will have to do more than take modest risks among themselves to try to heal their psyches. They will have to take big risks in trying to abolish the race, class, and gender hierarchies that damage us all. They will have to learn to create communitas in struggles for justice.

NOTES

A slightly different version of this essay appears in M. Kimmel and M. Messner (Eds.), *Men's Lives*, third edition (Boston: Allyn and Bacon, 1995). It is an abbreviated version of a chapter from my book *Unlocking the Iron Cage: Understanding the Mythopoetic Men's Movement* (New York: Oxford, 1995).

1. Robert Bly, *Iron John: A Book About Men* (Reading, Mass.: Addison-Wesley, 1990).

2. See Kay Leigh Hagan, editor, *Women Respond to the Men's Movement* (San Francisco: HarperCollins, 1992); Kenneth Clatterbaugh, *Contemporary Perspectives on Masculinity* (Boulder, Colo.: Westview, 1990), pp. 85–103; Susan Faludi, *Backlash: The Undeclared War Against American Women* (New York: Crown, 1991), pp. 304–312; R. W. Connell, "Drumming Up the Wrong Tree," *Tikkun* 7, no. 1 (1992): 31–36; Sharon Doubiago, "Enemy of the Mother: A Feminist Response to the Men's Movement," *Ms.*, March/April (1992): 82–85; Fred Pelka, "Robert Bly and Iron John," *On the Issues*, Summer (1991): 17–19, 39; Diane Johnson, "Something for the Boys," *New York Review of Books*, January 16 (1992): 13–17.

3. For a sampling of other writings in the mythopoetic genre, see Robert Moore and Douglas Gillette, *King, Warrior, Magician, Lover: Rediscovering the Archetypes of the Mature Masculine* (New York: HarperCollins, 1990); Wayne Liebman, *Tending the Fire: The Ritual Men's Group* (St. Paul, Minn.: Ally, 1991); Christopher Harding, editor, *Wingspan: Inside the Men's Movement* (New York: St. Martin's, 1992).

4. Michael Schwalbe, *Unlocking the Iron Cage: Understanding the Mythopoetic Men's Movement* (New York: Oxford, 1995).

5. Victor Turner, *The Ritual Process* (Ithaca, N.Y.: Cornell, 1969), pp. 94–165.

6. Ibid., pp. 131–132.

7. Ibid., p. 139.

8. For an introduction to the basic concepts of Jungian psychology, see Calvin Hall and Vernon Nordby, *A Primer of Jungian Psychology* (New York: Penguin, 1973); or Frieda Fordham, *An Introduction to Jung's Psychology* (New York: Penguin, 1966). For more detail, see Edward C. Whitmont, *The Symbolic Quest* (Princeton, N.J.: Princeton, 1991).

9. Turner, p. 154.

10. Many of the poems frequently read at mythopoetic gatherings are collected in Robert Bly, James Hillman, and Michael Meade (eds.), *The Rag and Bone Shop of the Heart* (New York: HarperCollins, 1992). Many of the fairy tales told at gatherings, including Bly's "Iron John," originally known as "Iron Hans," are taken from the Grimm brothers' collection.

11. Turner, p. 141.

12. A description of the sweat lodge ritual can be found in Joseph Epes Brown (recorder and editor), *The Sacred Pipe: Black Elk's Account of the Seven Rites of the Oglala Sioux* (Norman, Okla.: University of Oklahoma, 1953), pp. 31–43. This account was a source of inspiration for some of the mythopoetic men. See also William K. Powers, *Oglala Religion* (Lincoln, Neb.: University of Nebraska, 1977).

13. Catherine Bell writes about how ritual "catches people up in its own terms" and provides a "resistant surface to casual disagreement." See Bell, *Ritual Theory, Ritual Practice* (New York: Oxford University Press, 1992), pp. 214–215. Other observers have noted how the improvised rituals at mythopoetic gatherings had this power to draw the men in. See Richard Gilbert, "Revisiting the Psychology of Men: Robert Bly and the Mytho-Poetic Movement," *Journal of Humanistic Psychology* 32 (1992): 41–67.

14. Turner, p. 165.

IV

THE PERSONAL IS PERSONAL: THE POLITICS OF THE MASCULINIST THERAPEUTIC

Homophobia in Robert Bly's *Iron John*

GORDON MURRAY

I WANT TO START WITH A STORY. I'm deep in a redwood forest on the Mendocino coast with a hundred men. Night has fallen. We take off our clothes by the light of stars. Men lift large smooth river rocks from a bonfire and put them in the pit of a small round sweat-lodge built of branches and tarps. Naked, 6 of us file into the pitch black lodge, close the door, sit in a tight circle, and begin to heat up. It is an unusual way for me to get to know a group of men. We name men who have mattered to us—we evoke their spirits, their memories, or the ways we have incorporated them into our lives. Men invite in fathers, grandfathers, sons, mentors, brothers, ancestors and gods. When it is my turn I close with ". . . and my lover Paul." The next day a man shared his reaction: "When you said 'my lover Paul' I felt an icy wind blow through me. I froze: the silence felt dangerous." Homophobia can be an unexpected icy wind.

This event took place during a week-long gathering of men led by Robert Bly, mentor of the "mythopoetic" men's movement. My story might be titled: "Mythopoetic Men Meet Gay Liberation." Bly's book *Iron John*[1] was the best selling non-fiction book of 1991; this branch of the men's movement is growing phenomenally, which thrills some of us and scares others. I want to share my mixed feelings about this book, and illustrate how this wing of our movement inappropriately protects itself from the unexpected icy winds of homophobia that I brought into that sweat lodge that night.

In his book, Bly retells the Grimm Brothers' fairy tale "Iron John" with commentary that casts the story as an initiation tale. He draws connections to traditional cultures, Greek myth, and contemporary dilemmas of the soul. At times I am moved to tears. When Bly describes how the Kikuyu men offer their blood in a bowl to nourish the initiate, he comments: "Can he have any doubt now that he is welcome among the other males?" I feel an empty, frightened place in me that has never been welcomed into the community of men in such a primal, unmistakable way, a part that still strives to belong.

This is Bly at his best. He is a poet, he writes beautifully, intuitively. I can see myself or men I know in lines such as these:

> men with an ideal father in their heads need to build an entire room for the father's twisted, secretive, destructive, vulgar, shadowy side . . . The son who always knew about his father's cruel and destructive side . . . needs to build a second room to house the generous and blessed side of his father.

> A man in guilt may decide to fail during the first half of his life. That's his punishment for not having saved his mother.

> A mentor can guide a young man . . . to build an emotional body capable of containing, more than one sort of ecstasy.

But there are gaping holes in Bly's book, and one is his discussion of homosexuality. Or rather, his lack of discussion. There are only three explicit references to homosexuality in the book. In one he refers to the threat of homosexual rape used to intimidate Michael J. Fox in a movie on Vietnam. (p. 85). In one he mentions that in the mythological garden, a man can fall in love with a woman, or with a man. (p. 133). The most extensive reference is in the preface, where he tries to account for his silence on the subject. "Most of the language in this book speaks to heterosexual men but does not exclude homosexual men." He goes on to explain that: "It wasn't until the eighteenth century that people ever used the term homosexual; before that time gay men were understood simply as a part of the large community of men. The mythology as I see it does not make a big distinction between homosexual and heterosexual men." (p. 10).

Now there has been a lively debate in the current gay cultural and historical renaissance about exactly this issue: whether homosexuality is something "real" and "essential" that transcends its historical manifestations, or, on the other hand, whether the homosexual/heterosexual distinction is socially constructed. In telling us that the term "homosexual" makes a distinction that's only a century old, Bly weighs in on the side of the social constructionists, but so does everyone else! Historian John Boswell points out that no one involved in this controversy identifies as an "essentialist," although constructionists accuse others of being that way.[2] Everyone agrees that whatever we denote by "homosexuality" manifests in other cultures and other times very differently. But this should be the starting place for exploring the homoerotic, not the end. To dismiss a discussion of everything homoerotic by claiming homosexuality is a social construction is intellectually irresponsible.

Let me give you some examples of what Bly leaves out, with the help of Christine Downing's *Myths and Mysteries of Same-Sex Love,*[3] and Bernard Sergent's *Homosexuality in Greek Myth.*[4] The Greek gods Bly refers to most often are Zeus, Apollo and Dionysius. Bly exhorts us to raise up Zeus energy, "which encompasses intelligence, robust health, compassionate decisiveness, good will, generous leadership." But he doesn't mention Ganymede, the beautiful young man Zeus brought to his side as, some say, an initiate. Plato describes how Zeus teaches Ganymede about love:

> The lover Zeus cannot contain all the love that flows into him, so some of it reenters the beloved, Ganymede, fills him with love. He feels a desire, like the lover's yet not so strong, to behold, to touch, to kiss him, to share his couch, and now ere long the desire, as one might guess, leads to the act.

Is this not a beautiful description of, to quote Bly, "a mentor guiding a young man . . . to build an emotional body capable of containing, more than one sort of ecstasy"?

Bly speaks of Apollo, a golden man who stands for wholeness, radiance, sun-like integrity, morality, perfection. And he mentions Hyacinthus, the uninitiated boy who dies in ritual sacrifice. But he doesn't tell us that they were lovers, that Apollo is, of all the Greek gods, the one who had the most male lovers, and that Apollo was infatuated with Hyacinthus, as Ovid says, "beyond all other mortals," and that Hyacinthus chooses Apollo from among his several suitors. Apollo is the paradigmatic lover and the model initiator who accidentally kills his beloved Hyacinthus while teaching him the arts of sports and hunting. Is this not a bittersweet description of the death of the boy in us, our sons and nephews, as we become men?

Bly speaks of Dionysus, born from the thigh of Zeus, eaten by the Titans, reconstructed from his heart which survived. Dionysus, says Bly, stands for the "ecstasy that can come from tearing and being torn, for the dark, alert, dangerous energy," which like Zeus and Apollo energy, he encourages us to evoke in ourselves. But why does he avoid telling us how Dionysus carves the branch of a fig tree to resemble a phallus, and sits on it to fulfill an erotic promise to the dead Prosymnus? Is not the homosexual intercourse in Dionysian rites the "ecstasy that can come from tearing and being torn?"

Bly speaks at length of tribal initiation rituals, particularly those in Paupua

New Guinea, where he finds living examples of his main thesis—which I find compelling and true-to-life—that men need a second birth, this time from men, not women. He tells us "men have lived together in heart unions and soul connections for hundreds of thousands of years." He tell us "A boy cannot change into a man without the active intervention of the older men." He goes so far as to tell us that "a substance almost like food passes from the older body to the younger . . . as the boy stands next to the father, as they repair arrowheads, or repair plows" and so forth.

What he doesn't tell us is that men have lived together not only in heart unions and soul connections, but sexual unions as well. What he doesn't tell us is that the "active intervention of the older men" often includes years of sexual partnership. What he doesn't tell us is that the "substance almost like food" that passes from the older body to the younger is often semen, passing not as the boy stands next to the older man, but as they engage in fellatio or anal sexual intercourse.

To give you some examples from Gilbert Herdt's *Ritualized Homosexuality in Melanesia*.[5] Many tribes believe that the ritual ingestion of semen is necessary to grow a boy into a man. Among the Marind-Anim tribe a stable relationship may arise between the boy and the older man, who call each other "anus father" and "anus son." When the boy is older he may marry his anus-father's daughter. In the Etoro tribe, the semen is drunk, and "a youth is continually inseminated from about age 10 until he reaches his early mid-twenties." The father of an 11- or 12-year-old boy in the Kaluli tribe picks an older man to engage in homosexual intercourse for several months, and they "point to the rapid growth . . . the appearance of peach fuzz on beards, and so on, as the favorable results of this child-rearing practice." Some anthropologists theorize that in taking the passive role in intercourse, the boy is "integrating a continuing feminine component into the masculine psyche," necessary to being a full man.

What are we to make of practices that we might call child abuse, but in other cultures are literal or symbolic descriptions of male initiation? If they were isolated instances from an exotic culture they would be intriguing enough, but what makes them compelling is the links that Sergent and others are beginning to explore between, for example, the initiations of ancient Crete, of ancient Greece, and of Melanesia before the missionaries arrived. Herdt points out that they pose a challenge to all of us interested in understanding the development of gender identity. Bly does us a service by dusting off and re-interpreting, the legacy of our own pre-industrial cultures but a disservice by his selective attention to that legacy.

Why does he pick and choose from the mythological and tribal data, excluding references to homosexuality? I think it's homophobia, a making-invisible, which goes something like: "It's OK to be gay, let's just not talk about it, let's just treat gays and lesbians like everyone else." This homophobia is seductive, for we gay people want to be treated like everyone else in many ways: in housing, jobs, healthcare, the right to serve in the military and have legally sanctioned domestic partnerships. But we also want our differences and unique perspective to be seen, and we, who are newly excited as we discover our hidden history across cultures and centuries, want to share the insights and riddles of those discoveries.

The two branches of the men's movement, the mythopoetic branch and the pro-feminist, gay-affirmative branch, are at a critical juncture in their relationship. Those of us in the pro-feminist, gay-affirmative branch must recognize the phenomenal growth of the mythopoetic movement and carefully ask ourselves "why?" What part is anti-feminist backlash and what part a healing voice that speaks to the wounds and needs of contemporary men? And what part of our response to this growth is envy, since no book on homosexuality or homophobia or feminist men has enjoyed the popular acclaim of *Iron John*? We need dialogue with the mythopoetic men not only for their insights, but to prevent a whole segment of men entering the men's movement indoctrinated in the homophobia of making-invisible.

The mythopoetic branch needs to move beyond the pretense that, since the word "homosexual" is only a hundred years old, that homoerotic relations are not part of the deep masculine. We need to acknowledge and examine our individual and collective homoerotic shadow. We need to recognize the astonishing prevalence of homoerotic behavior in conjunction with male initiations and male myths across cultures and history, if we are to do justice to that history and come to a full understanding of what it means to be a man today.

NOTES

1. Bly, Robert: *Iron John: A Book About Men*. Reading, Mass.: Addison-Wesley, 1990.

2. Boswell, John: "Revolutions, Universals and Sexual Categories," in Duberman, Vicinus & Chauncey, ed.: *Hidden From History: Reclaiming the Gay and Lesbian Past*. Meridian, 1990.

3. Downing, Christine: *Myths and Mysteries of Same-Sex Love*. New York: Continuum, 1989.

4. Sergent, Bernard: *Homosexuality in Greek Myth*. Boston: Beacon, 1984.

5. Herdt, Gilbert, ed.: *Ritualized Homosexuality in Melanesia*. Berkeley: University of California Press, 1984.

The Shadow of *Iron John*

PAUL WOLF-LIGHT

ROBERT BLY'S BOOK *Iron John* has cast a long shadow over contemporary ideas concerning men and masculinity and the practice and shape of 'Menswork' generally, whether therapeutic, antisexist etc. It clearly struck a chord in many men, particularly in the United States where it remained on the best sellers lists for over a year. In this country, although its influence seems to have been more peripheral there are few men involved in 'Menswork' who do not know of it.

At a time when the issues of men and masculinity seem to be becoming more prominent in the public sphere it feels appropriate to examine in more depth what is an important and seminal work. Structured around the Brothers' Grimm fairy story *Iron John*, the book offers a rich and poetic view of manhood and masculinity. It attempts to reconnect the sense of being a man with both Nature and modern civilisation, in doing so trying to offer alternatives to more 'macho' and destructive stereotypes of masculinity without losing what could be called the 'male soul'. Using parts of the *Iron John* story as metaphors for different stages of masculine development, Bly attempts to describe a process in which men can discover their maleness and mature as men without losing touch with their connection to the Earth and the historical and anthropological roots of masculinity. Yet although inspiring, illuminating and worthwhile in what it aspires to, it is also riddled with serious contradictions and flaws.

The very name *Iron John* conjures up the image of a dark and foreboding figure, armoured, inflexible and grim. As a symbol for the transformation of men away from the rational, rigid, unfeeling and destructive stereotypes of the past he seems grotesquely inappropriate. Yet the figure is clearly impor-

214 : PAUL WOLF-LIGHT

tant to Bly. So much so that the book is named after him rather than the Wild Man, with whom he appears interchangeable during the story as told by Bly.

I believe that many of the flaws and contradictions in the book emanate from the dark qualities contained in this figure, qualities that Bly does not appear to recognise. They appear to reflect his own disowned and unconscious shadow which emerges time and again throughout the narrative. This shadow seems much closer to the social and historical legacy of men and masculinity both in terms of values and behaviour. It is authoritarian and autocratic, impersonal, contemptuous and violent. In short, the very image of patriarchy. Bly, rather than attempting the more difficult task of integrating this shadow with the more human and intimate qualities that his idealised *Iron John* espouses, instead splits this dark side off and projects it onto the 'macho man' and the savage man. This enables him to subtly lay claim to those enormous benefits that we as men have derived from such behaviour, particularly in terms of power and material wealth, without having to own the darkness from which they have been derived.

What seems at first glance to be a deeply personal book becomes on closer examination strangely detached and impersonal. Bly's personal history and his own experiences of living through the developmental stages depicted in the story are fragmented and lacking depth. Much of the time he is talking about others or giving his interpretations. Although critical of others for sloppiness and lack of rigour, *Iron John* is no less guilty of confused and muddled thinking, lacking discipline and intellectual clarity. As a poetic vision, it offers flights of illumination for the soul, but when brought down to earth and examined more closely a darker shadow emerges.

To reveal this shadow more clearly I wish to examine six themes that occur throughout the book and seem central to Bly's work. These are the themes of fatherhood, initiation, mythology and fairy tales, the 'soft' man, politics and the warrior. I believe that all of these themes are important and Bly's acknowledgement and exploration of them is both a significant contribution and of value. Yet too often they are treated in rather too simple and idealistic a way, ignoring the darker depths that these themes also embrace.

The theme of fatherhood runs as a constant thread through *Iron John*, yet Bly's approach to it seems both reactionary and idealised. He appears to adhere to a model of parenting whereby the mother is initially responsible for child care, and then at a certain age, usually around puberty, the father has to separate the boy from his mother and become the main parent in terms of attachment. He gives many examples of this occurring in other cultures. The notion that a child can be brought up and be nourished and nurtured from birth by the mother and father together seems outside Bly's framework. The type of parenting both described and advocated in *Iron John* creates the very conditions of overattachment to mothers and distance from fathers that Bly recognises as problematic, yet he appears blind to this contradiction.

From my personal experience of having three children whose ages range from 3 to 18, I know that it is not only possible for both parents to bond equally with a young baby from birth, but that separation is then much less of an issue. By being attached to more than one parent the dependency on each becomes lessened. But sharing parenting means prioritising child care over work and ambition for a significant period of time, and this involves necessary sacrifice. A further consequence is that parental authority is shared between the parents and the father becomes less special and more ordinary. In particular it means being involved on a daily basis with all the anger and 'boundary pushing' that children are constantly directing towards those individuals who are responsible for restricting and caring for them.

The need for men to be involved with parenting from birth onwards, and to redefine the role of father to include being a parent and nurturer from the beginning, rather than merely being a protector and provider, is not one that Bly acknowledges. A significant number of men have been doing just this for many years now, yet *Iron John* reflects little of this. Instead the book harks back to an idealised time when mothers' and fathers' roles were segregated and separate, a time that allowed fathers to avoid the sacrifice of parenting and to maintain their position of detached authority within the family.

This idealisation and selective interpretation of the past is further reflected in Bly's approach to initiation, which is muddled and misleading. He fails to differentiate between two very different types of initiation, mixing them inappropriately to suit his arguments. The first of these types is what can be called collective gendered initiation, which consists of a formal and traditional ritual that each boy has to pass through. The function of this is to separate him from his mother and give him a collectively defined male identity. It takes no consideration of him as an individual, instead imposing a socially defined identity upon him that demands a conformity reflected in collective allegiance and obedience within a rigid gender role. In the book Bly shows a great deal of admiration for this form of initiation.

The second type of initiation is very different. This is best described as a shamanic initiation. It is not concerned with the socialising function of collective initiation but rather with the spiritual and psychological development of the individual. It requires an internal recognition from the initiate of his calling and the process is informed in considerable part by the initiate's own experiences including dreams and visions. The separation that takes place in such a process is not merely from his mother and family but from the very ground of his being, with the very real danger of becoming psychotic. Relatively few individuals have ever experienced this form of initiation and the guidance given was individual and spiritual rather than collective and political.

Bly's muddling of these two types allows him to claim that by going through a collective initiation men will become more independent individuals. In fact whilst it may result in them becoming independent of their mothers, they become in turn passive and dependent upon a collective approval based upon the prevailing cultural stereotypes of men. This is what appears to have happened in much of the part of the American men's movement that has derived from Bly. Here macho stereotypes and blatant misogyny revolve around the rallying call of mens rights and gender segregation. Although Bly openly disowns and condemns much of this, it is easy to see its roots in *Iron John*.

Bly's political naivety is further reflected in his attitude to myths and fairy tales. He claims that 'ancient stories are a good help because they are free of modern psychological prejudices.' Whether even this is true, he ignores the fact that they are steeped not only in the prejudices of the time they were originally written but also that they will have been subsequently coloured by those prejudices of the intervening years as they were passed down. The development that takes place in *Iron John* unfolds in a distinct social framework, reflecting the political values of the time in which it was set. These values included the subordination of women, slavery, racism, religious intolerance, a strict hierarchical structure built upon wealth and power, and the acceptance of violence as a means of obtaining what you wanted, particularly through warfare. The psychology of the story includes and reflects these values.

Unfortunately, by turning a blind eye to the historical framework and romanticising the stories, the prejudices become enshrined rather than recognised and challenged. If we wish to work with myths as reflecting deep psychological truths we must be fully aware of the political values that they are embedded in. We need to recognise their prejudice and incompleteness as guides as well as their richness and psychological depth.

This political naivety and some of Bly's attitudes towards women are revealed further when we examine his claim in *Iron John* that men today have become soft as a result of being too connected with their feminine side and that they therefore need to re-connect with their masculinity. Setting aside for the moment whether this is true or not, it is worth examining his definition of this feminine side of men. In *Iron John* this appears to be in the main defined as being passive, lacking vitality and being unable to be assertive, the masculine thus representing active, assertive vitality.

This representation in fact is not so much a description of masculine and feminine as a recapitulation of the stereotypical qualities socially assigned to men and women. These so called feminine qualities are those that women were, and to an unfortunate degree still are, supposed to identify with and embody in our culture. This expectation of women to be passive, unassertive and lacking in vitality has been part of the means by which they have been kept as subordinate to men, for by internalising these life denying qualities women become participants in the everyday reinforcement of their lack of equal status. By identifying these as feminine, Bly subtly reinforces the very sexism and inequality that he claims to abhor, attempting thereby to give it some archetypal and essential validity that easily becomes a justification of men's superior status.

The identification of basic human qualities such as assertiveness, vitality and being active with any gender is problematic and unnecessary. Although Bly and others may state that feminine and masculine do not denote man and woman, this is an intellectual statement that denies the deeper emotional identification and resonance between man and masculinity, woman and femininity.

An interesting point to be made here is that in Bly's earlier book, *A Little Book of the Human Shadow*, whilst still denoting the soft passive qualities as being feminine he states that what is missing in such men is their witch, another feminine quality, whose value lies in her assertiveness and who also embodies activity and vitality. In the interim he has effectively removed these qualities from the feminine and set up a polarity between what becomes the 'life giving' masculine and the 'life denying' feminine. He attempts to avoid this in *Iron John* by describing the 'soft' passive qualities as 'life preserving', but this is nonsensical. You need to be able to be active, vital and assertive to preserve life, as any parent could acknowledge.

The second question that arises is whether Bly's claim that men in general have become 'soft' is true. As has been pointed out by Mick Cooper in *Achilles Heel* issue 12, there is little evidence to support this. The vast majority of men seem far from acknowledging any value in being 'soft', let alone behaving in such a way. My own personal experience has been that it is only in the New Age, therapy and anti sexist sub cultures, which together make up a rather small fraction of the male population, that men are generally found to be soft in the way Bly describes. My experience of men during years spent working in the business world, in being involved in community politics on council estates, and in my current work as counsellor for men who behave violently, is that they are far more identified with being hard than soft. As a generalisation I would say that most men are still cut off from feelings other than anger and rage, avoid any acknowledgement of vulnerability, and still expect to be the dominant partner in relationships with women.

My own history has more in common with these men than with those Bly describes. I have had to shift from aggression to assertion, learn to express my pain and anxiety as grief and fear rather than rage and withdrawal, and accept relationship, intimacy and compromise over independence, distance and selfishness. This has made me neither passive nor guilty, but I have become more vulnerable, more human, more warm and more willing to say sorry when I am in the wrong. This willingness to be vulnerable is a softness I value and is not only vital and alive but an essential part of my assertiveness. My experience of working with men is that these vulnerable qualities are what are missing, often alongside an inability to be assertive rather than aggressive. Becoming more feminine or masculine does not come into it, broadening their human qualities and experiences to become more inclusive does.

A generalisation I would make is that the majority of men have not gone soft but are confused about their identity as men. This seems to be a reflection not only of the changing status of women but also of a more fluid and educated society which renders rigid gender roles increasingly irrelevant and even dysfunctional. With men's identity and status so bound up with their gender role rather than their personal sense of self this confusion and uncertainty is understandable. But it needs to be tolerated and explored so that a more genuine sense of self as a man can emerge, rather than being fled from in a desperate attempt to recreate a bygone age of certainty.

In *Iron John*, Bly seems unable to tolerate this confusion, which appears to be reflected in his political views. There is a longing for certainty and dominant leadership running through the book, and there are several occasions when he makes derogatory remarks about alternative political approaches. His reactionary attitudes to parenting and women have already been touched upon, yet the absence of race and homosexuality as significant factors in *Iron John* is equally telling.

Whether eliciting positive or negative responses, both race and homosexuality exert enormous influence on the political landscape of America. Yet there is scarcely a mention of them in *Iron John*. The workshops that Bly runs also seem to be almost exclusively white and heterosexual. But then, how would such a story in such a setting speak to a black or gay man? If it spoke to them at all, it would probably be in a very different way to the interpretation Bly gives. For if there is one thing we ought to have learnt by now, from gay men in particular, it is that it is not masculinity but masculinities that we need to be addressing and that this diversity has to be acknowledged.

Bly himself, whilst criticising the New Age and therapy movements for not being more politically involved, seems happy to run his workshops on those same circuits, charging high fees that render them immediately exclusive and privileged. Capitalism does not appear to be on the agenda for questioning and those who do not have the financial means are ignored. The giving of a few bursaries in a group of over a hundred men seems an example of political correctness rather than political awareness, all surface and little substance. In this he mirrors the marginalisation that takes place in society as a whole whereby white, affluent heterosexuality is the model for all men. He seems to prefer to ignore this problem rather than struggle with what are very difficult and challenging issues. In this his shadow looms large, a veritable reactionary Mr. Hyde exploiting that which his liberal Dr. Jekyll condemns.

Perhaps where this split is most marked is in Bly's romanticising of the warrior. He attempts to put all the dark parts of the warrior into the soldier, leaving the warrior as some kind of golden ideal who fights and even kills, yet in an almost bloodless and honourable way. Although abhorring guns and modern weapons which are only fit for soldiers, Bly appears to condone and admire hand to hand combat with swords. He seems to have no notion of the terrible damage swords and knives can do, that such combat results in limbs being hacked off, bodies being pierced and ripped, blood, gore, enormous physical pain and often death. These harsh consequences are ignored behind a romantic idea of honour and respect. There is no empathy for the dead or wounded or for their children, wives and families. In fact these men appear unconnected to close others, seeming to be separate men fighting separate men. Such combat becomes as clean and clinical, detached and impersonal as any example of modern warfare, the only difference seeming to be the respect and honour the combatants show each other as they hack themselves to death!

This romanticising and split seems to be rooted in Bly's personal history. Bly says of himself that he was not in touch with his warrior energy when he was a child and a young man. This lack of experience as a youth of 'being a warrior' seems to have affected him profoundly, with the unfortunate result that he has compensated by romanticising and advocating 'warrior' qualities without understanding what they actually mean. The ability to protect oneself and others is an important one to have regardless of gender, but equally it carries a potentially grim and dark consequence with it. The burden of damaging and perhaps killing another human being even in self defence is a heavy one to carry, and has little to do with romance and triumph. Rather it casts a dark cloud over the heart that needs to be slowly and painfully dissolved in human relationship, with a residue perhaps always remaining. Bly is right when he states that the soldier avoids facing this by his detachment and rationality, yet his view of the warrior is equally dangerous and detached with a similar denial and avoidance of this darkening of the heart.

Amongst the shadow I have laid bare there does of course lie my own, for in part it is the darkness in my own heart that enables me to see Bly's. Since I was a child I have been aware of my ability to kill and my wish to wreak vengeance on those who crossed me. I have been both harsh and violent at times with people who I perceive as having damaged either myself or those close to me. My own long standing love of mythology was never simply rooted in the magical and spiritual qualities evoked. The threads of vengeance, conquest and power that pervade many of these stories were equally attractive.

The shadow I carry within is not merely unfulfilled potential and unexpressed pain that needs transforming and healing. It includes a grinning demon who delights in others' misfortune, a messianic angel of light with a ruthless and self righteous demand for purity, a slavering wolf with a hunger for blood and flesh, and a grim faced man who derives sadistic satisfaction in the brutal destruction of everything warm and human. And yes, some, though by no means all, of this grim faced man in particular I see in the figure of *Iron John*. Projection it certainly is, but I believe that I have demonstrated that there are substantial 'hooks' to my projections in both Bly and the book.

Yet it is of no more value to be blinded by this darkness than it is to be blinded by the light of idealism. They need to be recognised as inextricably linked. The darkness and density of the shadow cast by *Iron John* is a direct consequence of the richness and light that pervades the book. There is much of value and beauty in Bly's writing and a deep love of men resonates throughout. I recognise a genuine wish to address the conflict between men and women honestly and a desire to heal the damage that men and women alike have experienced both as children and in relationship. His failures as demonstrated in my criticisms and others are not a cause for dismissing either Bly or *Iron John*. Rather by naming the shadow contained therein a deeper and broader understanding becomes possible. The book then becomes less important for the answers it offers but more so for the questions it raises. And for that Bly deserves respect and gratitude.

Soft Males and Mama's Boys: A Critique of Bly

TERRY A. KUPERS

ONE MUST CERTAINLY ACKNOWLEDGE ROBERT BLY'S contribution to the evolving men's movement. He has helped bring men together to share their stories and their feelings, to explore their "shadows," to re-awaken their vitality, their respect for elders, their need for spirituality and so forth. These are important contributions. And clearly, judging from the popularity of his appearances and tapes and the sales of *Iron John*, his message has struck a deep chord within a large number of (mostly white, middle class and middle aged) men.[1]

THE POSITIVE CONTRIBUTIONS

Some of Bly's formulations are quite useful. For instance, when he instructs men on the need to finally forgive their fathers and get on with their lives, he brings us a step closer to making psychotherapy terminable. He believes men must resolve leftover conflicts with their fathers if they are to be whole. Men need to acknowledge their fathers if they are satisfied with the way they were raised; if their fathering was not optimal they need to grieve for the father they never had and then make amends with the disappointing one who exists; or, if their father is not alive, they can forgive him for his short-comings and honor his memory. Bly's advice is quite sound, *if* it is well-timed. Some men, even at midlife, have never gotten in touch with their anger toward and disappointment in their fathers; for them, forgiveness would be premature. But the suggestion that men grieve and forgive serves to short-circuit the kind of endless resentment that makes therapy such an interminable project.[2]

And Bly says some important things about male individuation. For instance, in Bly's (1990) telling of the story of Iron John, the wildman is captured in the forest and locked in a cage in the center of town.[3] A boy is playing with a golden ball. When the ball rolls into the cage, the boy asks the wildman to return it and he refuses—unless the boy will free him from the cage. The boy protests he does not have the key. The wildman retorts that the key is under his mother's pillow. In other words, if the boy is to get in touch with the wildman deep within, with his desires and his power, he must break with his mother. There is a valuable truth to discover in the story—as long as we can somehow avoid the misogynist and politically reactionary conclusion that mothers (and women) are ultimately to blame for men's sense of unfreedom. Unfortunately, Bly offers no words of caution here.

I will mention one more example of Bly's useful "pearls" for men. He and Michael Meade claim that "the male mode of feeling" is very different than the female mode, for instance men are not as interested in face-to-face discussions of personal matters, preferring instead to stand shoulder-to-shoulder facing a common task or adversary.[4] The point is valid: men do have different ways. When women writers mock male shoulder-to-shoulder relating and imply that face-to-face relationships are the only kind that are truly intimate, they alienate men who might otherwise listen to what women are trying to tell them about sharing and intimacy. But, at the same time, shoulder-to-shoulder intimacies can be rather limiting, and men would do well to learn more about the face-to-face variety.

THE IMPLICIT POLITICAL MESSAGE

In spite of Bly's useful contributions, his message contains some alarmingly regressive implications. For instance, the evolving men's movement, even while refusing to support a traditional notion of the "real man," is beginning to construct hierarchies and categories of deviance of its own. Bly's intolerance of "softness" in men is a prime example. The basic idea is that certain men are "Mama's boys" or "pussy whipped," meaning they were too tied to their mothers as children, and as adults they are too tender, too emphatic, too interested in women's issues. But against what standard is this "too" measured? Of course, the standard is a new version of that familiar old concept, the "real man." Traditionally, a "real man" is strong, brave, independent, relatively unemotional, unflinching, *and properly distanced from the female perspective and from identification with women.* The new concept, more acceptable to sensitive men, is that a "real man" gathers with other men, tells his story, talks about feelings, plays drums, takes part in primitive dances and rituals, *and is properly distanced from the female perspective and from identification with women.*

Bly's (1982, 1990) notion of "soft males" fosters stigmatization. He begins by describing the "soft males" of the seventies:

> They're lovely, valuable people—I like them—they're not interested in harming the earth or starting wars. [In the 1982 interview, Bly added "or working for corporations"—perhaps a corporate executive talked him into removing that clause from the 1990 book.] There's a gentle attitude toward life in their whole being and style of living. But many of these men are not happy. You quickly notice the lack of energy in them. They are life-preserving but not exactly life-giving. Ironically, you often see these men with strong women who positively radiate energy. (1990, pp. 2–3)

Bly believes that the man who wishes to be liberated from the bonds of the traditional male image must traverse two further stages of adult development. First he must get in touch with his feminine side, his "interior woman," and second he must get in touch with the wildman inside him, the "deep male." In order to accomplish the second step, the man must resolve certain issues with his father, and go to other men for help finding his way. The male who is attuned to the issue of gender equality has traversed the first stage but not the second.

I agree with Bly there is another step men must take, and I agree that men must talk to other men about this, not just to women. But I do not think it is merely a matter of distancing women and getting in touch with the "wildman" within, the source of life and power that has been repressed in the "soft male." I believe Bly takes a wrong turn here, attempting to delineate what ails men without looking to gender relations. He thinks there is something innate and universal about (straight) masculinity that can be understood without reference to the experience of women and gay men, and without reference to historical change or to the kinds of domination that frame the experience of both genders.

Bly is blaming and devaluing women when he repeatedly accuses mothers of smothering sons. He rarely mentions the mother's role in nurturing and raising the son. Juxtaposing this observation with Bly's emphasis on forgiving the errant father, it seems fair to conclude there is a significant bias against women and against dependency on women.

When asked by Bill Moyers in a television interview if the phenomenon of men's gatherings in the 80's and 90's is not an outgrowth of the women's movement of the 60's and 70's, Bly makes light of Moyers' suggestion and insists the men's movement developed independently. He seems concerned lest his masculinity seem reactive to women, so he has to devalue women and refuse to acknowledge their contribution to a heightened gender consciousness. Meanwhile, he rarely mentions the fact that men oppress women and says nothing about the need for men and women to join in the struggle to put an end to sexism. In fact, in the Moyers interview, he says that women are unhappy mainly because they, like men, did not get enough of their fathers' attention. What about sexual oppression, exclusion from positions of power, unequal pay, rape and other forms of sexual oppression? Bly is silent. In addition, Bly practically ignores the experience of gay men (see Murray, in this volume).

Bly colludes in the disturbing tendency for sensitive men to move on from the stage of supporting women's struggles to evolve a new, more "sensitive" and "spiritual" form of sexism. For instance, with so much focus on avoiding passivity and feeling powerful, too little attention is given to the need for men to admit to weakness, painful emotions and dependency needs, and to develop the capacity to tolerate these qualities in others and to nurture.

I was in a leaderless men's group for five years in the early seventies, at the beginning of what is now called the men's movement, and I readily admit the group I was in and many others like it were formed by men who had a deep respect for the women who were demanding their rights. We not only did not want to be left out, but also we believed we had much to learn from the women's precedent—and we struggled to evolve ways to transcend the male posturing that had kept us apart and isolated us until that time. Men's groups of that era typically began with discussions of men's problems relating to women. The successful groups eventually turned to the problems men have relating to each other, and solutions to those problems often led to improved relationships with women as well. Many of the men at gatherings I have attended come from similar backgrounds, or attend men's events because the women in their lives encourage them to do something about their alienation from their own inner life and from other men.

LEARNING FROM WOMEN

Let us assume for a moment that the women's movement is generally correct, and a significant part of what ails our society is uncontrolled male posturing; for instance, men cannot back down from a fight, not on the street, not in the competitive world of business and not in the international arena where they regularly challenge each other to wars. And let us assume for a moment that what is needed is more emphasis on qualities that are popularly held to be feminine, such as the capacity to nurture and care about the fate of others, to work cooperatively with others instead of always competing, to respect and protect natural resources including our bodies and our rain forests, to be open about feelings and include feelings in our decision-making process, and so forth. Then the last thing we would want to do is stigmatize men's willingness to admire women for these qualities and to learn as much as they possibly can from them.

Here I risk jumping into the middle of a large debate about gender differences, essentialism and social constructivism. Essentialism maintains that there is something different about women, something innate and universal. If there are feminists who take this stance (I do not know any who would admit they do), this would have to mean something better than what is innate and universal in men. The other side holds that our gender roles and gender relations are socially constructed and change with history—and therefore there is reason to hope and to struggle for differently engendered, and thereby improved, social relations.

The debate about essentialism vs. social constructivism goes astray in implying that just about anyone who theorizes about sexual differences is guilty of essentialism. For instance, Katha Pollitt claims Carol Gilligan is an essentialist.[5] Of course, it would be better for Gilligan to restrict her generalizations about women to the subgroup she studied—largely white and middle class—but I doubt that Gilligan actually believes we live our gendered lives outside of culture and history.

At public workshops and lectures I am frequently accused of generalizing, or creating a stereotype, when I talk about gender. The accusation implies that I am guilty of essentialism. I always try to caution readers and audiences that I am speaking mostly about men like me, and that I do not find it useful to think in biological and universal terms about psychology and human relations. But I do generalize. For instance, I believe that men, in general, tend to dread disclosure of their dependency needs. Of course I can only generalize about white middle class men in the nineties in the U.S.A., but I also wonder about the degree to which this generalization characterizes men of different classes and races.

Am I trying to establish an ageless, universal notion about men, or am I attempting to find words to speak to a large number of men who know exactly what I mean when I refer to men's fear of confessing dependency? Of course not all men possess the quality I am describing. Many readily admit their dependency needs to their intimates, while a certain number of women tend to deny their dependency. But how can we talk about gender without generalizing about gender differences at some point? We must be able to talk in the abstract about gender differences without implying a timeless, universal, gendered human essence. It would help if, at each level of abstraction, we continually tested and qualified our generalizations. Generalizations about gender are always provisional and subject to change as we move on to more sophisticated levels of analysis.

When we are ready to move on past the debate about essentialism *vs.* social constructivism, another question emerges: As women in large numbers enter public life and rise to the top of hierarchies that are currently reserved for men, will they bring with them their feminine ways (the capacity to be open about personal things while still getting the job done, the capacity to make friends and collaborate on projects, etc.) and thus serve to ameliorate some of the vicious competition and ruthlessness that currently characterize the workplace and public life; or will the women who rise to the top, selectively, more resemble men in their ways? (To be consistent, social constructivists must agree that a woman can become as cutthroat and merciless as any man.)

I think the jury's still out on that question, and the verdict depends on the success of the feminist struggle and all the other struggles that aim to transcend social domination. Meanwhile, it does seem clear that given current gender relations in middle class American society, women disproportionately carry the burden of nurturing—their children, men, each other—and doing various other peaceful and nature-respecting things. Other women in other places might have very different ways, but median contemporary American middle class women's ways seem to contain important clues about how we might solve some of the world's present problems—for instance war and ecological disaster. "Male" proclivities—including competition, concern about status in hierarchies, isolation, obsessional steadiness of pace and the use of women to enlarge one's ego—have led to our current political predicament. Perhaps a shift in the balance so that women have more of a share of power would lead to a more just and equitable society. Perhaps this hope is shared by the unprecedented number of voters who are electing women to important offices today. The hypothesis seems to be that women's larger sense of connection with others and their greater capacity to nurture prepare them better than men to cope sensitively and cooperatively with the nation's and the world's problems.

In this context, calling men Mama's boys, soft males and pussy whipped because they listen too much to women is quite counterproductive—the wrong male qualities are being stigmatized. It is precisely the men who admit to the strong influence of women—the men who do not feel a strong need to "dis-identify" with women at every opportunity—who can contribute most to changing gender relations and devising ways to keep in bound the greed and violence that are rampant in today's world. According to Bob Blauner, "Men in the movement are likely to have grown up closer to their mothers than to their fathers. Therefore there are a sizable number of "Mama's Boys," and the denial of this reality contributes to the movement's flight from mother—this is because we accept the male prescription and want to fulfill the criteria of adequacy in the new men's movement."[6]

THE PROS AND CONS OF "SOFTNESS"

What, precisely, does Bly mean by "soft men"? On the one hand, he seems to be referring to men who have a highly developed feminine side, who have a deep respect for women and their power, who prefer connectedness and nurturing over combat and competition, and who eschew traditional male pursuits that involve cruelty, misogyny and homophobia. To the extent Bly devalues these qualities in men, he is leading us down a false path. He also seems to be referring to men who are passive, unformed as individuals, entirely reactive to others' wishes and demands, and so frightened of anger and combat that they tend to back down and disavow what they stand for in the face of strong opposition. Here is where Bly has a point, this kind of "softness" is very limiting. Sam Keen offers an alternative to this kind of softness: "The historical challenge for modern men is clear—to discover a peaceful form of virility and to create an ecological commonwealth, to become fierce gentlemen."[7]

But why should we apply the point exclusively to men? Women who are passive, unformed as individuals, entirely reactive and afraid of their anger and strength are also quite limited human beings. This kind of "softness" is not good for either gender. In other words, when Bly links "softness" in men with excessive or prolonged connection to women, he makes two errors. First he stigmatizes certain "feminine," nurturing qualities in men. And second he assumes that passivity and an inability to stand up for oneself are only problematic in men. In other words it is more acceptable for women to be passive and not entirely formed as human beings.

There is another way that Bly's link between closeness with women and softness in men misses the mark. Bly implies that if men would stop being "soft" they would stand up to the women who have gained so much power in recent years, and doing so would make men feel powerful again. This message appeals to many men who feel inadequate while they perceive women gaining power in our society. But this is a message of backlash.[8] The reason men feel powerless and inadequate is not that women have taken their power away. Shifts in the economy, high unemployment, plant closures and massive lay-offs, higher taxes for the middle and lower classes with fewer social services, racism, homophobia, a crisis in health care, inflated insurance premiums and other unfortunate social developments over the last fifteen years have made it more difficult for men to feel adequate and powerful. Bly allies with ultra-conservative forces when he blames the plight of the American male on the emergence of powerful women in the public arena.

Finally, Bly's use of the term "soft" reflects another underlying assumption: that men's ways are strong and powerful while women's ways are "softer" and powerless. I do not accept that assumption! Cooperation, concern about the plight of others, respect for nature and a host of other qualities we associate with women today are the ingredients for a greater power than men now have. For instance there is the power to make the personal political, to meet together and talk personally while at the same time making plans to change the social arrangements, the power to save the environment by rationally disposing of our waste products, and the power to avert nuclear annihilation.

I have discussed the need for men to stand up to the women in their lives in order to be able to resolve some of the tensions that regularly arise in heterosexual couples, and sometimes men must work through unresolved conflicts regarding their mothers in order to develop their capacity to stand toe-to-toe with women as adults.[9] But this is not the same as saying women are to blame for men's feelings of inadequacy. If there is to be social progress, men and women must stand together against the wrongs of a patriarchal culture. Otherwise, power would be left to those who are more competitive, greedy and ruthless. Men and women must be anything but "soft" (in the sense of passive, reactive and unwilling to stand up for their interests) if we are to redraw the lines that constrict gendered behavior. But the right balance of sensitivity and toughness will not come from stigmatizing men who are deeply connected with women and the feminine within.

CONCLUSION

I agree with Bly's critics when they protest the sexism and homophobia that are implicit and unexamined in his message. I cannot go along when these same critics poke fun at the large number of men who gather at men's events seeking new rituals, a new kind of connectedness with other men and a new burst of spirituality in their lives. The social alienation that drives these men to seek alternatives to their "keep-them-close-to-your-chest" everyday life is the same social alienation that progressives and pro-feminists are struggling so hard to change. Let's recognize potential fellow-travellers. Men who drum because they would like more rhythm in their lives, men who tell their stories around campfires because they would like to be known by other men, and men who want to hug other men and establish rituals of joy and of sorrow—these are all men who might as easily grow to understand that the antidote to their alienation is not ultimately contained in the magic of their primitive forest gatherings. Rather it requires that straight men ally with women and gay men to radically alter our gendered social relations. Meanwhile, radicals could use some rhythm too, and some celebration of our manliness.

NOTES

1. Robert Bly, *Iron John: A Book About Men* (Reading, Mass.: Addison-Wesley, 1990).

2. Terry Kupers, *Ending Therapy: The Meaning of Termination* (New York: New York University Press, 1988).

3. See also Robert Bly, "What Men Really Want," interview with Keith Thompson, *New Age* (May 1982): 30–51.

4. Robert Bly, *The Male Mode of Feeding* (Audiotape: Pacific Grove, Calif.: Oral Tradition Archives, 1989).

5. Katha Pollitt, "Are Women Morally Superior to Men?" *The Nation* (28 December 1992): 799–807.

6. Robert Blauner, "The Men's Movement and Its Analysis of the Male Malaise" (Unpublished manuscript, 1991).

7. Sam Keen, *Fire in the Belly: On Being a Man* (New York: Bantam Books, 1991), 121.

8. Susan Faludi, *Backlash: The Undeclared War on American Women* (New York: Crown, 1991).

9. Terry Kupers, "Feminist Men." *Tikkun* 5(4) (1990): 35–38; and *Revisioning Men's Lives: Gender, Intimacy and Power* (New York: Guilford Press, 1993).

Psyche, Society, and the Men's Movement

CHRIS BULLOCK

THERE ARE SIGNS OF DECLINE in the men's movement. In my local alternative newspaper, the section that used to contain at least a full page of men's events now has barely two or three listings. My friends in other cities tell me the same story: declining numbers of men's groups, great difficulty in raising money for anything to do with men's projects. (Canada's White Ribbon campaign, a high profile men's movement against violence towards women, recently announced a major funding crisis.)

Probably the biggest sigh of relief will come from those happy to see the demise of the mythopoetic men's movement, that part of the men's movement associated with the American poet Robert Bly and also associated, in the popular media, with images of naked men drumming in the woods and turning themselves into macho savages. This hostility to the mythopoetic men's movement is not just a matter of television jokes about wild men and wimps. Feminists (of both sexes) have been persistently concerned with what they see as a 'mythopoetic' distortion to the *social* dimension of men's and women's lives, especially to the power differential between men and women.

In this article I hope to open a dialogue between the mythopoetic men's movement and its feminist social critics by looking at a central theme in Robert Bly's writing on men—the understanding of men's wounds. I focus on Bly because he is the "indisputable star of the men's consciousness movement,"[1] because he is the writer on men's issues from whom I have learned the most, and because his is the name that comes up again and again in Kay Leigh Hagan's *Women Respond to the Men's Movement*,[2] as the feminist writers in that collection define the branch of the men's movement they find most threateningly oblivious to questions of power and social structure. My way of proceeding will be to outline briefly some of Bly's treatment of the theme of the wound in *Iron John* (1990) and elsewhere, followed by an examination of the feminist social critique of this treatment of men's pain, and then to evaluate both the feminist and the mythopoetic perspectives on men's suffering.

In the Grimm Brothers story on which *Iron John* is based, as the young male hero of the story releases the Wild Man from a cage in his parents' palace, he receives a wound to the finger. Bly describes this wound as an initiation wound, an outer wound that reminds the bearer of his inner wounds, that is, of the damage to his inner sense of value and significance. In contemporary men, these inner wounds can come from shaming or beating by parents, being betrayed by older men, or enduring competitive and superficial male relationships.[3] However, being wounded is not a simply negative experience; though the culture tells men that "a wound that hurts is shameful," "[w]herever the wound appears in our psyches . . . is precisely the place [from] which we will give our major gift to the community" (p. 42).

A common response to wounding is what Bly calls "ascension" (p. 33), that is, rising above the pain by becoming very intellectual, very successful, very cheerful, or very special in some way that takes a man away from his body and his feelings. Correspondingly, the healing of the wound requires a return to the experience of pain, a return to things left 'below'; it requires what Bly calls the descent. Descent is the movement from a false cheerfulness to grief, seen as "a door to male feeling."[4] It is the decision to "follow the grief downward" at one of the "little turns" in conversation (p. 14). It is "taking the road of ashes," accepting failure and humiliation. It is moving back to a valuation of physical labour, and thus the physical in general.[5] It is confronting the shadow, that dark "part of our personality that is hidden from us."[6] It is "going down to that missing water, the unconscious."[7] Indeed, at one point in *Iron John*, Bly claims that allegiance to the much-discussed figure of the Wild Man simply "amounts to a trust in what is below" (1990, p. 224).

This, then, is (in broad outline) Bly's view of men's wounds. It is clear that the contributors to *Women Respond to the Men's Movement* do not hold that view in great esteem. The most dismissive comment in the collection comes from Margaret Randall; after comparing Bly's ideology to Reagan's defence of America's Vietnam adventure and to Bush's defence of the invasion of Iraq, she argues that Bly's theory of the wound is one of the "poverty-builds-character or abuse-makes art doctrines . . . [that] nurtures sickness itself as a source of power."[8] Gentler, but equally dismissive, is Barbara Kingsolver's admonition that

> if there is kindness in us, we will not belittle another's pain, regardless of its size. When a friend calls me to moan that she's just gotten a terrible haircut, I'll give her some sympathy. But I will give her a lot more if she calls to say she's gotten ovarian cancer. Let's keep some perspective. The men's movement and the women's movement aren't salt and pepper; they are hangnail and hand grenade.[9]

The criticism of the mythopoetic approach to men's wounds most evident in *Women Respond* is, however, a criticism of that approach's "social amnesia" (to use a term from Russell Jacoby). This case is put so eloquently by Elizabeth Dodson Gray that it seems worth quoting her comments at length. Gray claims that Bly fails to be

> clear about the role of the patriarchy as a systemic repressive phenomenon, causing boys and men to bury their feelings and become remote father figures who cannot express love.
>
> Bly apparently does not see how, generation after generation, patriarchy has coerced us all so that men are reared by women, ignored by fathers, and then want to flee women in order to "discover their true masculinity." These social roles that patriarchy designs, coerces and perpetuates *cause* the very inner wounds Bly describes so eloquently and seeks to heal.
>
> Bly tries nobly to lance men's inner wounds. But he does not perceive their root cause in the power system of patriarchy. So he is helpless to interrupt this process as the generations roll on.[10]

I do not find all these different feminist critiques of Bly on men's wounds equally pertinent. The comparison of Bly with Reagan and Bush, and the association of his views on the wound with a Horatio Alger-like glorification of poverty, seem very misguided, given Bly's long-standing anti-Republicanism and his vocal opposition to both the Vietnam and Persian Gulf wars. The claim that the mythopoetic approach ignores the social basis of men's wounds, however, needs serious attention and careful evaluation. It seems to me it would be a mistake for me to pretend to be able to evaluate this claim without involving my own gendered and social positioning. So what I propose to do is to return to the theme of wound and ascent/descent, this time writing the persons of Bly and myself into the picture, and then exploring what a social analysis of this theme can and cannot offer, from my own particular vantage point.

The theme of ascent from and descent to the wound has a special poignancy for Bly. He has often spoken and written of the pain he received from his father's withdrawal into alcoholism and of his response to this pain: his cheerfulness as a child, his "longing for purity, 'to be above it all,' not to be involved" (1990, p. 58). As I noted earlier, for one who has 'ascended' in this way, descent is essential and it seems that Bly underwent his descent during the three years in New York which he spent "being mostly blocked depressed and poor" (Solataroff, p. 271). This theme also has a special poignancy for me. I grew up in a family where my working-class father was remote through age and illness, and, in any case, generally sent me to my middle-class mother for decisions and guidance. The atmosphere of the family was one of worry about the present and anxiety about the future. I responded by trying to become an 'intellectual,' going away to University, escaping to another country. In the mid-seventies, Ph.D. freshly completed, I sank into a major depression, a frightening voyage into darkness with no guide to make me aware of what the meaning of descent might be.

In seeking to understand the social origins of this pattern of ascent and descent, I came across a description of the petit bourgeois family by the English social psychologist David Smail which resonated powerfully with my experience of family life. For Smail, the petit bourgeois family's position "perched on a ledge a little way up the social pyramid" produces

> [r]igid conformity to narrowly ideal standards and denial and repression of emotions, perceptions and values which do not meet them, resentful respect for authority and uncritical acceptance of social institutions, breed[ing] an atmosphere . . . which, not surprisingly, is one of the most psychologically mutilating in which one can find oneself.[11]

The petit bourgeois family is not universal, but it has a special typicality at the present time in that

> It is in this stratum, and those close to it, that the course of development most typical of our society is perhaps most obviously to be found—the transformation of a lively and promising human infant . . . into an emotionally constricted, competitively hostile adult. . . . This is the great inertially stable backbone of our society, the guardian of its values and the target of its mass media. . . . (P. 117)

I find this social and class analysis of my experience valuable in a number of ways. First it helps curb any tendency I might have to assume my experience is universal, to translate petit bourgeois male into world being. It thus serves the project that feminism has found so important: the elimination of the equation between white Western masculine and the universal. Second, it serves the almost opposite function of translating, to use a phrase from C. Wright Mills, my private trouble into a public problem. If this pattern of experience is not universal, it is not solely personal either, but possesses a social typicality. Besides averting a collapse into self-blame, this insight also provides a social basis for Bly's claim for wound and community; if many people are wounded as a result of the petit bourgeois family, then those who acknowledge this wound are surely of potential service to others in this situation. Third, I find Smail's description of petit bourgeois socialization an excellent description of gender socialization, of the making of "emotionally constricted, competitively hostile" masculinity. From this description I understand how men with only a little power might nevertheless use that power against those with less power than they have, which most often (but not always) means women and children. Thus it helps me understand better the occasional unexpected emergence of authoritarianism in my own work and personal life.

Social analysis is not absent from *Iron John*. Notably there is Bly's claim that the replacement of an agricultural society by an industrial society has weakened the "bonding between father and son, with catastrophic results" (p. 94). This argument seems valid but lacking in sharpness. Does this argument refer to all fathers and all sons equally? Is the son of a blue-collar father more affected than the son of a managerial father? What about the effect of the industrial revolution on the role of mothers? The claim lacks sharpness because it lacks the reference to power and class, and because it lacks discrimination among the universal, the socially typical, and the particular; both this reference and this discrimination I take to be necessary to critical social analysis.

Thus, I am led to acknowledge the justice of feminist claims like Margo Adair's that "It is taboo to name power. . . . Nowhere in the pages of *Iron John* is the subject raised" (1992, p. 56). And I hope I have shown, through brief comments on the petit bourgeois family, that critical social analysis has a contribution to make to the understanding of themes which are obviously close to Bly's heart. And yet, having defended the value of the analysis of class and power for understanding men's issues, I now want to qualify this defence by acknowledging that Bly's mythopoetic analysis provides me with something which the tradition of critical social analysis recommended by many of the contributors to *Women Respond to the Men's Movement* cannot provide. To explain what this is, let me focus again on the theme of men's wounds.

In *Taking Care* (1987), from which I drew the description of the petit bourgeois family, Smail argues that our society tries to distract us from pain and distress, but their presence keeps us in contact with what is really going on. Thus, "Our most reliable guide in the formulation of our conduct . . . is the private knowledge of pain . . . pain . . . calls us back from disembodied reverie" (p. 141). To put this in gendered terms, if, as Elizabeth Dodson Gray argues, "patriarchy as a systemic repressive phenomenon . . . caus[es] boys and men to bury their feelings" (p. 163), then these buried feelings, and especially the feeling of pain, become the appropriate starting point for men's awareness and transformation. Now, my point is that, while social analysis promotes an understanding of "patriarchy as a systemic repressive phenomenon," the paradox is that in the condition of ascent, intellectual understanding is more often a vehicle for avoiding pain rather than for experiencing it. Certainly for me, understanding the general contours of my childhood experience was and is not enough to put me in contact with that experience, to allow me to experience it with feeling and body sensation. To allow pain to act as a "guide for conduct," I need to feel the pain, and yet my way of enduring my childhood years was to avoid feeling this pain. To understand a background or a social condition but not to feel it is, in my view, to remain in the state Smail calls "disembodied reverie." To escape from "disembodied reverie" requires, I would claim, not only understanding cognitively where pain comes from but also experiencing that pain with bodily and emotional depth, a depth that Bly's work points us towards.

To explain what I mean by depth, let me expand on some of Robert Bly's comments on men's wounds. In *Iron John*, after that part of the story in which the young boy has dipped his finger in a sacred spring to ease the pain of his wound, Bly comments: "If we are to live in this story rather than merely observe it, we have to ask ourselves 'What wound do we have that hurts so much we have to dip it in water?'" (1990, p. 31). To prime the imagination, he lists some injuries from the father, climaxing in a brief retelling of an African story in which a boy fails his father and the father strikes him with an axe handle. He then lists some shaming comments from mother, comments like "'You're very frail, you know; you shouldn't play with those boys. . . . You're too big for your britches'" (pp. 30–31). Finally there are wounds delivered from older men and from peers: the lies told to young soldiers before they went to Vietnam, the absence of older men in the lives of gang members, the wounds from having only superficial barroom conversations with other men (pp. 32–33).

It would be hard to make a discursive generalization from these details; instead of supporting the development of an intellectual argument, they act as particulars inviting the reader to identify and descend into his or her own experience. Just possibly nothing on Bly's lists catches fire with individual readers, but the range is broad enough to make this unlikely. For me, the comment on frailty sinks deep; it is a conditioning comment that I've never before thought of as an injury. Nor had I thought of bar conversations as wounding, despite the bleakness I remember feeling on many walks home. At the start of *Iron John*, Bly justifies calling on fairy stories by claiming that "The images the old stories give . . . are meant to be taken slowly into the body. They continue to unfold, once taken in" (1990, p. ix). This process of slowly entering the body happens, I believe, not just with the images from the story of *Iron John*, but also with many of the other images that Bly offers during the book, including these images of wounds received from parents and others. It is this entering into the body, engaging the feelings, that I am calling *depth*.

Depth, as I am describing it, is an appeal to the embodied reader, and it is this appeal that I find lacking in social analysis with its inevitable employment of "ideal-typical procedures."[12] Notice that I am speaking of procedures here and not of content. In his very interesting review of sociologies of the body, Chris Shilling defends sociology from "accusations that it has adopted an entirely disembodied approach to its subject matter" by pointing out that classical sociology has at least focussed "selectively on certain aspects of human embodiment."[13] But this is to make a claim about matter (content) as a defence against a charge that also seems to be about manner (approach). On the level of content, there are important distinctions to be made between, for example, theorists like Michel Foucault who argue a "view of the body as only existing in discourse" (cited in Shilling, p. 198) and those who, like Giddens and Shilling, find this view of the body reductionist. However, all these discussions, like the recommendation that men simply adopt a critical social understanding of patriarchy, belong to the body of critical social science with its "cognitivist perspective."[14] And Brian Fay is correct, I believe, in arguing that cognitivism has a hard time describing the "somatic knowledge" that is an essential part of assimilating a culture (p. 149).

The difficulty social analysis has in dealing with "somatic knowledge" lies, I would argue, in its commitment to "external description" and to "psychic distance, the existence of a rigid barrier between observer and observed."[15] These terms come from historian Morris Berman, who claims that "Academic discourses generally lack the power to shock, to move the reader. . . . [because they] fail to address the felt visceral level of our being . . ." (p. 110).

Berman contrasts the assumptions of these discourses with the earlier almost universal assumption—evident, for example, in the pre-Homeric Greek concept of *mimesis*—that "participating consciousness" is necessary for knowledge (p. 112). Social analysis, one could say, often "gets written with the mind holding the pen. What would it look like, what would it read like, if it got written with the body holding the pen?"[16]

My answer to this question is that analysis "written with the body" might very well look like *Iron John*. Throughout *Iron John* there are passages like the following, where Bly shifts from expository definition to a directly participatory rhetoric:

> Religion here does not mean doctrine, or piety, or purity, or 'faith,' or 'belief,' or my life given to God. It means a willingness to be a fish in the holy water, to be fished for by Dionysus or one of the other fishermen, to bow the head and take hints from one's own dreams . . . to eat grief as a fish gulps water and lives. (1990, p. 38)

Interestingly, just as I was about to connect "participating consciousness" with the bodily and emotional depth I find in Bly's work, I noticed that Berman makes the connection himself. He records Bly's comment that a "twinge in his gut" told him a certain line belonged in a poem, and says that while he doubts that " 'gut twingeing' can serve as an adequate methodology for historians. . . . it's [not] a bad start" (1989, p. 118). He then goes on to claim that with mythology and storytelling "the body and its concomitant emotions are immediately engaged, along with the mind" (1989, p. 118), and to examine the contribution these modes could make to the discipline of history.

In Berman's view, mythology and story are not history but they are not separate from history either, and this kind of relationship is exactly the kind of relationship I am trying to establish between critical social analysis and mythopoetics in their understanding and portrayal of men. So, on the one hand, it should be clear that critical social analysis and mythopoetics are not the same thing; one provides an activist analysis of the social and historical structures in which both men and women participate, while the other provides a vehicle for evoking the state of things in men's psyches and bodies, viewed from the perspective of "participating consciousness." The gap between the two perspectives is obvious from some of the comments on men's pain in *Women Respond to the Men's Movement*. From the perspective of critical social analysis, men's pain may well look like the pain of a "terrible haircut" or a "hangnail" (Kingsolver, p. 40), experienced by a "dependent appendage of . . . social power relations."[17] From the perspective of "participating consciousness," pain is pain and to learn its lesson, men must "find again their interior lives which for so long have been largely ignored by them" (Gray, p. 162). However, on the other hand, it seems to me that the perspectives are not separate from each other, and, indeed, that to dwell exclusively in one perspective invites trivialization of the 'loss of father bond' or the 'men's pain as hangnail' variety.

This sense of incompleteness in the social analytical and mythopoetic approaches seems to suggest the falsity of methodological separations among body, psyche, and society, and to argue for the need of an integrative approach. In searching for a model for such integration, Morris Berman finds in the work of Gregory Bateson an encouraging image of the possibility of integrating analytical and participational modes:

> In a Batesonian framework, as opposed to archaic consciousness, we can actually focus on the circuit, not just be immersed in it. . . . The hope is that we can have both *mimesis* and analysis, that the two will reinforce each other rather than generate a "two cultures" split.[18]

Yet when I contemplate the integration of social analysis and mythopoetics, instead of a sense of satisfaction, I find myself in a state of disquiet, which comes from a growing unease with the way that I myself have tackled this discussion. I have tried to describe the different contributions to the understanding of men that can be made through the "external description" of social analysis and the "participating consciousness" of mythopoetics. Still, though I have been trying for balance, and though I have written myself into the discussion in a couple of places, my main mode of argument seems clearly to be much more that of external description than that of participating consciousness. In a discussion focussed on the subject of wounds and damage, I have allowed a glimpse of my family background but have said very little of the wound that resulted from this background, and the damage I believe I have done as a result of it. I notice that David Smail, though he talks of pain as a guide to conduct, speaks little of his own pain. And that's just the point; even the most revisionary forms of social analysis do not revise the avoidance of vulnerability, the avoidance which seems to me to be so central to conventional masculine socialization.

The lesson I learn from my own practice is, then, that when social analysis and mythopoetics are brought together, the "ideal-typical" procedures of social theory will almost inevitably dominate the partnership. Robert Bly shows his awareness of a very similar problem in an article on the initiation of the rider (approximately the ego), the horse (approximately the body), and the hawk (the transpersonal or spiritual aspect of the person); he concludes his discussion of the initiation of the horse with the comment that he "prefer[s] not to use psychological jargon in order to define the horse more clearly—that would merely be to ignore the whole problem by letting the rider control the argument."[19] The rider will control the argument because, as Berman points out, modern academic discourse refuses participating consciousness, and because currently prestigious theories that focus on society, language, ideology and power, whatever their other contributions, intensify rather than diminish this refusal.

However if approaching the body and psyche in men with the "ideal-typical" procedures of sociology involves "ignor[ing] the whole problem," so, too, does avoiding the issue of power and offering sweeping generalizations instead of differentiated social analysis. In searching for a way in which mythopoetics could make a contribution to critical social analysis without being rewritten by its partner, I came across a discussion of the relationship between depth psychology and socio-political understanding in Andrew Samuels' *The Political Psyche:*

> The central features of depth psychology . . . may also be the ways and styles in which it should make its contribution to social science. Not only saying something *about* irrationality, emotion, personality, creativity, morality—but saying something *with and through* these thematics, and with and through dream, fantasy and passion.[20]

If I translate his argument into the terms of my discussion, I come up with the following: the contribution of mythopoetics to social analysis may be to discuss issues of irrationality, emotions, the body, and so on in men in ways that not only say something about these topics, but say something with and through these thematics and with and through image, myth, and the passion of participating consciousness.

When I began this article, I was hoping to establish a dialogue between mythopoetic and feminist social perspectives. Specifically, I hoped that my discussion of the theme of men's wounds and pain would lead to a clearer sense of the differing contributions that each of these perspectives could provide and to a proposal for a closer working relationship between the two. If I still find a difficulty with this last part of the project, I do not think it is simply because I recognize justified feminist suspicion of mythopoetic obliviousness to class and power. It is also because I see men, as well as women, as a shifting territory where the unconscious, the emotions, the sensations, the experience of social situatedness, the use and abuse of power all relate but are not identical with each other. I can just about imagine a way of writing that would do justice to this territory, that would move between *mimesis* and analysis, that would be sometimes imagistic and exploratory and sometimes linear and explanatory, but I, for one, can't yet do it. What I can do is conclude that mythopoetics point to an essential part of this project, and its loss would most likely move us back to a discourse that is entirely *about* men. Such a discourse is inevitably incomplete. Thus, I view the decline of interest in mythopoetics, if decline it is, with much more gloom than most of my academic colleagues.

ACKNOWLEDGMENT

This paper began in a series of conversations with my friend Dr. Max Innes, whose responses have been very valuable to me but who, of course, bears no responsibility for what I have done with them.

NOTES

1. Don Shewey, *In Defense of the Men's Movements* (St. Paul, Minn.: Ally Press, 1992), 11.

2. Kay Leigh Hagan, ed., *Women Respond to the Men's Movement: A Feminist Collection* (New York: HarperCollins, 1992).

3. Robert Bly, *Iron John: A Book About Men* (Reading, Mass.: Addison-Wesley, 1990), 31–36.

4. Bill Moyers and Robert Bly, *A Gathering of Men*, transcript (New York: Public Affairs Television, 1990), 5–6.

5. Robert Bly, *"Being a Lutheran Boy-god in Minnesota,"* in *Growing Up in Minnesota: Ten Writers Remember Their Childhoods*, ed. C. G. Anderson (Minneapolis: University of Minnesota Press, 1976), 213–15.

6. Robert Bly, *A Little Book on the Human Shadow*, ed. William Booth (San Francisco: Harper & Row, 1988), 7.

7. Ted Solataroff, "Captain Bly," *The Nation* (9 September 1991): 272.

8. Margaret Randall, " 'And So She Walked Over and Kissed Him . . .' Robert Bly's Men's Movement," in *Women Respond to the Men's Movement: A Feminist Collection*, ed. Kay Leigh Hagan (San Francisco: HarperCollins, 1992), 146.

9. Barbara Kingsolver, "Cabbages and Kings," in *Women Respond to the Men's*

Movement: A Feminist Collection, ed. Kay Leigh Hagan (San Francisco: HarperCollins, 1992), 40.

10. Elizabeth Dodson Gray, "Beauty and the Beast: A Parable for Our Time," in *Women Respond to the Men's Movement: A Feminist Collection*, ed. Kay Leigh Hagan (San Francisco: HarperCollins, 1992), 163.

11. David Smail, *Taking Care: An Alternative to Therapy* (London: Dent, 1987), 117.

12. Anthony Giddens, *Modernity and Self-Identity: Self and Society in the Late Modern Age* (Stanford: Stanford University Press, 1991), 2.

13. Christopher Shilling, *The Body and Social Theory* (London: Sage, 1993), 8–9.

14. Brian Fay, *Critical Social Science: Liberation and Its Limits* (Ithaca: Cornell University Press, 1987), 146.

15. Morris Berman, *Coming to Our Senses: Body and Spirit in the Hidden History of the West* (New York: Simon and Schuster, 1989), 110–11.

16. Morris Berman, 1989, 110.

17. Rosemary Ruether, "Patriarchy and the Men's Movement: Part of the Problem or Part of the Solution?" in *Women Respond to the Men's Movement: A Feminist Collection*, ed. Kay Leigh Hagan (San Francisco: HarperCollins, 1992), 17.

18. Morris Berman, *The Reenchantment of the World* (Ithaca: Cornell University Press, 1981), 275.

19. Robert Bly, The Hawk, the Horse and the Rider" in *Choirs of the Gods*, ed. J. Matthews (London: HarperCollins, 1991), 25.

20. Andrew Samuels, *The Political Psyche* (London: Routledge, 1993), 21–22.

Cultural Daddy-ism and Male Hysteria

DAVID M. WEED

There is a proverb which says, A pig may fly, but it isn't a likely bird.
Augustus De Morgan, *A Budget of Paradoxes*

THIS ESSAY HAD ITS GENESIS AT 2 A.M. near the beginning of a cold April a couple of years ago. A week earlier, my wife had brought home a library copy of Robert Bly's *Iron John: A Book About Men*.[1] I had opened the book a few times at random and had become more troubled each time at Bly's notions of masculinity. Then one evening I read the Preface before going to bed, which was, I suppose, rather like eating a mental pepperoni pizza: I woke up a few hours later thinking about it—and feeling angry. I was just then becoming familiar with the early anthologies on masculinity such as *Men in Feminism*[2] and *Engendering Men*[3] and studies such as Klaus Theweleit's *Male Fantasies*.[4] Academic texts all, they had seduced me into thinking that nowadays masculinity must be written as a "progressive" story, which deconstructs and undermines "traditional masculinity": that set of historically received (though also historically variable) assumptions about men's gender role and gendered power that determines, for the most part, both the textual and political reality of contemporary Western culture. Bly's book challenged me with a popular, retroactive vision, which shook me out of my reverie of happy theoretical consensus. It also, however, reinforced for me the importance of gender politics as an everyday cultural practice: if academic studies of masculinity cannot work their way outside the "ivory tower," then any understandings that we gain are no more than empty signifiers. We may discuss, for example, the seduction, simulation, and breakdown of the unity of the male subject, but cultural forces embodied by agents such as Bly ideologically reproduce a masculinity that has embedded within the real dangers of the history of patriarchy.

In a sense, I understood how it feels to be politically disoriented, positioned on the margins of a culture that continues to reproduce traditional masculinity. Despite general claims of sympathy with feminism, the "men's movement" has established itself, ironically, as the caretaker of those ideological constructions of men and women against which feminists have battled most adamantly. Its radical conservatism, behind its mask of progressivism, shows that profeminist men need—for now, at least—to force a plurality of politics: a sense of "men's movements." One of our first tasks, therefore, must be to show why the "mythopoetic" vision of masculinity must be discredited. Not only does Bly reproduce a species of traditional masculinity (though, because it is threatened, a hysterical version of it), but he does so on some disturbing grounds, ranging from a misuse of psychoanalysis to a misunderstanding of the history of the forces that have shaped contemporary masculinity. "Popular culture" is Bly's main social target, because it has made men "soft." His fear of the feminization of contemporary men leads him to propose a "mythic" version of masculinity, which seems designed to suppress or at least provide male regulation of that dangerous femininity:

> It is in the old myths that we hear, for example, of Zeus energy, that positive leadership energy in men, which popular culture constantly declares does not exist; from King Arthur we learn the value of the male mentor in the lives of young men; we hear from the Iron John story the importance of moving from the mother's realm to the father's realm; and from all initiation stories we learn how essential it is to leave our parental expectations entirely and find a second father or "second King." (Pp. ix–x)

Bly wishes to shore up what he sees (erroneously) as a masculinity beleaguered by women, especially through their threatening sexuality, among the generation of men that he positions as his "cultural sons." This essay, therefore, serves as a step toward disputing the "cultural father" of patriarchy, an anti-Oedipal, anti-text to help serve as an antidote to *Iron John*.

First, I want to sketch one of the major problems with Bly's notions of gender. Bly's answer to his recurring complaint that men, young men in particular, have become soft, weak, and feminine is that they must recapture a sense of their own power and masculinity through the cultural "reservoir" of "fairy stories, legends, myths, hearth stories" (p. xi). That he sees men as powerless is, of course, both inaccurate and dangerous. He marks a cultural disjuncture between traditional masculinity and what he implies, derisively, is "New Age" masculinity, whose main fault is that it has become the victim of an "active feminine" in women. In fact, there has hardly been a rupture: "man" is still "king of the road." He owns public space and may use it as an arena in which to rape, steal from, and generally attempt to reify women as victims. The oversight appears as only one way that Bly ignores our political and cultural reality in order to promote his fantasies.

Those who accept Bly's version of endangered masculinity will do so because they already know other versions of this story. Men may *feel* powerless, but that feeling, encoded into men by their culture, allows them to rationalize and justify misogynistic practices. Throughout men's lives, history and culture have trained them to translate sexual difference into male power. Society's "discourses of sexual difference" are

> complex and heterogeneous sign systems that encode—and enforce—differences between the sexes. . . . Anatomy is not destiny, but biological differences between the sexes have, throughout human history, been translated by social institutions into codes of behavior and law that privilege men over women irrespective of class.[5]

By misunderstanding the social and historical implications of Bly's program, men may feel entitled to reproduce the misogyny for which *Iron John*, as a modern monument to misogyny, stands. We must not allow men to walk ignorantly into the same old stories of masculinity, applauding on the way, as does the reviewer for *Fortune*, who calls *Iron John* "an antidote to 25 years of strident feminism. . . . It's also dumb. But better dumb than numb. Go, Bob!"[6]

The cheerleading misogyny of the *Fortune* reviewer bothers me less than the more insidious misogyny of *Iron John* itself, in which Bly attempts to disavow his project's antifeminist stance. He generally does so obtusely, by gratuitously tossing "and women" into his text at odd and usually inappropriate times. He makes a similar move in relation to homosexual men, whom he mentions—condescendingly—once, in his Preface, by saying that "this book speaks to heterosexual men but does not exclude homosexual men. . . . The mythology as I see it does not make a big distinction between homosexual and heterosexual men" (p. x). To be both serious and facetious, however, the boy in the "Iron John" tale that serves as Bly's key to masculine mythology does not become Iron John's lover, but rather reaches the end of the story in a traditional heterosexual dénouement of marriage to the king's daughter. The sudden disavowals of difference always serve most strongly to condemn the rest of the text by creating monstrous ironies. In this essay, my eventual focus will be discussion of my problems with Bly's attempt to define his and my masculinity. I also want to examine two more of Bly's disavowals: the first because it most clearly highlights the problem of men trying to recapture (as though it were ever lost) traditional masculinity, and the second because it holds the key to Bly's hysteria about his position as a man in contemporary culture.

The first disavowal concerns Bly's elision of the power structure in patriarchy that has allowed and even tacitly promoted violence against women. Near the beginning of his book, Bly argues that, to stop men from being "soft" and "receptive," they need the "ability . . . to shout and be fierce." Then he disavows the power relationship that such behavior suggests: this ability, he says, "does not imply domination, treating people as if they were objects, demanding land or empire, holding on to the Cold War—the whole model of machismo" (p. 27). He also disavows the violence of fierceness by calling violent men "stuck in the warrior mode," the cure for which—in a point to which I will return—becomes male mothering and a ritual homosocial bond (p. 191). Bly's disavowals, within the framework of *Iron John* itself, supposedly counteract the swords, war, wounds, and fighting that Bly repeatedly reinscribes as models of "the masculine." Bly desires to separate the rituals of masculinity from everyday social reality; he fails to recognize, however, the extent to which those rituals inform and mold reality. Such rituals have been analyzed as "mythology" by Roland Barthes[7] and as "ideology" by Louis Althusser[8] and others. In all cases, the writers have made clear that such social rituals are not disconnected from but rather are part of the fabric of material reality. Bly elides the question of violence in other ways, too: for example, he skips discussion of the part of the "Iron John" tale in which Iron John kills men and dogs. Such occlusions within the confines of his book, though questionable, may be innocuous, but on a cultural level, such pretended innocence shows how thoroughly Bly's conscience lies in the realm of the fairy tale. The grim(m)ness of the fairy tale lies in the pretense that we can reproduce an innocent masculinity based on metaphorical violence because we intend it to remain metaphorical.

To band together two of Bly's favorite figures from the Western literary tradition as examples, we can examine Zeus, whose "positive male energy" represents "male authority accepted for the sake of community" (p. 22), whom Bly wants to recuperate for the modern mythopoetic male, and William Butler Yeats, whom Bly fondly quotes—yet never, of course, from "Leda and the Swan," where we see "positive male energy" played out "for the sake of the community." Zeus, in the form of a swan, rapes Leda, whose union will give birth to Helen and Clytemnestra. Yeats figures the rape as the "annunication that founded Greece": "A shudder in the loins engenders there / The broken wall, the burning roof and tower / And Agamemnon dead."[9] To try to re-legitimate "male authority," the patriarchal glue that, for Bly, holds Western culture together, he presents that authority as innocent of any wrongdoing: he wishes us to ignore the rape, war (starting with the Trojan War inaugurated by Helen's beauty), and murder (Clytemnestra, in murdering Agamemnon, performs a symbolic castration) engendered at the same mythic level he piously invokes. Bly uses myth selectively to rewrite Western cultural history, attempting to convince us that—to move from one bird to another—patriarchy is walking and quacking but isn't a duck.

Bly presents us with a bowdlerized version of patriarchal history, then follows with a certainly duplicitous move. I have mentioned one of Bly's readings of history because I want my concern about the serious issues that Bly's text raises for women not to get obscured in my own reading of Bly's text. Because Bly and I share positions as white heterosexual men—though our positions differ quite markedly beyond those broad political categories—my reading of the book, which concentrates on reading it from those positions, cannot have cultural implications equivalent to readings that women and other men may provide. I may be politically opposed to Bly, but I cannot fear him precisely because he reinscribes my position at the apex of a cultural hierarchy. Rather, my work may serve a better function—in a turn on Bly's subtitle, *A Book About Men*—as a paper *for* men. Such a reaction to Bly becomes an intricate matter, to which I will finally return, in that men have to find a way to reject Bly's vision that will equal breaking with the history with which Bly remains consistent: a history that pretends to be for our manly good but that must strain to argue its innocence to assuage its guilt over preserving manhood at the expense of others—primarily women.

Bly's second disavowal concerns his use of psychoanalytic configurations of "mother." Given his penchant for mythology, his use of Jungian archetypes comes as no surprise, but more challenging and odd are his readings of Sigmund Freud. That his reading of Freud is neither particularly deep nor current indicates why *Iron John* becomes in many ways a straw target: he seems occasionally aware of but unable to use fruitfully anything that has happened recently in feminist or psychoanalytic theory. He seems to understand, for example, poststructuralist notions of identity: he opens his first chapter by mentioning that the "identity of the American man has not been constant . . . over decades, or even within a single decade" (p. 1). But he also takes repeated pains to base masculinity in genetics, hoping to naturalize the old stories of masculinity: "Men receive the warrior gift . . . from imper-sonal warrior mansions high in the genetic heavens" (p. 191). If, on the level of the nature of masculine identity, *Iron John* becomes laughable as it strains to posit a definitive masculinity, then his use of psychoanalysis becomes a more serious matter. His interpretation of Freud's version of the father's role becomes so unproblematic, and the mother's role becomes so overly vilified, that he manages, incredibly, to outgun Freud in the matter of mi-sogyny.

"Mother" becomes the main scapegoat for everything currently "wrong" with American men; "wrong" translates into contemporary men's failure to conform to traditional masculinity—their naiveté, softness, and reluctance to wield the phallic power that Bly constantly employs as metaphor. His fear that women have come to dominate men appears in the way that Bly chas-tises the contemporary "strong or life-giving" women that he pretends to praise. Contemporary women choose "soft men to be their lovers" so that they can become mothers; the soft men are "in a way, perhaps . . . their sons" (p. 3). If he occasionally praises women, noting their capacity to nurture or their "marvelous" role as mothers—and even these compliments, in the con-text of contemporary feminism, appear backhanded and patronizing—such praise amounts to no more than another disavowal, an attempt to mask the repeated passages that bespeak men's castration anxiety. "Keith," for exam-ple, who has been "closer to women than to men" and who "works with women and [is] alert to the concerns of women" dreams that he runs with a clan of she-wolves: they all arrive at a riverbank and, as they all look in the water at their own reflections, he sees that he has no face (p. 17). The domi-nant-woman-as-mother is not the only target for Bly's misogyny—as we will see, he includes "feminized" men—but he makes it clear that women must (again) bear the blame for men's feminization because of their desire to castrate them: in this case, by robbing "Keith" of his face. Bly's book is largely a primer for men to learn to dominate their mothers, and he appears to intend that lesson as a means for them to learn to dominate all other women. *The Odyssey* becomes a primary mythic legend for Bly's retelling of the way men are supposed to display their phallic power: Odysseus must "lift" his "sword" when he approaches Circe, "who stands for a certain kind of maternal energy" (p. 4).

Bly makes man's main obstacle to his phallic masculinity (allegedly only mythic) battle with "the dark side of the Great Mother," who, in "ordinary life is an enraged woman" (p. 77). Bly discovers his poetic language in de-scribing her: she is "the black darling, the one with boar tusks coming down from her lips . . . the Rageful one, the Dark side of the Moon, the Ogre who lies on the back side of the moon with bat wings and ripped-apart birds" (p. 77). (Should we wonder that he meets so many enraged women?) The mother's role continually becomes an attempt to steal or to diminish male phallic power: if the mother wounds a man through her "possessiveness," he feels "inadequate and too small" (p. 72).

Bly's "Mommy-bashing" finds perhaps its most troubling component in the way that it rewrites the Freudian Oedipal drama. According to Freud, the boy must undergo a tremendous psychic battle to overcome his fixation on his mother. Bly erases the boy's Oedipal feelings for his mother, however; the problem becomes, not the boy's, but the *mother's*. "Too much mother" means, for Bly, a "psychic incest" in which the mother's clinging, smothering desire becomes all-important, as though, in terms of the Greek drama, the fault lies solely with Jocasta rather than with Oedipus as well. Bly's fear of but respect for contemporary woman lies in her "emotional richness" (p. 186): of course he finds her traditionally feminine "emotion" most praiseworthy. As a mother figure, however, woman's "feelings" allegedly create a pressure on the boy—her "psychic incest"—which, again in covertly sexual terms, make the boy feel "shame over his inadequacy" (p. 185). The union, on a "feeling" level, between mother and son is always caused by the mother: "American mothers sometimes confide details of their private lives to their small sons, details that might better go to adults their own age" (p. 185). Bly's ultimate horror over Mother's sexuality occurs in one of Bly's imaginary scenarios, when the young boy yells that he wants to "let the Wild Man out!" and Mother responds, "Give Mommy a kiss" (p. 12). Thus, for the boy to give up desire for his mother becomes a simple matter, because, Bly tells him, it's all his mother's fault. He can feel comfortable with himself, Bly suggests, because his sense of shame derives from the woman who has tusks hanging from her lips: an image implying that mother's tusked vagina threatens to penetrate him with her sexuality and emotion.

Compared to Bly's use of "Mommy," "Father" merits little invective. That American culture has "Too Little Father" (p. 93)—again the man's role becomes one of (loss of) phallic power—is, of course, Bly's point. In psychoanalytic terms, however, Bly practically erases the boy's perception of a competition between himself and his father over the mother. Bly notes at one point that, "for thousands and thousands of years," the Oedipal drama played itself out because fathers and sons lived "in close—murderously close—proximity" (p. 19), but the idealized relationship between fathers and sons never again carries any other force than a positive one in *Iron John*. All of his overdetermination of the sexual tension between mothers and sons becomes minimized when he discusses fathers and sons. Bly quotes Bruno Bettelheim, who

> noticed . . . that in most traditional cultures Freud's version of father-son hatred doesn't hold. The wordless tension, which he assumed to be universal and based on sexual jealousy, was, in Bettelheim's opinion, true mostly in Vienna in the late nineteenth century. (P. 93)

Curiously, Bly has no other problems with universalizing Freud. His use of Bettelheim seems understandable, however, considering that, for Bly, father and son have no reason to be jealous of each other, since all the sexual tension derives from the mother anyway. Because, at heart, Bly's prescription for our culture lies in reinscribing "plenty of father" (p. 93), he occludes any psychic difficulty in the relationship between fathers and sons, making, as we will see, the ritual, homosocial union between father and son the "happily ever after" of *his* fairy tale. "Plenty of father" makes the father the agent of a "body-on healing" (p. 93) of his son: a healing necessary because of the implied sickness of all those "female frequencies" (p. 94).

We need, therefore, to question why Bly proposes such a radically retroactive, misogynist vision. In other words, what does Bly want? Bly says he is looking for contact, perhaps, with his own father (p. 24), but that answer only mystifies the way he positions himself within his text. In terms of *cultural* filial relations, Bly notes that, during his twenties and thirties, he fulfilled the Oedipal role of the son: "I attacked every older man in the literary community who was within arrow range, and enjoyed seeing the arrows pass through his body, arrows impelled by the tense energy bottled in my psyche" (p. 23). Bly's apprehension that his position as "son" has passed places him now, he suggests, in the position of a cultural father. The reason for his occlusion of any psychic turmoil between the father and the son becomes clear when we look at how *impenetrable* Bly wants his current position as cultural father to be. That the traditional father, also embodied in the figure of the king, becomes the real hero of *Iron John* should not be surprising. But fathers and kings—those men (and of course it is men) "in . . . position[s] of power" (p. 22)—must, for Bly, occupy positions of unquestioned authority. Sons, of course, must obey, must not assume that power equals corruption and oppression (p. 22). The Greeks become his model because they "understood and praised a positive male energy that has accepted authority" (p. 22). Our culture, Bly says, has a "hunger for the father," which "transmutes into a hunger for the King" (p. 103).

Bly figures the "King" as traditionally masculine: scopophilic from "his room high in the castle among the air and sunlight" and a force of dominating mental power who "suggests solar power and the holy intellect" (p. 105). Most important, the king represents a nostalgia for a coherent male subjectivity and for visible masculine power. He sheepishly pines for the Middle Ages: "I am not saying that the king-killing was an error," he notes, but he also figures the end of kingship as the source of our political and psychological distress, because "our visual imagination becomes confused when we can no longer see the physical king" (p. 109). Bly longs for a masculine representative who "has arrived at unity; he is undistorted, unmingled . . ." (p. 105).

His reading of the male subject indicates how thoroughly *Iron John* participates in contemporary male hysteria. Bly's work appears as a testimony to

[t]hat fateful point where the specular coherence of unitary male subjectivity shatters, and what remains is but the violent residues of the death of the old male cock. Crash male subjectivity . . . as the hysterical sign of the fatal breakdown of the symbolic order of the unitary male subject.[10]

Bly has to wave his phallic weapons at Mommy and her stand-ins out of fear that his power won't be recognized. The phallus cannot be hidden any longer, he implies: only hysterical phallic exhibitionism can restore men to power. Bly's men's movement is about power, of course, as Susan Faludi notes in *Backlash*.[11] In her section on Bly, in fact, she gives us a portrait of the artist as hysterical male subject: he shouts, scowls, and paces during a lecture, sticking his face in that of "a frail, elderly woman" and yelling into the microphone (pp. 310–11). Faludi's portrait finally shows egotism and insensitivity. The mention of non-violence (Faludi records that one man in the audience mentions Gandhi) becomes one of the "weak ideas" of "soupy philosophers" to Bly (p. 311). Bly's book and his public self as an extension of that work appear emblematic of contemporary "crash male subjectivity." The problem lies not only in that subjectivity's realization of its lack of masculine coherence and unity but also in its sense of the historical fracture that has caused the crash. Bly implies that popular culture has been the sole, and more important (though also historically inaccurate), the recent, demon that has attacked "the respect for masculine integrity" and is "determined to destroy respect" for "Zeus energy" (p. 23). Bly's misreading of the history of masculinity in popular culture—his belief that the generation of men that follows him is the first one to suffer the allegedly debilitating effects of effeminacy—lends a note of alarm to *Iron John*. His misinterpretation has arisen, it seems, from his attempt to gain access to a patriarchal power that his culture has promised (particularly through its myths, legends, and fairy tales) but (so it appears to his crash male subjectivity) has not delivered. In other words, if younger men, because of popular culture, are suddenly not *really* men, then he has no one over whom he can wield his authority. In his attempt to legitimate his position as father, therefore, he tries to mend the breaks between his sons' and his own "masculine" subjectivity: the father's authority must be unquestioned, and his relationship with his sons must be only a lesson in the reproduction of a perfect, unthreatened, and "healthy" masculinity.

Indeed, a homosocial bond between father and son, in which the father asserts his dominance, becomes Bly's ritual prescription—his book's happy ending. In the "boar ritual," which Bly derives from *The Odyssey*, the "grand-fathers" wound the son and leave a scar. Even though "[i]t seems" to Bly that the wound "is not specifically a sexual wound" (p. 216), at other places in the book, which I mentioned earlier, the boar becomes part of the Great Mother figure, who has "boar tusks coming down from her lips" (p. 77). In the section about the "boar ritual," Bly tries to disassociate the boar from his notions of femininity, but he cannot escape making the two analogous. He calls the boar a "he," but the images associated with it are feminine: the boar is a figure of "the terror of impetuous forces in nature, such as floods, firefalls, waterfalls, wind-weather"; "he" is also associated with the "new moon" (p. 212; see also Theweleit). Bly does not directly associate the boar ritual with his idea that men need "male mothering" (p. 190), partly because he seems to need to distance himself from the sexuality and "femininity" present in the boar ritual. Bly appears alternately to need but to be unnerved by the proposition of occupying the position of the mother. The need to occupy the "masculine" and "feminine" parental roles also appears to be part of his male hysteria. In essence, Bly's project—his fantasy, perhaps un-conscious—is to make motherhood safe by eliminating those dangerous women from it. The project seems partly to terrify him, however, because of the sexual undertones of the homosocial bond.

His compulsion to co-opt the position of mother for men but to shy from the "femininity" that such a move implies is also symptomatic of the anath-ema that Bly reserves for any traces of the feminine within the masculine, a move that appears to begin innocently enough. He says that there is "some-thing wonderful about . . . the practice of men welcoming their own 'femi-nine' consciousness and nurturing it"—though we could question the irony in his tone, the way he makes those "feminine" words "wonderful," "welcoming," and "nurturing" appear somehow swarmy—but then he adds, "yet I have the sense that there is something wrong" (p. 2). Within a page, he has challenged men by questioning their virility in terms that suggest sexual dysfunction: the "soft male" has "little vitality to offer" (p. 3). Curiously, Bly also displays a trait that occurs frequently in misogynist texts. The man who hates women also hates men who exhibit any traces of femininity: gender traitors are serious criminals. Gender-reversal among "younger men"— his cultural sons—preoccupies and terrifies Bly. He claims that the traditional roles of a "passive feminine" and an "active masculine" are being reversed: women are "coming out into activity just as the men are passing them going the other way, into passivity" (pp. 60–61). Though he attempts to praise women for their "coming out," he eventually must repeal women's power in order to re-establish male authority. Men, he suggests, must outactive the active woman to insure patriarchal dominance, particularly in the home. For Bly, men's "passivity" takes root in the domestic sphere, where the man becomes a mouse in his refusal to stand up to his wife. The "domestic front" thus becomes the battleground in which men must learn to wrest power from women (Faludi, p. 310). Bly's portrait of contemporary men as victims to their wives and mothers leads Bly to analyze domestic situations in ways that have dangerous implications. For instance, the child who has suffered from incest, Bly says, "can do nothing about it" (p. 147). True enough, but Bly also suggests that the child remains a victim as an adult, feeling the "confusion of shame" (p. 148) partly by repeating the abuse. Bly ignores that the adult's role in incest, however, is no longer as victim but as *victimizer*.

His patronizing attitude toward those "soft males," who are "lovely, valuable people—I like them" (p. 2), rhetorically weights his work in order to let Bly position himself as "the man," the definer of masculinity. From my position—in my mid-thirties, I suppose I am one of those "lovely, valuable" younger men he challenges—I question his denigrating portrayal of his "unmanly" cultural sons. Ironically, as a textual embodiment of a cultural father, Bly appears more intellectually foolish than the popular culture that he derides for its representations of fathers as fools and more boyish than the generation of men whose masculinity he questions. In the first case, he somehow supposes that popular culture (if, indeed, it is even feminizing to men as he indicates) can supplant thousands of years of patriarchy in Western culture: Dagwood Bumstead supposedly usurps Odysseus as the model for masculinity. In the second case, he continually derides popular culture, at one point calling it "Disneyland culture" (p. 81), while trying, ironically, to base his model of masculinity on a fairy tale.

From my position, however, I do have to recognize the potential for my critique to become merely an Oedipal drama, in which I attack an older man in the literary community. To begin to refute that narrative, I want to mention the few parts of *Iron John* with which I agree, notably the section entitled "Learning to Shudder" (pp. 84–86). And one sentence of Bly's in particular stands out: "Eventually a man needs to throw off all indoctrination and begin to discover for himself what the father is and what masculinity is" (p. 25).

I like that sentence because it works against the very indoctrination that the rest of *Iron John* proceeds to enact. I don't agree that individually, as men, we can make that discovery: culture is too complex to suppose that men, as "free agents," can make discoveries about masculinity outside its parameters. Thus, a "men's movement," as a political movement that investigates the cultural forces—particularly masculinity itself—that act upon men, seems to me, in essence, a good thing. Bly, however, has gotten us started on the wrong foot: his work points uncomfortably and awkwardly backward, and it stinks of a history that has attempted to keep women beneath it. Thus, simply to "kill" Bly critically cannot be the answer. That tactic is part of a violent cultural heritage of which Bly represents the most recent agent. We need, perhaps, to disinherit him. We need to refuse to accept his patrimony by understanding the seriousness behind the grim(m) fairy tale and by recognizing the injustice involved in accepting such an inheritance, which keeps us, as men, in power at an awful cost to ourselves and others.

Bly's book can be helpful, but only if it can be used to show how many of our problems stem from its ideology of masculinity. In these days of feminist backlash and the hysterical male, we must combat the powerful drive to recuperate "the old male cock." The drive shows up continually in *Iron John:* for example, Bly writes of a man who, one day while meditating, "saw a man of light at the end of the corridor, nine feet tall with a spear. The man of light approached and said, 'If you don't make something of your life, I will take it from you'" (p. 92). Fears about phallic size and the equation of size with power—"nine feet tall with a spear"—don't just get played out in Bly's fairy tales and anecdotes. According to research by the Kinsey Institute, American men figured the average length of an erect penis to be ten inches.[12] Tania Modleski may be right that "the father" must be "frankly confronted and the entire dialectic of abjection and the law worked through or else the project to beat out (or write out) the fathers is doomed to failure."[13] But the most intense pressure lies in making sure that any reformulation of the law does not rewrite itself along the lines of the old model, or the father indeed *will* "at any time . . . emerge from hiding with a vengeance" (Modleski, p. 70). The move will never be easy to make, but at least we have "fathers" such as Bly to make traditional masculinity look ridiculous under scrutiny.

I want to end with one piece of mythology Bly relates that might hold some hope for our future:

> Ancient Celtic myth has an image for the end of patriarchy. . . . Eagles sit on the top branches of the sacred tree, with dead animals underneath their claws. Rotting bits of flesh fall down through the branches to the ground beneath, where the swine eat them. (P. 122)

In Bly's reading of the myth, men are the swine, and they are starving (p. 122). He does not interpret what the eagles represent, and thus his reading doesn't make particular sense. It seems to me that the eagles represent patriarchy itself as a system. Men, then, may be the pigs (chauvinist pigs?) who have had to eat the rotten meat that the patriarchal system has dropped. If men recognize the eagles and the meat for what they are, then they have two alternatives: to pretend that the meat tastes good or to stop eating. At any rate, the image allows us to see the absurdity of patriarchy, a system which so distorts men's vision that we believe that pasting eagles' wings on pigs we will be able to fly.

NOTES

1. Robert Bly, *Iron John: A Book About Men* (Reading, Mass.: Addison-Wesley, 1990).

2. Alice Jardine and Paul Smith, eds., *Men in Feminism* (New York: Methuen, 1987).

3. Joseph A. Boone and Michael Cadden, eds., *Engendering Men: The Question of Male Feminist Criticism* (New York: Routledge, 1990).

4. Klaus Theweleit, *Male Fantasies*, 2 vols. (Minneapolis: University of Minnesota Press, 1987).

5. Margaret W. Ferguson, Maureen Quilligan, and Nancy J. Vickers, eds., *Rewriting the Renaissance: The Discourses of Sexual Difference in Early Modern Europe* (Chicago: University of Chicago Press, 1986), xxi.

6. Gil Schwartz, "Inner Warriors," *Fortune* (26 August 1991): 115–16.

7. Roland Barthes, *Mythologies* (New York: Noonday-Farrar, 1972).

8. Louis Althusser, "Ideology and Ideological State Apparatuses (Notes Towards an Investigation)," in *Lenin and Philosophy, and Other Essays* (New York: NLB, 1971).

9. William Butler Yeats, "Leda and the Swan," in *The Norton Anthology of English Literature*, ed. M. H. Abrams et al., 5th ed., 2 vols. (New York: Norton, 1986).

10. Arthur Kroker and Marilouise Kroker, "The Hysterical Male: One Libido?" in *The Hysterical Male: New Feminist Theory*, ed. Arthur and Marilouise Kroker (Montreal: New World, 1991), xiv.

11. Susan Faludi, *Backlash: The Undeclared War Against American Women* (New York: Crown, 1991).

12. "Harper's Index," *Harper's* (March 1991): 19.

13. Tania Modleski, *Feminism Without Women: Culture and Criticism in a "Postfeminist" Age* (New York: Routledge, 1991), 70.

Iron Clint: Queer Weddings in Robert Bly's *Iron John* and Clint Eastwood's *Unforgiven*

MARK SIMPSON

In the seventies I began to see all over the country a phenomenon that we might call the 'soft male'. Sometimes even today when I look out at an audience, perhaps half the young males are what I'd call soft. They're lovely, valuable people — I like them — they're not interested in harming the earth or starting wars. . . . But many of these men are not happy. You quickly notice the lack of energy in them. They are life-preserving but not exactly life-giving. Ironically you often see them with strong women who positively radiate energy.

   US men's movement guru Robert Bly[1]

Listening and talking little was the one non-convict in the group, Harris Breiman, a specialist in the men's movement who made contact with the prison through the movement council he runs in Woodstock . . .

   'It's the warrior notion of the youngsters,' said Mr Velez, 37. 'So much focus on being a warrior. When I was first on Rikers Island [the prison], you had to have the right walk, the right display of aggression'.

   As the group focused on prison swagger, Mr Harris cautioned that 'the warrior can have a positive direction, too. The warrior in and of itself is part of what we are. If you give away the warrior energy you're going to be a passive victim.'

   New York Times (23 February 1993)

IN HIS BOOK *Iron John* (1990), a Jungian mythopoetic allegory-with-commentary extravaganza based on the Brothers Grimm fairytale 'Iron Hans', the poet and self-styled spiritual leader of the US men's movement Robert Bly has argued that the problem facing men today is that they have become too soft, too concerned about their 'feminine' side. They are, he says, too eager to please women, with the result that they are out of touch with the 'deep masculine', the 'warrior' who is an essential part of their psyche, making them miserable, passive and unsure of their identity. The story of Iron

John is interpreted by Bly as an instruction on how to reclaim that 'deep masculine' and the male energy that is said to go with it.

The story tells of a wild man covered from head to foot in hair (whose rusty iron colour gives him the name 'Iron John') who is kept in a cage in the courtyard of a castle. The key to the cage is kept by the Queen under her pillow. The young prince, playing in the courtyard, loses his prized 'golden ball' through the bars of the cage. Iron John persuades the boy to steal the key and release him in exchange for the return of his ball. But once Iron John is released, the boy is frightened of being punished by his parents and runs off to live in the forest with Iron John. Their partnership does not last, however, and the boy returns to civilization (in fact a kingdom adjacent to his parents') disguised as a peasant. Nevertheless he is able to call on Iron John's assistance from the edge of the forest whenever he needs it, and in this way wins great battles and eventually the hand of the princess.

Bly stresses the timeless, pre-Christian origins of the story and offers it as an antidote to what he sees as the present-day dearth of images of 'real men' in popular culture and the prevalence of 'stereotypical sissies like Woody Allen—a negative John Wayne.'[2] It becomes apparent that Bly's obsession with ancient narratives of manhood is a liking for a kind of heritage masculinity, an Olde Worlde natural virility with added bran: 'One of the things we do is to go back to the very old stories five thousand years ago when the view of a man, what a man is, is far more healthy.'[3]

In effect Bly is telling us that the 'unhealthy' soft men, constipated on their modern diet of processes, domesticated manliness are in *sore* need of a change in their intake of role models; what is needed is the raw *fibrous* manhood of Iron John (™ Robert Bly Bakeries Inc.) to restore their 'authentic' regular maleness and relieve them of their haemorrhoidal 'feminine' condition.

To restore his strength, Bly suggests, the soft man must stop taking his cue from 'mother', ignore the negative John Waynes and 'descend down into the male psyche and accept what's dark down there':[3] get in touch with the 'wild man', the 'hairy man': release Iron John from his cage.

Bly's ideas, which may appear bizarre and even comical to an English readership, have gained a remarkable popularity in the United States. Since the mid-1980s tens of thousands of American males have attended weekends in the forest based around his Wild Man masculinity and the 'need' to counteract the 'feminization' of modern men. As *Iron John* became a bestseller, the American men's movement went mainstream and gained respectability, its representatives often consulted on the burning men's issues of the day and even involved in prisoner rehabilitation schemes (Bly's ideas are shamelessly employed to explain the opposite phenomenon of 'soft men': the violently non-feminine behaviour of maladjusted males, suggesting that they are overcompensating).

American popular culture too began to show evidence of being influenced by these ideas, most notably Clint Eastwood's *Unforgiven* (1992), which is analysed below and compared with the Bly philosophy as told in *Iron John*. The two texts are examined alongside one another not simply to demonstrate the permeation of Bly's ideas in American popular culture but also to illustrate their remarkable *symmetry* with the work of Eastwood (a masculinity 'guru' from an age before the men's movement) as well as the secret of their appeal and the reason why they will probably not export well: their intimate connection, not to 'ancient' conceptions of manhood, but to the New World and the American Western tradition.

Unforgiven features Clint Eastwood as William Munny, a widowed Kansas pig farmer struggling in the 1880s to raise his two children single-handedly and live by the values which his dead wife, a strong Christian, instilled in him—putting his murderous past as the 'meanest sonofabitch in the West' behind him. We see him trying unsuccessfully to separate his pigs which are dying of fever. Into this scene of uneasy domesticity rides an impetuous young man by the name of The Schofield Kid (Jaimz Woolvett). In awe of Munny's reputation as a gun-slinger he tries to persuade him to be his partner for a contract killing in Big Whiskey, Wyoming, a revenge killing of two cowboys for 'raping and killing a prostitute' (in fact her face was slashed). Munny refuses. 'My wife,' he says, covered in pig shit, looking tired, old, and defeated, 'cured me of my sinful ways.'

Munny has become a sad, soft man, trying to please his dead wife. The boy rides off disgusted: 'You're not William Munny!' he shouts, rejecting this 'negative John Wayne'.

Munny looks at his dying pigs (are they dying of shame?), his hungry children and his filth-covered clothes and realizes his failure as a 'soft man'. Finally the need to feed his children sends him out after the Schofield Kid and his disowned past. But he still has not 'accepted what is dark down there', he is still in thrall to his dead wife: he is still without masculine energy. So we see him fail to hit a single bottle when practising with his revolver and his horse shies away from him when he tries to mount it, causing him to fall flat on his back (the horses, like the pigs, instinctively *know* when their master is a weak, soft male). His young son looks on ashamed.

Mounted at last—but looking very *queasy* in the saddle—Munny looks up Ned Logan (Morgan Freeman), his black partner from the bad old days and persuades him to join him while Ned's Indian wife looks after Munny's children; the pair of them catch up with the Kid and ride on to Big Whiskey.

In Big Whiskey the fragile Munny has caught a chill as a result of the heavy rain during the ride (and quite possibly his Christian refusal to partake in the cockle-warming liquor the other men drink to keep the rain out). True to the memory of his wife he remains downstairs in the saloon while the other two visit the whores upstairs. In swaggers Sheriff Little Bill Daggett (Gene Hackman) with his deputies. He has heard about the bounty and is determined to keep hired guns out of 'his' town. Daggett demands and gets Munny's weapon and then proceeds to kick seven shades of shit out of him. Munny does not resist Daggett's boot as it drives into his chest and stomach. Later, he is found by his partners and carried away to a barn where the whores nurse him. 'I can't believe he didn't do anything,' exclaims The Schofield Kid.

Munny still has no energy, he is still passive, he is without his 'golden ball', because he has yet to steal the key from under his wife's pillow, escape her power and set his wild man free. In Bly's words:

> We see more and more passivity in men. . . . If his wife or girlfriend, furious, shouts that he is a 'chauvinist', a 'sexist', a 'man', he doesn't fight back, but just takes it. . . . If he were a bullfighter he would remain where he was when the bull charges, would not even wave his shirt or turn his body, and the horn would go directly in. After each fight friends have to carry him on their shoulders to the hospital.[4]

In 'hospital' Munny develops a terrible fever and nearly dies. But when the fever breaks and he recovers, it transpires his skills and self-assurance are returning; he has begun to accept his 'true' nature; and with that acceptance comes his *virility*. With The Schofield Kid and Logan he corners the partner of the cowboy who mutilated the whore. Munny asks Ned to do the shooting because, as we know, he is now such a poor shot. Ned only manages to wound the boy and, hearing his moans and pleas, cannot bring himself to finish him off. Taking Ned's rifle Munny kills the boy—with one shot. He has become a killer again and a *man*. But his restoration is still not complete: he shows far too much compassion for the boy, allowing his friends to bring him water before murdering him. It takes another 'fever', another 'kicking', to send him into the very darkest depths of his psyche.

That 'kicking' comes in the form of Ned's death. Distressed by the killing of the cowboy and his loss of nerve, Ned tries to return home to his wife. He pays dearly for his attempt to renounce his past and his 'warrior' inside. On the way he is captured by a posse and handed over to Daggett who tortures and then kills him.[5]

When Munny hears this he is grief-stricken but instead of showing it he finally takes the elevator ride to the basement of his psyche and embraces whole-heartedly its darkness. He rides into town, single-handedly killing Daggett and most of his deputies, ordering the quaking survivors to bury Ned's body which has been propped up in an open coffin outside the saloon with the sign 'This is what we do to assassins' around his neck. They obey him, now recognizing him at last as William Munny, *'the meanest sonofabitch in the West'*.

In terms of the film's development he is finally restored as 'William Munny', having decided to embrace his dark destiny; in terms of the audience's relationship to the film he is Clint Eastwood again, a reassuring Good Bad Guy, replacing the tormented, ineffectual, *embarrassing* Good Good Guy; and for Bly he is a soft man made hard, a Woody Allen self-doubting figure transformed into John Wayne, no longer life-preserving but life-taking and thus life-giving (it is the destroyer, the warrior who has the power to grant life just as surely as to take it). He is imperfect, certainly; pained, definitely, but he is an authentic man, no longer trying to please women, true to *him*self. As Eastwood himself has said, 'Munny gave her his word that he wouldn't pick up the guns, but it's what he knows; it's the accident of who he is.'[6]

In his preface to *Iron John* Bly goes out of his way to reassure that his masculinism does not present a threat to women.

> I want to make it clear that this book does not seek to turn men against women, nor to return men to the domineering mode that has led to repression of women and their values for centuries. The thought in this book does not constitute a challenge to the women's movement. The two movements are related to each other, but each moves on a separate timetable.[7]

Unfortunately the 'separate timetables' are very much in conflict: there is only room for one train on Mr Bly's railroad, something that he is not afraid to admit out of print. At a two-day lecture at the Jung Centre in San Francisco he harangued a mixed audience shouting, 'There's too much passivity and naivete in American men today. There's a disease going around, and women have been spreading it. Starting in the sixties, the women have really invaded men's areas and treated them like boys.'[8]

Women *are* the problem. It is women's influence and power that must be destroyed in order to free Iron John and save the 'soft' men. Bly's 'ancient', 'healthy', 'warrior' masculinity is one that women will recognize as not so very ancient or healthy at all; just the social imperative for male dominance/ domination at any cost ('If you give away your warrior energy you're going to be a passive victim'—i.e. a 'pussy') that they only very recently began to roll back. Bly's prescription of how men should escape the 'power of mother's bed' is also familiar: employ the threat of violence. In his book he advises men to show women 'the sword', being careful to add, 'But showing a sword does not necessarily mean fighting. It can also suggest a joyful decisiveness'—the joy of a bully, in other words.[9]

The bully's power, as any woman or man who has suffered under one will tell, does not rest upon his *use* of his fists, so much as the threat of them. This seems to be what Bly is encouraging men to do. But of course the threat of violence eventually has to be backed up by something more substantial than 'mythopoetics'. According to Susan Faludi, at a 1987 seminar Bly revealed just what 'showing the sword' meant. A man in the audience complained, 'When we tell women our desires they tell us we're wrong.' 'So, then bust them in the mouth,' Bly instructed. After someone pointed out that this promoted violence against women Bly modified his statement, 'Yes. I meant, hit those women verbally!'[10]

Bly's *Iron John*, for all its careful prevarication and prefaces, its airy-fairy 'mythopoetics' and its earnest scholarliness, is really a paean to male violence: 'show the sword', 'get in touch with the wild man', 'accept what's dark down there', 'bust them in the mouth!'

Unforgiven, made by a director/actor famous for his use of violence to achieve his ends, is a better story than Bly's *Iron John* and better told. Somehow a lesson in violence comes across better as a taciturn visual tutorial from The Man With No Name than the wordy, flighty 260-page volume written by a soft-bodied, white-haired, cravat-wearing poet trying on Whitman's clothes and playing with Hemingway's hunting rifle.

What is interesting about Eastwood in *Unforgiven* is the way in which, like Bly, he seems anxious to present violence no longer as a Spaghetti Western hedonistic experience, but rather as something fated: in place of the Spaghetti Western we now have the Gothic Western. 'Violence always hurts,' he told the *Guardian*. 'The new thing about *Unforgiven* is the way it hurts the perpetrators too.' Violence is no longer celebrated for its fun but for its 'nobility', its 'human tragedy'.

And like Bly's book, *Unforgiven* has a preface that appears to pre-empt any reading of the film as misogyny. At the beginning of the film a young prostitute has her face slashed for laughing at a cowboy's penis. The sheriff initially wants to horsewhip him but the brothel-owner demands compensation instead: 'After all, it's my property that has been damaged.' Daggett orders the cowboy to hand over his horses to the man. But the prostitutes refuse to accept this male 'justice' and decide to pool their savings to hire a gunman who will dispense their *own*. 'They might ride us like horses,' vows the whore 'mother'. 'But we'll show them we're not horses.'

But this nod to feminism, as in *Iron John*, is rapidly taken over by the internal logic of the plot of a film that demands that women be characterized as 'the problem'. Initially treated sympathetically, their grudge against the cowboys turns to vindictiveness. They refuse the attempts of the slasher's cute young partner to make amends by keeping his best horse from the brothel owner and offering it to the scarred girl instead. In fact the first cowboy killed is the nice boy, whose agonizing death Logan cannot stomach. Women, whether Madonnas (Munny's wife) or whores, bring trouble into this Wild West world, trouble between men and trouble with men: 'there's a disease going round and it's spread by women' (and it kills pigs).

This is why Bly's famous weekends in the forest are men-only affairs. Forget Odysseus and the Iliad; the age-old 'universal' myths of manhood that he lays claim to in an attempt to legitimize his philosophy, are as local, as close to hand, as *American* as the myth of the Western. Bly's *Iron John* is nothing more than a bad Western: 'bad' because it looks to Europe to 'authenticate' a mythology that is as home-grown as John Wayne and Huckleberry Finn. The 'healthy man' that Bly looks for in high-falutin' translations of fancy European folk-tales and Greek myths is right on his doorstep in good ol' American chaps and stetson, thumbs hooked over his gun-belt, chewing baccy. Eastwood, in his leathery, old-timer way, knows this, and that is why he won Best Picture and Best Director from the Academy Awards for his retelling of this myth.

Both men are American romantics (but give me Eastwood's grim romanticism any day over Bly's lush prose trying to be plain), in love with the wilderness Eros, an Eros founded on the exclusion of women and the 'pure' love of male for male, the object of which is, as Leslie Fiedler put it, 'to *outwit* woman, that is to keep her from trapping the male through marriage into civilization and Christianity. The wilderness Eros is, in short, not merely an anti-cultural, but an anti-Christian, a Satanic Eros.'[11] The Queen must be outwitted and the key stolen from under her pillow to allow the Wild Man to escape from the cage of marriage and civilization and flee with him into the forests. Bly's emphasis on the pre-Christian status of his myths is a belief in their pagan/Satanic power to roll back the 'feminization' of man in Western Christian civilization, in the same way that in the Western the frontier is 'unsettled' and beyond the rule of law; Bly looks to the past while the Western looks to the horizon to achieve the same ends. (Of course, the Hollywood Western also looks to the past: the horizon is that of nineteenth-century America before the closure of the frontier.)

In *Unforgiven* the pure love of male for male, the romance of the West, is that of 'partners': it is taken for granted that *both* cowboys, rather than just the slasher, should pay the penalty: the bond between such men is closer and even more indissoluble than marriage. This is also the story of Munny and Ned: Ned leaves his wife the moment his old partner comes riding by.

And as so often happens in American dreams of the wilderness, the 'partner' sought by the white man 'lighting out for the territory' is black. For once 'civilization is disavowed and Christianity disowned. . . . The wanderer feels himself more motherless child than free man. To be sure, there is a substitute for wife or mother presumably waiting in the green heart of nature: the natural man, the good companion, pagan and unashamed—Queequeg or Chingachook or Nigger Jim.'[12] Ned is Munny's first port of call on leaving his farm. Ned appears to agree to his request only because his old flame has asked him to, rather than out of any real desire for the bounty. In the tradition of masculine passion denoted by its very understatement the film makes clear their deep and 'pure' love for one another, one that is unspoken but fought to the death for.

This is precisely what Munny is prepared to do when he learns of Daggett's killing of Ned (whose own death can be read as a punishment for turning his back on Munny). This is the diabolical denouement of this Western: in embracing 'what is dark down there', calling Iron John from the edge of the forest, Munny is making a Faustian pact. Munny rides into town at night and sees Ned's corpse propped up in a coffin outside the saloon lit by flickering candles, ghastly and satanic: As Fiedler points out, 'the dark-skinned companion becomes the 'Black Man', which is a traditional name for the Devil himself'. In avenging/saving Ned, Munny is making an infernal vow, putting him forever outside the reach of his wife, Christianity and civilization. He is Huckleberry Finn, determined not to give in to Aunt Sally's threats and reveal the whereabouts of his beloved Nigger Jim, embracing damnation.

'All right, then I'll *go* to Hell' . . . It was awful thoughts and awful words, but they was said. And I let them stay said; and never thought no more about reforming. I shoved the whole thing out of my head, and said I would take up wickedness again, which was in my line, being brung up to it, and the other warn't.[13]

'It's what he knows, the accident of who he is.' The Faustian pact is a 'queer' marriage. Munny is Ishmael clinging to Queequeg's coffin in Moby Dick, saved but damned by Ned's corpse, married to him forever in a way that the living Ned would not or could not allow; it is a marriage that puts Munny forever outside civilization, sends him to Hell—but in his own way.

But however 'queer' the marriage, it must never be physically consummated: the diabolical, pagan homosocial world of men is atoned for in the 'purity' of their love for one another. Ned's death guarantees the chastity of Munny's marriage to him.[14]

Likewise in *Iron John* the preface tells us that 'Most of the language in this book speaks to heterosexual men but does not exclude homosexual men.'[15] In fact *all* of the language speaks to heterosexual men; homosexuality is as *necessarily* invisible (but always present) in the world of Bly as that of Eastwood's West; 'the past' is used as a circumvention of the irresolvable problem of homo-desire: 'It wasn't until the eighteenth century that people ever used the term homosexual; before that time gay [*sic*] men were understood simply as part of the community of men.' In other words, 'I deal in timeless mythologies of masculinity and since homosexuality is not timeless I shall ignore it.'

As usual Bly employs disingenuousness dipped in an 'inclusive' aniseed liberalism to throw his enemies off the scent. Despite the claim to a 'universal' myth, he makes a very clear distinction between homosexual and heterosexual men. His whole mythology, like that of the West, depends upon it—but only to *exclude* homosexual men. Bly's masculinism and the tale of Iron John depend upon the implicit myth of 'pure love' between men: explicitness—i.e. actual homosexuality in general or the homosexual in particular and especially—threatens to bring it low and spoil it for everybody. This wilful blindness becomes laughably clear in Bly's analysis of the ending of the Iron John story:

The young man's father and mother were among those invited to the wedding, and they came; they were in great joy because they had given up hope that they would ever see their dear son again.

While all the guests were sitting at the table for the marriage feast, the music broke off all at once, the great doors swung open, and a baronial King entered, accompanied in procession by many attendants.

He walked up to the young groom and embraced him. The guest said: 'I am Iron John, who through an enchantment became turned into a Wild Man. You have freed me from that enchantment. All the treasures that I own will from now on belong to you.'[16]

What could be clearer? The real romance of the story has been consummated. But Bly, the expert mythologist and translator, cannot recognize a queer wedding when he sees one. The ending tells us, he writes, that we need not only to 'free ourselves from family cages and mind sets' but also to free 'transcendent beings from imprisonment and trance'. Yes. . . . But what about the symbolism of the wedding scene, the embrace, the sharing of worldly goods? And any child could tell you how you turn a frog into a prince. 'I think that we have said as much as is proper here about the Wild Man,' is Bly's final word on the matter. Perhaps Bly should be less concerned about 'transcendent beings' and work on freeing himself from his own 'imprisonment and trance'. His insubstantial analysis reveals the bogus notion that is at the very heart of Bly's credo: 'descend deep down into the male psyche and accept what is dark down there' is a call to end repression if it is anything at all—and yet Bly's interpretation of the most crucial scene in the whole Iron John story is itself a lesson in disavowal, a refusal to accept 'what is dark down there'.

The end of the Iron John story shows that, just as in the Western, the overriding romance was homosexual: 'woman' has been outwitted again, prevented from 'trapping the male through marriage into civilization and Christianity' even at the very moment of the boy's readmission into the family ('they had given up hope that they would ever see their dear son again') and holy matrimony: instead of the bride, Iron John comes through the 'great doors'. Freed from his enchantment by the boy's love, Iron John is 'tamed'; he loses his hair and becomes a baron (in effect he turns 'white') and thus can return to civilization to join the boy, to save him from it in the nick of time.

The ending also demonstrates that Iron John is more than just an aspect of the boy's own psyche, as Bly would have it. The romance has been a mutual attraction of opposites: the soft boy's attraction to Iron John's toughness and *Iron John's attraction to the boy's softness;* in the end the romance had the effect of both giving the boy just enough 'wildness' and giving Iron John just enough 'civilization': a perfect exchange, a perfect couple. Thus the ending appears to balance the incompatible: marriage and queer romance, familial acceptance and masculine freedom, civilization and the forest.

But this is just a fairy tale. In the 'real' world of adult literature and cinema these opposites cannot be reconciled and the resolution must be darker: there can be no 'queer wedding' or Fiedler's 'holy marriage of males'. Instead there is the usual fatal sublimation: the dark-skinned Queequeg dies but lives on through white Ishmael's love for him, adrift in an endless blank wilderness of ocean; black Ned dies but lives on through white Munny, an outlaw cast adrift in a wilderness of crime.

NOTES

1. Robert Bly, *Iron John* (New York: Vintage, 1992), p. 2.

2. Quoted in Susan Faludi's *Backlash: The Undeclared War Against Women* (London: Chatto and Windus, 1991), p. 340.

3. Bly, *Iron John*, p. 6.

4. *Ibid.*, p. 63.

5. 'An intelligent man with no stomach for killing, despite his proficiency with a rifle, his distaste for the job at hand is obvious and his reluctance to participate ultimately proves his undoing.'—production notes.

6. The production notes offer this succinct and revealing description of the Munny character: 'William Munny is a complex, taciturn man whose perspective is tempered, not only by his past, but by the love for his late wife and his children. He becomes caught between who he was and who he is, struggling with the knowledge that he can make himself solvent by calling upon the very darkest elements of his personality.'

7. Bly, *Iron John*, p. iv.

8. Faludi, *Backlash*, p. 345.

9. Bly, *Iron John*, p. iv.

10. Faludi, *Backlash*, p. 345.

11. Leslie Fiedler, *Love and Death in the American Novel* (New York: Stein and Day, 1962), p. 212.

12. *Ibid.*, p. 26.

13. *Ibid.*, p. 352.

14. In *The Eiger Sanction* (Eastwood, US, 1975), Eastwood gave us an unambiguous example of his attitude towards homosexuality. In it he plays an expert mountaineer and part-time CIA operative whom a mincing queer villain, complete with a lapdog by the name of Faggot, tries to have killed. Rather than demean himself by killing such a monstrosity he merely leaves him out in the desert to die—he lets *nature* wreak its revenge on this freak. Even heterosexual men cannot be trusted. Another

268 : MARK SIMPSON

character, a friend of Eastwood's, oversteps the limit of friendliness; 'Don't go sloppy on me,' Eastwood warns disgustedly. So it comes as no surprise to learn later that he is the enemy agent Eastwood has been looking for all along.

15. Bly, *Iron John*, p. v.
16. *Ibid.*, p. 232.

V

THE STRUGGLE FOR MEN'S SOULS: MYTHOPOETIC MEN RESPOND TO THE PROFEMINIST CRITIQUE

Thoughts on Reading This Book

ROBERT BLY

I WAS FASCINATED IN READING THIS BOOK to see how clearly and passionately most writers here state their point of view: for example, "There is no such thing as deep masculinity because there is no such thing as masculinity." But we have to be careful. No one could see subatomic particles, but physicists finally agreed that they exist. Moreover, physicists now agree that matter can take the form of particles or waves, and not in some either-or manner, but matter can be both at once. Just as there are mysteries that even well-trained physicists could not see for a long time, it's possible there are mysteries that the sociologically trained mind cannot see.

In science there has been a general agreement that all workers are moving toward a common goal of understanding. Physicists of all stripes, for example, have agreed to be honorable opponents. But in this book the contributors exhibit an urge to turn an opponent into a monster. I ask: Have the profeminist men here understood the nonpatriarchal quality of inclusiveness? I am charged throughout this collection with so many crimes that it would take hours to reply to them all: I pick the wrong story, I am an essentialist, I am a Jungian, I am a men's rights person in disguise, I am a Pharaoh, I am a secret patriarch. It's clear that many of the contributors would like to take me to a Chinese neighborhood meeting and have me confess my sins.

Rather than replying to these charges, it may be helpful just to talk a bit. I agree that men, white men particularly, have claimed for themselves a place of privilege that forces women to accept mistreatment in hundreds of ways. I value the persistence with which the contributors talk about masculine arrogance. The question is what to do about this arrogance. Scolding has not helped. When men learn to experience the deep grief they are already carrying in their bodies, that grief dissolves for some their cultural arrogance and bravado. The work on grief is a part of the battle against male hardness and arrogance; it is not a retreat from the battle.

Men should stand up and speak about the pain that millions of women feel. And yet declaring women's pain is quite different from declaring that everything which comes out of the masculine voice is false or deeply wrong in essence. "There is no such thing as deep masculinity because there is no such thing as masculinity." If there is no such thing as masculinity, then a man has no center in himself from which he can speak. Some of the writers in this book are as afraid of their own 'I' as homophobic men are of gay men. Such writers feel that their 'I' has to be purified by feminist doctrine before it can be trusted. Poems written by a man, then, are naturally full of errors. All poems are full of errors. That can be a stimulus for sorrow rather than self-hatred.

I feel that we as men are making a serious mistake when we give up our voice and speak "for our mothers," or "for all women." Speaking as a married man, I can say that when we speak for our mothers, we usually are disloyal to our wives. So there is no easy path here. Moreover, saying what sincerely aggrieved women want us to say makes us acceptable in the short run and allows us to speak a certain kind of truth, but at the same time it may damage some voice that we hardly know about, which is just beginning to be heard. That voice which we can hear inside ourselves on our best days is not a patriarchal voice. It is a voice trying to come from the heart.

I think we have to be patient in order to allow that voice to come out and not decide ahead of time what the voice should say. None of us wants to reestablish patriarchy. The destructive essence of patriarchy, which I feel vividly in the story of Herod, moves to kill the young masculine as soon as it appears anywhere within range. I felt that Herod quality coming from some professors when I was in college move directly towards me; and that is one reason I dropped out of the university environment and supported myself separately. Herod also moves to kill the young feminine. That's very clear to anyone who works in the university. I have daughters, and the last thing I want is for this Herod energy to move against them. I want all women to have a fair chance when they come up for jobs in the university. I don't want anyone stealing wages from my daughters, or self-esteem either.

I prefer the word "expressive" rather than "mythopoetic" as an adjective to the men's work that many of us do. At conferences we urge men to respect their own fathers and to respect fathering. Our best influence, I think, has been in teaching young men who are fathers to deepen and intensify their fathering from the day their daughter or son is born. I agree with Michael Kimmel that, "It is through the social practices of parenting that men may connect with the emotional qualities they rejected in real life—nurturing, compassion, emotional responsiveness."

The conferences have been broadening so as to include men of color, and that has intensified this work. The conference at Buffalo Gap in Virginia, for example, included half African-American men and half white men. Michael Meade, particularly, labors with great devotion to create mixed conferences and to bring new teachers in. At Buffalo Gap there were six teachers, two African-American teachers, two African teachers, and two white teachers.

The book before us does not give an accurate picture of the teaching done by men working in the expressive or mythopoetic movement. The profeminist writers become the "people" and all other teachers become the "bad others." Oppositional thinking is by definition misleading. Worst of all, simplified versions taken from inaccurate media coverage are passed on in this book for truths. For example, I taught many workshops for women during the 70s, and summed up much of that work in a long essay I wrote called "I Came Out of the Mother Naked," which defends the matriarchal and pre-matriarchal consciousness. I placed that essay in the middle of a book of poems still in print called *Sleepers Joining Hands* so it would be easily available; it has also been reprinted in several anthologies, but none of the writers in this book mention having read it. It's sad to see writers here, as those in the media, literalize or concretize the Wild Man so that it appears I am defending a biker or a macho. The being under the water is a god, namely Dionysus, who was in Greece a god for both men and women. The word *iron* refers to the color of his hair and his imprisonment inside iron bars. But writers literalize the word "iron" as hardness, as in Iron Man or "pumping iron," or make up misinterpretations, and argue against these.

I like Michael Kimmel's invitation to the two sides evoked in this book to respond to each other's ideas and argue. But surely if we are to be honorable opponents, we need to take a hint from the physicists and agree that we are moving toward a common goal. I would like to think it possible to introduce images, or myths, and not have them misinterpreted through linear thinking. Those trained to think in a linear way will also think literally, so that if iron is mentioned, it must refer to weapons and so be patriarchal. But we know that any given story, such as "Iron John," can be patriarchal and also matriarchal, particle and also wave. If either-or readers insist on approaching stories with a linear mind, looking for traces of the patriarchal devil, then such readers will end up throwing away all stories and eventually all literature.

This collection makes the point that mythological thinking is flawed, but linear thinking is also flawed. Efforts to welcome gay men into the expressive movement have been flawed—Jed Diamond is right about that. Current attempts to reunderstand and reestablish ritual are flawed, and certainly my efforts to understand and speak of initiation are flawed. But we have to be patient with each other. The writers of this collection and I agree on a number of matters. There is a danger, now that the old Father has been seen through, that some people, some voters, frightened, will try to reestablish as President a fake father or fascist father or manufactured father. The election of Ronald Reagan showed that danger very clearly, as does the recent rise of Newt Gingrich.

Marion Woodman and I have been working with men and women the last eight or nine years, and I'll leave you with a thought I have often heard her express. When she talks to either men or women, she says to them, "The next step for us who care is to make clear distinctions between patriarchy and masculinity." We know that patriarchy has damaged masculinity—perhaps not as much as it has damaged the feminine—but still severely. If patriarchy has damaged masculinity, and continues to do so, then they cannot be the same. Spokeswomen for gender feminism made a mistake thirty years ago in failing to make the distinction between patriarchy and masculinity, and, as a result, many young men, rather than being ashamed of being patriarchal, are ashamed of being men. We must be more clear. To be ashamed of your gender is not healthful for anyone.

The Postfeminist Men's Movement

AARON KIPNIS

INITIALLY, I WAS DELIGHTED TO BE INVITED to contribute to this book. In recent years, I have had several fine discussions with profeminist men. They seemed both interested in reconciling their ideas with our postfeminist views and desirous of taking the good will toward men they experienced in our mythopoetic gatherings into their own communities of men. I was hopeful that this would be the beginning of a vigorous dialog that might start building bridges between our disparate camps. Instead, what I have read is more of a polemic, which sadly has little grasp of the essential arguments which it proposes to debate. In recent years, my male-affirming, feminist partner and I have facilitated forums with thousands of women and men facing one another for thoughtful, well-informed, mostly good-willed debates on controversial gender issues. So, I welcome being challenged in this arena, but the articles here are, for the most part, sadly not up to speed on the conversation.

Much of the feminist writing in this anthology is so mean-spirited and riddled with epistemological and empirical errors, and other academic impoverishments, that the only spirit in which I can respond is that which I would use to address any student trying to pass off sophomoric ideology as a genuine contribution to the field. As a polemic uttered by ideologues who appear to be somewhat out of touch with the lives of men outside their privileged class, this book undercuts dialectical process rather than stimulating it. My greatest disparagement of this book, however, is not its ideas, but rather its severely limited review of the literature of, and dialogs within, the postfeminist men's movement. Instead, these articles react to a few popular books and media distortions, picking on a few off-hand comments or decontextualized quotes as representative of an entire body of thoughtful, revolutionary, and revitalizing literature on the postfeminist men's movement's incipient revisioning of Western masculinities.

Clearly you are all intelligent guys. But this book does not present its questions in the spirit of an intelligent academic inquiry. So, this makes me wonder—what is the real purpose of this book? The pursuit of knowledge is endangered when ideologies and academics merge. Standards of evaluation become weakened as the spirit of inquiry succumbs to the tyranny of fundamentalism's polemic. This book doesn't start from a well-developed enough place to truly warrant a response. It fails to rise to the level of dignity the revisioning of masculinity deserves. Yet, after several decades of ubiquitous academic feminist assault on men and masculinity, I find myself in the quandary of no longer being willing to let blatant distortions about our work stand unchallenged in print.

Professor Kimmel privately asserts that he has adequately researched this topic. It is clear, however, from both their comments and bibliographies, that most feminist contributors to this book have not. Is it possible that feminists are so repulsed by the emergence of a new pole of gender dialectic, outside the constraints of the women's movement, that they cannot bear to read our literature or attend in significant numbers open forums in which this conversation is being hosted?

The gender perspective of the postfeminist men's movement resides in a third position, somewhere beyond the militant poles of feminism and so-called patriarchy. Indelibly informed by both, we are also in the early years of articulating an entirely new perspective on men, masculinity, and their relationship to women, nature, spirit, and culture. I welcome a critique that begins at the same level of sophistication as the contemporary social dialog on gender. For the most part, however, that conversation is only happening outside the walls of the academy in forums where men, and women as well, can safely speak about the truth of their experience, freed from the constraints of politically correct doctrines.

Most profeminist men in this book are not responding to a known phenomenon, but rather a poorly researched and highly imagined one. The ad hominem attacks on Robert Bly and attempts to reduce the postfeminist men's movement to a monolithic cult of personality are so blatant and off base that they scarcely deserve mention. Bly, valuable artist that he is, is also simply one of many voices in a broad-based movement concerned with the social, psychological, and spiritual revisoning of masculinity.

The rhetoric of this book reminds me somewhat of that of the mid-6os when Nixon started reframing the student anti-war movement as a communist plot. We were incredulous then, since many of us thought of ourselves as patriots with a higher vision of our nation's moral responsibility. But then, Nixon never came to any of our meetings or really investigated what we thought and felt. His view was tainted by his political perspective.

Now, instead of the right imagining communist plots everywhere, the academic left finds "patriarchal" ones. In a stranger-than-fiction marriage, feminists have somehow joined the mainstream perspective of materialistic modernity in decrying something they must have mostly seen through the media's eyes and the distortions of their own ideology, both of which have blinded their capacity to see our texts or contexts. The media, with the exception of Bill Moyers, never really investigated the issues either. They merely sensationalized the more colorful aspects of men's break from both traditional heroic stereotypes and new limits placed on masculine imagination by decades of feminist revisionism.

In order to create an adequate forum for debate, profeminist men must *significantly* familiarize themselves with the fundamental texts of the postfeminist men's movement. Where is your commentary on Mark Gerzon's pioneering *Choice of Heroes*,[1] which began reimagining old masculinities over a decade ago? Where are the references to Shepherd Bliss' widely published calls (in dozens of men's journals and anthologies over the years) to discard the warrior as the dominant male-congruent image in favor of an evocative image of men who dance, make music, protect nature, and love women?[2] Where is regard for Sam Osherson's attention to healing the father-son wound?[3] Where is the analysis of John Lee's excellent work helping thousands of men recover from addictions and manage anger in healthy ways?[4]

Also missing are any genuine reading of my first book, *Knights Without Armor*,[5] which calls for a significant spiritual, psychological, and social revisioning of masculinities, and Sam Keen's philosophical commentary.[6] This maliciously careless review of the literature also overlooks Jed Diamond's views on ways men can heal their lives and thus the earth[7] as well. It is probably too late to press for these authors, but also important to this particular mythopoetic theme is Joseph Jastrab's heartfelt *Sacred Manhood, Sacred Earth.*[8]

Other mythopoetic works which have fallen into the profeminist lacunae are: the thoughtful work on Phallos by Eugene Monick,[9] any thorough reading of Robert Moore and Douglas Gillette's five scholarly volumes on masculine archetypes,[10] the Colemans' work on the Earth Father,[11] William Anderson's scholarly *The Green Man*,[12] Gordon Dalbey's mythopoetic Christian perceptive on *The Masculine Soul*,[13] Michael Gurian's imaginative *The Prince and the King*,[14] Michael Meade's elegant, *Men and the Water of Life*,[15] and many more works with which anyone investigating our field should have at least passing familiarity.

Astonishingly, even more mainstream postfeminist academic works on masculinity are overlooked such as Ruben Fine's profound psychological analysis in *The Forgotten Man*,[16] David Gilmore's anthropological insights in the *Making of Manhood*,[17] and social psychologist Alexander Mitscherlich's *Society Without the Father*,[18] to name but a few. Since several equations between mythopoeses and men's rights advocacy have been made here, one would think that profeminist men would acquaint themselves with at least a few fundamental postfeminist social commentators such as Herb Goldberg,[19] Asa Baber,[20] and Warren Farrell[21] before they dismissed their ideas.

There are hundreds of other credible postfeminist books, anthologies, and articles which, over the last decade, have insightfully detailed previously uncharted territories of the deep masculine psyche. These works simultaneously view the social construction of gender from a significantly different analysis than that done by feminists. All escaped your eye. You have not even done a literature review comparable to that required for a term paper, much less developed the authority to comment on an entire movement and nascent psycho-social-spiritual philosophy. It also appears that several authors in this book did not even conduct a careful reading of the few relevant texts they cited.

It is only because male-bashing is de rigueur in today's academy that such a poorly researched, blatantly misleading, politicized, and unbalanced critique could even be published by a reputable university press. Even though I admire the editor's courage and attempt at fair play through inviting a few leaders of the postfeminist men's movement to respond, the expanded view still fails to validate this work. Since the profeminist positions in this book represent a sequence of recapitulations and narrow variations on ideologically constrained ideas, I will not comment in depth on each article but rather touch on some of the overarching ideas throughout. (1) Bly's ideas, or the rest of ours for that matter, are not "universally rejected by feminism as patriarchal." Many *male-affirming* feminist women admire and support the positive changes the men's movement is generating through its dedication to: fathering, recovery work, environmental protection, reducing violence, mentoring, confronting racism and homophobia, and supporting egalitarian partnerships with women. This latter view may be better understood through reading my *Gender War, Gender Peace* co-authored with Elizabeth Herron,[22]

Carolyn Baker's "Confessions of a Recovering Feminist,"[23] Christina Sommers' *Who Stole Feminism?*[24] and other works by "new" feminists who reject the pathologizing, male-denigrating sentiment so prevalent in "old" feminism. A good anthology, which includes Elizabeth Herron and former head of NOW, Karen DeCrow, can be found in Jack Kammer's *Good Will Toward Men.*[25] (2) Ironically, feminist sources are more frequently cited in this book than the postfeminist texts it critiques. In the feminist authority oft-cited here, *Women Speak about the Men's Movement* [sic. ed.] Spretneck, Steinem, and others extol the image of the soft, obedient feminist male who serves women, carries their pain, and has few needs of his own for women to contend with.[26] Rianne Eisler, here and elsewhere,[27] distorts the valuable idea of partnership between the sexes by imagining a matriarchal world devoid of an autonomous sacred masculinity equal in value to the essential feminine. Starhawk assures us she wants men to be potent as long as they are not "assholes." Yet we would find it "patriarchal" or, in the strange new language of political correctness, europhallologocentric thinking, if men said they wanted women to be empowered as long as they weren't witches or "bitches." Why, then, should we not regard this source text as eurogynothymicentric, heterophobic, reverse sexist doggerel?

The authors in Kay Leigh Hagan's vituperative, twisted, and insidiously conspiratorial volume completely overlooked the excellent postfeminist works on life-affirming masculinity, failed to interview any of us, and declined to attend most public forums in which they could openly dialog with us. They ignored complex, overarching ideas in favor of a myopic, knee-jerk response to something clearly not understood nor sufficiently investigated. Therefore, I find it repugnant that their book is cited as a predecessor to the present volume since as a misandric diatribe it represents an astonishingly weak foundation for a dialectic on gender issues to progress. (3) Rather than threatening the revolution, the postfeminist men's movement is on the precipitous edge of social revision and is, in fact, the male-affirming antithesis of patriarchy rather than its re-entrenchment. Many of its leaders were also on the front lines during the anti-war movement, the free speech movement, the civil rights movement, the environmental movement, and yes, even the women's movement, where many of us spent a decade or two before realizing that men's legitimate social, psychological, and spiritual needs were being utterly forsaken by our feminist comrades. The men's movement is a logical development from feminism, just as women's consciousness was advanced by the civil rights movements, which progressed from democracy's often unimplemented but otherwise liberating visions. We have the same antecedents and destiny: a gender justice movement that will consider the needs of both genders *equally* in all our institutions. (4) Epistemological approaches can be examined but not dismissed as invalid until vigorously applied to knowledge and then analyzed. This volume's critiques of archetypal psychology are based upon a paucity of research which does not even include its foremost thinkers like Hillman[28] or Jung[29] and fails to demonstrate even a passing understanding of the basic principles of the field. On a similar note, since feminist literature has thrived on the anecdotal, and subjectivity is increasingly becoming the "reasonable woman" standard for new social contracts, how can feminists dismiss the subjective experience of men concerning their social, spiritual, physical, and psychological privation?

It is ridiculous to debate subjectivity or "essentialism" as a men's movement fallacy since feminism, for all its extolling of objective social constructivism, is clearly riddled with essentialist thinking. The blatant heterophobia of MacKinnon,[30] androphobia of Daly[31] and Spretnack,[32] misandry of French,[33] matrimoniphobia of Steinem,[34] and factual distortions by Faludi,[35] to mention but a few, all contribute to a feminist ontological premise which promotes a fallacious, inimical, *essentialist* caricature of a denigrated father that flies in the face of the nurturing, protecting, and sacrificing character of most men.

Provocative comments by some men, though often taken out of context in this volume, deserve critical comment. They are, however, certainly no less vituperative than the rampant misandry in feminist literature and thus, by feminism's own standards, not sufficient to discredit our work or even deem it antifeminist. After decades of unrestrained male-bashing, men have good cause for anger toward the women's movement. This is not backlash; it is a legitimate response to abuse of academic, social, media, and literary power.

We do confront the shadows of masculinity in our work: not, however, to codify attempts to shame men into changed behavior but rather to help men understand themselves more deeply and thereby develop healthier lives. More important, however, we balance the dialog on perceived patriarchal "privilege" through also analyzing the objective realities of men's privation. Men have significantly higher rates than women of suicide, addiction, injury, victimization by violence, death on the job, and death from the 15 major illnesses, as well as skyrocketing rates of homelessness, incarceration, and impoverishment.[36] In light of these and many other ugly facts, it is not spurious for some of us to wonder seriously about how well men are faring in our culture and to tender the position that some damage may have been done to the masculine soul as well.

On the basis of women's excessive and escalating violence toward children, shall we conclude that women are essentially infanticidal? No. Of course not. This, however, is the bizarre juncture at which feminism rejects the same essentialism it uses to demean men by proposing that women's abuse of power is socially constructed. The postfeminist men's movement is merely reiterating the same premise: if men behave badly, it is because something has happened to their masculinity that obscured its essential goodness. In our own, often still experimental ways, we are attempting to repair some of the damages done to masculinity by the onslaughts of modernity. (5) Concerning wounds and power, it is valuable that feminists have raised our consciousness about the gender-specific wounds of women. In fact postfeminist men actively support women's demands for social, political, and economic equality. It is a given. We also, however, express similar concerns for men and boys. This is the primary element separating the profeminist and postfeminist men's movements. Blatantly missing from feminist analysis of gender entitlements is an understanding of the disproportionate, gender-specific ways in which males suffer, are disempowered, and are at risk for abuse and neglect. Why fault the men's movement for merely recapitulating the same gender sensitivity feminism developed toward women? Apparently, we have learned our lessons well from their example.

Many men are undergoing a major restructuring of the basic paradigms governing masculine consciousness and behavior. If feminism is not primarily interested in helping boys and men, why not support the men who are? Feminist critiques would be much better directed at men who have abandoned their sons and daughters, neglected the planet, and eschewed egalitarian partnerships with women. But those men are harder to reach than the poets, therapists, community activists, and educators who are trying to give the same sort of attention to men's gender-specific needs that women have received over the last few decades.

Social constructionist theory rarely addresses the possibility that male violence is often a desperate response to psychological, social, and emotional trauma. For example, men who batter as adults were often abused themselves as children. Most treatment programs, however, do not address these untended wounds, but merely attempt to deal with the behaviors. In California, the statutory rape of boys by women was not even made illegal until 1993. Yet in our men's groups, it is apparent that sexual abuse and female battery of boys happen frequently and create just as many psychological problems for males as the reverse does for females. In my opinion, the social tolerance for *all* forms of abuse toward males is one of the primary causes of male rage and violence.

Feminist attitudes breed many double standards for men. They now affect almost every social institution. For example, schools have recently become very concerned about the ways girls lag behind in math and the sciences. And this needs to change. Feminists fail to mention, however, that boys lag just as far behind girls in reading skills, have lower grades overall, and, more important, have significantly higher high school dropout rates than girls. In many schools, over 5 percent of boys are given behavior modification drugs to get them to conform to a regimented, feminized school environment. The vast majority of teachers and counselors who refer them to psychiatrists for this treatment are women. Girls are not given drugs to make them more assertive and inquisitive. Nor should they be. But why do we tolerate this widespread chemical restraint of boys? Profeminist men would certainly protest similar practices against girls.[37]

In other arenas, self-esteem task forces have become very concerned about girls' mental health. This is good; however, boys' suicide rates are five times higher than girls. Isn't this a measure of a serious self-esteem problem among boys? There are massive public health campaigns to educate women about breast cancer, but little information for men about prostate cancer, a disease affecting 1 in 11 men that kills about thirty-five thousand annually. Because feminists falsely believe that men are, in every case, more privileged and less sensitive than women, they fail to bring the same level of care to men and boys that is extended to women. This is the down side of profeminist male chivalry. Certainly, profeminist men would be alarmed if women were dying over 7 years earlier than men, but the reverse statistic brings little concern.

Feminists usually fail to note that males account for: 70 percent of all assault victims, 80 percent of homicide victims, and 85 percent of the homeless. Males represent the fastest growing impoverished group in America, with over ten million now living in poverty.[38] Ninety percent of persons with AIDS, 93 percent of persons killed on the job, and 95 percent of prisoners are men.[39] In prison these men, many of whom are nonviolent, are raped in numbers matching those of free women. But we have no rape crisis centers or social programs—with the exception of a few, largely postfeminist men's groups—which deal with the posttraumatic stress-induced disorders of men victimized by the American penal system. Why are profeminist men not more concerned about issues which decimate their own gender? Through helping men to recover from their traumas, women are ultimately served as well, something one would think all feminists would welcome.

At last count there were over 600 academic women's studies programs, yet not a single one examining the rapidly changing needs of men in our society. There are about 15,000 courses devoted to women's studies, yet only 91 courses on men's studies, i.e., courses that *specifically* look at the gender-specific, social, and psychological issues of men and masculinity with the same vigor applied to women's issues. It is little wonder that, in this increasingly antimale academic environment, men have become a steadily diminishing minority of new college students and those preparing for graduate studies.

The study of male roles, male psychology, and interiority has not yet claimed a forum even remotely equal to the feminist initiative. In many instances, male-affirming voices on campus are actually repressed by feminists on the grounds that any views which challenge feminist doctrines must be inherently misogynist.[40] While men still dominate the Senate and the Fortune 500, women's voices even more disproportionately dominate the academy today on the subject of gender. There is no other academic field that I know of that regards open debate on issues as inimical. That sort of fundamentalism is usually only reserved for religion.

Men in America are just beginning to realize the extent of their wounds as they struggle against both traditional male and feminist inhibitions to find their own voices to challenge gender oppression. They are also rediscovering the depth of their masculine spirituality and beauty through mythopoetic men's work. Certainly there is much room for thoughtful criticism of our work. We still have much to learn and can benefit from legitimate challenges. It is equally important to create a forum where critique of feminism can be legitimized as something other than chauvinism, backlash, or counter-social revolution, and where proactive male perspectives are not paranoically distorted as implicitly antifeminist.

My postfeminist colleagues and I welcome serious inquiry. Many male-affirming women have already joined us in that conversation. The gender reconciliation movement emerging from that dialog is lively in the workplace and private educational centers, but still pretty much at bay in academia where, in gender studies, indoctrination still takes precedent over dialectical process. I hope profeminist men will soon expand their mandate to become also inclusively pro-male, for it is only through developing positive regard for both genders that we will ever create gender justice.

In conclusion, I say: Impose on yourselves the same discipline you would require of us. In the face of feminism, most of my colleagues and I have attended numerous feminist conferences, engaged in many dialogs on gender that were dominated by feminist perspectives, and read dozens of feminist books and hundreds of feminist articles. Read at least a dozen of the books cited in the notes and use the bibliographies within some of those texts as a further resource. I look forward to a better day when we can actually have a real debate on these issues instead of this sad excuse for a genuine pursuit of new knowledge.

NOTES

1. Mark Gerzon, *A Choice of Heroes* (Boston: Houghton Mifflin Company, 1982).

2. See, for example, Shepherd Bliss, "Kokopelli: Ancient Fertility God as New Model for Men," *The Sun* (December 1991).

3. Sam Osherson, *Finding Our Fathers: The Unfinished Business of Manhood* (New York: The Free Press, 1986).

4. John Lee, *Facing The Fire: Experiencing and Expressing Anger Appropriately* (New York: Bantam, 1993).

5. Aaron Kipnis, *Knights Without Armor: A Practical Guide for Men in Quest of Masculine Soul* (Los Angeles: Jeremy P. Tarcher Inc., 1991).

6. Sam Keen, *Fire in the Belly: On Being a Man* (New York: Bantam Books, 1991).

7. Jed Diamond, *Inside Out: Becoming My Own Man* (Marin, Calif.: Fifth Wave Press, 1983); and *The Warrior's Journey Home: Healing Men Healing the Planet* (Oakland, Calif.: New Harbinger Publications, Inc., 1994).

8. Joseph Jastrab, *Sacred Manhood, Sacred Earth* (New York: HarperCollins, 1994).

9. Eugene Monick, *Phallos: Sacred Image of the Masculine* (Toronto: Inner City Books, 1987).

10. See, for example, Robert Moore and Douglas Gillette, *King, Warrior, Magician, Lover: Rediscovering the Archetypes of the Mature Masculine* (San Francisco: Harper, 1990).

11. Arthur Coleman and Libby Coleman, *The Father: Mythology and Changing Roles* (Wilmette, Wash.: Chiron Publications, 1988).

12. William Anderson, *Green Man: The Archetype of Our Oneness with the Earth* (London: HarperCollins, 1990).

13. Gordon Dalbey, *Healing the Masculine Soul: An Affirming Message for Men and the Women Who Love Them* (Waco, Tex.: Word Books, 1988).

14. Michael Gurian, *The Prince and the King: Healing the Father-Son Wound* (New York: Putnam, 1992).

15. Michael Meade, *Men and the Water of Life: Initiation and the Tempering of Men* (San Francisco: HarperCollins, 1993).

16. Ruben Fine, *The Forgotten Man: Understanding the Male Psyche* (New York: Harrington Park Press, 1987).

17. David Gilmore, *Manhood in the Making: Cultural Concepts of Masculinity* (New Haven: Yale University Press, 1990).

18. Alexander Mitscherlich, *Society without the Father: A Contribution to Social Psychology* (1963; reprint, New York: Harper Perennial, 1993).

19. Herb Goldberg, *The Hazards of Being Male* (New York: The New American Library, Inc., 1976).

20. Asa Baber, *Naked at Gender Gap: A Man's View of the War Between the Sexes* (New York: Birch Lane Press, 1992).

21. Warren Farrell, *Why Men Are the Way They Are* (New York: McGraw-Hill, 1986); and *The Myth of Male Power* (New York: Simon and Schuster, 1993).

22. Aaron Kipnis and Elizabeth Herron, *Gender War, Gender Peace: The Quest for Love and Justice between Women and Men* (New York: William Morrow & Co., 1994).

23. Carolyn Baker, "Confessions of a Recovering Feminist," in *Man!* (Out of print. Reprints are available at no charge from Carolyn Baker. Send self-addressed stamped envelope to 1901 Cleveland Ave., No.2, Santa Rosa, Calif. 95401).

24. Christina Sommers, *Who Stole Feminism?* (New York: Simon and Schuster, 1994). See also, Sommers "Hard-Line Feminists Guilty of Ms.-Representation," *Wall Street Journal*, (New York: 7 November 1991.

25. Jack Kammer, ed., *Good Will Toward Men* (New York: St. Martin's Press, 1994). See especially Karen DeCrow, interview by Kammer, pp. 52–62.

26. Kay Leigh Hagan, ed., *Women Respond to the Men's Movement* (San Francisco: HarperCollins, 1993).

27. Rianne Eisler, *The Chalice and the Blade* (San Francisco: Harper and Row, 1987).

28. James Hillman, *The Myth of Analysis* (Evanston, Ill.: Northwestern University Press, 1972); James Hillman, *Re-visioning Psychology* (New York: Harper and Row, 1975); and James Hillman, ed., *Puer Papers* (Dallas: Spring Publications Inc., 1979).

29. C. G. Jung, *Archetypes and the Collective Unconscious, vol. 9, pt. I, Collected Works* (New York: Pantheon, 1959).

30. Catherine MacKinnon, *Only Words* (Cambridge: Harvard University Press, 1993).

31. Mary Daly, *Gyn/Ecology* and *Pure Lust* (Boston: Beacon Press, 1978, 1984, respectively).

32. Charlene Spretnak, ed., *The Politics of Women's Spirituality* (New York: Anchor Books, 1982).

33. Marilyn French, *The Women's Room* (New York: Summit, 1977).

34. Gloria Steinem, *Outrageous Acts and Everyday Rebellions* (New York: Holt, Rinehart and Winston, 1983).

35. Susan Faludi, *Backlash: The Undeclared War Against American Women* (New York: Doubleday, 1991).

36. Centers for Disease Control, *Vital Statistics of the United States, vol. 11, Mortality, 1987–88* (Washington, D.C.: National Center for Health Statistics, 1993).

37. Irwin Hyman and James Wise, eds., *Corporal Punishment in American Education* (Philadelphia: Temple University Press, 1979).

38. U.S. Bureau of the Census, *Money, Income, and Poverty Status in the U.S.* (Washington, D.C.: GPO, 1989).

39. U.S. Department of Justice, *Source Book of Criminal Justice Statistics* (Washington, D.C.: GPO, 1990).

40. Aaron Kipnis, "Male Privilege or Privation? A Call for More Vigorous Social Activism on Behalf of Boys and Men" (paper presented at the 1994 conference of the American Men's Studies Association in Chicago, Ill. Copies of speech available for $5.00 from: The Gender Relations Institute, Box 4782, Santa Barbara, CA 93140).

Healing, Community and Justice in the Men's Movement: Toward a Socially Responsible Model of Masculinity

ONAJE BENJAMIN

AS AN AFRICAN AMERICAN WHO HAS SURVIVED fifty years in a Eurocentric and racist society, I have developed a pessimistic and cynical view of any process—whether political, therapeutic, economic, or spiritual—which emanates from the predominant European American culture. It was with this attitude that I cautiously approached the various activities that collectively are defined as the Men's Movement.

My initial experience was to attend a six-day Multicultural event sponsored by MOSAIC, a nonprofit organization formed by Michael Meade to promote cross-cultural events for men and women. It was held in Buffalo Gap, West Virginia, and was attended by over one hundred men, about half of whom were "men of color," with gay men on both sides of the racial line.

During the course of the event, Native-American, African-American, Latino and European-American men met in community and engaged in conflict, ritual, dance, grief, and celebration. The collective personal histories, pain, strength, and convictions that emerged were significant and powerful. By nature and composition, this event integrated the personal and the political.

After Buffalo Gap, I was invited to two subsequent men's gatherings in California and North Carolina. Unlike Buffalo Gap, only one other African American was present at each event. Without the presence of a large number of "men of color," I felt compelled to defend my existence. This was particularly true since I chose to challenge what I perceived to be white male paranoia—racist thinking and self-indulgent victimization among those present.

Although I have since become more empathetic to the wounds that Euro-

288 : ONAJE BENJAMIN

pean-American men experience, it was difficult listening to clearly privileged, upper-class, European-American men talk about their suffering and
victimization. The level of denial and feigned ignorance triggered my distrust of European Americans, making it difficult to participate in community building.

During this period of introduction to what I define as Men's Work, I
joined the staff of a program that provided counseling services for men who
were abusive to women. Both the model and the majority of men who staffed
this program defined themselves as profeminist and had been active in the
evolution of the *National Organization for Men Against Sexism* (NOMAS).
Identifying myself as being associated with what some call the mythopoetic
wing of the men's movement stimulated much tension and discourse between myself and the other staff.

However, working within a profeminist work environment forced me to
take a look at my sexism and challenged my commitment to social change
across lines of gender, as well as race and class. A requirement of all men
working with this domestic violence treatment program was to look at the
ways in which we were abusive to women. I initially entered this activity with
a great deal of denial and resistance, but eventually was able to look at my
"shadow" as it related to my interaction with women. I learned to identify
and change my behavior that was verbally and emotionally abusive to my
partners. This exercise, which I continue to practice, has been beneficial in
working on my own sexism and better relating to women.

The disdain that many profeminist men have for men in general, or at
least those they perceive as not unquestionably supportive of all feminist
doctrine, is in my opinion unfortunate, and ultimately counterproductive to
the struggle for gender justice. This anti-male sentiment is prevalent in profeminist writings and frequently in programs treating men who are abusive
to women. My experience working in a program—one of the oldest and
largest profeminist agencies for "batterers" in the country—and my review
of other models convinced me that an empathetic approach is discouraged
or viewed as a form of "collusion" with the "perpetrator."

I witnessed the physical and sexual abuse of my mother by men, and have
had partners who were victims of male violence. Therefore, I support and
participate in efforts to stop violence—against both women and men. In order for a treatment model for abusive and violent men to be effective, it must
(1) hold these men accountable for their behavior, (2) deconstruct patriarchal and sexist belief systems, and (3) be empathetic to the traumas and
wounds these men have experienced which greatly contribute to their violent

behavior. I define these integrated components as a model of "empathetic accountability."

A report published by the American Psychological Association on youth and violence and research on violence and victimization in the African-American community by Dr. Carl Bell indicate that many individuals who exhibit violent behavior, as children, either witnessed or were victims of violence. As is the case with many children who are exposed to urban warfare or familial abuse, many men who are violent and/or abusive may suffer from Post Traumatic Stress Disorder (PTSD). A significant number of the hundreds of men I counseled for their abusive behavior reported that they were childhood victims of violence.

Men's social conditioning greatly contributes to the overall level of violence in this culture—the vast majority of whose victims are themselves men. Therefore, it is essential that violence prevention, and other programs serving men, be grounded in the emerging school of Masculine Psychology. In addition to challenging sexism and other discriminatory constructs, there should be a focus on developing models of masculinity that are socially responsible, foster justice, and support equality.

I agree—at least in principle—with a number of the concerns profeminist men have leveled at the so-called mythopoetic men's movement, but they do not accurately and fairly address the overall experiences and needs of men. The dogmatic concept that men have "all the power" does little to accurately reflect the oppression that men experience along lines of race, class, and sexual orientation. This is not to deny the privilege experienced by men in this culture and the oppression of women perpetuated by sexism and violence, but rather to recognize the need to view oppression and victimization in ways which are not hierarchal or ideologically rigid. The recent emphasis on multiculturalism and diversity within the mythopoetic wing of the men's movement has challenged its participants to become more aware and sensitive to these forms of oppression.

I do not support the way in which the male victimization is presented by some individuals associated with the "men's rights" wing of the overall Men's Movement. Yet, I do believe that models and/or programs for addressing the needs of men and "restructuring" their masculinity in ways that are conducive to creating "gender justice" are necessary. Models and programs should utilize a gender-specific approach in addressing the high mortality rates, suicide, homelessness, drug addiction, inadequate medical care, depression, work-place and domestic violence, sexual assault, and other problems that are prevalent among men in our society.

There must be a political component to *all* "men's work" that addresses the full spectrum of issues related to inequities in our society. As men, we should be open to challenges regarding our commitment to confronting those systems which perpetuate gender and other injustices. As a presenter at men's retreats and workshops, I have advocated a more socially responsible focus in men's work and the idea that Men's Work must incorporate at least three essential integrated principles—Healing, Community, and Justice. Men's work must not only concern itself with the psychological and/or ritual aspects of personal development, but also speak to the political realities of social injustice.

Experts in the emerging field of masculine psychology have written extensively about the male psyche and those issues that adversely affect the development of what I call "socially responsible masculinity." Shame and an inner sense of powerlessness are issues with which most men struggle. These issues evolve out of Patriarchy. Patriarchy does not benefit all men equally. In fact, it is a major cause of much of the wounding men experience in this culture. Like sexism, racism, and classism, it is a manifestation of oppression within our capitalistic power structure that clearly most benefits the wealthy.

I am opposed to the demonization and pathologizing of masculinity in the interest of exorcising patriarchy from society. The deconstruction of patriarchy is quite possible without socially stigmatizing the male gender. While much of what is associated with gender, race, and class is socially constructed, there are psychologically archetypal as well as biological aspects that play a part in how each gender develops and functions—none of which necessarily lead to oppression. Attacking and shaming men is counter-productive to creating meaningful social change and, void of the development of socially responsible models of masculinity, an exercise in feminist fundamentalism and political elitism.

As a father who has been involved in the growth and development of a daughter, two step-daughters, a step-son, and two grandchildren, I have both a personal and political commitment to seeing sexism and gender injustice eradicated. It is for these and other reasons that I believe that the work of creating short-term communities, support groups, ritual, and other cultural-specific events for men are essential for creating a culture which is gender equitable and committed to social change.

My hope and vision is that there can be a dialogue and collaboration between those groups of men that make up the men's movement and that we can find common ground to enhance our collective efforts to address gender and other forms of social injustice. My commitment to healing, community, and justice has guided my work in teaching at men's conferences: working with the southern rural poor, imprisoned men, and gays in the African-American community; and developing anti-violence, mentoring, and counseling programs.

I plan to continue my work to build a men's movement that promotes personal healing, builds gender and socially equitable communities, and addresses issues of injustice. I am committed to working with men and women of all cultures, ethnic groups, and sexual orientations. It is clear to me that the models which will bring about meaningful changes and justice in the world cannot and will not function like those institutions which characterize our culture today.

Mythopoetic Men's Movements

SHEPHERD BLISS

NOTE: RATHER THAN RESPOND DIRECTLY TO THE ATTACKS, misunderstandings, and ill-informed judgments on men and mythopoetic men's movements by the majority of this book's essays, my response will be indirect. I have edited and expanded my comments from a debate with Michael Kimmel on April 22, 1992, at a Symposium on Men and Masculinity at the University of California, Berkeley. A multicultural, mythopoetic team of musicians and poets from the Kokopelli Lodge accompanied me. However, I do want to say a few direct words of response, trying to contain some of the sadness, anger, and other feelings I had upon reading these essays.

Such anger toward men! Such hatred! So much blaming and shaming! I do not share it. Nor the distortions such anger and hatred bring. So many lies here. I am sorry that these men, and others of both sexes, have been hurt by some men. And others hurt by some women. Let us heal those wounds, rather than perpetuate them. There is much work to be done. I choose to do mine in certain ways. Others choose different ways. You do not need to be like or think like me. Nor do I need to think like, be like, or act like you. Let us honor diversity. We can live here together. And work to improve things.

I first brought the word "mythopoetic" (then an obscure literary term) forward in the mid-1980s, to describe the development of men's movements seeking to revision masculinity. At the time it was being called "the Robert Bly men's movement," after its most visible activist; I did not like associating it with one person. "Mythopoetic" does not mean "myth and poetry" or the contraction "myth 'n poetry," as some think. It comes from the word "mythopoesis," which refers to re-mythologizing. It means re-making, so the mythopoetic approach means revisioning masculinity for our time. Men, women, and children would benefit from new masculinities. That this word and our movement are misunderstood and so maligned in these pages brings me pain and sadness. The ideologies of most of these writers cloud them from seeing what other men—different from them—are saying and doing. We speak of movements, plural, rather than singular, since there are many—varying by ideas, methods, and geographical regions, as there are many masculinities. A long tradition of nurturing, generating men exists, which the mythopoetic approach to men affirms. This tradition includes historical figures such as Francis of Assisi, Henry David Thoreau, and Walt Whitman. Mythological figures representing this tradition include the ancient Greek father of music and poetry, Orpheus, the Mexican plumed serpent, Quetzalcoatl, and the Native American humpbacked flute player, Kokopelli.

Let me admit that we have made major mistakes within our men's movements, though I do not feel the attacks made in the essays here help us. For example, I have published numerous articles in many men's publications questioning the use of the word "warrior." The use of this term opens us to misunderstanding.

I call my brothers away from self-loathing and their castigating of other men. Such attacks are the essence of traditional masculinity. We would all benefit from being more tolerant and increasing our range of being uncomfortable with others and their differing ideas while still accepting them as persons. Let us love one another, rather than cast stones. The loving of men is the best thing we can do to improve gender relations and the world. I call us all to love both men and women. It is time to get beyond and over being so conflictual with each other and so mean to each other, even in the guise of academic objectivity and the search for truth.

Some of the untruths, fantasies, and fears regarding the mythopoetic men's movement presented in many of the essays in this book have come to unfortunate reality in another men's movement—called the PromiseKeepers. This right-wing Christian group has filled football stadiums with over 50,000 men to challenge feminism and gay rights. Founded by University of Colorado football coach Bill McCartney, they plan to mass a million men to a revival in the Mall in Washington, D.C., during the 1996 presidential election campaign. Men are encouraged by this group to return to Jesus and the Biblical image of men who control, dominate, and lead their wives and families. Feminism is blamed for the world's problems. This growing group is a serious threat to women, gay people, and all of us advocating changes in gender relations.

This is the talk: Let me clear the air. I will need more than words for such a clearing. I want to appreciate the musicians from The Kokopelli Men's Lodge for joining me to play their rhythms. I want to establish a different ground on which to discuss men than that presented by Professor Michael Kimmel. In contrast to his socio-political approach, I will take a mythopoetic approach. Being here at the university is like being in a strange forest. I do not recognize these unusual trees and words and ways which sociologists have. So please permit me to prepare my own ground for our discussion of men. I am in a distinct minority in this room, so I hope you will extend me the courtesy of an indirect response to the material presented.

My good friend Capt. Ray Gatchalian serves with the Oakland Fire Department. He is Filipino-American, and we are members of a multi-cultural men's group. He is also a fine musician; I invite you to listen to the ancient sound seeking modern minds which he plays on the *huaca*, a Peruvian clay flute used to "summon the gods." Perhaps it will clear a space so you can hear about the mythopoetic men's movements from the inside, experience it for yourself and participate in it directly, rather than making theoretical judgements based on observation from outside. (Ray plays the *huaca*)

Thank you Ray—for your music and for your work every day as a firefighter in the face of disasters such as the recent East Bay firestorm and the earthquake. Ray is one of the many good men—the "majority report" on men who do good for women, men, and children, men who love and care for other human beings. Such men make mistakes, yes, but do not condemn us as a whole group. We would benefit from remembering the good men and praise them for the hard work they do for the community. Men doing good work deserve our support and encouragement. Good will toward men and good will toward women would help us all; then we can work to improve ourselves and gender relations on the basis of that compassion.

As we approach the twenty-first century, it gives me great pleasure to be in Berkeley, where today's men's movements were born in 1970, with the Berkeley Men's Center. So we are relatively young movements, one might say adolescent. We make lots of mistakes. My nephew, who recently moved in with me from Omaha, was born at the same time as the men's movements. They are both in their 20s. He makes lots of mistakes. He learns from them, and we learn together—this middle-aged man and that young man. We avoid attacking each other, even though our differences are substantial; attacking can worsen rather than help situations.

I want to echo the Berkeley Men's Center's Manifesto of the early 1970s, which still guides my own work. My brothers wrote:[1]

We, as men, want to take back our full humanity. We no longer want to strain and compete to live up to an impossible oppressive masculine image—strong, silent, cool, handsome, unemotional, successful, master of women, leader of men, wealthy, brilliant, athletic, and "heavy." We no longer want to feel the need to perform sexually, socially, or in any way to live up to an imposed male role, from a traditional American society.

. . . I am proud to be a descendant of that legacy. I came to the men's movements directly from the women's movement in the mid-1970s. One way of looking at the history of the men's movement is as follows:

- 1970s—focus on male-female relationships and men supporting women
- 1980s—focus on father-son relationships and men relating to older men and mentors

In the 1990s, mythopoetic men's movements have gotten a lot of media, most of it unwelcome, most of it inaccurate. The powers that be have figured it out correctly: mythopoetic men's movements are a threat to traditional masculinity and power in this country, which is why *Esquire* and *Gentlemen's Quarterly* have attacked us. This was to be expected. What disappoints me is the alliance these powerful conservative forces have made with some feminist women and men in their campaigns against our challenges to traditional masculinity.

While continuing the work begun in the 1970s and 1980s, a main issue for men in the 1990s, in my opinion, should be working to preserve our threatened Earth. We need eco-masculinity rooted in the struggles against war, against violence, and for the environment and ecology. We need to go beyond the warrior. The old stories are not enough. We need new archetypes, masculinities for our time—the 1990s and for the twenty-first century. We need husbandmen of the Earth. We need New Masculinities which do not oppress women, men, or children.

I speak as a member of mass movements, plural, of men in motion to change consciousness. We say movements, plural, rather than singular, because we differ so much by geographical region and local color; we have no common doctrine, ideology, leadership, or even vision, in spite of the media and others who see that gray-haired poet Robert Bly as our leader. It is difficult in this academic forum to describe what the mythopoetic movements are, though it is easy to function in mythopoetic modes, which is one reason we have musicians here. What we do is as important as what we say. We are unlike other movements in history. I do not speak for our movements, but from their contexts. We have no central organization, so I speak for myself, an individual who participates in many diverse groups. I am a leader in our movements, a ritual leader, which is quite distinct from a political leader. My central concern is the psyche, soul. My key tools are language, music, movement, and other ceremonial arts.

SOCIOLOGY, SCIENCE, POETRY, AND DRUMMING

Sociology and poetry are two distinct ways of knowing, two often contrary modes of understanding reality, as different as men and women. The sciences and mythology are unique sets of stories, each attempting to explain what is. Linear reasoning differs from narrative logic, both being valid. The twentieth century has witnessed the domination of the sciences, and the consequent development of technology, including its use in modern warfare and the devastation of total war in our century. We are on the edge of collapse, through means such as nuclear war and environmental disaster, *not* because of the men on the front lines, as some would suggest, but because of systems of industrialism and technology and the inappropriate use of the sciences, including the social sciences, to control those men active at the front.

Men and women together have built systems of production and consumption which are run on sexist agreements about the division of labor on the basis of rigid sex roles. We have colluded in building this system together. Those in the active role, men, get blamed, but this system is built with the passive collusion of women. It is unfair to blame the active men and absolve women from responsibility for the world we have built together. The good woman/bad man dualism is too simple. It is in all of our interests to dismantle our sexist system. We must see ourselves as allies, rather than adversaries, if we are to destroy this system. It is time for working together, amidst disagreements, rather than resting in self-righteousness. Poetry, music, mythology, and the mythopoetic men's movements can be crucial in dismantling this sexist system. You have just heard a political sociologist speak. Now I invite you to listen, perhaps with different ears, to a mythopoetic approach to men and gender. I encourage you beyond either–or thinking to both–and thinking, beyond the defective good–bad dualistic paradigm.

We drum in the mythopoetic men's movements for many reasons, including the following: It is cooperative, rather than competitive, drawing men together, breaking isolation and facilitating participation. Drumming provides a container for the development of community, offering a means of side-by-side intimacy. It is play, rather than work. Too many men are workaholics. Drums can take men back to boyhood. It gets men out of our heads into our hands, bodies, and hearts. Drumming is a body experience which can heighten feelings and animate men's emotional bodies. Men cooperating on drums together are not a threat to women, children, or each other. Men who play tend to be healthier, live longer, and relate better to children. We alter consciousness with our use of the arts and lift men into nonordinary reality, without the abuse of substances such as alcohol, drugs, and other addictions. We drum to get men back to the feminine, to that heartbeat rhythm which we all first heard in our mothers' wombs. We do honor our mothers, women, the feminine, and feminism.

Pleasure can be included in learning. When we took the teachers out of the woods and placed them in classrooms, we lost something. When we took learning out of its context, nature, we lost something. When we divorced beauty and pleasure from teaching and learning, we lost something. When men moved from the country to the city, from farms to factories, we lost something. We need to do some recovery work. We must re-associate learning with direct experience, with animals, plants, and nature itself. It is time to recover such glories as beauty, pleasure, love, and, yes, the feminine. It is important to get back to the basics—especially to the land itself—as that nineteenth century naturalist Thoreau did, an ancestor to those doing today's mythopoetic men's work. Humans used to see themselves as part of the nonhuman world; our disassociation from the Earth is the source of our gender problems, which modern technology heightens. On this Earth Day, April 22, I want to draw our attention to the Earth and our stewardship of it.

IN PRAISE OF TEACHERS AND ELDERS

Many of the assaults upon poet Robert Bly made in the media and by other mis-informed people may have less to do with him and more to do with these people's disappointments with their own fathers. People who have never seen or read Bly (except for perhaps his *Iron John*) somehow feel free to attack him personally and politically—knowing little or nothing about his politics or his person. Perhaps our problems have less to do with that evil patriarchy (which means rule of the fathers) and more to do with our culture's massive problems of absent fathers, which produce father hunger, and projecting upon men, especially older men. Studies reveal that the average father in America spends less than five minutes a day with his children, which is not long enough.[2] Perhaps we have too little father, rather than too much! It is easy to blame fathers for this neglect, but perhaps we need to examine our economic system which keeps men at work away from the home and the family, as some feminists writers indicate. Complaints against the patriarchy (the father) may in fact be longing for the good father. That longing often comes toward older men in forms of passive and active aggression. Being old, gray-haired, and willing to speak his truth, Bly becomes the target for such displaced hunger, which he does not deserve.

I met Bly 25 years ago, when I was a young officer in the U.S. Army on my way to Vietnam. Bly's acts of courage against that war placed him in the poet's prophetic role, where he has remained. Bly helped me leave the army, in spite of my military family, which gave its name to Ft. Bliss, Texas, and has contributed many soldiers and generals to the U.S. military. I am indebted to Bly, as are many young men, because he helped me see the futility of war; I engaged in direct acts against the U.S. military and resigned from the U.S. Army. During the more recent Persian Gulf War, Bly once again was active on a national scale against war. Bly's history of political activism on behalf of peace is one of the most extensive of any major U.S. writer. I do not agree with all Bly's ideas; in fact, I have argued publicly and privately with him for years. But his passion for life has benefited me and many others. I admit to a great love for Robert Bly. I do like being around him. I have struggled with him for a quarter of a century now. Bly is stimulating. I feel alive in his vibrant presence. I enjoy his maleness and the fact that he is an old man who speaks his truth. Perfect he is not. Bly stands for what the ancient Greeks called *alethia*—truth beyond mere facts.

I was raised by the women's movement in the 1960s, as I came into manhood. I have listened to women speak on gender, and will continue to listen. Men must hear women's just complaints about sexism. Feminism is forever in my bones, not just my head; it has entered my blood, my body, and my heart. I cannot separate it from my sense of self, my sense of reality, my sense of purpose and my sense of the "other sex," a term which I prefer to the adversarial and militaristic "opposite sex." These days I am most drawn to spiritual feminism and those parts of the women's movement committed to working with men and to gender reconciliation. As I consider our potential survival on this threatened Earth, images of my teachers come to mind. Nelle Morton opened the door for me in 1966; she wrote *The Journey Is Home*. Carol Gilligan taught me while I was at Harvard University about women's different voice. May Sarton led me to the muse. Three mature psychologists—Jean Shinoda Bolen, Marion Woodman, and Linda Leonard—have continued to inspire me. These women are part of the women's spiritual movement.

She's coming back—after a long exile. Once again, her names can be heard across the land. A spiritual awakening is occurring. Every year for the last twenty years a group of us have had an annual Great Mother conference, organized by Bly. Its teachers have included women such as Jungian analysts Woodman and Leonard. I want to share a line from a Bly poem that is running through my mind. It is one of Bly's many love of women poems, which perhaps Prof. Kimmel has not read, or he would not distort Bly so, take him out of context, and falsely accuse him of being against women.

> In the month of May,
> when all leaves open,
> I see when I walk
> how well all things lean on each other . . .
> then I understand,
> I love you with what in me is unfinished.
> I love you with what in me is still changing.[3]

It's from Bly's book *Loving a Woman in Two Worlds*. I am tempted to spend the rest of my time reciting love poems, but I will refrain. I do want to add another one. It is spring, a time of change, which I feel in my body. As a mythopoet I want to suggest, rather than declare. I want to draw a circle, rather than a rigid line. Rather than a linear, analytical approach, I want to use the languages of feeling—poetry and music. The nineteenth-century American poet Edwin Markham wrote "Outwitted":

> He drew a circle that shut me out.
> Heretic, rebel; a thing to flout.
> But Love and I had wit to win.
> We drew a circle and took him in.

This poem reveals contemporary mythopoetic approaches to all men—the good, the bad, and the ugly—"take them in," care for them. We practice what another nineteenth century men's movement ancestor, Walt Whitman, called "manly love." During the Civil War, Whitman worked as a nurse, loving men in both blue and gray uniforms, writing, "All men ever born are my brothers." We echo our great gray poet today. Mythopoetic men's movements are movements of lovers of men, women, and children. We work with gay, straight, and inbetween men. With men from their teenage into retirement years. With men of many different cultures and races. At the risk of seeming sentimental, let me say that the only solution for our serious gender problems today is the love of men, the love of women, and the love of and caring for children. The hatred and blaming of women will get us nowhere. Nor will the hatred and blaming of men. We must get beyond self-loathing and shame to a place of inclusion. Shame and blame do not motivate people to change; inclusion and love can catalyze people to be transformed.

THE MYTHOPOETIC APPROACH TO MEN

Mythopoetic refers to re-mythologizing, not merely repeating the old stories. I study the old myths to learn their teachings, and then evolve them. When Bly appeared on the men's scene in the early 1980s, those who moved in response to his ideas were called "the Bly men's movement." I did not like that description. I do not have a great man theory of history. There is much more than one man here. There are authentic movements already involving hundreds of thousands of men. So I spent months studying literature and came upon the somewhat archaic term "mythopoetic." Though the term is awkward and academic, it has stuck in the media and among men. In a 1986 *Yoga Journal* article, I write, "Rather than employing rational, analytical or political thinking, the mythopoetic approach to men uses symbols, metaphor, and archetypal images."[4] The mythopoetic approach is change and future oriented, rather than conservative and past oriented. A mythopoetic approach to men seeks to transform men, masculinities, and manhood.

Our approach is also psychoecological, by which I mean a primary concern with repairing, mending, healing. If we use a merely sociopolitical approach, we may keep ourselves in the gender prison. It is cure that I want. We need to describe the problems of our rigid sex roles and gender inequality in language which can facilitate change, not merely one which creates a bad man/good woman dualism blaming one gender, and leaving the other feeling self-righteous. Hence, instead of blaming men for our problems, and then shaming them, I prefer a holistic approach designed toward a solution. We must all take responsibility for this world which we have colluded in making.

Mythopoets are not separatists. We hate neither women nor men; we are not misogynists or misandrists. We have both men's only and gender gatherings. My partner Bruce Silverman lives with his wife and two daughters, pleasantly surrounded by the feminine. Bruce teaches weekly drumming classes to women. We do not believe in male domination of the drum, as has historically been the case, or of any other aspect of life. We believe in the equality and mutuality of both genders. Bruce directs the Sons of Orpheus, a men's mythopoetic community, of which I have been the Literary Director. Orpheus was the Greek father of music and poetry who played the lyre so beautifully that rocks, mountains, fish, trees, and birds swayed to it. In one year alone we had about half a dozen marriages, among three dozen men in the Sons. Part of our work is to get men and women closer; blaming either gender does not help. Recently, for example, one of the men who is having his first child asked for support. The fathers came forward to help him by telling their stories. A few weeks ago a man was remembering pain from his childhood. So he asked that we sing him a lullaby. We surrounded and cradled him. These are the kinds of things we do in the mythopoetic men's movements, hardly being demons who defend that enemized "patriarchy." When a woman friend of Bruce's was being harassed racially, some of us volunteered to stay in her home to help protect her and her young daughter from the racist attacks—hardly a defense of "the patriarchy."

TOXIC MASCULINITY VS. THE DEEP MASCULINE

There are many masculinities. Masculinity is not singular or monolithic. Masculinity varies from man to man, from family to family, and from culture to culture. As he ages a man's sense of what it means to be a man changes. Internal dynamics, family and friends, and the environment influence each man's developing masculinity. Masculinity is learned behavior and as such can be changed. Masculinities are made, not born. They become, rather than are. Masculinities emerge; they are processes, rather than events, dynamic rather than static, though an individual man can become frozen in his sense of manhood. Masculinities can be unlearned, relearned, and transformed.

As you can tell, I am not that straw man that some ultra-feminists describe as an "essentialist." I do believe that archetypes influence our behavior, but I also believe in the social construction of reality. The prevailing archetypal psychologist in the mythopoetic men's work, James Hillman, has written a book on social reality.[5] Once again, it is not either-or, that you either believe in archetypes or the social construction of reality; you can have both-and, unless you are a fundamentalist.

Among the allies of mythopoetic men are those men and women working for recovery from addiction. In recent years the recovery movement has stimulated me to consider our addictive society. In the mythopoetic work we tell classic fairy tales and myths; I have learned to combine the stories of Homer and Dante with stories from my own life and those of the men and women with whom I work. Mythopoetic men's movements overlap with other men's movements—especially the recovery, gay, and feminist movements, and less with the men's rights activists.

Toxic Masculinity poisons through means such as neglect, abuse, and violence. Toxic Masculinity can wound and even be fatal to men, women, children, and the Earth. Masculinity itself is not inherently negative, in spite of some contemporary writings about "men who can't love," and "men who hate women," and "refusing to be a man." Healthy masculinity does many wonderful things—father children, fight fires, harvest food, love the feminine, write poetry, play music. These qualities contribute to what Bly calls the Deep Masculine. It is generative, earthy, nurturing, playful, forceful, and zany.

Let me contrast Toxic Masculinity, which I see as our problem, with the Deep Masculine, which I see as part of the solution. Toxic behaviors can be accumulated in a sexist society. They are not essential and inherent; but they can become addictive. Men are not essentially bad. Boys are born loving. In our sexist society too many men and women continue to play our inherited roles. Together we make a sexist system, which must be dismantled for the sakes of women and men, as well as our children.

Getting beyond blaming, merely political, language and a model which conceptualizes women as victims of masculinity and men as oppressors is important. We would benefit from language from the health and recovery fields which is change-oriented. The addictive system in which we all live is more complicated than simplistic either-or thinking. According to Yale psychologist Helen Block Lewis, our society "injures the two sexes differently."[6] Women have been describing how this society wounds them; men are just beginning to identify how rigid gender distinctions also damage us. Lewis characterizes the society as channeling men into "expendable warriors" and women into "inferior childbearing." Men become economic symbols and women become sex symbols.

It is time for men to join women in speaking out against the ways sex roles damage us, not only as allies to women in their just demands for political and economic equality, but as humans also wounded by rigid sex roles. When men add our voices to those of women we can move toward gender justice and gender reconciliation designed to end the sexism which injures both men and women. Since "both are victims," according to Lewis, rather than fight against each other, "it seems more sensible for them to join in a common struggle." Part of this joint struggle can be against the addiction of Toxic Masculinity.

The difficulty with some current thinking and writing on men and on gender is that it postulates a good woman/bad man dualism which blames men and glorifies women. Such scapegoating is not healthy or conducive for change or recovery. It can lead to self-righteousness for one gender (refusing to take any responsibility and imaging the-self-as-victim) and shame for the other (being a man is inherently bad). The Toxic Masculinity/Deep Masculine continuum is a dialectical, dynamic alternative to the frozen bad man/ good woman dualism. Rather than trying to imitate women or become "honorary women," the path I suggest is to overcome Toxic Masculinity and recover the Deep Masculine, which lies at the base of each man. The Deep Masculine is within him and within the legacy of positive male ancestors who have gone before and taken responsibility for families, tribes, villages, and entire peoples. It interacts with historical reality, and can emerge, or be repressed.

The women's movement describes how women are damaged by what is variously defined as "inequality," "sexism," and "the patriarchy." Though the critique seems basically correct, the language used to describe the problem can separate and imprison us, rather than release us. As Anne Wilson Schaef writes in *Escape from Intimacy*, "Victims never recover. They just stay victims."[7] Yes, women have been victimized by sexism. But we need to understand how to move from that damage to freedom—processes which can be described as healing or recovery and framed in terms of health. In the essay "It's Time for Feminists to Make Amends," Schaef adds, "To hold on to bitterness, anger, defensiveness or a victim status is to stay in the Addictive System."[8]

Men are only beginning to see how our inherited concepts of masculinity damage us. Yet how obvious it is, once we look—men die eight years younger than women in the U.S. today: they have higher rates of cancer, heart attacks, and suicide. More substance abuse, risk-taking, and automobile accidents. At the turn of the century the difference was only two years in the U.S. and it remains two years in some other countries, such as Russia. The male sex role is hazardous to our health. The basic difference in mortality rates is not biological or genetic; it is behavioral and social.

ECO-MASCULINITY AND MANY FEMINISMS

We live in a time when the Earth itself is threatened, not so much by those mean old men, as some would contend, as by the forces set loose by industrialism, including technology, nuclear weapons and power, and all that pollutes our air, land, and water. Our ways out of these problems are not to condemn men, but to balance the feminine and the masculine, so unbalanced today. The love of mothers and of women, and the love of fathers and of men, both seem crucial to me, if we are to survive. As the goddesses return, they bring with them the gods of the ground, to use metaphors, as poets are prone to. That cooperative masculinity which manifests itself in forms such as raising barns, harvesting food, and volunteering to fight fires is returning. Earthy masculinity does not have time to waste bickering, snickering, and being sarcastic, snide, mocking, and putting down.

The consensus about what it means to be a man in America has eroded. We live in a time when masculinity as we have known it is deteriorating. As a result of economic realities, the changing international situation, and the women's movement, we are witnessing the de-structuring of traditional masculinity. I welcome this dissolution, confusing and even painful as it is for many men and women. I am tired of male violence in the forms of rape, abuse, neglect, and competition. I am tired of men dying eight years younger than women. I am ready for change. Our men's and gender work is a matter of life and death. Our work has saved the lives of many men—from alcoholism, violence, and early death. The stories I have heard and could tell! Men's lives are no less important than women's, nor more. We are not sociological statistics. Mythopoetic men's movements enhance the quality and length of men's lives and hence improve the lives of women and children, providing environments for men to become more loving, better fathers, to care for their families, helping us all.

There are many feminisms, as there are many masculinities. My sociological brother advocates one feminism. I advocate another. I want men and women to work together. My goal is to build a post-patriarchal society. Feminisms which leave men out or place us in a secondary rather than equal role will never end sexism. Feminisms which draw a circle to include men contribute to the ending of sexism. We do not need to be "honorary women" or "imitation women," as shame-based, man-hating writers such as Sonja Johnson and John Stoltenberg advocate.

Poetry and sociology are two distinct ways of knowing. In *Woman and Nature* Susan Griffin[9] contends that we must re-associate ourselves with nature. This has become one of the key methodologies of mythopoetic men's movements—getting back to animals, plants, and nature itself. When we playfully act like animals on all fours it is easy to mock us, as it was easy to mock the early bra-burning women. There is a long tradition of identifying with animals in indigenous cultures and among poets such as Gary Snyder. Sure, it does look silly to see grown men acting like boys. But for the men participating—rather than for the sociologists observing—it often helps connect them to each other and to the larger nature of which humans are an integral part. We need eco-feminism and eco-masculinity. We can return to earthy masculine archetypes, such as Kokopelli.

We need to get beyond warriors, even gender warriors, and beyond heroes, even feminist heroes, as Allan Chinen documents in his wonderful book *Beyond Heroes*.[10] Let me offer another poem, which points beyond the warrior. It is from the thirteenth century—our ecstatic Sufi ancestor Rumi: "Out beyond ideas of wrongdoing and rightdoing,/there is a field. I'll meet you there."[11]

Let us get beyond blame and shame to meet each other in such a clearing.

In my many years in school, including five years in graduate school working on my doctorate, I was taught to be a Lone Ranger. Now I never teach or do public speaking without colleagues at my side. Mythopoetic men's movements have to do with men breaking isolation, which we see as a key cause of problems such as violence. Hence we emphasize men being together, working in groups and building community. Much of male intimacy is side by side, rather than face to face. Rather than always being verbal, it includes doing-together. Men die eight years younger than women in the United States. Our lives are about 10 percent shorter, not for biological but for behavioral reasons. My conclusion—there is something hazardous about the male sex role in America today. Fortunately for humanity, and other species, as we seek to evolve into the twenty-first century, we are witnessing a re-awakening of ancient wisdom, a return to mythology and its languages, poetry and storytelling, and a re-awakening of interest in nature and ecology, as compared to industry and technology.

GENDER RECONCILIATION

Sociologists and political scientists offer facts. Poets and mythologists offer metaphors. Both facts and metaphors seek to describe reality. The ancient Greeks spoke of *alethia,* the higher truth which they knew was more than mere facticity. It is *alethia* which interests me, and to which the goddesses and spiritual feminism point. Our discussion of men and gender belongs within this larger context. Along with modern science we can turn to more ancient wisdoms in our attempts to understand men and gender. Then we must go beyond the old stories to the development of new stories for men and for gender.

I advocate an ecumenical spirit in men's movements. I disagree with Michael Kimmel. It does not mean that he is wrong, or that I am right. Just that we differ. As a mythopoet I find reality more complex than simple good woman/bad man. Such dualistic, polaristic thinking is the old paradigm. I prefer the holistic, synthetic thinking of the new paradigm in the physics of Fritjof Capra.[12] I appreciate Michael's passion and concern for justice. I hope you can hear other approaches and not feel you have to choose either–or. We live in a both–and world.

Women's and men's movements are maturing toward a movement of men and women for Gender Reconciliation. Some of the adherents of the original women's and men's movements remain stuck in the early stages of blame, anger, shame, and dualistic thinking. Others have matured to inclusive thinking, a systems approach, and dialetical thinking, rather than polaristic thinking, either–or. Together men and women can end sexism, which injures both genders. As adversaries, we do not have a chance to end sexism, which is rooted in the adversarial relationship. We need to be allies, partners, even when we differ.

NOTES

1. Berkeley Men's Center Manifesto, in *Men and Masculinity*, ed. Joseph Pleck and Jack Sawyer (Englewood Cliffs, N. J.: Prentice-Hall, 1974).

2. Osherson, Sam, *Finding Our Fathers: How a Man's Life Is Shaped by the Relationship with His Father* (New York: Fawcett, 1987).

3. Bly, Robert, "In the Month of May," *Loving a Woman in Two Worlds* (New York: Dial Press, 1985), p. 77.

4. Bliss, Shepherd, "Beyond Machismo: The New Men's Movement," *Yoga Journal*, November–December, 1986.

5. Hillman, James, and Michael Ventura, *We've Had One Hundred Years of Psychotherapy—and the World Is Getting Worse* (New York: HarperCollins, 1993).

6. Lewis, Helen Block, *Shame and Guilt in Neurosis* (New York: International University Press, 1994).

7. Schaef, Ann Wilson, *Escape from Intimacy* (San Francisco: HarperCollins, 1990).

8. Shaef, Ann Wilson, "It's Time for Feminists to Make Amends," *MenTalk* (Minneapolis, Minn.: Twin Cities Men's Center, 1990).

9. Griffin, Susan, *Woman and Nature: The Roaring Inside Her* (San Francisco: HarperCollins, 1979).

10. Chinen, Allan, *Beyond the Hero: Classic Stories of Men in Search of Soul* (New York: Tarcher/Putnam, 1992).

11. Rumi, *Open Secret*, translated by John Moyne and Coleman Barks (Putney, Vt.: Threshold Books, 1984), p. 8.

12. Capra, Fritjof, *The Tao of Physics* (Boston: Shambhala, 1991 revision).

We've Come a Long Way Too, Baby.
And We've Still Got a Ways to Go.
So Give Us a Break!

MARVIN ALLEN

I FIND IT DISTRESSING THAT FEMINISM and the media have given such rapt attention to the enigmatic, mythological aspects of the men's movement while ignoring the more grounded and psychologically efficacious elements. A movement rich with diversity, leaders, and goals has been, in the eyes of the media and feminism, reduced to a cult of white-collar drum bangers with visions of kings, warriors, and wild, hairy men dancing in their heads. According to countless newspaper and magazine articles, these seekers of the "deep masculine" were followers of the poet Robert Bly. Whatever Bly said, whether it made sense or not, suddenly became the voice of the Men's Movement. If Bly came across as a bigot or sexist, then the Men's Movement was bigoted or sexist. If Bly was a closet patriarch, then *his* movement was a clandestine attempt by threatened men to win back all the power and virility they lost to the Women's Movement. Why didn't they pay more attention to such well balanced and apparently emotionally healthy leaders as Aaron Kipnis (*Knights Without Armor*), Bill Kauth (*A Circle of Men*), or Sam Keen (*Fire in the Belly*)? Other men's leaders like Herb Goldberg (*The Hazards of Being Male*), Warren Farrell (*The Myth of Male Power*), and Asa Baber (*Naked at Gender Gap*) also have some very salient, if controversial, ideas to offer the men and women of this country. Without diversity in leadership, a movement gets top heavy and extremely vulnerable to criticism— much as a thousand acres of corn can be devastated by a single type of bug. By creating an easy target like Bly as *the* leader, and by focusing on only the sensational or unusual elements of men's gatherings, the media was able to discredit and dismantle much of the Men's Movement in short order.

Most of the 20 percent of American people who have even heard of the

Men's Movement actually believe that the whole thing is about a bunch of white, middle-aged, middle-class men in the woods dancing around in animal skins, drumming wildly, hugging each other, primal screaming, and whining about their lot in life. Yes, there are drums and dancing and some screaming in many of the outdoor gatherings for men. But that's only a small part of what goes on.

For instance, the Wildman Gatherings I designed, and continue to facilitate with my friend and colleague Dick Prosapio, are weekend retreats dedicated not only to helping men become more emotionally aware and alive, but to assisting them in becoming more available, more nurturing husbands, fathers, and friends. Yes, we use certain Native American ceremonies that we believe will help white, middle-class Americans become more connected with the beauty and the spirit of this Earth. To develop a passion for our planet is one of the goals of the weekend. And, yes, we sing a Native American chant, but we also sing "Amazing Grace." Too bad the media and the feminists couldn't hear the glorious sound of "America the Beautiful" sung by a hundred men's voices rising up through the pines and into a crisp, starlit night in the mountains of Nevada.

And what of the white, middle-class men who are whining about their unfair lot in life? What's that all about? Is it possible that for the first time in their lives many of these men are facing the fact that, as impressionable little boys, they were hurt by an unrealistic masculine code that made a shambles of their natural feelings and pushed them into a robot-like existence? Is it possible that these same men who seem so cool and collected on the outside, have been hiding the fact that they were deeply hurt by neglectful emotionally unavailable, or even abusive mothers and dads? And is it whining to finally give vent to all that buried pain, grief, and rage? Is it really so weird to want to be liberated from all those troubling feelings and belief systems that have driven us into aggressive competition, workaholism, alcoholism, perfectionism, passivity, or raging? Is it so strange to want to seek comfort and validation from other men who have endured the same masculine conditioning process and many of the same experiences as we have? Isn't this, after all, what it's all about? Trying to become more emotionally healthy, balanced men? Are we supposed to be able to transform ourselves by just deciding to pull ourselves up by our bootstraps? Or by going to Sunday School? Or in a Saturday afternoon chat with our wife or lover? Is it possible that working in groups of men may be the most effective and efficient way for males to break out of their emotional armor, defensiveness, and isolation?

It seems ironic that some feminists (and by the way, I consider myself a feminist who wants to see true equality and fairness between the sexes) complain bitterly about what jerks men are and yet they also complain when men get together to try to change themselves. It seems to me that men need some time and space to understand what's happened to them; to see the relevance that their personal history has in their present day lives; to realize that certain ways they have of thinking, feeling, and behaving may be hurting themselves or their loved ones; to take responsibility for what they've done and are doing; and, finally, to get whatever help is necessary to create positive change in their lives. I know of no better way for the average male to achieve these goals than to be in the company of other like-minded, nonblaming men.

You see, men have come a long way, too, baby. And a significant part of our journey has been through hell in this twentieth century. First there was World War I, then World War II, then the Korean War, the Cold War, the Vietnam War, the Persian Gulf War, and several "skirmishes." Remember, too, that during most of this century men who didn't volunteer were forced to fight the wars or go to prison, or, at the very least, were considered cowards. To be effective and efficient in these wars and in earning a living, males had to be "toughened up" by parents, schools, churches, media, and the military. As they grew into adulthood, these males were expected to display characteristics of leadership, independence, toughness, courage, responsibility, and quiet stoicism. These traits became synonymous with manliness and played a major role in keeping our country free and our standard of living high. Traditionally, men from other cultures around the world have been conditioned in similar ways.

Unfortunately, however, while millions of men in our country have had the traditional masculine traits drilled into their heads and hearts, they've been taught very little about the traditional "feminine" ways of being. Without the feminine—I prefer to call them human—qualities of patience, vulnerability, gentleness, compassion, and empathy, these men are destined to become emotionally unbalanced. Millions of American boys continue to be emotionally stunted in this way before they reach their 18th birthdays. Many of these boys who didn't get enough good parenting will try to compensate for their low self-esteem and insecurities by following the rules of manhood in an exaggerated fashion.

Thus, under such circumstances, "Be stoic and don't let your feelings get in the way of positive action," becomes "Don't ever cry or show your vulnerable emotions, no matter what." "Be strong enough to get the job done and don't give up too soon," becomes "Don't ever be weak, don't compromise, and never give up." "Be brave," becomes "Don't ever be scared, but if you are, never let anyone know." "Be capable of leading when necessary," becomes "Prove your manliness by controlling and dominating those around you." "Be a responsible provider," becomes "Prove your worth to bosses, co-workers, and wives by pleasing them and achieving at all costs."

After working with thousands of males in our country, I am convinced that a significant number of men have been so influenced by one or more of these exaggerated masculine rules that their ability to enjoy meaningful relationships or even life itself has been deeply diminished. Although following the manly code may have paved the way for men to achieve success in business, sports, or war, the toll on their wives, their children, their friends, their planet, and themselves has been unacceptable.

Millions of American men spend a lot more time trying to prove themselves than they do celebrating themselves. They spend more time feeling numb, anxious, or angry than they do feeling joyful. To make matters worse, many of these men just go through the motions in their relationships. Because they can't be vulnerable and haven't developed the necessary communication skills, they are often unable to experience the deep inner satisfaction that should come from intimate relationships with wives, children, and friends. Instead, they may find themselves outside the loop in their own families, spending much of their lives trying to cope with soul wrenching isolation and loneliness.

Emotionally unbalanced men fall prey to very "unmasculine" feelings of inadequacy, anxiety, depression, and dependency. To avoid or to cope with these painful and embarrassing emotions, millions of men have turned to such manly solutions as excess work, alcohol, TV sports, food, sexual compulsions, and even aggression and violence. Unfortunately, these "solutions" not only don't work, they create more problems. I sincerely believe divorce, addictions, wife battering, child abuse, suicide, and crime could all be reduced by 75% or more if men could just become a little more emotionally balanced. While men who use violence against their wives and children must be stopped and prosecuted to the full extent of the law, we must also realize that incarceration alone will not heal these men's problems. They need help in the form of effective and appropriate counseling and treatment. Otherwise, they will just serve the time and repeat the same crimes with their families or with new ones.

While rape and wife battering are serious and widespread, we must understand that these criminal acts are only the visible and extreme tip of the iceberg. There are also millions of other emotionally unbalanced men who would never rape or physically batter but who continue to be excessively critical, controlling, and emotionally abusive to their wives and children. In millions of other men, emotional imbalance takes the form of sulking, stony silence, and passivity.

These serious maladies affecting so many American men must be addressed if our families and our communities are to flourish. As a nation, we must understand that the vast majority of American men are goodhearted, well-intentioned people who, as a group, are reflecting both the positive and the negative effects of traditional masculine conditioning. If we are to replace sexism, racism, and violence with mutual respect, dignity, and equality, surely a first step must include a new masculinity that demands emotional honesty, wholeness, and balance. Certainly this new masculinity must also recognize that excellence in relationships is every bit as manly a trait as excellence in business, sports, or war. To do this, men and women must work together in fresh, nonblaming ways to raise awareness and to encourage meaningful dialogue that fosters understanding and compassion. To help them develop healthier ways of thinking, feeling, and behaving, men must be encouraged and supported to get the assistance they need from counselors, men's groups, classes, relevant books, and friends. Finally, we must find the wisdom and the courage to raise our sons to be the well-balanced, emotionally healthy men that our Creator intended them to be.

So for God's sake, let's support the elements of the men's movement that foster true growth and development. Don't throw the baby out with the bath water. Why not take the energy that's being spent fighting Bly and turn it into a resource that supports the practical, down to earth, psychologically sound aspects of the men's movement? The truth is, that part of the men's movement that smacks of patriarchy or lacks substance and groundedness will go down the drain without much outside intervention. In fact, if you listen closely you may hear a giant sucking sound right now!

Twenty-five Years in the Men's Movement

JED DIAMOND

I AGREE WITH MICHAEL KIMMEL that the articles titled *Profeminist Men Respond to the Men's Movement* "leave(s) the dialogue incomplete" and am pleased to accept his invitation to offer my own thoughts and feelings.

I have been actively involved in men's work since 1969 when my first son, Jemal, was born. Holding him for the first time, moments after his birth, I made a vow to have a different kind of relationship with him than the one I experienced growing up. To do that, I knew I would have to help create a different kind of world for us all to live in.

My life work is to help people escape the current dominator culture (what some call patriarchy) that is destroying men, women, children, gays, people of color, indigenous peoples, and ultimately the entire human race. I want to help build a new partnership society in which we can once again live as equals in balance with the totality of life. I believe we don't have the luxury of sniping at each other. The ship of civilization is sinking and we need all the allies we can muster if we are going to survive on this planet.

Since so many of our views on men, masculinity, sexism, and the men's movement are colored by our own lives, I think it is helpful to share some of my own life experiences. I hope this will allow my own biases, fears, concerns, and passions to surface. When we truly understand where the other is coming from, we are better able to appreciate our similarities and differences without attacking each other.

MY ROOTS IN LIFE

I entered the world on December 21, 1943, in New York City, the first and only child born to parents who were Jewish by tradition, but intellectually opposed to religion. I attended my first march and rally when I was six months old, and though I didn't hear the term "red diaper baby" until much later, it captures the politically charged atmosphere of my youth.

We moved to Los Angeles and bought a small house in the all white suburbs of the San Fernando Valley. While my mother stayed home with me and earned money typing manuscripts for soon-to-be-black-listed writers, my father, an actor in New York, tried desperately to break into the emerging television industry. Repeated failures to find meaningful work led to a nervous breakdown and eventual hospitalization when I was six years old. I didn't see my father again until I graduated from college.

I was raised by a mother who loved me desperately, hated "weak" men like my father, and became a self-sufficient, independent, politically active feminist. (She didn't use the term "feminist," but described herself as "just a woman trying to survive and raise my kid.")

MY ROOTS IN THE MEN'S MOVEMENT

When I met my first wife, Candace, in 1964, she insisted I read Betty Friedan's *The Feminine Mystique,* and I learned that "the problem that has no name" was my problem too; though I had no idea what to do about it other than to read more books and dialogue with my wife. In the summer of 1971 we attended a feminist conference with 700 women and about 20 men, which both excited and terrified me. Though I felt a lot of anger from some of the women, many welcomed my presence and encouraged me to join with them in attacking the problem of sexism. It took me another year to find enough like-minded men to form a men's group, which lasted until I moved out of the area four years later. In 1979 I joined my present men's group, which has been meeting regularly for 15 years. A year and a half ago we joined with an Asian men's group to explore issues of racism.

When Candace and I separated in 1976, I was shocked to see how much rage we had toward each other, particularly around issues of child support and custody. She wanted more money than I felt I could pay, and I wanted a kind of involvement with our two children that she found unacceptable. During that time I found a good deal of support from a group called *Equal*

Rights for Fathers and later attended a number of local and national conferences on "Men's Rights."

In 1982 I was finishing my first book, *Inside Out: Becoming My Own Man,* when I read the *New Age Journal* interview with Robert Bly. In Bly I recognized a man who was wrestling with many of the same demons that haunted my life: the loss of my father, my ambivalent feelings toward women, my sense of powerlessness, my pain and rage, my addictiveness, and my vindictiveness. Since then I have probably attended forty or more gatherings with Bly and others he works with.

In 1983 I attended my first NOMAS Conference in Ann Arbor, Michigan. I loved the intellectual atmosphere and appreciated the presence of men of color, gay and bisexual men, and a few feminist women. What moved me the most were the evenings of music, poetry, song, storytelling and dance when we got out of our heads and into our bodies. I brought my son and daughter to the next two conferences and both attended a number of the California Men's Gatherings with me. I have been active over the years in the Men's Studies Task Force. I have probably attended thirty or more profeminist men's gatherings.

In recent years I have felt the importance of extending my therapeutic, political, and social action to healing our relationship to the Earth.

I have found many allies in the last thirty years in many parts of the movement. In my recent book, *The Warrior's Journey Home: Healing Men, Healing the Planet,* I acknowledged a few of them: Shepherd Bliss, Robert Bly, Warren Farrell, Betty Friedan, Herb Goldberg, Fred Hayward, John Lee, Joseph Pleck, and Anne Wilson Schaef.

POSSIBLE BLIND SPOTS

As a whole the articles by the profeminist men are quite negative in their view of "the men's movement." Like Kenneth Clatterbaugh, most seemed to reject the movement as being "patriarchal or at least as patriarchy friendly." That is not my experience. Perhaps I am blinded by my own biases, or perhaps the men who wrote the articles are missing something.

The first difficulty I see is that the title of the publication is *Profeminist Men Respond to the Men's Movement,* yet most of the response is to Robert Bly. I counted 191 references to Bly. Robert Moore was mentioned 17 times, Shepherd Bliss 7 times, James Hillman 6, Michael Meade and Doug Gillette 4 each, John Lee and Aaron Kipnis 2 each, and Sam Keen once.

To me that would be like saying I was going to critique the Profeminist Men's Movement and then putting 90 percent of the focus on John Stoltenberg and his book *Refusing to Be a Man.*

I have seen many people inflate Bly's importance, then, having blown his influence out of proportion, proceed to attack him. "If a person continues to see only giants," observed Anais Nin, "it means he is still looking at the world through the eyes of a child." I wonder if the men who see Bly worthy of 191 mentions and all the rest of the men in the movement a total of 44 are missing something important.

The second difficulty I see is that the men who have written the response seem to have made their judgments based on limited experiences attending workshops and a reading of Robert Bly's *Iron John.* Bly is first and foremost a poet. I wish there had been more focus on *Loving a Woman in Two Worlds* or *The Man in the Black Coat Turns* or his *Poems of Kabir* or *Poems of Rumi* or his translations of Antonio Machado.

Shepherd Bliss, who coined the term "mythopoetic," is mentioned only in passing. I would hope that those who want to understand the men's movement would read some of the numerous articles that Bliss has written over the past twenty-five years.

The third problem I see is that those who have written the most critical responses to the mythopoetic men's movement are writing as academicians. They are using the logic of the university mind to judge an experience that cannot be understood in those terms. This is like trying to understand the early consciousness-raising groups of feminist women by holding them to the standards of male academia. This approach misses the point for the same reasons that most scientists fail to understand the wisdom contained in Native American cosmology. The critics seem to be reading *Iron John* as though it were a doctoral dissertation on the men's movement rather than a rough summary of a ten-year ritual dialogue between Bly and thousands of men and women throughout the country.

SPECIFIC CONCERNS

There seem to me to be six major concerns that profeminist men have with mythopoetic men. I'd like to state them and then comment briefly on each.

1. *The movement is patriarchal or at least is patriarchy friendly.*
In the years I have been leading workshops and attending gatherings with

Robert Bly and others I have found much that supports my work in dismantling the patriarchy and little that is patriarchy friendly. The patriarchy is supported by unconscious men (and women) who are blind to the destructive effect the dominator culture has on themselves and others. Men coming together to acknowledge their wounds, feel their pain, release their rage, own their responsibility, and share their love are not patriarchy friendly.

Some would wish us to be more outwardly political, more direct in our commitment to women, gays, and lesbians, people of color, and those trapped in poverty. I would remind our critics that the women's movement began with a similar personal agenda. The feminist understanding that "the personal is political" is no less true for men. Many of us are moving beyond the personal and taking on social issues of consequence. These moves are far less publicized by a media that, for the most part, would trivialize our work (as they did with the early women's movement). Feminist women were once portrayed as angry, sexually repressed bra-burners. Many of us are portrayed as inarticulate, sexually oppressive drum-beaters.

2. *In contrast to the profeminist movement, we lack a clear agenda for social change.*

The concern seems to be that we are fuzzy-headed and illogical and, though we may have good intentions, we are politically naive and prone to drift with the patriarchal tide. As a result, Kenneth Clatterbaugh argues that "the mythopoetic men's movement is unlikely to go in any direction other than toward some version of patriarchy."

Having attended many profeminist and mythopoetic gatherings I can well understand the confusion. Mythopoetic gatherings are more like sacred rituals than conferences. They are closer to the world of indigenous spiritual ceremonies than to the world of academic argument.

I believe that is a strength, not a drawback. We also feel free to test our ideas, to say the most outrageous things, to be illogical, to celebrate the joy of being male, to express our pain and anger, to tell Robert Bly (and others on stage) they are full of shit. It is only the media and some critics who portray Robert Bly as the Grand Old Man of the Movement, The Patriarch. Those within the movement see him as a brother. Sometimes we see him as a naive and boisterous younger brother. At other times we see him as a wise and considerate older brother.

3. *We overemphasize wounds from the personal and familial and exclude exploration of the social and institutional contexts.*

This concern, I believe, stems directly from overemphasizing Robert Bly as a spokesman for the movement and taking *Iron John* as the primary expression of Bly's views on men.

I think there is great value in exploring the personal and familial roots of our pain. If we don't do that we end up, as many men and women in the movement have, projecting unresolved issues from our childhood onto our friends and critics. This contributes to conflict and misunderstandings and damages the movement.

Those who haven't recognized our commitment to social and institutional change have failed to delve deeply enough into the work of Bly, Bliss, Keen, Kipnis, or Hillman, to name only few. For example, in his book written with Michael Ventura, *We've Had a Hundred Years of Psychotherapy and the World's Getting Worse,* James Hillman is very critical of a movement that would have us heal our inner wounds without dealing with the oppression in the outer world. He says that every time we take our pain and rage over social injustice to a therapist or personal growth group, "We're depriving the political world of something. And therapy, in its crazy way, by emphasizing the inner soul and ignoring the outer soul, supports the decline of the actual world."

4. *We emphasize heterosexual experience and deny or minimize the homosexual experience.*

I agree with this concern. I think it is a major failing of the mythopoetic work. Unacknowledged homophobia keeps us from fully expressing who we are as individuals and as change agents in the society. I agree with men's leader Keith Hennessy who says he wants

> more direct acknowledgment of homophobia, a weapon used against every boy, which inflicts deep wounds that breed everywhere men gather. Homophobia takes up so much space in our movements! Most of the land we call *dancing* is occupied by homophobia. Most of the land we call *touch* is fenced off by homophobia. Most of the public land we call *friendship,* including asking for and providing care, is fenced off by homophobia. All of the oceans we call *emotions,* except for anger and depression, are fenced off by homophobia.[1]

I feel hopeful that there are enough men in the mythopoetic movement who agree that this major omission in our work will be addressed and healed. "I believe that in this gender-torn world," says Hennessy, "men meeting together to tell stories and pray and touch and challenge and commit to love is a world healing r/evolutionary act."

5. *The movement fails to appreciate the limitations of stories and myths as a basis for understanding men.*

Though I believe that all labels have their drawbacks, I believe the term "mythopoetic" is useful in describing the work of Robert Bly and Michael Meade. It becomes less useful when we use it to encompass the work of other leaders associated with the movement such as James Hillman, John Lee, Robert Moore, Malidoma Some, and John Stokes.

To criticize the movement because it emphasizes myths and stories fails to recognize the contribution of therapists, social activists, recovering addicts, dancers, tribal elders, aikido masters, ecologists, and many more who offer forms other than myth and poetry for expressing the truth of the male experience.

6. *In drawing men together the movement perpetuates the separation between men and women and contributes to male rage and violence toward women.*

This critique of the movement seems to be based on the media stereotype of men in the woods baring their chests, beating their drums, bemoaning the plight of oppressed white men being attacked by angry women, and generally wanting to return to the good old days when men were men and women knew their place. That stereotype has as much truth as feminist women being portrayed as ball-breaking bitches, bent on blaming men for all that is wrong in the world. Though there may be a few men and a few women whose words and behavior fit the stereotypes, they are a very small minority of men and women in the movement.

My experience with men in the wilderness has allowed me to feel my connection to the nonhuman world, to experience and heal some of the wounds I received in childhood, to release the shame of feeling less than a man because I was different, to dance joyfully with other men, to feel gratitude to women for waking me up to the deadly dominator culture, and, as Robert Bly challenges us, "to discover the sound that male cells sing."

But men meeting together in the wilderness is a very small part of the work we do. It also involves men and women coming together to air our differences and find our common ground. Some of the best workshops I have attended have focused on gender reconciliation. These include those led by Angeles Arrien and Robert Bly, Clarissa Pinkola Estes and Michael Meade, Malidoma Some and Sobonfu Some, and Elizabeth Herron and Aaron Kipnis.

I believe the men's movement has the potential to transform our society. Our strength comes from our commitment to change, the diversity of our various approaches, and the good will and common purpose that are at the core of our work. I look forward to our joint efforts in the coming years and echo the words of the poet Rumi, who said, "Out beyond ideas of wrong doing and right doing, there is a field. I'll meet you there."

NOTE

1. Keith Hennessy, "Queer Healing," a workshop at the 18th National Conference on Men and Masculinity, July 8–11, 1993, San Francisco, Calif.

VI

CONCLUSION:
CAN WE ALL
GET ALONG?

Why Mythopoetic Men Don't Flock to NOMAS

MICHAEL SCHWALBE

IN SEPTEMBER 1990 I BEGAN TO STUDY a group of men engaged in mythopoetic activity. From then until June 1993 I attended 128 meetings and gatherings of various kinds; observed and participated in all manner of mythopoetic activities; read the movement's guiding texts; read small mythopoetic publications from around the country; and listened to audio tapes of talks by movement leaders. I also interviewed twenty-one of the local men at length.[1]

Any sociologist who has studied a group from the inside will tell you that there is always more diversity within the group than most outsiders see. This is true in the case of the mythopoetic men. People often ask me for a quick account of who the men are, what they are doing, and why—as if the men are all alike and one explanation fits all. While there are commonalities of experience and outlook among the mythopoetic men, there are also differences. With regard to gender politics, which is my concern here, the mythopoetic men embrace a range of views from profeminist to men's rights. I want to acknowledge this diversity at the outset, because in what follows I'm going to refer to the men as a group.

The question I'm trying to answer here is this: Why don't men who get involved in mythopoetic activity flock to the National Organization for Men Against Sexism (NOMAS)? On the surface it seems that there's no good reason why the mythopoetic men should be unwilling to endorse NOMAS-style profeminism. Most mythopoetic men would endorse, in principle, NOMAS's goals of ending all forms of violence against women, ending racism, affirming gay relationships, and enhancing men's lives. Indeed, some men involved in mythopoetic activity do support NOMAS and attend its national conferences on men and masculinity. Yet most mythopoetic men disidentify with NOMAS and its profeminist stance. Examining some of the reasons for this may shed light on both the mythopoetic phenomenon and gender politics in the United States.

FEELING BETTER ABOUT BEING MEN

First, it is necessary to consider what the mythopoetic men are seeking. For the most part they seek self-change, not social change. The men want to feel better about themselves as men; to feel things more fully and to live richer, more authentic emotional lives; to act with more self-confidence; to know themselves better as emotional beings; and to experience emotional communion with other men. That men are gathering to try to help each other achieve these goals is in itself an important bit of social change. But it is not a change effort that examines or targets the larger political, economic, and cultural arrangements that created misery for women and men.

The foremost goal for many of the men who participate in mythopoetic activity is self-acceptance. They want to feel better about who and what they are as individuals, and especially as individual men. The Jungian psychology that guides mythopoetic activity helps tremendously. It tells the men that their wounds, weaknesses, and shadow sides are potential sources of strength and wisdom. This is exactly what the men want to hear; it is a healing message in itself. Jungian psychology also allows the men to deflect "shaming messages" because it says these messages come from people who are projecting elements of their own shadows. Hence critics, whoever they might be, can be readily discounted.

Jungian psychology also helps the men revalue the category (men) to which they belong and from which they derive their central identity. It does this by celebrating the goodness of masculine energies that are supposedly essential parts of every man. The men can thus feel better not only about their defects, which are redefined as potential strengths, but also about belonging to a category of beings who possess energies said to be valuable for the healthy survival of the human species. Jungian psychology—especially as used by Bly, Hillman, Meade, and others—helps the men redeem themselves as flawed individuals and redeem the category to which they belong.

No matter what psychology provided the theory behind the practice, the warmth and supportiveness found at mythopoetic gatherings would be therapeutic in their own right. Being listened to, accepted, and even comforted as they talk about their suffering helps the men feel better about who and what they are. The small support groups to which many of the men belong also serve this function. It's clear that many of the mythopoetic men find that their therapeutic needs can be met without engaging in political analysis and action around gender issues. In fact, as I'll explain later, such analysis and action would probably keep the men from getting what they want out of mythopoetic activity.

It's easy to lampoon twelve-step programs and New Age psychobabble about wounded inner children. The mythopoetic men, perhaps a third of whom also have a foot in the recovery movement, have been likewise lampooned for their jargon and unusual therapeutic practices. But I've seen that many of these men really do have serious psychic wounds to contend with. These may stem from childhood experiences of being shamed for their behavior or appearance, from being sexually abused as children, or from failures in their adult lives—including failures to live up to the ideals of traditional masculinity. Belonging to a *group* that is relatively privileged *materially* has not spared the men these troubles as individuals.

So when I look at these men as flesh-and-blood people, and not as members of a social category, I can see that their psychological distress is real. I can also see the strength of their needs for self-acceptance. This is in part why they join a therapeutic movement based on a psychology that encourages guilt-free self-acceptance. And even if it is true that their material privileges allow them the luxury of doing "inner work" instead of just struggling to survive, this doesn't mitigate the seriousness of their psychic pain.

One reason the mythopoetic men don't flock to NOMAS should thus be clear: it offers no comforting psychological theory. It offers no guilt-absolving, guilt-deflecting "healing messages." In fact, NOMAS's profeminism is perceived by many mythopoetic men as offering just the opposite. As one mythopoetic publication put it, the profeminist branch of the men's movement is declining because its "critical attitude toward men alienates many potential supporters and newer branches offer more positive alternatives."[2]

It seems to many mythopoetic men that NOMAS accepts the "shaming messages" that come from radical feminist women. This is why many mythopoetic men see NOMAS as the guilt wing of the men's movement. The profeminist stance is seen as guilt- and shame-inducing, and disempowering, because it gives angry women too much power to define the nature and worth of men and masculinity. Given what these men are experiencing psychologically, and the therapeutic quest they are on, NOMAS's profeminism strikes many of them as toxic.

NONSOCIOLOGICAL THINKING ABOUT
GENDER AND FEMINISM

While I think the mythopoetic men misunderstand feminism and NOMAS, there is a grain of truth in their view. The truth is that if men take feminism seriously they must engage in self-critique. Part of this critique is recognizing the sexist impulses that are ingrained in us by virtue of our socialization into a male-supremacist society. If this leads men to see the ways in which they are unfairly privileged in this society and how their unconscious sexist behavior hurts women, then some guilt is entirely likely.

Perhaps it is that many men drawn to NOMAS can distinguish between productive guilt and neurotic guilt, the former being what motivates us to change, the latter being what erodes our sense of worth. To make this distinction it is necessary to think sociologically—that is, one must be able to see unjust gender arrangements as historical conditions that predated and shaped men who are alive today. From a sociological point of view, it makes no sense for men today to feel guilty for the sexism they inherited. Yet this same view imposes responsibility for working to change sexist social arrangements and metes out deserved guilt if we do not.

The problem is that few of the men involved in mythopoetic activities think sociologically about gender. They do not see gender as a social construction that depends for its existence on humanly created ideologies and institutions. Rather, following Jung, they see gender as an essential, timeless feature of males and females. In light of the psychological distress many of the men suffer, it is more comforting for them to embrace an essentialist view of gender than to acknowledge their ingrained sexism, recognize its harmful effects, and take responsibility for changing themselves and society. That's a tall order even for the healthiest of people.

Because the men don't think sociologically, they take feminist criticism of men personally. Part of the problem here is a misunderstanding of feminism. To many mythopoetic men, feminism is exaltation of the feminine; it is militant action in pursuit of equal rights for women; it is strident criticism of men and masculinity; it is women telling men to be more like women; it is women seeking to turn the tables and dominate men. Men who embrace feminism therefore must be self-denigrating and weak, since this means accepting the view of angry, wounded women that there is nothing good about "maleness."

The big thing the mythopoetic men have missed in feminism is the analysis of unjust social arrangements that produce gendered beings all too suitable for enacting dominant and subordinate roles. Because they think in psychological terms and operate with an essentialist understanding of gender, the men take feminist criticism of patriarchal institutions personally and seek to defend themselves against it. They experience this social criticism as an indictment of their moral worth as men.

Many of the men react especially sharply because they see themselves as advocates of equality for women. (Most of the men in the group I studied supported liberal feminist positions.) What this means is that some of the men have experienced *radical* feminist criticism of men as a kind of betrayal. Many of the men tried hard all their lives to please women. And then women, or at least some women, turned on them, criticizing them for what they could not help being: men.

What the mythopoetic men want to do is to reinvest the identity 'man' with new moral value. Anything feminist or profeminist is seen as a threat to this project. The NOMAS profeminist position is thus tainted. Profeminist men, as seen from the mythopoetic perspective, have bought into the feminist perspective that shames men. This is not what mythopoetic men want, which is anything but more shame and guilt. NOMAS may claim to "enhance men's lives," but it doesn't celebrate masculinity or manhood *per se*, and so it promises little or nothing by way of immediate gains in self-acceptance or in feelings of worth as a man.

To sum this up: another reason the mythopoetic men don't flock to NOMAS is that the profeminist NOMAS stance is perceived as feminist-inspired political dogma, which is accepted by men who are willing to let themselves be shamed by, or used by, women. The profeminist NOMAS stance is not seen as growing out of a sociopolitical analysis of unequal gender arrangements because the mythopoetic men don't see gender as a social construction; because they don't have a clear view of structural inequalities between women and men; and because they are focused on their own psychological troubles.

POLITICS AS AN OBSTACLE TO SELF-KNOWLEDGE AND COMMUNITAS

I don't think the mythopoetics are an unusual or unusually troubled group of men. For the most part they are quite ordinary. This means that in being socialized to manhood they were taught to repress many of their feelings. It also means that as they pursued careers and raised families, they experienced much isolation from other men. What they're now seeking, in addition to self-acceptance, is to receive the emotional part of themselves that has been repressed, and to achieve emotional communion with other men. A political analysis of their circumstances would probably not be of much help in doing these things.

Part of the mythopoetic philosophy is that men raised in our society are taught to "live in their heads," that is, to be rational to the point of being emotionally numb. Getting out of this debilitating way of being is said to require taking a risky, emotional path into the psyche. A sociopolitical analysis of gender inequality simply wouldn't do the trick. In fact, it would probably have the opposite effect of encouraging the men to think and talk in an abstract, intellectual manner. This kind of talk would "come from the head and not the heart." It thus wouldn't do much to help the men explore the inner reaches of their psyches or to gain knowledge of themselves as emotional beings. The sociopolitical discourse that is associated with NOMAS's gender politics is thus unappealing.

The other problem with collective political analysis is that it leads to arguments. This is not what the mythopoetic men seek at their gatherings. They do not want to compete over whose interpretation of social reality is correct. They want to make emotional connections with other men. They want untroubled brotherhood in which their feelings are validated. They want what Victor Turner calls "communitas."[3] When discussions at mythopoetic gatherings turn political, inadvertently, and disagreements surface and tensions arise, someone will usually say, "we're getting away from the important work here." The important work being maintaining a mood of fellow-feeling.

The main problem is that the mythopoetic movement does not provide men with tools for reflecting on the sexism that is deeply ingrained in all men socialized in male-supremacist societies. In fact, in celebrating maleness and masculinity, albeit nontraditional masculinity, there is inevitably a great deal of sexist baggage that comes along for the ride. When the group doing the celebrating consists of men only—men who want acceptance and validation of their feelings from other men—challenges to expressions of sexism are less likely to be made. While the mythopoetic men by and large do not engage in "woman bashing," there is a great deal of low-level, unconscious sexism evident in their talk and behavior.

Two qualifications to this account are necessary. One is that the mythopoetic men are generally not apolitical in the sense of being uninformed, apathetic, and socially unconscious. The men in the group I studied are generally left-liberal in their politics, informed about current political events, and supportive of progressive causes. But they are willing to compartmentalize politics and emotion work so that they can get what they want out of their mythopoetic activities. As one man said in response to an earlier version of these remarks, "I don't go into the woods to be socially responsible. . . . When I want to be socially responsible I march, write letters, and sign petitions."

The second qualification is that at least one prominent mythopoetic teacher, James Hillman, disparages the easy separation of the emotional and the political. He has argued that men's feelings of grief and anguish often have a real basis in the lousy state of the eternal world, and that if we dissipate these feelings in therapy instead of using them to propel political action, then we're not doing what we should.[4] In Hillman's view, political action can be a path to personal growth. Some mythopoetic men are taking Hillman seriously and looking for ways to turn their emotional energies toward social action. Others cling to the notion that personal healing must be complete before such action is undertaken.

HOMOPHOBIA AND INVISIBLE PRIVILEGES

The mythopoetic men are predominantly self-identified as heterosexual, although a substantial proportion (a fourth to a third, by my estimate) have interest in homoerotic contact with other men. Despite their recognition that homophobia is a problem—because it keeps men isolated from each other and afraid to show affection for each other—the mythopoetics definitely want to reaffirm their heterosexual identities. This is evident in the practice of qualifying any expression of desire for physical affection or touch from other men with the caveat that the desire is for *nonsexual* contact. Homophobia is also evident in the concern the men show for public perceptions of their activities. In an interview a man told me that one reason he didn't like media coverage of men's retreats was that it fostered misperceptions. "The camera might show us dancing," he said, "and people would think we're a bunch of gay guys."

NOMAS is known to the mythopoetic men to include a large number of gay men. One mythopoetic publication labeled the profeminist branch of the men's movement the "profeminist/gay affirmative" branch, thus highlighting the association with gay men. Even more revealing was the statement, in the same place, that "heterophobic gays and bisexuals far outnumber straight men" in the profeminist men's movement.[5] This statement reflects a perception of NOMAS as hostile territory for heterosexual men. How might such a perception have been formed? I would guess that it is the result of challenges to heterosexist behavior.

If the mythopoetic men reject homophobia in principle, why should the presence of gay men in NOMAS bother them? I think part of the reason is a vestige of the homophobia that gets instilled in men raised in heterosexist societies. But something more is revealed by the use of the term "heterophobic" to describe the gay men involved in the profeminist men's movement. One thing that is revealed here is a resistance to giving up two invisible privileges of middle-class, heterosexual, white manhood. The first privilege is not having to defend the value of one's identities. The second is not having to critically reflect on the habits—the assumptions of superiority or at least normality—that come from being socialized as a member of the dominant group.

The term heterophobic also implies a symmetry of oppression between gays and straights. The suggestion is that if gay men object to heterosexist behavior on the part of straight men, this is being heterophobic, which is no different from homophobic straights criticizing gays and lesbians. I see reflected here the same absurd notions of symmetrical oppression upon which men's rights thinking is based.[6] Just as feminist criticism of men is dismissed as "neo-sexist," gay criticism of heterosexist behavior is dismissed as heterophobia. The immense power imbalances that characterize relations between gays and straights and women and men are thus swept from consciousness.

The mythopoetic men are allergic to criticism, all of which tends to be discredited as shaming or wounding. Only a group that is secure in its power and status can get away with dismissing its critics in this way. The mythopoetic men have the privilege of ignoring feminist criticism and so they're not going to go out of their way to get more of it in NOMAS. By the same token, the mythopoetic men are unused to being members of a minority. Hence they fear being outnumbered by allegedly heterophobic gays. The common thread here is a desire to protect a safe place—the mythopoetic movement— where they can feel strong and close ranks against threats to their invisible privileges.

CONNECTING HEADS AND HEARTS

The story of the mythopoetic movement is still unfolding. I think the movement can be steered, which is part of what I'm trying to do. I want to document, interpret, and intervene. I think it is possible to inject more feminist consciousness into the movement, if it's done right. Two things that have to be done are, first, to respect where the men are at psychologically, and two, to show how a sociological analysis of gender inequalities can be not only guilt and shame alleviating, but ultimately more empowering than any psychological view.

If the mythopoetic men can be shown how their desires for self-acceptance, authenticity, and supportive community can be achieved only through a transformation of society that includes eliminating class, race, and gender inequalities, then they will come along. Their hearts are in the right places in many ways. The hard part will be the recognition, and the resistance it evokes, that such a transformation will entail the loss of some of the power and privileges these men now take for granted.

What I would like to see, in other words, is the mythopoetic men link their rejection of the iron cage of rationality, of alienated work, of competitive relationships among men, and of soulless culture, to a project that recognizes how these things harm us all, men and women—and more so people of color and working-class women and men than relatively well-off middle-class white men. This will require sociological thinking and a more radical political consciousness—as some feminist women argued almost twenty years ago. In speaking of "men's liberation," Carol Hanisch hoped that men would get in touch with what the mythopoetics might today call their lover and warrior energies:

> Women want men to be bold—boldly honest, aggressive in their human pursuits. Boldly passionate, sexual and sensual. And women want this for themselves. It's time men became boldly radical. Daring to go to the root of their own exploitation and seeing that it is not women or "sex roles" or "society" causing their unhappiness, but capitalists and capitalism. It's time men dare to name and fight these, their real exploiters.[7]

Taking up this challenge will require embracing an analysis that recognizes the role of elite white *men*—those who run the capitalist economy and its lapdog government—in orchestrating the reproduction of the iron cage, of alienated work, of homogenized culture, and of competitive social relationships. Feminist theory offers some of the most powerful intellectual tools available for making these connections. As I see it, the task is to get mythopoetic men to recognize the moral imperative, which ought to resonate with what is already in their hearts, to take up these tools, or their equivalents, and work to dismantle the iron cage rather than just to spring themselves from it temporarily.

NOTES

This is a revised version of a talk given at the 17th National Conference on Men and Masculinity, sponsored by the National Organization for Men Against Sexism, July 1992, Chicago. Thanks to Sherryl Kleinman for helpful comments on earlier drafts.

1. For a full account of my study, see *Unlocking the Iron Cage: Understanding the Mythopoetic Men's Movement* (New York: Oxford, 1995).

2. *Wingspan: Inside the Men's Movement,* ed. C. Harding (New York: St. Martin's, 1992), xiv.

3. See V. Turner, *The Ritual Process* (Ithaca, N.Y.: Cornell University Press, 1969), 131–65.

4. Hillman has made this point in statements at mythopoetic gatherings and in a number of articles reprinted in mythopoetic publications. This is the main theme of his book of conversations and letters with Michael Ventura. See J. Hillman and M. Ventura, *We've Had a Hundred Years of Psychotherapy—and the World's Getting Worse* (New York: HarperCollins, 1992).

5. *Wingspan: Inside the Men's Movement,* ed. C. Harding (New York: St. Martin's, 1992), xiv.

6. For an analysis of the tortured logic upon which men's rights thinking is based, see K. Clatterbaugh, *Contemporary Perspectives on Masculinity* (Boulder, Colo.: Westview, 1990), 61–83.

7. C. Hanisch, "Men's Liberation," in ed. Kathie Sarachild, *Feminist Revolution—An Abridged Edition with Additional Writing* (New York: Random House, 1978), 76. I first saw this quotation in bell hook's essay, "Men: Comrades in Struggle," which appears in her book *Feminist Theory: From Margin to Center* (Boston: South End Press, 1984).

In Defense of the Men's Movements

DON SHEWEY

AN EXERCISE IN SACRED SPACE

Think about something tender. Think about something sacred. Think about something that makes you cry. Think about a romance that made you love every living creature, a loss you didn't think you could bear, a death that opened the bottomless pit of mortality below you.

Now imagine talking about it to someone you barely know standing in a noisy bar in Grand Central Station at rush hour.

That's what it's like trying to discuss what's called "the men's movement" in the media.

But a crowded bar in Grand Central Station is not the right place to talk publicly about love or inner life. You need sacred space—ritual space. "Change or transformation can happen only when a man or woman is in ritual space," poet Robert Bly elaborates in his bestseller, *Iron John*. "A man or woman remains inside this heated space (as in Sufi ritual dance) for a relatively brief time, and then returns to ordinary consciousness." Just as the feminist movement emboldened women to do consciousness-raising and ritualizing without men, men have discovered that they can only do certain kinds of soul work without women present to perform for or to try to please. Around the country, men are creating ritual space where they can enter and sustain a discourse on the male psyche, initiation, poetry, excess, desire, grief, shame, and the Three Stooges.

Women would probably be surprised at how little time is spent at these gatherings talking about them. The subtext of the question "Where are we at as men?" is not men's relationship to women but to the world. What can be done about the environment, the economy, education, AIDS? What can men do? How come good men don't seem to get things done these days, while the retrogressive Republican ideologues behind Reagan and Bush seem to have no trouble moving their agenda? One thing that can be said about right-wing conservatives is that they're generally religious people or, at any rate, churchgoers, meaning that they recognize some transpersonal commitment. Many Americans (including many on the left) have no such navigational system, no attachment to something beyond material reality. It's unfashionable even to talk about God.

Robert Bly and the other teachers who lead men's gatherings hardly ever invoke the deity, and when they do, they talk about the gods. What they're doing is holy work nevertheless. Fortunately, they don't claim to have all the answers. "We're going to talk about the male psyche tonight, a subject about which we know almost nothing," I once heard Bly say at the beginning of a program. "We always say a few things that are true, but we don't know which ones they are."

WHO ARE THESE MEN?

It's a beautiful Saturday morning on the campus of the New Mexico School for the Deaf, and 500 men fighting spring fever are lining up to enter the James A. Little Theater through the stage door. In the hallway, a shirtless man is dancing wildly and whooping; from behind him wafts the rumble of drumming. As we get closer to the entrance, a sense of chaos radiates, ever-stronger, from the other side. A tunnel of pine branches has been constructed as a sort of ritual birth canal. Just before I stoop to go through, the gatekeeper (a balding man in a flannel shirt and jeans) leans to whisper in my ear, "Let your movements be a blessing."

In a flash I'm through. I stumble into bright lights, a thicket of drummers, men coming at me, the steady pulse of clapping. Where am I? Suddenly, there's Bly, in my face, his blue eyes going all googly behind his steel-framed glasses, his long arms waving and wiggling like flapping wings. He's dancing like a big, silly silver-haired walrus in Tom Wolfe-white trousers and a blue brocade vest. I lock into his gaze and go into my own basic boogaloo, and we dance together across what turns out to be the stage of the auditorium before he shakes my hand and points me down the stairs to the audience. Pleased to meet ya.

I look back and notice that some guys accept the invitation to dance, but most just stagger offstage looking dazed. The house is already full of guys standing and clapping. Led by mythologist and frequent Bly collaborator Michael Meade, a fireball of energy who beats out the tempo on a cowbell, they're chanting "Go back-back, go back-back, go back-back, go back!" At least half the men are locals; they're the ones with tans wearing shorts and greeting one another with hugs. The rest of us make small talk with the first friendly face or circulate like lone wolves looking to connect with that secret buddy in the crowd. I would venture to guess, though, that I'm not the only one wondering, "Who are these men?"

That's what everyone wants to know. What kind of men go to men's gatherings? And what goes on there? Looking to answer those questions, partly out of personal interest and partly out of journalistic curiosity, I've spent the last year attending men's gatherings of various descriptions, including three different conferences conducted by Bly, Meade, and psychologist James Hillman. The first was the event in Santa Fe, a two-day seminar last April in Santa Fe sponsored by the C. G. Jung Society of New Mexico. For the First Multicultural Men's Conference, held in May in Buffalo Gap, West Virginia, those three guys invited three black teachers—playwright Joseph Walker, poet and essayist Haki Madhubuti (ne Don Luther Lee), and Burkina Faso-born scholar Malidoma Some—to spend a week sharing cabins in the woods with 50 black men and 50 white men. Early in November, Bly, Hillman, and Meade (sounds like the men's movement equivalent of Crosby, Stills and Nash, doesn't it?) took over the Manhattan Center ballroom on West 34th Street for another two-day seminar sponsored by a local men's group, On the Common Ground.

The week in Buffalo Gap was a historic occasion beyond anyone's expectations, and it deserves its own in-depth report. This article will focus on the two-day events in Santa Fe and New York in some detail, as a way to get beyond the media stereotypes to the substance of what Bly has called "men's work."

The media—TV, magazines, newspapers—have picked up the scent of something fresh and wild and intriguing going on with these men, but they don't know exactly how to deal with it. The usual media handles are missing; the men with the ideas don't consider themselves celebrities, so they've declined offers to go on *Donahue* and *Oprah.* Spiritual transformation cannot be televised. So the media basically make fun of the whole thing. Mock the leaders, mock their attire, mock their rituals, reduce their ideas to cartoon cliches, mock the cliches, ignore the content, chase the animal into a trap and kill it. How many articles have you read about "guys out in the woods banging on drums and dancing around fires" that make it all sound like the most ludicrous kind of pretentious, self-indulgent, corny, macho bullshit behavior in the world?

The general impression seems to be summed up in one of Matt Groening's "Life in Hell" cartoons, an ad for "Akbar & Jeff's Wild Man Weekend," which advises participants to bring "1 loincloth (or bikini-style underpants), 1 jar of warpaint (wife or girlfriend's lipstick OK), 1 large cigar, and $300." The schedule of activities includes nude jumping jacks at dawn, chest pounding, flower sniffing, and a lecture on "How to Fantasize About Sleeping with Lots of Attractive Women." It's a hilarious cartoon, and it perfectly illustrates that hip, sophisticated way we have of equating things with their marketing—dismissing a movie because of its trailer, judging candidates by the quality of their television commercials, discussing books on the basis of their reviews. Why not? You can learn a lot about animals by examining their shit. Not everything, though.

Here are some of the kinds of men people *think* go to men's gatherings: macho men wanting to be macho together; wimpy men wanting to be macho men; gay men wanting to fuck each other. These, of course, are categories (along with "yuppie" and "New Age devotee") that few self-respecting middle-class American men would admit to belonging to. I've been to enough men's gatherings, though, to know that all these varieties are indeed likely to show up.

Here are some other varieties (none of them mutually exclusive). *The isolated*—these guys are hungry to be around other men, especially men who will talk more than TV-talk (instant opinions, soundbites, punch lines). *The wounded*—wounded by divorce, alcoholism, substance abuse, medical mistreatment, bad luck. A surprising number of men turn out to have been sexually abused as children. Then there are *the numb*—they've got all the exterior signs of success (good career, happy home life) but they have no inner life. They've just turned 35 or 45 or 55 and they feel life is passing them by; they realize they've been sleeping and they need to *wake up*.

There's another bunch of guys heavily represented at men's gatherings who don't get mentioned much. They might be called "the responsible men." These are men who accept that almost any urgent problem facing the world today (homelessness, racism, destruction of the planet's natural resources, poor education, abuse of women and children) can be traced directly to the male sex—to the greed, low self-esteem, sexual insecurity, cynicism, and spiritual poverty of individual men. They accept that men, too, are victimized by patriarchal values. They accept that electoral politics and mass demonstrations are a limited solution at best. They accept that every man who has the strength, ability, education, and courage to do something to change the world for the better has a personal responsibility to do so.

They accept that the capacity to change has to be cultivated within oneself before it can be expressed outwardly, but then it *must* be expressed outwardly. They accept that—despite some women's fear and suspicion that male bonding is exclusionary, dangerous, and destructive—there is great creative potential in men working together for change. They accept that getting men to love, value, and honor the child within, the man within, the woman within is a giant step toward loving, valuing, and honoring men, women, and children outside. They don't necessarily know how to do that or even how to begin, but many of the men who show up at men's gatherings recognize that the work has to start somewhere and they're ready to do it.

At least that's the impression I get from the men I encounter at gatherings. The median age is early forties. (This men's work doesn't speak to young men as dramatically as it does to those who've been around the block and had the stuffing knocked out of them once or twice.) It doesn't surprise me that there are a lot of doctors, health-care workers, and therapists around; soul work is essentially healing work. It also doesn't surprise me that there are few men of color. American society is ruled by straight white men, and that's the group within whom profound changes must take place before profound changes can be made in the world.

But finally, the most truthful answers to the question "Who are these men?" are specific ones. Among the men I meet in Santa Fe are: Steven, a divorced potter who lives in Taos; Jim, a schoolteacher from Michigan who lives on a Navajo reservation where his wife works as a doctor; Thomas, a gay priest from the Midwest who was forced to resign from his job after being outed by a fellow priest; and Scott, a farmer who grows alfalfa for cattle in Colorado.

In New York, I mostly hang out with Dirk, a cabinetmaker from Katonah whom I met at Buffalo Gap, and the three friends he's nudged into taking the workshop. Russell, a red-haired, wise-cracking, emotionally free carpenter, has been on a spiritual journey for a couple of years since he took his wife and kids to North Dakota to spend time with a Native shaman. Walter, a black social worker who trains inner-city kids in workplace literacy skills, is drawn to the men's work specifically to get ideas about mentoring young black men. Meanwhile, Al, an Italian-American lawyer from Westchester who probably spends most of his professional life playing it close to the vest, seems nervous, intrigued, and a little over his head in this hotbed of masculine expressiveness.

Talking to these men, I recognize in each of their stories reflections of my own quest to hitch the wagon of my talents, education, and good intentions to a larger purpose. And as a group, these individuals represent a perfect cross-section of the different degrees of readiness and apprehension with which people approach the men's work.

SLIPPERY DEVIL

There's no question that most people are drawn to these events because they want to be around Robert Bly, who after decades of renown as a poet, translator, and antiwar activist has become the indisputable star of the men's consciousness movement. Though hardly the first to gain prominence writing about contemporary men, Bly has been leading men's conferences since 1981 and developing his ideas in print since his landmark 1982 interview with Keith Thompson called "What Men Really Want."

But Bly entered the mass American brain almost overnight when his interview with Bill Moyers, *A Gathering of Men,* was broadcast on PBS in January of 1990. That documentary has become practically the Magna Carta of the men's spirituality movement; I once heard an elderly man say he'd watched the video three times in one week and found himself sobbing each time. In our post-literate culture, any TV show reaches more people than any book. Still, *Iron John,* Bly's unclassifiable volume of literary analysis, philosophy, and cultural criticism, was on the *New York Times* hardcover best seller list for over a year.

It's funny what that "leader" business brings out in people, though, and it's fascinating to see how Bly deals with it. When someone steps into the spotlight and commands attention, two things tend to happen. That person instantly attracts resentment, suspicion, attitude. Especially among the intelligentsia, anything that smacks of spiritual or visionary leadership kicks off an allergic reaction to gurus. Notice how in recent years the word *guru,* a beneficent Hindu term for teacher that literally refers to one who leads people "from the darkness to the light," has been transformed into a pejorative term, synonymous with *charlatan.* That probably has to do with the other strong reaction to leaders deeply embedded in the American character, which is the thirst for a savior, the willingness to surrender one's own flawed self to follow note-for-note the program of someone who seems to know better.

Bly circumvents those knee-jerk reactions by being as off-putting and unpredictable as possible. Just when you're beginning to see him as a wise old man, he reveals a little boy's delight in dirty jokes. Just when you're admiring him as a repository of guru-like wisdom, he makes some insulting remark about Tibetans. Just when you're ready to dismiss him as a gruff macho poseur, he whips out some delicate bit of verse or remarks knowingly about joy or ecstasy. Try to compliment him, and he'll either thank you or bite your head off. He's a trickster, a clown, a slippery devil.

I was very put off by him at first. Watching *A Gathering of Men*, I hated his voice with its combination of Midwestern mushmouth, mean-father barking, and sarcastic mimicry. As a writer, I chafed at the vagueness of his language ("There's a lot of grief around men these days . . ."). Listening to an audiocassette (the post-literate equivalent of the literary essay) called "The Naive Male," I found myself torn between agreeing with compelling and surprising truths and violently objecting to vast overgeneralizations and undue putdowns. And I couldn't stand his habit of snapping "You understand me?" or "Is that clear?" to bully a response out of audiences.

When I finally got over my resistance to Bly and sat down with *Iron John*, I was pleased to discover that he not only practices that quality in Roland Barthes that Susan Sontag superbly describes as "a festive (rather than dogmatic or credulous) relation to ideas" but also encourages it in others. It's surely no accident that Bly begins many of his readings with a poem by Antonio Machado called "Walker," which deflects the guru worship of would-be cult followers by declaring the non-existence of The Way: "We make the path by walking."

Women have a whole other set of fears about this men's work. Some women see the idea of a men's movement as a kind of nightmare, especially at this moment in the wake of the Clarence Thomas–Anita Hill hearings. As one friend says over dinner, "Women feel totally oppressed by men, and the idea of them going off in the woods to worship maleness makes me very nervous." One of the most commonly heard sentiments was expressed in *Newsweek*'s cover story, "What Do Men Really Want?": "If middle-class males have the lion's share of economic, political and sexual power in this country, why are many of them so unhappy?"

There's no denying the inequities between men and women in American society. But it's also a mistake not to notice that men are asking the same questions. "If men have all the power in the world, why do I feel so powerless?" A lot of the hostility between men and women stems from misunderstanding and miscommunication (as Deborah Tannen so lucidly lays out in *You Just Don't Understand*). One thing that we fall into is making vast generalizations about men and women that quickly take the form of polar opposites. If men are powerful, women are powerless. Another way that works is that the categories become mutually exclusive. If men are competitive, then women are not and cannot be. Or that if women feel pain, men don't.

The media have stoked women's fears by portraying the men's movement as hordes of men gathering in packs trying to become the same man: a wildhaired, chest-thumping, cigar-chomping, woman-crushing he-man. And there are various factions of the men's movement that provide ammunition for that attack. There are groups of aggrieved men who want to circulate "The New Male Manifesto" and wear buttons that say "Save the Males." And there are numerous men's gatherings where the leaders put participants through paramilitary exercises with the idea of getting them to reclaim their abandoned masculinity, snap out of their passivity around women and authority figures, "get their balls back." I've been to one of those men's weekends that promises nothing less than "a 20th century initiation into manhood." Those gatherings sometimes do a lot of good, especially for men who've been walking around asleep for 40 years. The danger of turning out these cookie-cutter "new warriors," of course, is that it locates the essence of a man on the outside—how he walks, how he talks, how he looks. And that's hardly an alternative to the philosophy of the ghetto or the Army that you can turn a boy into a man by giving him a gun.

To me the most impressive thing about the mythopoetic men's movement, as exemplified by Bly, Hillman, and Meade, is that it scrupulously avoids indoctrinating men with some est-like formula of behavior. When Bly talks about men getting in touch with the "wild man" inside, he's not suggesting that corporate types go marching into business meetings with warpaint and a tomahawk any more than he's advocating taking teenagers from Crown Heights into Prospect Park, starving them for three days, and circumcising them without anesthetic.

I've noticed that many people have opinions about Robert Bly without knowing anything about the ideas he and others doing men's work disseminate. It doesn't surprise me. After all, more people have seen the parody of Bly on *Murphy Brown* than the Moyers interview on PBS. More people have seen pictures of Bly in his trademark, multicolor-striped vest than have bought *Iron John*. And I think it's safe to say that more people have bought the book than have read it. So I'll mention just a few of the key ideas that run through Bly's writing and speaking about men.

One is that many contemporary American men suffer from a lack of initiation—by which he means not just the brutal physical trials we usually associate with male initiation (fraternity hazing, army basic training) but also the emotional and spiritual instruction from elders required for men to grow into maturity as integrated individuals. Without initiation (whose ingredients include separation from the mother, symbolic wounding, an encounter with another reality, and being welcomed into a community of older men), a man often has no understanding of his capacity for pain, no concept of rites of passage or cycles of life. He remains a boy in an adult man's body, to whom life just seems like one blurry skidmark from graduation to the grave.

The behavior of uninitiated males, Bly contends, has given a bad name to masculinity, which is surrounded entirely by negative associations and held responsible for all the ills of the world. This situation has given rise to what he calls the "soft" or "naive" male who, in rejecting the aggressive and obnoxious male traits that women dislike, has also abandoned the forceful and heroic aspects of masculinity, to the detriment of society.

To analyze what's missing from contemporary men and to seek reparation, Bly turns to folk tales and myths from ancient cultures to find richer, deeper, more complex images of masculinity than those in today's pop culture, which glorifies the macho (Arnold Schwarzenegger) and the money-mad (Donald Trump) and ridicules almost every other kind of man as impotent, foolish, or wimpy. In stories, as in dreams, every character is you, so mythology offers men a variety of kings, magicians, warriors, lovers, and clowns to model. In particular, Bly has latched onto the Grimm Brothers' story "Iron John," whose central character is a wild hairy man whom Bly discusses as an initiatory figure, a source of spontaneity and natural wisdom through whom a young man gains tools with which to face the ups and downs of life.

To combat women's complaint that men have no feelings, Bly has proposed his own set of underrecognized male modes of feelings, and first among them is grief. Sometimes that grief is traceable to an absent father, a failed romance, a lost child, a shattered dream, but often, says Bly, "Men feel a very deep grief that has no cause." To honor that grief and not deny it, he stresses the need for periods of "dwelling in the ashes." As he pointed out to a Philadelphia radio interviewer, "Our agricultural system is a disaster, our relationship with children and the schools is a disaster, the relationship to the blacks is a disaster, to single women raising children, the whole thing—and we're hiring president after president who says, 'This is wonderful, and we're doing great.' "

Another masculine tradition Bly likes to emphasize comes from David Gilmore's anthropological study *Manhood in the Making.* In most cultures, Bly reports, "A man is defined as a person who goes to the center of the village and speaks his mind. If you don't, you're considered a trash man." Bly himself doesn't hesitate to speak up—maybe you've noticed—and he doesn't mince words. Last spring, at the height of patriotic revelry over the triumph of Operation Desert Storm, Bly repeatedly reviled the Gulf War as "shameful," the media coverage as "disgusting," and the display of yellow ribbons as "cowardly."

Appearing with Deborah Tannen at Cooper Union the night before the men's weekend, Bly wasted no time voicing his opinion on the Clarence Thomas-Anita Hill affair. "She was obviously telling the truth," he said, to thunderous applause. "There's no greater reason for the men's movement than to look at this hearing," he continued. "Hatch, Simpson—these guys are fossilized fragments of the patriarchy disguised as Republicans. On the other side, we have the Democrats, who are nothing. *Is that it for men in the United States??*"

On the lecture circuit, Bly could make a fortune going around by himself preaching his Wild Man gospel. And he does do a fair share of solo poetry readings and "A Day for Men with Robert Bly" workshops. Most of the time, though, he travels with Meade, the Seattle-based mythologist whom he met in 1979 through their shared love of Irish storytelling, and James Hillman, the renegade psychologist who was director of studies at the Jung Institute in Zurich after Jung's death and subsequently turned Jungian theory upside down with books like *Re-Visioning Psychology* and *The Dream and the Underworld.*

Other fellow travelers on this journey sometimes include Robert Moore, the Southern-drawling psychologist best-known for his study of male archetypes *King, Warrior, Magician, Lover* (co-authored with Douglas Gillette), and wilderness expert John Stokes, who earned his reputation as a tracker by undergoing wilderness training with native teachers in North America, Hawaii, and Australia. After the multicultural men's conference in West Virginia, Bly expanded the crew to include Haki Madhubuti, who offers poems and perceptions from his provocative studies of African-American culture (most recently *Black Men: Obsolete, Single, Dangerous?*), and Malidoma Some, who rivets men's gatherings with his recollections of his initiation as a member of the Dagara tribe.

Appearing with a posse serves two functions: it cuts the ego inflation and media attention that gravitates to lone superstars, and it gives the men who come to these conferences a living, breathing model of a community of men in which joking, grieving, disagreeing, being silly, and saying important things are not only possible but encouraged.

PLAYING IN THE BAND

Every men's gathering I've been to has had a touch of theatricality to it: there's generally a scenario, a script of sorts, often a star, some audience participation. The Bly, Hillman, and Meade weekends seem especially like theater, and by theater I mean the way the Greeks originally thought of it—as an opportunity for the community of citizens to gather and, in a formal way, discuss the things that matter to them. Over the course of the weekend, the guys on stage read poems, tell stories, play music, lead songs and chants, ask questions, interact with the audience, tell jokes, and instigate anger and dancing, returning again and again to matters of importance to men in American society. It feels like nothing so much as a town meeting, only the community in question exists not on the map but in the hearts of men.

The theme for the weekend in Santa Fe is "The Community of Men and the Language of Desire," so the program begins with a round of poems about desire. Meade, a round-faced Irishman with a Prince Valiant haircut, accompanies himself on Cuban tackhead conga, while Bly occasionally plucks at a bouzouki, which, he admits, is more of a stage prop than an instrument he knows how to play. It fascinates me that this branch of the men's movement revolves around poetry; going to poetry readings seems like the ultimate sissy pastime. I suppose only someone as big and gruff and eminent as Robert Bly could make the case for reclaiming eloquence and verbal decoration as male virtues. Throughout the weekend, the poems are not beside the point, not a lull or a diversion from the real stuff—they provide some of the major statements and images that recur in the discourse. Good stuff, too: Auden, Neruda, Garcia Lorca, William Stafford, Sharon Olds, Bly's own work (of course), a surprisingly wild piece from Carl Sandburg. "We didn't get that one in high school," notes Bly, "we just got the *fog* creeping in on fucking *cat's feet*."

After Meade reads the Blake poem that begins "Man was made for joy and woe," Bly asks him to repeat it, this time dedicated to Etheridge Knight, the black poet who died recently of cancer at the age of 55. Addicted to heroin after being wounded in the Korean War, Knight spent years going in and out of prison, where he started writing. Bly befriended him and coaxed him into the usually all-white environment of men's gatherings. Knight made one of his last appearances at a reading with Bly in Indianapolis, looking every bit as sick as he was. A friend who was there told me that, after Knight left the stage, Bly bawled for two minutes before he could continue.

Today Bly reminisces a little about Knight and reads a wonderful, salty self-interview poem called "Welcome Back, Mr. Knight, Love of My Life" ("How's your pussy problem?/Your lady-on-top-smiling-like-God-titty-in-your-mouth problem?"). Hillman continues with more Knight, a litany of imprecations: fuck this, fuck that, "Fuck everything/I want my woman back so my soul can sing." "A Jungian theme song," Hillman suggests. "Fuck Scotty Peck," Bly throws in (a reference to the author of the self-help best-seller *The Road Not Travelled*). This quickly becomes the all-purpose expression of the weekend. When Meade says, "Women have access to a wide range of emotions and can switch from one to another—men are slower at it, so they get accused of not having feelings," someone in the audience calls out, "Fuck that!"

Some men's gatherings, even ones that revolve around celebrated guests, hew to a circular structure that encourages group intimacy, easy exchange of ideas, and socializing. Sooner or later, you pass a talisman or talking stick around the circle and say who you are and why you're here. Not at this event. It's strictly a frontal situation, The Big Guys onstage, the rest of us locked in theater seats with limited leg and elbow room. They talk, we listen. The number of people taking notes reinforces the university-lecture feeling.

But if you're going to listen to three guys talk all weekend, this is a pretty good group. For one thing, they're all strikingly different from one another in looks, demeanor, and expertise. And in the course of the weekend each has a role to play, both in the sense of function and of character. Bly is the bard who looks inward for the truth of a situation, the grand old man whose seniority and temperament cast him as the master of ceremonies—he decides when it's time to move along. Meade is the communal storyteller who constantly monitors the temperature of the group feeling and tries to keep everyone happy (often smoothing the feathers Bly ruffles). And Hillman is the resident intellectual whose references to philosophy, psychology, and classical mythology create a challenging mental obstacle course along the path to the male psyche. Not just an academic but an original thinker, he gives each idea his own crazy spin; replace his tweedy wardrobe with a cape and staff, and you'd call him a sorceror or holy fool.

The camaraderie among them is also inspiring to observe, especially for men exploring how to do soul work in groups. Rather than sprawling across the stage, they huddle quite close together, almost in formation, like a doo-wop group. (Each has his own microphone, though. The entire weekend is being recorded—of course!—and you can order the tapes before the show and pick them up a half-hour after it ends.) Actually, a jazz combo would probably be the better analogy. The three of them have played together a lot, but not so much that they've memorized the script. They like to keep things loose and surprise one another. So it seems as much for their own sake as for the audience's that they begin the conference in earnest with each making a statement—taking a solo, as it were, on the theme of Why I'm Doing This Men's Work.

Hillman addresses the social value of men's work head-on. "In the early '70s," he says, "you frequently heard this expression: 'Let me share this with you.' Now you hear 'I don't want to know about that' or 'I know.' It seems to me the one thing of uppermost importance now is that men meet to talk with each other about the contemporary world, from their hearts. If not, we turn all talk over to the media.

"What matters now is: where is the republic going? Have we crossed the border into empire, where all that's important is circuses, propaganda, and centurions? This is serious. The Jewish French philosopher Levinas says that the fundamental aspect of human life is ethics, and that ethics is constellated by a face. But in technological warfare, you see blips, not faces. We can't have an ethical reaction if we haven't see the faces of the enemy; we only see the commentators on CNN. So our reactions are paralyzed. Shame, paralysis, responsibility, anger—these things have to be expressed, and not privately. That's why I'm here: we have to express our feelings, so that we don't stop talking."

It's not surprising that Hillman should talk more about ideas than about himself, but he does say one thing you don't hear men say very often: "The ability to bring my intellect out into the public and share it is enjoyable—a blessing."

By contrast, Bly links his soul work directly to personal history. "In high school my emotions were a complete mystery to me," he says. "I went to my father and asked for protection, but he was wild and dangerous psychologically, and he said no. When my mother said yes, I went numb from my neck to my knees. To accept my mother's protection, I had to learn to think and feel like a woman—that was the deal. I decided to have no emotion at all, rather than have a woman's. I learned to fake it," he adds slyly, "by quoting poems from Yeats.

"My mother didn't really protect me, though. A lot of stuff went on in the household that she ignored. So where's the protection going to come from? In my twenties, if a woman seemed strong, I'd enlist. Does that work, to let a woman protect you?" Men in the audience call out various answers (including, "She's the one who we need protection from"). "I found more and more I was receiving protection from men," Bly says, "especially when I started doing some work with Joseph Campbell. What I said *interested* him, and that interest was a blessing. It made me more able to be with other men. I get a blessing from these three men," he says, gesturing toward the others onstage.

"The other thing is this," he continues. "Every family gives you a wound. In mine, it was my father's alcoholism. Where does healing take place? In the family? Isn't that crazy? The wound has to be healed by the gender that gave it to you. Groups of men have done it for me. I urge you, when you leave here, to join a small group of six or seven men. It's a fundamental experience."

"Ho," someone calls out. I cringe a little inside. This is one of the things people make fun of about men's gatherings. "Ho!" is a Native American expression that can mean "Amen, brother" or "Good point"—it's the butch equivalent of a drag queen's snapthology. Acceptable in the ritual atmosphere of, say, a sweat lodge, it seems hokey in this setting. I think I'd prefer "Fuck that!"

"My father's been dead for 12 years," begins Michael Meade's narrative. "He died from depression and loss. He was a truck driver, and when I was a boy I became seriously curious about what was keeping my father alive. The best answer came one day when I found a violin stored away in the basement. He'd had it since he was a child. He'd never learned to play it, but he never got rid of it. That's what brings me to these things—I'm trying to avoid giving up my desires in life. Many men, when they take on the responsibility of family and work, they stop dancing. That feeling of being big inside goes away. It's the love of art, music, languages, the foolishness of our own desires that keeps us alive."

He pulls out a quote from Albert Camus: "Man's work is nothing but a slow trek to rediscover through the detours of art those one or two images in whose presence his heart first opened." He reads it again to let it sink in.

"I'm here looking for more opportunities to do that, to go back," Meade says. "The other side of it is that I feel the eyes of my children watching me.

I spend a lot of time with adolescents, and they're scared about what's going on in the world. They don't hear enough conversation among adults. What's needed to heal their confusion and despair is art and ritual. That's what's missing in our society, men displaying their beauty rather than force or brutality."

PROLETARIAN PRINCE

It's strange to hear this talk about male beauty in a room full of mostly heterosexual men. The word *male* is more commonly a prefix for domination, violence, and chauvinist pig. Having heard those words for years, flung like spears by angry feminists, many men have gotten used to ducking them, backing away from asserting their maleness lest it be labeled machismo, effectively neutering themselves so as not to be identified with the enemies of women. To hear male beauty spoken of is curious, confusing, intriguing, almost unbelievable.

Which is not to say that these leaders have found a miracle cure for homophobia. There's plenty of that around—not just fear of gay men but also men's fear of their own feelings of warmth or desire for other men. People frequently comment on the amount of hugging that goes on between men at these events; the *Boston Globe*'s coverage of one 1989 men's weekend revolved around the reporter's biggest fear: "Could he escape being hugged?" Bly and Meade always make a show of physical affection, but it's usually what I call "the straight men's hug"—their chests may be touching, but they're standing two feet apart so they form an A-shape.

Part of this is just plain erotophobia. The Bly, Hillman, and Meade events are always more talk than action, because the leaders themselves are more in their heads than in their bodies. Toward the end of the New York weekend, one man calls out, "Where is the sex and lust in this story?" Meade replies, "Why are you expecting it? Was it in the brochure?" Hillman is more comfortable with physical stuff than Bly or Meade; he's given whole series of lectures on the asshole, and he's the only one who dares to bring up homophobia as a major obstacle to mentor relationships between older men and younger men.

But the fear of gay men is not to be discounted. My gaydar tells me that up to 30 per cent of the men in the Santa Fe and New York weekends are gay, bisexual, or undeclared. Gay men have some things to learn from these gatherings about overcoming passivity and asserting their purposefulness, and they have many things to teach: male display as a substitute for combat, expressing grief, celebrating diversity. For gay men, coming out is an initiation, sometimes benign, often brutal. They've already learned half the things Bly and Meade are trying to teach. But they're not encouraged to share their gifts, and most of the time their presence in the room goes completely unrecognized. At conferences all across the country, gay men have gone up afterwards to complain.

Bly and Meade try to be welcoming, bless their hearts, but gay culture is clearly alien and threatening to them; after all, Meade went to Catholic schools all his life, and Bly was a teenage mama's boy who wrote poetry and who was probably scared to death that people would think he was queer. So they can hardly be expected to speak for gay men; if anything, their jitteriness is a burning reminder of the need for gay men to tell their own stories and myths. At the same time, I suspect Bly and Meade purposely want to limit the amount of gay expression at their events for fear that too strong a gay presence will drive away the straight men who are terrified even to dip their toes into this kind of soul work.

That it's possible for these groups of ordinary men to talk about soul work or male beauty at all is a tribute to the character of Michael Meade. Unlike Bly and Hillman, Meade has practically no credentials to speak of—no titles, no degrees, no books. He's just a guy, a working-class Irish Catholic kid from Queens who knows how to do this cool thing of playing a drum and telling stories at the same time. And he's become a populist hero. The men adore him. He's the perfect foil to Robert Bly. If Bly comes off as a lion, king of the jungle, Meade is more like a frog—homely, close to the ground, a proletarian prince. Anyone can relate to him. He's Everyman's brother. Any concern that this mythologizing and poetry reading is sissy stuff flies out the window when Meade opens his mouth. Blunt, direct, street-smart, he sounds just like Columbo.

Meade exudes a distinct male authority that's comradely and unthreatening. And he's thoroughly grounded in the legends and mythology that have been his passion since he was 13. For instance, one key piece of research Meade has turned up in his cross-cultural survey of masculine mythology is the universal principle that the Masai tribe of East Africa calls *litima:* "that violent emotion, peculiar to the masculine part of things, that is the source of quarrels, of ruthless competition, possessiveness, power-drivenness, ambition and brutality"—as Meade points out, "They're not pulling any punches here"—"but is also the source of independence, courage, upstandingness, wildness as opposed to savagery, high emotions, ideals, of the movement toward individuation." And during the New York weekend, when Dirk's friend Walter challenges The Guys Onstage to come up with a model of mentoring that's not Eurocentric, it's Meade who has at his command African tales of knighthood in which smiths make powerful talismans with their own blood and Asian stories about princes who seek out wise old men.

Meade's main contribution to men's gatherings is, in a way, their most theatrical, hard-to-describe, you-have-to-be-there element. Accompanying himself on drum, he tells stories — some of them five-minute "dilemma stories" that lead up to an open-ended question, others elaborate hero's journeys that take all weekend to narrate — and then breaks them down for discussion, character by character, episode by episode, image by image. The theme of the seminar in New York is "Making a Hole in Denial," which Meade introduces with a story called "The King with the Cannibal Tastes."

The stories Meade tells serve two purposes. First they invite men to enter the realm of mythology, to relate to different characters as archetypes or aspects of themselves. It's Jung 101: "How am I like the king? What part of me does the Old Hag represent?" But discussing the stories is also a way to begin building trust in the room, to test the ability of the group to contain the emotions that might come up — not unlike what goes on at an AA meeting. (If any one thing has laid the groundwork for a movement of men making time in their lives to explore emotional, psychological, and spiritual issues, it's been the proliferation of 12-step programs.)

As the weekend progresses, the safety of ritual space enables men to voice remarkably personal sentiments. "Someone sexually abused my young daughter," one man mourns, setting off a ripple of gasps and moans throughout the room. Another sprays the crowd with anger over his wife's infidelity as if his rival were among us. Bly himself reveals a touching fragility. "My favorite aunt died yesterday at the age of 94," he confesses. "I feel lonely." Perhaps the most unusual thing about these sharing sessions is that whatever feelings are aroused, men are invited not to fix them but just to feel them.

RITUAL COMBAT

Tenderness is not the only way to build trust among men, though. Another of Bly and Meade's tried-and-true theories is that a group of men can't truly bond until there's a possibility of violence that's averted.

One afternoon in Santa Fe, Bly is going on and on (a bit too much for my interest level) about what family therapist John Bradshaw calls "the inner child." It's a concept Bly values, but he suggests that there's danger in spending too much time coddling that part of ourselves, that the time comes when the inner child has to be killed so the adult male can emerge.

Suddenly, a flash of heat erupts in the room. "This talk about killing the inner child sounds like the craziest thing in the world to me," declares a man who identifies himself as a therapist and goes on to testify as to the usefulness of the inner child in his own life.

"I thought we were talking as human beings. You're talking as a therapist," Bly responds in a tone that makes it clear how fond he is of therapists.

"What we're talking about is an inner divine child," Meade explains, quickly trying to calm the waters. "When we metaphorically kill it, it can still come back as an image."

"We're not talking about the historical child but the divine child," Hillman chimes in. "The imagination doesn't spend enough time with the divine child because it's so wrapped up in 'My father didn't play ball enough with me.'"

"Something in this guy's smugness irritates me," Bly announces, zeroing in on the therapist. "The way he talks about his inner child sounds like the way England used to talk about India."

Whoa, Nellie! The feeling in the room turns combative. Tension rises. No one can believe Bly is singling someone out for attack. The dynamic is fascinating. Being tough with the guy, Bly openly challenges him to be tough right back. But the therapist gets intimidated and clams up. Urged on by others in the audience to defend himself, all he does is give Bly the finger.

This is felt throughout the room as an inadequate response.

"Power comes from hearing your own voice," Bly advises. "Get your adult masculinity into your voice."

"To feel you are powerless and we are powerful brings the child into the room," Hillman notes. "This constant talk about empowerment and identification with the inner child is what paralyzes the body politic, which doesn't vote."

Someone in the audience accuses the men onstage of pretending to ignore the power differential in the room. "You're on a higher platform," he points out, "and you're making definitions."

"That's what I'm getting paid to do," says Bly. "What would you rather I do?"

"Express your opinions without being judgmental."

"Impossible!" Bly snaps.

Expressing impatience with the spineless attitudes of sensitive-New-Age-guys is what gets Bly labeled "arrogant." It's also one of his great gifts in life. He cuts through the bullshit, and he has fun doing it. "I understand that you have to get rid of the child inside you to become a man," says someone in the audience, "but it's the word killing that bothers me. How about *transmute?*"

"Aw, you're eating too much yogurt," Bly snorts. "When you want a hamburger, you kill a cow. You don't *transmute* it."

Bly and Meade have their act together. They're like the rhythm section of this jazz band, relentlessly collaborative. But every so often throughout a weekend, they basically concede the floor to Hillman, who's more eccentric, a one-man band who gives a dazzling, half-composed, half-improvised rap on whatever topic seems pertinent to the occasion—mentoring, beauty, the cross-cultural associations of the word *white.*

I happen to think Hillman is brilliant, but I've noticed that he drives some Bly and Meade followers crazy. His patrician style of criticism strikes some men as "caustic," and his characteristically contrary thinking puts others' noses out of joint. In New York when Meade launches into a prepared talk on the distinction between neurotic suffering and genuine suffering, Hillman summarily announces, "I'm not interested in suffering." And he takes a dim view of this "inner child" stuff. "By worshipping the inner child, we cling to the abuse of 20, 30, 40 years ago rather than attending to the abuse in our daily life."

What most enrages the Madison Avenue ad exec sitting near me in the New York seminar is that, unlike almost everyone else in the room, Hillman speaks with virtually no reference to his personal experience. I don't share that objection, but on the other hand whenever I feel overly intimidated by Hillman's erudition it does help to remember that he was born in Atlantic City and that his hobby is tap dancing.

In Santa Fe Hillman's moment of glory is his solo on the subject of needs, wants, and desires. He begins with three thoughts: 1) we take our needs literally; 2) we believe our needs can be fulfilled; and 3) we believe if they're fulfilled, they'll go away. "I'm suggesting that none of these is true," he says. "Needs are statements of the soul. You have to ask: what does the need need? Let need really come up. Say it aloud. Listen to it in your own body. Sing the blues. Complain. Feel the lack as a lack rather than focusing on what would fill it."

"Do that eeee thing," coaches Bly, sounding every bit like a groupie requesting his favorite song.

Hillman obliges by demonstrating the plaintive, whiny sound in *need*, *please*, and *weak*. "That's not what a woman wants," he says. "A woman wants to be wanted, not needed. Need produces long marriages where the people need to be together but don't want to be." Need, he says, creates an infantile, passive feeling in the body, whereas want moves out to get something—a step in the right direction.

Toward desire, that is. Not sexual desire, or rather not just sexual desire. He's really talking about the kind of mysterious yearning that can never be fulfilled. "Desire is a potent thing we lose early," he says. "Think of those moments you had as a teenager—your yearning for fame, for glory, the princess, the castle. We are born with wings of desire, then they're blocked, secularized, humanized into needs. The more therapy helps you meet your needs, the more it blocks the realization of your desires."

Say what? Bly asks him to run that one by us again, and he obliges. "The more therapy helps you meet your needs, the more it blocks the realization of your desires. Then you end up with small triumphs, like going shopping."

Someone starts to ask "How do you . . ." and Hillman cuts him off. "Let's put aside how-to questions for the moment. We have a huge addiction to how-to in this country. The first how-to we need to learn is how to listen to an idea that throws your other ideas around."

MEN'S WORK: THREAT OR MENACE?

As Hillman points out, a lot of men come to these gatherings begging for instruction, hungry for tools: what can I do? how do I become a man? how can I fulfill my dreams, serve my community, change the world? And judging from the volume of business in books and tapes at conference bookstalls, a lot of men would happily embrace Robert Bly's Rules of Order. The instructions they get, though, are somewhat frustrating: Go inside. Work on yourself. Don't skip steps. Ground yourself in study, inner work, purification. Use your imagination. Don't ask for something unless you want it. Know what you want. Don't give your power away. Don't expect other people to do it for you.

At the first International Men's Conference in Austin last month, I had a conversation with an African-American man from Houston named Abati Akinlana, whom I first met at the multicultural conference in West Virginia. He suggested that the ultimate effect of what's going on among men won't be the creation of a movement focused on memberships, legislative goals, and an articulated public policy agenda. Instead, the best way to think of it is as a revolution in consciousness. "This is the biggest threat to military madness," he said. "When Bush proposes something crazy like the Gulf War, the people won't let it happen. Men will stand up and say, 'This is bullshit.' But first they have to be able to say that to their parents, their wives, their bosses, whatever."

It has to be acknowledged, though, that American society does not want this consciousness to spread—perhaps precisely because it's an inquiry and not a movement, a process and not a product. Everything in America is about moving the merchandise. So get ready for the 15 minutes of Men.

Despite the best efforts of the media to create celebrities and promote a national men's movement, it remains largely a grass-roots activity, and that in itself contains a political threat. During the New York weekend, I had a conversation with James Hillman in which he mentioned his theory that ordinary men are increasingly being marginalized in American society—alongside women, gays, and people of color—so that the only political power resides with an elusive elite, Noam Chomsky's "government by conspiracy."

The media contributes to suppressing men's consciousness by its anti-spiritual bias. The men's movement is seen as silly because the substance is edited out. It's seen as trendy and superficial because that's what can be shown on TV or described in Timenewsweekspeak—they get the soundbites but not the Yeats poems. Men's work is seen as apolitical because the politics are censored.

During the Gulf War, which got high approval ratings because the American public liked the coverage on CNN, Bly and Meade were among those repeatedly expressing opposition in impassioned, provocative terms. Bly wrote an editorial that among other things compared Bush's squandering the peace dividend on the one-side bloodbath in Iraq to Agamemnon's sacrificing of his daughter; the *New York Times* refused to publish it, though the *Minneapolis Star Tribune* did. Bly says he gave an interview about his men's work to the *Los Angeles Times* on the stipulation that half the article would talk about the war; when it came out, almost everything about the war had been cut. Making a rare talk show appearance on CNN just after the cease-fire, Bly called the 60-mile corridor into Iraq (which allied forces described as "a turkey shoot . . . like shooting fish in a barrel") as "our My Lai." The interviewer changed the subject. "Are you just going to let that lie on the floor between us?" Bly asked. She said, "Yes."

Maybe Bly's remarks on the war were obvious. Maybe talk about censorship is paranoia. Nonetheless, there's a pattern to how the men's movement gets portrayed in the press. It's a pattern recognizable from the trivializing coverage—not so long ago—of feminism as a movement of "libbers" and "bra-burners," of man-haters and ugly women.

Robert Bly and his colleagues know what they're up against. It's why they keep going. In his closing remarks at the men's weekend in New York, Haki Madhubuti encourages idealistic thinking while acknowledging it isn't the safest or most popular path to tread, as the last few decades of American history have shown. At the risk of sounding like Oliver Stone, he puts the audience on notice that not everybody feels warm and fuzzy inside about the idea of men coming to consciousness. "There are people who have orders from on high to do you harm," he says. "You are a considerable foe. Many are prepared to eliminate you with extreme prejudice. Let them know they are in for a fight."

Betwixt and Between in the Men's Movement

MIKE DASH

INTRODUCTION

Of the many branches of the "men's movement," two branches in particular are like oil and water. These are the mythopoetic and the profeminist. They rarely mix and are often contemptuous of each other, though both are valuable. As if I had friends who couldn't stand each other, I find myself in-between; I would like to build a bridge.

My own experience is rooted in activist, profeminist politics. Thus, there is clearly much in mythopoetry that I find problematic. But I think we can have both, we need both, and the two movements need each other.

Mythopoetry focuses on what is missing—a vibrant, life-affirming masculinity—but has no focus on removing what is toxic in masculinity. Profeminism works to eliminate what is toxic—a death-dealing, patriarchal, violent masculinity—but has not developed a vision of what will take its place. Neither approach can succeed by itself.

As movements, these two branches need each other. Mythopoetry needs profeminism to save it from its current drift toward the reactionary politics of the men's rights movement. Profeminism needs mythopoetry's personal and communal richness as well as its large audience.

A synthesis or alliance between movements would be a significant step toward building a broader men's movement. At present, men separate their own personal work from the political work. Mythopoetry does intense personal work with politics left out, though it would like to carry its inner work forward into activism. Profeminists are intensely political but our personal work is not usually an explicit part of what we do together. What we stand to gain is a men's movement that combines activism with inner work.

MYTHOPOETRY

I first came to men's work in a community of nonviolent direct activists who were working against U.S. militarism. The women in the group challenged the men on our sexism. This led us to try forming a men's affinity group for consciousness-raising and other personal/inner work.

However, we never came to a shared vision of the group's purpose and it did not last long. In contrast, the women had a strong political/action affinity group as well as a strong personal/spiritual connection. I was left with the feeling that something—some kind of shared, personal men's work—was missing.

Around this time I read a short interview with Robert Bly, in which he said, "I am superficially masculine, but not deeply masculine."[1] I had no idea what "deeply masculine" might mean, but I wanted to know more. A year later, he scheduled a six-day conference nearby and I attended it.

For the first day or two of the conference, I was quite uncomfortable. I had expected it to have a consensus-based egalitarian style like the activist community I came from. I was completely unprepared for the orchestrated agenda and the clear delineation between leaders and participants. But I also found much to like. Whereas the men's community I came from had been unsuccessful in doing personal work, the Bly conference was quite successful. Mornings started with movement and meditation. Days combined storytelling, poetry, and lecture with role-playing and small-group discussions. Evenings were given to "night work"—ritual, poetry, and dance—and to personal testimonies.

The testimonies, in particular, were passionate and moving. Conference organizer Michael Meade set the tone on the first night, saying, "When men gather in seriousness of purpose, it is important for each man to be able to tell his story." Men spoke with great feeling about their lives and listened intently to each other. Some were in pain; some spoke of their longings; others were exultant, angry, or hopeful. I came away feeling that I had found a good place to accomplish some of the personal men's work I had been wanting to do.

In the years since, I have continued to do mythopoetic work along with profeminist work. My ongoing contacts with mythopoetry include another of Bly's six-day conferences plus workshops, ritual groups, retreats, and wisdom councils. From these experiences, I see several things that mythopoetry could offer to an alliance with profeminism.

- A recognition that contemporary masculinity is in trouble. "[T]he images of adult manhood given by the popular culture are worn out; a man can no longer depend on them."[2] Of course, this is not news to profeminists—but mythopoetry has been able to convey that recognition to a wide audience, with which profeminism has had little success. In its place, mythopoetry offers a model of masculinity that is grounded and inwardly oriented. The model is similar to the hero's quest described by Joseph Campbell. It says that a man's primary life work is in the psyche, in becoming whole—not in money, power, status, or the domination of women.
- A recognition that the solution requires inner work. As James Hillman puts it, "Unless his spirit ventures toward the invisible, a man will be unable to perform his daily round with purpose."[3] Mythopoetry also provides some tools for "making soul," as Hillman calls it: ritual, poetry, myth.
- A recognition that the solution requires working in a community of men; a man cannot solve this problem alone. Beyond simply recognizing this, mythopoetry provides some tools for building a supportive, nurturing fellowship of men. One example is the wisdom council, which gathers so men can speak openly and from their own experience. In Seattle, where I live, there are at least sixteen wisdom councils. The largest is seven years old and draws more than two hundred men each month.[4]

In addition, mythopoetry clearly has many faults. Because these have been well-analyzed by others, I will give only a summary. In particular, there are several that are especially relevant to the question of whether profeminists can build an alliance with mythopoetry.

- Mythopoetry wants to withdraw from rationality, as if intuition alone can guide us. My question for mythopoetry is this: unless we incorporate a political analysis (among others), how can we distinguish a healthy, intuitive sense of direction from a toxic one?
- There is a limited view of the root causes of the crisis in masculinity. Mythopoetry sees this crisis as arising from the loss of a tradition of manhood. That loss is seen as coming from the collapse of the defining mythology of our age and from the damage that the industrial revolution did to the father-son bond (by taking the father out of the home, so the son grows up without male guidance). This may be a workable starting place. But the roots of the crisis go back so far that they affect all aspects of life—political, psychological, socioeconomic, and so on. Mythopoetry needs to look at all factors—not just industrialism and the collapse of myth—if it is to achieve any significant changes in men's lives.

In addition to a feminist analysis, mythopoetry needs to add analyses of race, class, and heterocentrism. Bly, for instance, almost never mentions gay or bisexual men. In a rare exception, the introduction to *Iron John* says ". . . this book speaks to heterosexual men but does not exclude homosexual men" (Bly 1990, x). However, mythopoetry cannot become truly "male-positive" without understanding the oppression of men who love men. Similar comments can be made about the oppression of men who are not "white" or middle-class.

- Male privilege is generally invisible to men and mythopoetry does not address it. Mythopoetry thus can open a man's eyes to his own wounds while leaving them closed to the wounds of others. As a result, it sees no contradiction between feminism and the men's-rights movement. "I consider myself a feminist as well as an advocate for men's rights."[5]
- Mythopoetry misunderstands the difference between sex and gender, between what is inherent in maleness and what is learned. Thus, when feminism gives a critique of masculinity, mythopoets mistake this for being anti-male: "Anti-patriarchy . . . may arise from anti-male sentiment."[6]

BUILDING A BRIDGE

In an illuminating comment, Ken Clatterbaugh has pointed out that women have easy access both to a feminist political movement and to a feminist spirituality. Clearly, this is not the present situation for men. It is as if mythopoetry is luxuriating in perfumed gardens. Understandably, many men are attracted to this. Meanwhile, profeminism is out in the desert, living on bread and water—which doesn't appeal to many men. As a result, the profeminist movement is small and its members are prone to burnout and isolation. What we need is access to both: we need a profeminist mythopoetry or a bridge between movements.

What Mythopoetry Can Offer Profeminism

- A wide audience of men who are ready to examine their masculinity.
- A place to do personal/communal work, in which a man can "continue throughout his life working and playing with male companions who earnestly try to develop personal as well as collective soul."[7]
- The left, as has often been said, is no fun. It can be arid, isolating, and

overzealous; activists burn out. Mythopoetry would give us place to re-charge our batteries.

What Profeminism Can Offer Mythopoetry

Profeminism can offer mythopoetry the advantages of a broad-based analysis. As presently constituted, mythopoetry is vulnerable to wandering off-track because it relies almost exclusively on intuition and on the intuitive interpretation of myths, stories, and poetry.

Thus mythopoetry has no compass or reference point by which men can tell when their intuition is steering them in the wrong direction. Profeminism can help because it checks itself against the conclusions that others arrive at—that is, against the conclusions of women, men of color, and indigenous peoples—so that it is less vulnerable to self-delusion.

- Mythopoetry wants to translate its inner work into action. For example, *Men for the Earth: A Call to Action* says, "We ask men to stand as allies with aware women, indigenous people, social justice organizations, [and] environmental groups . . . to create bold and far-reaching action strategies. . . . We commit ourselves to the time, hard work and celebration required. . . ."[8] So far, however, mythopoetry has not created such strategies or acted on them. Profeminism can offer a clear vision of what work needs to be done and some good tools for doing it.
- Joining with natural allies. Sexism, racism, and heterocentrism are bad for everyone, including the privileged men who make up much of the "men's movement." Women, gay/bisexual men, and men of color are natural allies for mythopoetic men who want to confront the illnesses of current masculinity: profeminism already has these alliances.
- A way out of an increasingly embattled position. Mythopoetry sees itself as under siege: "Men doing Men's Work will come under attack as never before. . . . [and] the attack is already under way."[9] It finds itself in this position because it sees feminism as anti-male. This is amplified by the perception that *any* critique of mythopoetry is an attack on men: one writer refers to essays in the book *Women Respond to the Men's Movement* as "radical feminist [and] anti-male."[10] We can help mythopoetry see that what is under attack is male supremacy, not men.

Obstacles to Bridge-Building

- An on-going concern for mythopoetry has been the issue of blame. Thus, for example, mythopoets may fear that they are being personally and individually included when we say that we have to end male violence—and then feel that they need to defend themselves. Profeminists need to help mythopoetry understand the difference between individual and collective responsibility. Until this happens, it may not be possible for profeminism and mythopoetry to work together at all.

- Mythopoetry views itself as "male-positive" and part of its appeal is that it offers a heroic vision of maleness. However, this is seen as incompatible with feminism. We need to clarify that men can be profeminist and male-positive.

- Many mythopoetic men seem to believe that sexism is easily addressed and easily unlearned—that all we need to do, for example, is stop using sexist language. They are then surprised and hurt to hear the issue of sexism reopened when they feel they've already dealt with it. We need to help them see that unlearning patriarchy is an ongoing process.

- Profeminists also present an obstacle in the form of our zeal. We can get overzealous, lose perspective, and throw the baby out with the bath water. In working with mythopoetry, we need to decide when an issue is important enough to struggle over and when it is small enough to be let go.

- Finally, profeminism's disdain for mythopoetry has been part of the problem. What has happened is that the men's rights movement is trying to commandeer mythopoetry. So far, this effort is succeeding—partly because of the total absence of profeminist voices in mythopoetry. For the most part, men come to mythopoetry to learn about masculinity and about themselves; they do not come for reactionary reasons. Until we start talking to mythopoetry, we should not be surprised at the success that reactionary voices are having in swaying mythopoetic men.

CONCLUSION

Is it possible to build a profeminist mythopoetry? The answer is far from clear. Mythopoetry may already have set its course irrevocably. But if we don't try, mythopoetry will probably continue to be apolitical at best and antifeminist at worst.

If we succeed, the rewards would be significant. We may be able to find new allies. We may be able to reach outside our tiny circle of profeminist men. And we may get to have a men's movement with a personal/spiritual focus *and* an activist focus.

ACKNOWLEDGMENT

I would like to thank Ken Clatterbaugh for his insightful questions and comments, which have given rise to many of the ideas expressed in this paper.

NOTES

1. Robert Bly, interview by *Whole Earth Review* (Winter 1988): 68.

2. Robert Bly, *Iron John* (Reading, Mass.: Addison-Wesley, 1990), ix.

3. Robert Bly, James Hillman, and Michael Meade, *The Rag and Bone Shop of the Heart* (New York: HarperCollins, 1992), 417.

4. "Wisdom Council Size and History," *Seattle M.E.N. Newsletter* (April 1993): 12, 15.

5. Jed Diamond, "A Letter from Jed Diamond," *Seattle M.E.N. Newsletter* (April 1993): 2.

6. Rod Van Mechelen, "Two Cheers for Patriarchy," *Seattle M.E.N. Newsletter* (March 1993): 7.

7. Wayne Liebman, *Tending the Fire: The Ritual Men's Group* (St. Paul, Minn.: Ally Press, 1991), 1.

8. *Seattle M.E.N. Newsletter* (Seattle, Wash.: Men's Evolvement Network).

9. Bert Hoff, "From the Editor," *Seattle M.E.N. Newsletter* (February 1992): 2.

10. James Smethurst, "Alternatives to Fear Succumbs to Fear," *Seattle M.E.N. Newsletter* (January 1993): 2.

Afterword

MICHAEL S. KIMMEL

So I soon made up my mind about the poets too. I decided that it was no wisdom that enabled them to write their poetry, but a kind of instinct or inspiration, such as you find in seers and prophets who deliver all their sublime messages without knowing in the least what they mean. It seemed clear to me that the poets were in much the same case, and I also observed that the very fact that they were poets made them think that they had a perfect understanding of all other subjects, of which they were totally ignorant.

Socrates, in Plato, "The Apologia"[1]

WHEN I BEGAN THIS PROJECT, I shared Socrates's sentiments, partly, I suppose, as a way of defining turf. But I've been challenged—at times creatively and at times through confrontation—by much of the dialogue created here. William James, not ordinarily one of my favorite thinkers, once wrote that the best scholars were people who were driven by some particular passion but were always ready to be surprised. In my work, such sentiments are more prescriptive than descriptive; I hope all my work is animated by a passion for justice and that I remain open to find allies in that struggle in unlikely places.

So I'm surprised to find allies among the mythopoets—some of them at any rate—in the struggle for gender justice. This will certainly surprise those who know me as one of their more visible and vociferous critics. It will certainly surprise many of the mythopoets themselves. And I suspect it will surprise some readers of this volume, who see how much anger and defensiveness seem to drive the words of a few of those writers.

But I believe that if one clears away the thick underbrush of anger and defensiveness that dominates several of these essays the potential for that alliance will become clear. I consider the mythopoets partial and potential allies of the work with which profeminist men and feminist women have been engaged for the past several decades. But they have some work to do.

Reading the responses by many of the leaders of the mythopoetic men's movement left me both saddened and guardedly hopeful. I was unprepared for the defensiveness and anger in the reactions of some. Yet I also found them compassionate, sincere, and often harmlessly befuddled. I was startled—and most saddened—by the casual dismissal of the substantive claims made by their critics. Virtually none of the writers took on any of these substantive claims. These were met with either categorical dismissals, the defensive yowls of wounded men, or sarcastic bombast. It was as if once stung by the criticism, it was impossible to actually engage with the ideas in a healthy and constructive dialogue. Many of their essays felt like schoolboys taunting other schoolboys that words didn't hurt them after all.

Several of the writers did sound notes of reconciliation and healing, even if they did not explicitly take on any of the substantive arguments of their critics. I found, for example, Onaje Benjamin's sentiments most inviting, and believe that we could work towards a more constructive dialogue. I was also touched by the tone of Marvin Allen's piece, and included Don Shewey's article because it seemed the least defensive and guarded of any observer of these events.

Robert Bly's words were generous and conciliatory. I agree with him that "[o]ppositional thinking is by definition misleading." But it can also be temporarily clarifying, as it helps us define ourselves in contrast to another position, even as we then must work to break down the division such thought has created. If there was a time for stakes to be planted, for turf to be defined and defended, surely that time has passed. It's time to explore the common ground, the place where our visions intersect. And to confront our common enemies, those forces moving in our culture who would set back the gains of women, or people of color, and of gays and lesbians to some terrifying degree.

Given that political imperative, it is sad, though perhaps expected, that the two camps seem to continually talk past each other. The mythopoets consistently take the profeminists to task for not citing enough of their work, but none of them ever mentions the work of profeminist men as having had any impact at all on their thinking. This is especially strange since profeminist writers (like Joseph Pleck, Jack Sawyer, Bob Brannon, Peter Filene, Marc Feigen Fasteau) began exploring these issues over a decade *before* Bly's epochal 1982 interview in *New Age* magazine ignited the current interest.

Pleck's *The Myth of Masculinity* (1981) even has the word "myth" in it—you would have thought they'd gobble that one right up!

I write this not to play tit-for-tat, but to suggest that perhaps there are two distinct universes of discourse that each group relies upon for its analysis. On one side lies the world of the spirit, the soul—poetry, myths, legends and non-European ritual; on the other side lies the world of political and intellectual engagement—history, social science, journalistic narrative. These works feed and nourish different parts of a person. But there are ways to bring them together, and I think we need to explore what those ways might be. I find the poets to make poor analysts when they ignore the work of those of us trained to do that analysis; but I find the work of my academic colleagues invariably impoverished if we cannot draw inspiration, references (or even the occasional epigraph) from the poets. We need the others' work, whether we acknowledge it or not. Socrates had it only half-right in the lines that open this essay: poets may be ignorant and inspired, needing to ask the experts before they mouth off about what they don't know anything about, but perhaps many political academics do have rather thin and impoverished interior lives that might well do with some spiritual nourishment.

I confess I am still somewhat surprised by the anti-intellectualism that bubbles over in several essays, especially those by Aaron Kipnis and Shepherd Bliss. This is particularly odd, since both men have their doctorates, and since several of their profeminist critics are not in university settings but are therapists and political activists. Ours is a political debate, not a debate between academic eggheads who have no contact with the real world and activists who get down and dirty with real guys. All of us—whether our primary arena is the university, the therapeutic office, or the street—are activists with strong political commitments.

It's predictable, I suppose, that a university professor like me would believe that the mythopoetics could learn much from the academics. What could they learn? Well, for one thing, there's this thorny question of essentialism versus social constructionism. It *seems* right these days to argue that gender identity is socially constructed, that it is constituted within the framework of gender relations. But one can't stop here. What is the "framework of gender relations" but relations of inequality, of power? Masculinities and femininities come to mean what they do within a framework of privilege and power. These dynamics of privilege and power are painfully obvious to those who do not have privilege. But they are painlessly invisible to those who have it. Try getting a white person to understand that being white is, as Peggy McIntosh puts it, an "invisible weightless knapsack" which one carries around, loaded with "special provisions, maps, passports, codebooks, visas, clothes, tools and blank checks."[2]

Most social scientists who have explored the meaning of social constructionism would agree that the very use of the term now implies this unequal playing field on which gendered identities are constituted. In other words, social constructionism is irretrievably about power imbalances.

To social scientists, then, myths and legends provide a cultural road map to explore the grounds upon which such power imbalances are legitimized by the cultures where they originate. But it seems to me that the mythopoets put such myths and legends to quite another use, to search for something that, as Shepherd Bliss writes, "lies at the base of each man." Bly invites us "to discover the sound that male cells sing," as Jed Diamond cites approvingly. (Since Michael Kaufman and I make this point about Bly's work in "Weekend Warriors," I won't belabor it here.) This is the language of essentialism, whether one claims it or not. Frankly, if I were a mythopoet, I'd claim it as proudly and as loudly and as often as I could, since it would set me apart from the dreaded linear facticity of social science.

This question of power—what it is, who has it—underlies much of the difference between the two camps. Profeminist men often sound only one note: men have all the power. It's accurate, I suppose, at the aggregate level, even though the note becomes rather monotonically shrill after a while. Mythopoets listen more carefully than profeminists, it seems to me, when men say, "If I'm supposed to have all the power, then why don't I feel powerful? My wife bosses me around, my children boss me around, my boss bosses me around. I'm completely powerless!"

The feminist understanding of men having the power rested on a symmetry in women's lives. At the aggregate level, women were not *in power*. Just look at those corporate boardrooms, those collegiate boards of trustees, those legislatures and executive mansions. At the individual level, women did not *feel powerful*. Feminism, then, was a political movement to challenge women's social powerlessness and their individual feelings of powerlessness. But the symmetry breaks down when applied to men. Sure, men are *in power* at the aggregate level. But individual men feel powerless.

Other movements of men privilege men's experience of powerlessness. Antifeminists like Warren Farrell claim that male power is a "myth."[3] "Feel powerless?" he seems to say. "Of course, you do. Women have all the power. We're the real victims of reverse discrimination, affirmative action, custody and alimony laws. Let's get some of that power back from those feminists!" Some of the mythopoets also seem to privilege the personal feeling over the social and political. If you don't feel powerful, then you're not powerful. "Come with us into the woods," they seem to say. "We'll go get some power. Here's the power chant, the power ritual, the power drumming." I remember a few years ago when mainstream American men, who were supposed to feel such renewed power under Reaganism, resorted to wearing power ties and eating power lunches to demonstrate their power—as if power were a fashion accessory. What better expression of political and economic impotence than to be eating and wearing the signs of one's power!

Mythopoets and antifeminists often use Farrell's analogy of the chauffeur to illustrate their argument. Think about a chauffeur: He's in the driver's seat. He knows where he's going. He's wearing the uniform. So, they say, you'd think he has the power. But from his perspective, someone else is giving the orders, and he's not powerful at all.

I think this analogy has some limited value: individual men are not powerful, at least all but a small handful of individual men. But they're right for the wrong reasons. What if we ask one question of our chauffeur, and try to shift the frame just a little: what is the gender of the person who *is* giving the orders?

Then we shift from the analysis of the individual's experience to a different context, the relations between and among men as relations of power. Because men as a group do have the power, and that power is organized against women, but it is also organized against other men. Only profeminism possesses the tools to bring those levels together, to both adequately analyze men's aggregate power, and also describe the ways in which individual men are both privileged by that social level of power and feel powerless in the face of it.

It seems to me that mythopoetic defensiveness reaches its zenith around the question of power, as if to identify and challenge men's power was to ignore men's pain. Such a trade-off is unacceptable politically, and, frankly, a non sequitur. Men's pain is caused by men's power. What else could it be? Would we say that the unhappiness of white people was caused by black people's power? The pains and sexual problems of heterosexuals were caused by gays and lesbians? Profeminism requires that both men's social power and individual powerlessness be understood as mutually reinforcing, linked experiences, both of which derive from men's aggregate social power.

As I read through their essays, I began to notice a pattern to the defensiveness of the mythopoetic responses that was structural, not personal, and that revolved around the connections between these social and individual levels of analysis and experience. In this, I believe I saw a key difference between the two camps, and, at the same time, some possibilities for common ground. The responses of the mythopoets vacillate between an abstract and global understanding of the "bad" part of masculinity, and a reductive, personally concrete "good" part. Thus Shepherd Bliss, for example, rails against what he calls "toxic masculinity"—which he believes is responsible for most of the evil in the world—and proclaims the unheralded goodness of the men who fight the fires and till the soil and nurture their families.

There is something important in Bliss's notion of toxic masculinity, a claim that masculinity itself is not, by itself, the problem to be fought against, but rather a specific construction of it, a construction shaped by a mold of patriarchy and privilege. Here, too, Robert Bly's distinction between patriarchy and masculinity is useful to disentangle two facets of our identities as men that have become so knotted as to be almost indistinguishable.

But as anyone who has ever tried to knit would tell you, the way to untangle knotted yarn is not to pull tightly on "your end" but to gently shake the entire skein, letting the natural weight of the knots release some of their tension. I've spent a good portion of the past five years pulling on my end of the yarn. Perhaps it's time for us to take the mythopoetic men at their word and together shake the mess we men have created, extracting a healthy masculinity from tightly wound associations of power and privilege with our sense of ourselves as men.

It's in that spirit that I reflected on these essays, and especially on the defensiveness in several of them. I was reminded of the defensiveness that one encounters among white people when first confronted with the evils of racism. While they can often understand how racism is a heinous and oppressive system—something terrible being done to someone else—their response to a more immediate understanding of the ways in which racism constructs *their* lives is often angry and defensive. "Don't blame me!" they shout. "My family didn't own slaves!"—as if racism were simply the individual actions of individual slaveowners.

But as we have come to understand, even if one is not a racist, in the sense of subscribing to racist ideologies or acting in racist ways, we gain certain privileges simply for being white. This is more concrete than just talking about systemic racism or sexism. These are privileges which we get whether we choose them or not. Just last week, for example, the former mayor of New York City, a black man, was bypassed by several taxicabs who stopped for white people further down the block. There was nothing those white people did to generate that privilege, little, in fact, that they could do to avoid it. But it can be acknowledged as a component of our identities. Not with a self-loathing shame that would prevent us from hailing a cab, but a politicized anger that such invisible privileges make it impossible for racial equality to develop.

A similar defensiveness pervades the mythopoets' responses that celebrate the heroic individuals and lambast the toxic aggregate. "Don't blame me!" they shout in unison. "I'm not a rapist!"—as if rape were simply an individual act by one man against one woman, rather than a systemic, yet incoherent collection of individual acts against women, by which virtually all women are rendered defensive, frightened, defiant, or intimidated and silenced.

What's missing, it seems to me, is a middle ground between the generalized abstractions of toxic masculinity and the concretely personal level of the good and decent men who populate the mythopoetic universe. This is a place where both the analytic and the expressive can join forces, where profeminist and mythopoetic men can become powerful allies.

Let me illustrate what I mean by this middle ground by taking one of Shepherd Bliss's examples: his friend Ray Gatchalian, the firefighter. I am sure that Mr. Gatchalian is a good and decent, caring and nurturing man: "one of the many good men" whose countless good deeds go largely unnoticed in the swirl of tabloid notoriety. At the same time, there are few organizations which have been more fiercely resistant to women's equality than the nation's fire departments. Almost daily, we read of sexual harassment in some fire department, or a vicious rage among firemen at any woman who would even seek to become one of their fraternity. (The Los Angeles Fire Department recently circulated a videotape of women failing at certain exercises to demonstrate their continued opposition to women's entry in the department.) This misogyny is an *example* of what Bliss calls "toxic masculinity."

Let me be clear: I am not accusing Mr. Gatchalian of sexual harassment, misogyny, or anything else. I am arguing that the two levels of analysis must be joined, somehow linking the toxic abstractions with the concrete good men. The very institutions of toxic masculinity may be populated by many of those nurturing eco-masculinists whom Bliss celebrates. What does it mean that so many good men are to be found in such toxic institutions?

To me it means that they aren't fulfilling their mythopoetic mission, that they are not living up to their promise as the good, caring, compassionate men they almost certainly are. For to be fully nurturing and caring, one must bring that vision into the workplace and into the public arena and challenge the elements of toxicity even among those very good men.

In short, one must politicize—bring to public awareness—the good, caring, and compassionate parts of manhood that the mythopoets herald. Here, then, we enter the terrain of the profeminist—not through guilt, blame, or shame, but through the very structures of accountability and the feelings of nurturing and compassion that animate the lives of the mythopoets.

I also believe that profeminist men can learn a lot from the mythopoets. I think that they do valuable work, important work, even essential work. I am less interested in categorical dismissal than these essays might suggest; I believe that, in their original formulations, both written and in workshops, the mythopoets laid out an important thesis, to which profeminist critique has provided an antipode. I believe that there are several places where we can now begin to unite in respectful dialogue and debate, and in wary alliance.

For one thing, the mythopoets acknowledge one another's work. Did you notice how often they referred to the work of other mythopoetic men? I don't read this as a defensive circling of the wagons; they genuinely appreciate each other's work. We profeminists are often so busy picking politically incorrect holes in one another's positions, or vilifying each other for not completely living up to our ideals, that we forget to acknowledge and appreciate how hard we are working in our common struggle. Profeminist men's conferences have felt to me like meetings of the old left, where party-line hacks spent more time ripping each other to shreds for deviations than they did fighting to dismantle inequality and oppression. Political paralysis is the only result of such political cleansing.

Living up to one's ideals is messy business, since our ethical ideals come from our heads, and our feelings often seem to come from somewhere else. It's enormously difficult, sometimes painfully so, to enact one's principles in everyday life. Those of us who try find that discomfiting feelings seem to show up at the least opportune or predictable times. Often, profeminists would have us will those feelings away, in a kind of puritanical assertion of control. Alternatively, we could realize that we are simply irretrievably and irredemptively bad—that is, "male"—and thus we can only hope to spend our days in sniveling self-abnegation.

Many profeminist men seem to decide, politically, the right thing to feel, and then set about acting as if we felt it. As any therapist will tell you, this is part of the problem, not its solution; these untidy and incorrect feelings will eventually explode into resentment and rage that can attach to anything or anyone who happens to be close.

The mythopoets welcome these feelings, and, in so doing, pose an alternative that, when linked to a political vision and critique, can take us to the next stage. After all, it is the mythopoets who encourage men to express their feelings, especially the less pleasant ones like pain, anguish, anger, and deep sadness and grief. These are emotions that men often feel humiliated to express, let alone feel. In mythopoetic settings, they are encouraged to feel and express those feelings. Forget for a moment what may strike some as hokey ritualism: these are real feelings pouring out. And it's about time, too.

I don't think it's just the outpouring of feelings that makes the mythopoetic work so intrinsically valuable. In mythopoetic settings, men confront the deep fears that they have of other men, the pain that other men have caused them, the wounds they carry of that fear and hurt. To counter men's fears of other men is to counter *homophobia,* literally the fear of other men. I take homophobia—this generalized fear of other men, in addition to its more limited definition of fears of homosexuality and homosexuals—to be one of the animating conditions of American manhood.[4] And the mythopoetic men's movement is an explicitly counter-homophobic project, breaking down the isolation that men feel and encouraging men to express their needs for intimacy with other men. This is very valuable work, indeed, which has recently been broadened to include work explicitly drawn around race and sexuality. "Hate between men comes from cutting ourselves off from each other," wrote the great Viennese philosopher Ludwig Wittgenstein. "Because we don't want anyone else to look inside us, since it's not such a pretty sight in there."[5]

If emotional expression is the good news, then inadequate political contextualization is the bad news. It's possible that, by ignoring the social aspects of power and privilege, mythopoets have made the hard emotional expression a bit easier, but also somewhat less effective once one returns from the woods. Mythopoets don't seem to want to analyze those connections of privilege and pain, nor work through them so that the inappropriate explosions of rage—at mothers, for example—can be better directed at a structure of inequality that constrained their mothers from finding their own way in the world, that confined them to their homes and families as the only source of fulfillment and nourishment.

It is possible that a lot of men do feel significant rage at their mothers (and their fathers as well, for that matter). And it is possible that expression of that rage is a central part of virtually any therapy that employs psychoanalytic insight, and it is a vital part of some group work. But it is not sufficient to generate a causal analysis; mother-blame is not social theory. Social theory requires context. If you imprison someone, why blame the prisoner for acting like a prisoner and making herself feel at home in the prison? Why not go after those who built the prisons in the first place? The key may be under the mother's pillow, in Bly's retelling of the story, but the mother's bed may be a prison of its own.

Another reason I think that the mythopoets can take on these less pretty scenes is that they also know how to have fun. Not one of the mythopoets talked about this, but it seemed very significant in their work, perhaps even fundamental. All those mediagenic activities—the drumming and dancing and sweat lodges and crying and hugging—let's face it, those men's retreats are really fun. They're a lot more fun than conferences, sales calls, department meetings, and legal teleconferences. For many of us, the demands of manhood—the workplace and family responsibilities—place a damper on our ability to whoop it up now and then. (For many of us, I suspect, that carefully demarcated and rule-bound arena of sexuality becomes the only arena in which we feel like we let go at all.) For many men, being a man is a drag (both as a performance and as a bummer). And the mythopoets encourage men to cut loose.

I wouldn't go so far as to make a political sensibility out of it; in fact, as my essay with Michael Kaufman argues, such a politics is inevitably regressive. Childhood is a place of fantasy retreat, not the world in which one lives. All these evocations of kings and gods in myth and legend have a ring of infantile omnipotence to them, a celebration of power unfettered by parental admonition. For grown-ups, play must be connected to work, and celebration and joy must be tied to a politics of change. Sure, there must be dancing at the revolution, as Emma Goldman said, but there has to be a revolution for the dancing to be meaningful.

Is the goal of the movement to make men feel better about themselves as men? However worthy that might appear, such a goal would leave intact the existing aggregate power relations that constituted our gendered experiences in the first place. In other words, a movement that would simply encourage men to feel better about themselves as men, without linking such feelings to the social inequalities based on class, race, sexuality, and gender, would ultimately serve to reinforce that inequality. Call it sexism with a happy face.

The alternative cannot be antisexism with a constant frown. I may be uneasy about men who want to be kings, warriors, or even knights-errant, but I'm also uneasy about a profeminist political sensibility that seems to take out all the spontaneity, joy, and fun in gathering together. Profeminist men often take comfort in the fact that we deal, as we say, with the "hard stuff" — homophobia, sexism, and racism, and their attendant violence, abuse, and rape.

That can't be all. I remember once hearing Andrea Dworkin calling herself "a feminist, not the fun kind." I admire Andrea's work enormously, but that is not my path. I'd like to be "a profeminist man, the kind who can have fun." I believe joylessness impoverishes our work—it makes us ineffectual, dour, and incapable of moving people—just as making fun the goal of one's life depoliticizes and impoverishes that life.

The ability to have fun is made possible, I believe, by the ability to forgive. And I believe that we profeminist men express far too little forgiveness—of ourselves and of other men. Don't misunderstand: there is a big difference between forgiveness and the defensive resistance one hears from those loud and angry purveyors of men's rights who line up with the Rush Limbaughs or Warren Farrells. Defensive resistance comes from a refusal to take responsibility when others act implicitly in our name—when some men, for example, commit acts of racist, sexist, or homophobic violence. Defensive resistance is part of our privilege of pretending not to know, a deliberate deafness, a willed numbness to the pains of others, in part because the only sound we hear is our own voice. Defensive resistance is that voice that runs away screaming "don't blame me."

Forgiveness, by contrast, requires acknowledgment. Forgiveness depends upon acknowledging how privilege shields us from that pain, and then brings it to consciousness. Forgiveness requires that we feel their pain, commit to their struggle to overcome the conditions that cause it, and acknowledge the ways in which our privilege made it invisible for so long. Forgiveness is not about forgetting; it is about remembering in such a deep way that we integrate our knowledge into a commitment to act in new and different ways.

Feminism is about forgiveness. Sure, feminism is about outrage at injustice and compassion for the survivors of that injustice. Feminism is about stopping the violence and empowering women. But feminism is also about forgiveness—at least in theory. Feminism asks us to retheorize past behaviors in a new light, to rethink our own lives in new ways. Feminism challenges men to hold their lives up to the light of women's experiences of our actions, rather than our intentions, however honorable or dishonorable those intentions may have been. Feminism allows us to rename our actions, so that, for example, what we might once have called "dating etiquette" or simple "dating"—that incessant trying to score, the ignoring of what she wants, the willful inability to hear her "no" as meaning "no," and all that cajoling and coercing and pleading—is now to be understood as date rape, or at least attempted date rape. Feminism allows us to rename what we used to call "office behavior" and "flirting" or "picking up students" as sexual harassment.

Feminism naturally demands that such re-visioning of our past be accompanied by an ethical acknowledgment of our behaviors' effects on women, an analysis of the social and personal origins of such actions, and a political commitment to learning new ways of relating to women and men in everyday life, as well as joining a struggle to implement that new vision in the public sphere. What kind of feminism would it be that allowed, demanded, encouraged such retheorizing and transformation, but then did not forgive the past? And what kind of profeminist men's politics can be so unforgiving of our brothers?

Mythopoetic men often forgive without revisioning; profeminist men sometimes revision without forgiveness. We need both. Mythopoets show us how to break down the barriers that isolate us from one another, that keep us from finding a voice with which we can challenge other men. And they show us how to learn to embrace other men with compassion, tenderness, and love. Profeminist men bring into view the privilege that provides an invisible but indelible structure to our lives and the lives of others, and challenges us to act ethically and politically to create a world of sexual equality and gender justice. Mythopoet gatherings give profeminists a glimpse of compassionate manhood; profeminists tell mythopoets to bring that vision back from the woods—into their homes, their workplaces, the streets. Mythopoets seek to learn how to love; profeminists want to use that love to transform the world.

Perhaps James Baldwin, himself no stranger to feelings of marginalization and powerlessness, outlined this project best in his powerful indictment of racism, *The Fire Next Time*. "We, with love, shall force our brothers to see themselves as they are, to cease fleeing from reality and begin to change it."[6] This work will have made a modest contribution to that project if it can inspire a dialogue of compassionate challenge, of nourishing debate, of loving engagement.

NOTES

1. Plato, "The Apologia," in *The Collected Dialogues of Plato*, ed. Edith Hamilton and Huntington Cairns (Princeton: Princeton University Press, 1961), 8.

2. See Peggy McIntosh, "White Privilege and Male Privilege: A Personal Account of Coming to See the Correspondences Through Work in Women's Studies" (avail-

able for $4.00 from Petty McIntosh, Associate Director, Wellesley College Center for Research on Women, Wellesley College, Wellesley, MA 02181).

3. See, for example, his *The Myth of Male Power* (New York: Simon and Schuster, 1994).

4. This is a point that I develop at length theoretically in "Masculinity as Homophobia: Fear, Shame, and Silence in the Construction of Gender Identity," in *Theorizing Masculinities,* ed. H. Brod and M. Kaufman (Newbury Park, Calif.: Sage Publications, 1994); and historically in *Manhood in America: A Cultural History* (New York: The Free Press, 1995).

5. Ludwig Wittgenstein, *Culture and Value* (Chicago: University of Chicago Press, 1980), 46.

6. James Baldwin, *The Fire Next Time* (New York: Dell, 1962), 21.

Contributors

MARVIN ALLEN is the author of *Angry Men, Passive Men: Understanding the Roots of Men's Anger and Moving Beyond It* (Columbine/Fawcett, 1993).

TIMOTHY BENEKE is the author of *Men on Rape* and is currently writing a book on sexism for the University of California Press. He lives in Oakland, California, and works as a freelance editor.

ONAJE BENJAMIN is a political activist who has worked in various peace and justice movements during the past twenty years. He is founder and director of Men's Work, a consulting firm that provides training and counseling services that emphasize the development of a "Socially Responsible Masculinity." He resides in North Carolina.

SHEPHERD BLISS, an activist in the men's movement since 1976, directs the Kokopelli Lodge, a traveling troupe of ceremonial artists. Dr. Bliss has contributed to over a dozen books, recently co-authoring *A Quiet Strength.* He edits the "Men's, Soul and Gender Newsletter," free copies of which are available from P.O. Box 1040, Sebastopol, CA 95473.

ROBERT BLY, one of the country's most distinguished poets, is a storyteller, translator, and lecturer on the international circuit. His eight collections of poems include *The Light Around the Body,* winner of a National Book Award; *Silence in the Snowy Fields,* which earned him a Guggenheim Fellowship; *The Kabir Book;* and *News of the Universe.* Bly has written, translated, or in some way contributed to nearly eighty books over the last thirty years. And as the author of the bestselling 1990 book *Iron John: A Book About Men,* he is perhaps best known as a leader in the men's movement. He lives in Minneapolis, Minnesota, with his family.

HARRY BROD is Assistant Professor of Philosophy at the University of Delaware. He is the editor of *The Making of Masculinities: The New Men's Studies, A Mensch Among Men: Explorations in Jewish Masculinity* and (with Michael Kaufman) *Theorizing Masculinities*, author of *Hegel's Philosophy of Politics*, and he is a spokesperson for the National Organization for Men Against Sexism.

CHRIS BULLOCK is currently Professor of English at the University of Alberta in Edmonton, Alberta, Canada. He is joint author of *A Guide to Marxist Literary Criticism* (1980) and *Essay Writing for Canadian Students* (3rd ed., 1994). Involved in the men's movement since 1981, he is currently working on a series of studies of men's issues in modern short stories.

KENNETH CLATTERBAUGH teaches philosophy at the University of Washington, Seattle. He is the author of *Contemporary Perspectives on Masculinity* (Westview, 1990), a member of the editorial board of *masculinities*, an associate editor of the *Journal of Men's Studies*, and the author of several articles dealing with philosophical issues in gender studies.

R. W. CONNELL is Professor of Sociology at University of California, Santa Cruz. His books include *Gender and Power* (Stanford University Press, 1987), *Which Way Is Up?* (Routledge, 1986), and *Masculinities* (University of California Press, 1995).

MIKE DASH is active in both mythopoetry and profeminism. He is a founding member of Seattle Men Against Sexual Harassment, a member of Seattle NOW, and on the board of directors at Alternatives to Fear (a nationally known organization that teaches women self-defense against rape). He has also participated in numerous mythopoetic ritual groups, wisdom councils, ceremonies, and men's conferences.

JED DIAMOND is a social activist and a happily married father of five and grandfather of four. He is the author of *The Warrior's Journey Home* (1994), *Looking for Love in All the Wrong Places* (1988), and *Inside Out: Becoming My Own Man* (1983).

DAVID GUTTERMAN is a graduate student in Political Science at Rutgers University. He is a cofounder of Men Acting for Change (MAC), a profeminist, gay affirmative men's group at Duke University.

MICHAEL KAUFMAN, a writer and speaker, is the editor of *Beyond Patriarchy: Essays by Men on Pleasure, Power and Change* (Oxford University Press, 1988) and the author of *Cracking the Armour: Power, Pain and the Lives of Men* (Viking Canada, 1993). He is the originator and a founding member of the White Ribbon Campaign against violence against women, and a former professor at York University in Toronto. He lives in Toronto and has a school-aged son.

MICHAEL S. KIMMEL is Professor of Sociology at State University of New York at Stony Brook. His books include *Changing Men* (1987), *Men's Lives* (3rd ed., 1995), *Men Confront Pornography* (1990), and *Against the Tide: Profeminist Men in the United States, 1776–1990* (Beacon, 1992), a documentary history of men who have supported feminism in U.S. history. He edits *masculinities*, an interdisciplinary scholarly journal, a book series on Men and Masculinities at University of California Press, and the Sage Series on Men and Masculinities. His new book, *Manhood in America: A Cultural History*, is published by The Free Press. He is the spokesperson for the National Organization for Men Against Sexism (NOMAS) and lectures extensively on campuses here and abroad.

AARON KIPNIS, Ph.D., is a trainer and educator in clinical psychology. He has lectured on male psychology and gender relations at hospitals and universities, including Harvard Medical School, and is an advisor on gender-related issues to businesses and government organizations. He is the author of *Knights Without Armor* and (with Elizabeth Herron) *Gender War, Gender Peace: The Quest for Love and Justice Between Women and Men* as well as numerous articles and book chapters on gender-related topics.

TERRY KUPERS, M.D., a professor in the Graduate School of Psychology at The Wright Institute in Berkeley, practices psychiatry in Oakland. He is the author of *Public Therapy* (Free Press, 1981), *Ending Therapy* (N.Y.U.P., 1988), and *Revisioning Men's Lives: Gender, Intimacy and Power* (Guilford, 1993). He is married and has three young adult sons.

MICHAEL A. MESSNER is Associate Professor in the Department of Sociology and the Program for the Study of Women and Men in Society at the University of Southern California. He is co-editor (with Michael Kimmel) of *Men's Lives* (Macmillan, 1992) and (with Donald F. Sabo) or *Sport, Men and the Gender Order: Critical Feminist Perspectives* (Human Kinetics, 1990). He has authored *Power at Play* (Beacon Press, 1992) and (with Donald F. Sabo) *Winning Isn't Everything: Men and Sports* (The Crossing Press, 1994).

GORDON MURRAY is a Clinical Instructor at the University of California, San Francisco, School of Medicine, and on the faculty of the New College of California in Social/Clinical Psychology. He has been a member of the leadership collective of the National Organization for Men Against Sexism (NOMAS) and has contributed to several anthologies on men's issues. He is a psychotherapist and consultant in private practice in San Francisco.

TIMOTHY NONN attends Graduate Theological Union in Berkeley, where he is completing his Ph.D. dissertation on faith and masculinity among poor men. He has a background in community organizing among rural and urban poor and refugees. He has published several articles on religion, gender, and poverty.

DON SABO, Ph.D. is Professor of Social Science at D'Youville College, Buffalo, New York. He and Michael Messner have authored *Sex, Violence, and Power in Sports: Rethinking Masculinity* (Crossing Press). His research interests include social inequality.

MICHAEL SCHWALBE is Associate Professor of Sociology at North Carolina State University. He teaches courses in social theory, social psychology, and inequality, and is the author of *Unlocking the Iron Cage: Understanding the Mythopoetic Men's Movement* (Oxford University Press, 1995).

DON SHEWEY has been a journalist, writer, and editor in New York for over ten years. He was one of the founders and arts editor of *7 Days*, has been contributing editor at *Rolling Stone*, and theatre editor for *Soho News*, and is currently contributing writer for *The Village Voice*. His books include *Sam Shepard* (Dell, 1985), *Caught in the Act* (New American Library, 1986), and *Out Front* (Grove Press, 1988). He is currently writing a book about men's spirituality.

MARK SIMPSON is a freelance writer for *The Advocate* and such British publications as *The Guardian, Gay Times, The Independent, Time Out*, and *The New Statesman*. He is the author of *Male Impersonators: Men Performing Masculinity* (Routledge, 1994). He lives in London.

DAVID WEED teaches at Syracuse University. He is working on a study of representations of men and masculinity in mid-eighteenth century novels by Smollett, Cleland, Sterne, and Goldsmith.

PAUL WOLF-LIGHT is a psychotherapist who currently works as project coordinator and therapist at Everyman Centre in Brixton, London. He is a member of the collective that produces the magazine *Achilles Heel* and has been active in local politics at a community level for many years. He is the father of a son and two daughters.